T0214686

Communications
in Computer and Information Science   **846**

Commenced Publication in 2007
Founding and Former Series Editors:
Phoebe Chen, Alfredo Cuzzocrea, Xiaoyong Du, Orhun Kara, Ting Liu,
Krishna M. Sivalingam, Dominik Ślęzak, and Xiaokang Yang

More information about this series at http://www.springer.com/series/7899

Emmanouel Garoufallou ·
Fabio Sartori · Rania Siatri ·
Marios Zervas (Eds.)

Metadata and Semantic Research

12th International Conference, MTSR 2018
Limassol, Cyprus, October 23–26, 2018
Revised Selected Papers

 Springer

Editors
Emmanouel Garoufallou (iD)
Alexander Technological Educational
Institute (ATEI) of Thessaloniki
Thessaloniki, Greece

Fabio Sartori (iD)
Department of Informatics, Systems
and Communication
University of Milano-Bicocca
Milan, Italy

Rania Siatri
Alexander Technological Educational
Institute (ATEI) of Thessaloniki
Thessaloniki, Greece

Marios Zervas (iD)
Library and Information Services
Cyprus University of Technology
Limassol, Cyprus

ISSN 1865-0929   ISSN 1865-0937 (electronic)
Communications in Computer and Information Science
ISBN 978-3-030-14400-5   ISBN 978-3-030-14401-2 (eBook)
https://doi.org/10.1007/978-3-030-14401-2

Library of Congress Control Number: 2019932786

This Springer imprint is published by the registered company Springer Nature Switzerland AG
The registered company address is: Gewerbestrasse 11, 6330 Cham, Switzerland

Preface

Since 2005, the International Metadata and Semantics Research Conference (MTSR) has served as a significant venue for dissemination and sharing of metadata and semantic-driven research and practices. This year, 2018, marked the 12th MTSR, drawing scholars, researchers, and practitioners who are investigating and advancing our knowledge on a wide range of metadata and semantic-driven topics. The 12th International Conference on Metadata and Semantics Research (MTSR 2018) was held at the Cyprus University of Technology in Cyprus, during October 23–26, 2018.

Metadata and semantics are integral to any information system and important to the sphere of Web data. Research and development addressing metadata and semantics is crucial to advancing how we effectively discover, use, archive, and repurpose information. In response to this need, researchers are actively examining methods for generating, reusing, and interchanging metadata. Integrated with these developments is research on the application of computational methods, linked data, and data analytics. A growing body of literature also targets conceptual and theoretical designs providing foundational frameworks for metadata and semantic applications. There is no doubt that metadata weaves its way through nearly every aspect of our information ecosystem, and there is great motivation for advancing the current state of understanding in the fields of metadata and semantics. To this end, it is vital that scholars and practitioners convene and share their work.

MTSR conferences have grown in number of participants and paper submission rates over the past decade, marking it as a leading, international research conference. Continuing in the successful legacy of previous MTSR conferences (MTSR 2005, MTSR 2007, MTSR 2009, MTSR 2010, MTSR 2011, MTSR 2012, MTSR 2013, MTSR 2014, MTSR 2015, MTSR 2016, and MTSR 2017), MTSR 2018 brought together scholars and practitioners who share a common interest in the interdisciplinary field of metadata, linked data, and ontologies.

The MTSR 2018 program and the proceedings show a rich diversity of research and practice from metadata and semantically focused tools and technologies, linked data, cross-language semantics, ontologies, metadata models, semantic systems, and metadata standards. The general session of the conference included 12 papers covering a broad spectrum of topics, proving the interdisciplinary view of metadata. Metadata as a research topic is maturing, and the conference supported the following seven tracks: Digital Libraries, Information Retrieval, Big, Linked, Social and Open Data; Metadata and Semantics for Cultural Collections and Applications; Metadata and Semantics for Open Repositories, Research Information Systems, and Data Infrastructures; Track on Digital Humanities and Digital Curation; Metadata and Semantics for Agriculture, Food, and Environment; Knowledge IT Artifacts in Professional Communities and Aggregations; and European and National Projects. Each of these tracks had a rich selection of short and full research papers, in total 23, giving broader diversity to MTSR, and enabling deeper exploration of significant topics.

All the papers underwent a thorough and rigorous peer-review process. The review and selection for this year was highly competitive and only papers containing significant research results, innovative methods, or novel and best practices were accepted for publication. From the general session, only eight submissions were accepted as full research papers, representing 26.6% of the total number of submissions, and four as short papers. An additional 11 contributions from tracks covering noteworthy and important results were accepted as full research papers, representing 23.4% of the total number of submissions, and 12 as short papers, bringing the total of this year's MTSR 2018 accepted contributions to 35. The acceptance rate of full research papers for both the general session and tracks was 24.6% of the total number of submissions, while the cumulative acceptance rate for all papers was 45.5%.

Cyprus University of Technology aspires to become a modern and innovative university with international recognition, which promotes excellence in education and research in cutting-edge fields, aiming at the scientific, technological, economic, social, and cultural upgrading of the country. Its mission is to provide high-quality education and high-level training and to promote lifelong learning with modern pedagogical methods, to produce and disseminate scientific knowledge through research and teaching, and through contribution toward addressing challenges in the fields of science and technology, to become a catalyst for the state and society. In particular, the mission focuses on creating added value through actions on the following three axes: Education, Research, Innovation, Transfer of Know-How, and Social Contribution. The library's mission is to serve and support the members of the academic society, enhancing the scientific research and the educational procedure. The library actively participates in the university's mission of providing high-level education and research in important sectors. This fact is achieved with access to information and to registered knowledge, with the carrying out of seminars as well as with ensuring and organizing noteworthy source of information for the development of research and other skills from its user-members.

This year the MTSR conference was pleased to host a remarkable keynote presentation by Dr. Christos Papatheodorou, Professor in the Department of Archives, Library Science and Museology at the Ionian University in Greece. In his presentation "Library Data Models Under the Lens of interoperability and Quality," Professor Papatheodorou shared his extensive experience and insights about metadata quality approaches and their adaptation to the various models of bibliographic data and their interoperability.

We conclude this preface by thanking the many people who contributed their time and efforts to MTSR 2018 and made this year's conference possible. We also thank all the organizations that supported this conference. We extend a sincere gratitude to members of the Program Committees both main and special tracks, the Steering Committee and the Organizing Committees (both general and local), and the conference reviewers who invested their time generously to ensure the timely review of the submitted manuscripts. A special thanks to the program chairs, Ernesto William De Luca from Georg Eckert Institute – Leibniz Institute for International Textbook Research, Germany, and Athena Salaba from Kent State University, USA; to the workshop, tutorial, and demonstration chair, Dr. Getaneh Alemu from Southampton Solent University, UK; to Anxhela Dani and Marina Antoniou for supporting us throughout this event and to Iro Sotiriadou and Anxhela Dani who assisted us with the preparation of the proceedings; and to Nikoleta, Vasiliki, and Stavroula for their endless support and patience. Our thanks go to Springer Nature, Elsevier, EBSCO, ACS, IEEE, Cyprus Tourism Organisation, and Reasonable Graph. Final, our thanks go to all participants of MTSR 2018 for making the event a great success.

November 2018   Emmanouel Garoufallou
                                                                        Fabio Sartori
                                                                        Rania Siatri
                                                                        Marios Zervas

Organization

General Chairs

Emmanouel Garoufallou — Alexander Technological Educational Institute (ATEI) of Thessaloniki, Greece

Fabio Sartori — University of Milano-Bicocca, Italy

Program Chairs

Ernesto William De Luca — Georg Eckert Institute – Leibniz Institute for International Textbook Research, Germany

Athena Salaba — Kent State University, USA

Local Organization Chair

Marios Zervas' — Cyprus University of Technology, Cyprus

Workshop, Tutorial, and Demonstration Chair

Getaneh Alemu — Southampton Solent University, UK

Special Track Chairs

Paolo Bianchini	Università degli Studi di Torino, Italy
Miguel-Ángel Sicilia	University of Alcalá, Spain
Armando Stellato	University of Rome Tor Vergata, Italy
Angela Locoro	University of Milano-Bicocca, Italy
Arlindo Flavio da Conceição	Federal University of São Paulo (UNIFESP), Brazil
Nikos Houssos	IRI, Greece
Michalis Sfakakis	Ionian University, Corfu, Greece
Lina Bountouri	Ionian University, Corfu, Greece
Emmanouel Garoufallou	Alexander Technological Educational Institute (ATEI) of Thessaloniki, Greece
Sirje Virkus	Tallinn University, Estonia
Rania Siatri	Alexander Technological Educational Institute (ATEI) of Thessaloniki, Greece
Ernesto William De Luca	Georg Eckert Institute – Leibniz Institute for International Textbook Research, Germany
Fabio Sartori	University of Milano-Bicocca, Italy

Steering Committee

Juan Manuel Dodero	University of Cádiz, Spain
Emmanouel Garoufallou	Alexander Technological Educational Institute (ATEI) of Thessaloniki, Greece
Nikos Manouselis	AgroKnow, Greece
Fabio Santori	University of Milano-Bicocca, Italy
Miguel-Ángel Sicilia	University of Alcalá, Spain

Organizing Committee

Pavlos Metaxas	Cyprus University of Technology, Cyprus
Stephani Liasi	Cyprus University of Technology, Cyprus
Maria Haraki	Cyprus University of Technology, Cyprus
Stamatios Giannoulakis	Cyprus University of Technology, Cyprus
Eleni Kamberi	Cyprus University of Technology, Cyprus
Nasia Panagiotou	Cyprus University of Technology, Cyprus
Marina Antoniou	Cyprus University of Technology, Cyprus
Alexia Kounoudes	Cyprus University of Technology, Cyprus
Antonia Nikolaou	Cyprus University of Technology, Cyprus
Damiana Koutsomiha	American Farm School, Greece
Anxhela Dani	Alexander Technological Educational Institute (ATEI) of Thessaloniki, Greece
Chrysanthi Chatzopoulou	Alexander Technological Educational Institute (ATEI) of Thessaloniki, Greece
Iro Sotiriadou	American Farm School, Greece

Technical Support Staff

Ilias Nitsos	Alexander Technological Educational Institute (ATEI) of Thessaloniki, Greece
Petros Artemi	Cyprus University of Technology, Cyprus

Program Committee

Rajendra Akerkar	Western Norway Research Institute, Norway
Arif Altun	Hacettepe University, Turkey
Ioannis N. Athanasiadis	Democritus University of Thrace, Greece
Panos Balatsoukas	University of Manchester, UK
Tomaz Bartol	University of Ljubljana, Slovenia
Ina Bluemel	German National Library of Science and Technology TIBm, Germany
Derek Bousfield	Manchester Metropolitan University, UK
Gerhard Budin	University of Vienna, Austria
Özgü Can	Ege University, Turkey

Caterina Caracciolo   Food and Agriculture Organization (FAO)
                                          of the United Nations, Italy
Christian Cechinel   Federal University of Pampa, Brazil
Artem Chebotko   University of Texas - Pan American, USA
Philip Cimiano   Bielefeld University, Germany
Sissi Closs   Karlsruhe University of Applied Sciences, Germany
Ricardo Colomo-Palacios   Universidad Carlos III, Spain
Sally Jo Cunningham   Waikato University, New Zealand
Constantina Costopoulou   Agricultural University of Athens, Greece
Ernesto William De Luca   Georg Eckert Institute – Leibniz Institute for
                                          International Textbook Research, Germany
Milena Dobreva   UCL Qatar, Qatar
Juan Manuel Dodero   University of Cádiz, Spain
Erdogan Dogdu   Cankaya University, Turkey
Biswanath Dutta   Documentation Research and Training Centre
                                          (DRTC), Indian Statistical Institute, India
Juan José Escribano Otero   Universidad Europea de Madrid, Spain
Muriel Foulonneau   Tudor Public Research Centre, Luxemburg
Panorea Gaitanou   Ionian University, Greece
Emmanouel Garoufalou   Alexander Technological Educational Institute
                                          (ATEI) of Thessaloniki, Greece
Manolis Gergatsoulis   Ionian University, Greece
Jorge Gracia   University of Zaragoza, Spain
Jane Greenberg   Drexel University, USA
Jill Griffiths   Manchester Metropolitan University, UK
R. J. Hartley   Manchester Metropolitan University, UK
Nikos Houssos   IRI, Greece
Carlos A. Iglesias   Universidad Politécnica de Madrid, Spain
Frances Johnson   Manchester Metropolitan University, UK
Dimitris Kanellopoulos   University of Patras, Greece
Pinar Karagöz   Middle East Technical University (METU), Turkey
Pythagoras Karampiperis   AgroKnow, Greece
Brian Kelly   CETIS, University of Bolton, UK
Christian Kop   University of Klagenfurt, Austria
Rebecca Koskela   University of New Mexico, USA
Daniela Luzi   National Research Council, Italy
Paolo Manghi   Institute of Information Science and Technologies
                                          (ISTI), National Research Council (CNR), Italy
John McCrae   National University of Ireland Galway, Ireland
Xavier Ochoa   Centro de Tecnologías de Información Guayaquil,
                                          Ecuador
Mehmet C. Okur   Yaşar University, Turkey
Matteo Palmonari   University of Milano-Bicocca, Italy
Manuel Palomo Duarte   University of Cádiz, Spain
Laura Papaleo   University of Genoa, Italy
Christos Papatheodorou   Ionian University, Greece

Metadata and Semantics for Digital Libraries, Information Retrieval, Big, Linked, Social, and Open Data

Special Track Chairs

Program Committee

Rebecca Koskela	University of New Mexico, USA
Valentini Moniarou-Papaconstantinou	Technological Educational Institute of Athens, Greece
Dimitris Rousidis	University of Alcalá, Spain
Christine Urquhart	Aberystwyth University, UK
Evgenia Vassilakaki	Technological Educational Institute of Athens, Greece
Sirje Virkus	Tallinn University, Estonia
Georgia Zafeiriou	University of Macedonia, Greece
Marios Zervas	Cyprus University of Technology, Cyprus

Metadata and Semantics for Cultural Collections and Applications

Special Track Chairs

| Michalis Sfakakis | Ionian University, Corfu, Greece |
| Lina Bountouri | Ionian University, Corfu, Greece |

Program Committee

Trond Aalberg	Norwegian University of Science and Technology (NTNU), Norway
Karin Bredenberg	The National Archives of Sweden, Sweden
Enrico Fransesconi	EU Publications Office, Luxembourg, and Consiglio Nazionale delle Ricerche, Firenze, Italy
Manolis Gergatsoulis	Ionian University, Greece
Antoine Isaac	Vrije Universiteit, Amsterdam, The Netherlands
Sarantos Kapidakis	Ionian University, Greece
Peter McKinney	National Library of New Zealand Te Puna Mātauranga o Aotearoa, New Zealand
Christos Papatheodorou	Ionian University and Digital Curation Unit, IMIS, Athena RC, Greece
Chrisa Tsinaraki	Joint Research Centre, European Commission, Italy
Andreas Vlachidis	University of South Wales, UK
Katherine Wisser	Graduate School of Library and Information Science, Simmons College, USA
Maja Žumer	University of Ljubljana, Slovenia

Metadata and Semantics for Knowledge IT Artifacts (KITA) in Professional Communities and Aggregations (KITA 2018)

Special Track Chairs

Fabio Sartori	University of Milano-Bicocca, Italy
Angela Locoro	University of Milano-Bicocca, Italy
Arlindo Flavio da Conceição	Federal University of São Paulo (UNIFESP), Brazil

Program Committee

Federico Cabitza	University of Milano-Bicocca, Italy
Luca Grazioli	ICteam SpA, Italy
Riccardo Melen	University of Milano-Bicocca, Italy
Aurelio Ravarini	Università Carlo Cattaneo – LIUC, Castellanza, Italy
Carla Simone	University of Siegen, Germany
Flávio Soares Corrêa da Silva	University of São Paulo, Brazil
Cecilia Zanni-Merk	Insa Rouen Normandie, France

Metadata and Semantics for Digital Humanities and Digital Curation (DHC)

Special Track Chairs

Ernesto William De Luca	Georg Eckert Institute – Leibniz Institute for International Textbook Research, Germany
Paolo Bianchini	Università degli Studi di Torino, Italy

Program Committee

Maret Keller	Georg Eckert Institute – Leibniz Institute for International Textbook Research, Germany
Elena González-Blanco	Universidad Nacional de Educación a Distancia, Spain
Steffen Hennicke	Georg Eckert Institute – Leibniz Institute for International Textbook Research, Germany
Ana García-Serrano	ETSI Informatica – UNED, Spain
Andreas Weiß	Georg Eckert Institute – Leibniz Institute for International Textbook Research, Germany
Philipp Mayr	GESIS, Germany
Lena-Luise Stahn	Georg Eckert Institute – Leibniz Institute for International Textbook Research, Germany
Andrea Turbati	University of Rome Tor Vergata, Italy
Christian Scheel	Georg Eckert Institute – Leibniz Institute for International Textbook Research, Germany
Armando Stellato	University of Rome Tor Vergata, Italy
Wolf-Tilo Balke	TU Braunschweig, Germany
Andreas Lommatzsch	TU Berlin, Germany
Ivo Keller	TH Brandenburg, Germany
Gabriela Ossenbach	UNED, Spain
Francesca Fallucchi	Guglielmo Marconi University, Italy
Alessandra Pieroni	Guglielmo Marconi University, Italy

Metadata and Semantics for European and National Projects

Special Track Chairs

Emmanouel Garoufallou	Alexander Technological Educational Institute (ATEI) of Thessaloniki, Greece
Stavroula Antonopoulou	American Farm School, Greece

Program Committee

Panos Balatsoukas	City University, UK
Mike Conway	University of North Carolina at Chapel Hill, USA
Jane Greenberg	Drexel University, USA
R. J. Hartley	Manchester Metropolitan University, UK
Nikos Houssos	IRI, Greece
Nikos Korfiatis	University of East Anglia, UK
Damiana Koutsomiha	American Farm School, Greece
Paolo Manghi	Institute of Information Science and Technologies (ISTI), National Research Council (CNR), Italy
Dimitris Rousidis	University of Alcalá, Spain
Rania Siatri	Alexander Technological Educational Institute (ATEI) of Thessaloniki, Greece
Miguel-Ángel Sicilia	University of Alcalá, Spain
Armando Stellato	University of Rome Tor Vergata, Italy
Sirje Virkus	Tallinn University, Estonia

Metadata and Semantics for Agriculture, Food, and the Environment (AgroSEM 2018)

Special Track Chair

Miguel-Ángel Sicilia	University of Alcalá, Spain

Program Committee

Ioannis Athanasiadis	Wageningen University, The Netherlands
Patrice Buche	INRA, France
Caterina Caracciolo	Food and Agriculture Organization (FAO) of the United Nations, Italy
Johannes Keizer	Food and Agriculture Organization (FAO) of the United Nations, Italy
Stasinos Konstantopoulos	NCSR Demokritos, Greece
Claire Nédellec	INRA, France
Armando Stellato	University of Rome Tor Vergata, Italy
Maguelonne Teisseire	Irstea Montpellier, France
Jan Top	Wageningen Food and Biobased Research, The Netherlands
Robert Trypuz	John Paul II Catholic University of Lublin, Poland

Metadata and Semantics for Open Repositories, Research Information Systems, and Data Infrastructures

Special Track Chairs

Nikos Houssos   IRI, Greece
Armando Stellato   University of Rome Tor Vergata, Italy

Honorary Track Chair

Imma Subirats   Food and Agriculture Organization (FAO)
of the United Nations, Italy

Program Committee

Sophie Aubin   INRA, France
Thomas Baker   Sungkyunkwan University, South Korea
Hugo Besemer   Wageningen UR Library, The Netherlands
Gordon Dunshire   University of Strathclyde, UK
Jan Dvorak   Charles University of Prague, Czech Republic
Jane Greenberg   Drexel University, USA
Siddeswara Guru   University of Queensland, Australia
Keith Jeffery   Keith G. Jeffery Consultants, UK
Nikolaos Konstantinou   University of Manchester, UK
Rebecca Koskela   University of New Mexico, USA
Jessica Lindholm   Malmö University, Sweden
Paolo Manghi   Institute of Information Science and Technologies - Italian National Research Council (ISTI-CNR), Italy

Brian Matthews   Science and Technology Facilities Council, UK
Eva Mendez Rodriguez   Universidad Carlos III of Madrid, Spain
Joachim Schöpfel   University of Lille, France
Kathleen Shearer   Confederation of Open Access Repositories (COAR), Germany

Jochen Schirrwagen   University of Bielefeld, Germany
Birgit Schmidt   University of Göttingen, Germany
Chrisa Tsinaraki   European Commission, Joint Research Centre, Italy
Yannis Tzitzikas   University of Crete and ICS-FORTH, Greece
Zhong Wang   Sun-Yat-Sen University, China
Marcia Zeng   Kent State University, USA

ReasonableGraph.org
Thinking Ontologies

SPRINGER NATURE

Contents

Digital Libraries, Information Retrieval, Big, Linked, Social and Open Data

Cultural Collections and Applications

Knowledge IT Artifacts (KITA) in Professional Communities and Aggregations

Digital Humanities and Digital Curation (DHC)

European and National Projects

Agriculture, Food and Environment

Open Repositories, Research Information Systems and Data Infrastructures

Metadata, Linked Data, Semantics, Ontologies and SKOS

A Semantic Web SKOS Vocabulary Service for Open Knowledge Organization Systems

Jonas Waeber and Andreas Ledl$^{(\boxtimes)}$ (iD)

Basel University Library, 4056 Basel, Switzerland
`andreas.ledl@unibas.ch`

Abstract. In this article, the Basel Register of Thesauri, Ontologies & Classications (BARTOC.org) is introduced to raise awareness for an integrated, full terminology registry for knowledge organization systems. Recently, researchers have shown an increased interest in such a single access point for controlled vocabularies. The paper outlines BARTOC's technical implementation, system architecture, and services in the light of semantic technologies. Its central thesis is that if the KOS community agreed on BARTOC as one of their main terminology registries, all involved parties would benefit from linked open knowledge organization systems.

Keywords: Knowledge organization systems · Terminology registry · BARTOC · Skosmos · SKOS · Semantic Web

1 Introduction

In the public and private sector, institutions heavily "rely on structured schemas and vocabularies to indicate classes in which a resource may belong" [1]. These schemas and vocabularies can be summarized under the generic term *knowledge organization systems* (KOS). According to Hodge, KOS may be defined as "all types of schemes for organizing information and promoting knowledge management" [2].

The DCMI NKOS Task Group has identified 14 types of KOS: categorization scheme, classification scheme, dictionary, gazetteer, glossary, list, name authority list, ontology, semantic network, subject heading scheme, synonym ring, taxonomy, terminology, and thesaurus.[1]

Such KOS are crucial for information visualization, search engines, user interfaces, subject cataloguing, indexing, classification and linked data, and for digital curation in general.

However, "many potential, partial solutions involving the development of (...) controlled vocabularies are found scattered across the community" and therefore

---

[1] http://nkos.slis.kent.edu/nkos-type.html

© Springer Nature Switzerland AG 2019
E. Garoufallou et al. (Eds.): MTSR 2018, CCIS 846, pp. 3–12, 2019.
https://doi.org/10.1007/978-3-030-14401-2_1

"less usable for research and decision making" [3]. What is urgently needed is both, to be able to get an overview of available vocabularies in a certain field, and to gain deeper insight into vocabulary content - preferably all kept in a single place. To meet the "growing demand for unifying such efforts" [3], semantic technologies should be the method of choice.

2   The Basel Register of Thesauri, Ontologies and Classifications (BARTOC)

BARTOC (https://bartoc.org), a terminology registry for KOS developed by Basel University Library, precisely aims at achieving these objectives: to describe KOS in a uniform way (e.g. http://bartoc.org/en/node/15); to visualize them and to make them browsable for humans (e.g. http://bartoc.org/en/node/459/visual); to foster interoperability and machine readability by utilizing Semantic Web standards like metadata schemas (Networked Knowledge Organization Systems Dublin Core Application Profile NKOS AP[2], Asset Description Metadata Schema ADMS[3]), RDFa[4], URIs[5], and SKOS[6]; and to provide academics, researchers, and practitioners with a multidisciplinary, multilingual tool that facilitates searching, finding, and browsing KOS.

2.1   Overview of KOS

BARTOC has undergone a lot of transformation in its six year history. The primary focus has always been to find solution for one specific problem: to provide people from various academic disciplines with as much information about as many KOS in their field as possible.

The tool started as a blog called 'Thesaurusportal', but when the number of records had reached 350, a more sophisticated approach had to be chosen. To overcome difficulties like pointing to related, complementary collections, distributing it as a database for further use, and adding a license, the blog was switched to a content management system called Drupal in 2013. This completely changed the look and feel of 'Thesaurusportal', which has been called BARTOC ever since. It was the first important step towards a basic terminology registry.

Today, BARTOC groups metadata of more than 2,800 KOS and 87 other terminology registries in one place. It is curated by an international board of KOS experts from Austria, France, Germany, Greece, Italy, Netherlands, Norway, South Korea, Spain, Switzerland, and United Kingdom. BARTOC's metadata scheme provides fields for Title, Alternative Title, English Title, Author, Name Authority (VIAF), Abstract, English Abstract, KOS Type, Format, Access,

---

[2] http://nkos.slis.kent.edu/nkos-ap.html.
[3] https://www.w3.org/TR/vocab-adms/.
[4] https://www.w3.org/TR/rdfa-primer/.
[5] https://www.w3.org/2001/tag/doc/identify.
[6] https://www.w3.org/2004/02/skos/.

Wikidata, Link (to resource), Language, Address, Location, License, Year of Creation, Listed in (reference to other terminology registry), Contact, and subject indexing (EuroVoc[7], Dewey Decimal Classification[8], Integrative Levels Classification[9]). Thus, in the user interface, keyword searches with auto-complete function and advanced searches by pre-configured filters can be launched. (see Fig. 1) Across the individual types of KOS (multiple labels possible), BARTOC contains 810 classification schemes (28.85%), 700 ontologies (24.93%), 680 thesauri (24.22%), 243 glossaries (8.65%), 140 terminologies (4.99%), 95 taxonomies (3.28%), 80 subject heading schemes (2.85%), 72 name authority lists (2.56%), 62 dictionaries (2.21%), 25 lists (0.89%), 9 categorization schemes (0.32%), 8 gazetteers (0.28%), 6 semantic networks (0.21%) and 1 synonym ring (0.04%). In contrast to Linked Open Vocabularies (LOV)[10], which is to some extent a similar initiative focussing on ontologies [7], BARTOC covers the whole range of controlled vocabularies.

Metadata are put under the free license PDDL 1.0 (ODC Public Domain Dedication and Licence[11]) and can be downloaded via dumps in several formats (JSKOS, XML, CSV, DOC, TXT, XLS, JSON). Single entries can easily be displayed in a machine readable manner by putting their URI into e.g. the 'RDFa 1.1 Distiller and Parser'[12], since Drupal supports the W3C recommendation RDFa out-of-the-box.

For the above mentioned reasons, BARTOC is the most comprehensive terminology registry for KOS, both regarding number of vocabularies and provision of metadata. However, in literature there is a subtle difference between *basic* terminology registries, containing "only the metadata of KOS vocabularies", and *full* terminology registries, containing "also the members (e.g., concepts, terms, relationships) of the vocabularies" [4]. Until the end of 2016, it was impossible to take a look into the described vocabularies directly from BARTOC. In order to bridge this gap and become a *full* terminology registry, further measures had to be taken.

2.2   Insight into KOS Content

Through a public-private-partnership with the Semantic Web Company (Vienna), BARTOC has access to 'PoolParty Thesaurus & Taxonomy Management Software'[13], a world-class tool to build and maintain information architectures, which also has Drupal integration and provides a great browsable visualization of vocabularies available in SKOS format for users (See Fig. 2).

---

[7] http://eurovoc.europa.eu/drupal/?q=node.
[8] https://www.oclc.org/en/dewey/features/summaries.html.
[9] http://www.iskoi.org/ilc/.
[10] https://lov.linkeddata.es/dataset/lov.
[11] https://opendatacommons.org/licenses/pddl/1.0/.
[12] https://www.w3.org/2012/pyRdfa/.
[13] https://www.poolparty.biz/taxonomy-thesaurus-management/.

Fig. 1. BARTOC user interface

To make this work, SKOS files of vocabularies are being uploaded to a Virtuoso RDF triple store[14] hosted by Semantic Web Company. Besides visualization of existing SKOS vocabularies, PoolParty is particularly useful for BARTOC in terms of assigning URIs to concepts of vocabularies which are either still offline or published in formats not completely ready for Semantic Web yet (like CSV, HTML, MARC, PDF etc.).[15]

3   The BARTOC Skosmos Vocabulary Browser

PoolParty visualizations were important stepping stones along the path towards our ultimate goal of allowing keyword searches within concepts of different vocabularies simultaneously. Semantic Web Company, amongst others like project

---

[14] https://bartoc-virtuoso.poolparty.biz/sparql.

[15] But vocabularies can also be published with open source software like TemaTres (http://www.vocabularyserver.com/) or VocBench (http://vocbench.uniroma2.it/).

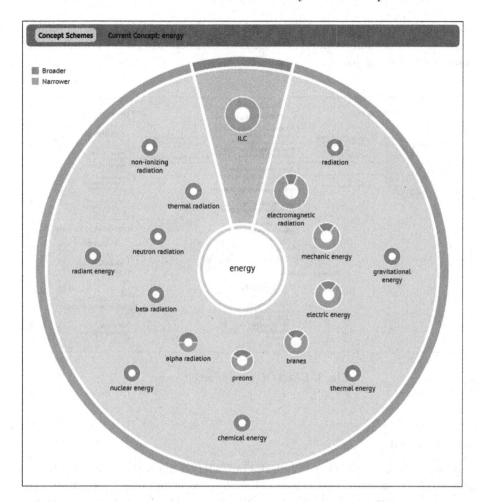

Fig. 2. PoolParty visualization of Integrative Levels Classification (ILC) concept "energy"

coli-conc[16], International Society for Knowledge Organization (ISKO)[17], TemaTres[18], and Data Archiving and Networked Services (DANS)[19], is an important partner for BARTOC to coordinate its technical development. But to get to the next stage of development, we had to choose another software. Since BARTOC has adopted an open source policy, 'Skosmos'[20], a web-based SKOS browser and publishing tool developed by the Finnish National Library [5], is being used.

---

[16] https://coli-conc.gbv.de/.
[17] http://www.isko.org/.
[18] http://www.vocabularyserver.com/.
[19] https://dans.knaw.nl/.
[20] http://bartoc-skosmos.unibas.ch/.

We also have to run a second RDF triple store (Apache Jena Fuseki), because Skosmos does not fully support Virtuoso, where PoolParty SKOS visualizations come from (See Fig. 3).

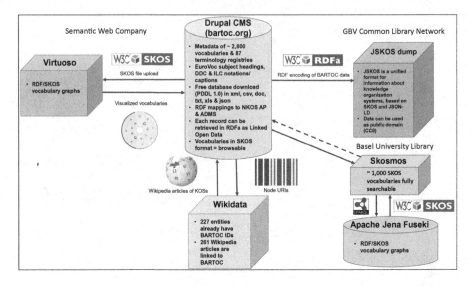

Fig. 3. BARTOC system architecture

3.1 Content

Currently, more than 1,000 vocabularies in BARTOC meet the criteria for being published in Skosmos, and new vocabularies are being added constantly. To increase the number of 'skosified' vocabularies, BARTOC regularly launches projects with institutions that indeed have a KOS, but not in SKOS format. [6] Where license permits, BARTOC also undertakes modelling independently. This makes a total of 2,831,363 concepts and 9,124,587 terms at the moment[21], which is, from what we see, by far the largest deployment of Skosmos. In many cases, we can use published SKOS files directly from the internet. If resources are not valid SKOS - even though they claim to - we either ask publishers to check[22] and repair or we upload an improved version to our own server. However, BARTOC Vocabulary Service sets out to do in large-scale effort what SKOS and RDF are meant for: "to represent knowledge organization systems" in a W3C "standard way", so that information can be "passed between computer applications in an interoperable way" and "be used in distributed, decentralised metadata applications".[23]

---

[21] As of August 24, 2018. See https://docs.google.com/spreadsheets/d/1TEgMdK3FU Ht2isnZaX0KQXfxAi-w6aGzShnSiXTxiUw/edit?usp=sharing.

[22] E.g. by SKOS Play! testing tool http://labs.sparna.fr/skos-testing-tool/.

[23] https://www.w3.org/2004/02/skos/intro.

By publishing KOSs in BARTOC's Skosmos Browser they become part of a network of concept schemes, concepts, and terms, which lays the foundation for "meaningful navigation between KOSs"[24] on the Semantic Web. Moreover, the SKOS Vocabulary Service provides a treasure trove "for establishing semantic relations between pre-existing concepts" (See footnote 24), the so-called 'mapping'. Even in its simplest application, it prevents KOS builders from reinventing the wheel and gives an overview of publicly available vocabularies/concepts they can reference to via URIs.

The representation of vocabularies collected in Bartoc Skosmos further differentiates this browser from LOV. LOV focuses only "property-and-class vocabularies in RDFS or OWL" [8], BARTOC Skosmos Browser only accepts vocabularies published as SKOS. This creates an emphasis on value vocabularies. As such the content of LOV and Bartoc Skosmos Browser have very little overlap. On the contrary, they are ideally complementary.

It would be preferable to have a quantitative study of BARTOC data similar to the one carried out by Nogales et al. for LOV to learn more about "use of vocabularies in the Web of Data". [9] First steps in this direction were taken by the paper from Voss et al. [10].

Some preliminary numbers can be gleaned from the statistic sheet. While on average the vocabularies have around 2,700 concepts, the median is only 21. This shows that the majority of value vocabularies are very small, with a few exceptions. Most of these exceptions are large thesauri such as the World Bank Thesaurus with 359,990 concepts.

3.2 Software Requirements

The Skosmos[25] software is published and maintained as open source by the National Library of Finnland. It is easy to run and has only open source dependencies. Currently Skosmos can only use the Apache Jena Fuseki triple store[26], as it depends on the specific Jena-Text Dialect of SPARQL.

To load and pre-process the data files from the various sources a script is used[27]. This script makes use of Skosify[28], which was developed by the National Library of Finland to improve SKOS data files for Skosmos. The script uses a Google Spreadsheet for configuration.

3.3 Hardware Requirements

The entire service runs on a single server. This server started out with only 2 GB RAM, 50 GB Disk and two cores. Soon after beginning to load vocabularies into Fuseki, we had to increase RAM to 16 GB and added a 480 GB SSD Disk

---

[24] https://www.w3.org/TR/skos-primer/.
[25] https://github.com/NatLibFi/Skosmos.
[26] https://jena.apache.org/documentation/fuseki2/.
[27] https://github.com/bartoc-basel/fuseki-update.
[28] https://github.com/NatLibFi/Skosify.

for storage. Once the service had run for a while we expanded the Server to 32 GB RAM and increased the number of cores to eight. Fuseki is very good at paralleling its workload and this helped a lot.

Requests are now answered in reasonable speeds, but for large vocabularies and general global searches Bartoc Skosmos is still fairly slow. It can take several seconds to resolve a search, but we no longer encounter time-outs as in the beginning.

3.4   Technical Implementation

One of the reasons Skosmos was chosen as a platform to make BARTOC SKOS vocabularies browsable, is that it is very easy to set up and maintain. It only takes about an hour to arrange everything and have a first working instance running. We adjusted the colour scheme of Skosmos to the one BARTOC uses and added a Logo with the twig templates used by Skosmos.

The Fuseki installation on our server uses the same configuration as provided on the wiki of Skosmos[29]. It would be possible to make some adjustments on how the index is built to expand the search capabilities of Skosmos global search, but we found the default configuration to be adequate for our use case.

Since the goal for Skosmos was to have as many SKOS vocabularies in one place as available, there had to be an easy way to upload new and update present vocabularies. It would be a lot of work to separately download and upload all 1000+ vocabularies and keep them up to date.

To this end a small script[30] was written in Python[31] to automate this process for most vocabularies. For this to work a vocabulary has to be available online as a single file in RDF/XML (.rdf), Turtle (.ttl), Notation 3 (.n3), N-triples (.nt) or JSON-LD (.json) format. The script is configurable with a Google spreadsheet to load new vocabularies. These vocabularies are then first pre-processed and checked before they are added to the Fuseki index. This is necessary to ensure, that the files downloaded have no easy to catch errors. First each file is parsed with the python library rdflib[32]. Several vocabularies provided online already failed at this stage, as they contained invalid characters (for example spaces in URIs) or syntactic errors. In case of maintained vocabularies we contacted the maintainers to fix the issue, or if this failed simply fixed the downloaded file and uploaded it to Bartoc.org server and download it from there with the script (Fig. 4).

Once parsed the graph is processed with Skosify[33]. The script checks the validity of the provided SKOS vocabulary and makes some simple changes. Only files properly defined according to the SKOS Reference[34] can be processed. No RDFS inference features are used, as they are much to specific to be of

---

[29] https://github.com/NatLibFi/Skosmos/wiki/InstallTutorial.

[30] https://github.com/bartoc-basel/fuseki-update.

[31] https://www.python.org/downloads/release/python-360/.

[32] https://github.com/RDFLib/rdflib.

[33] https://github.com/NatLibFi/Skosify.

[34] https://www.w3.org/TR/skos-reference/.

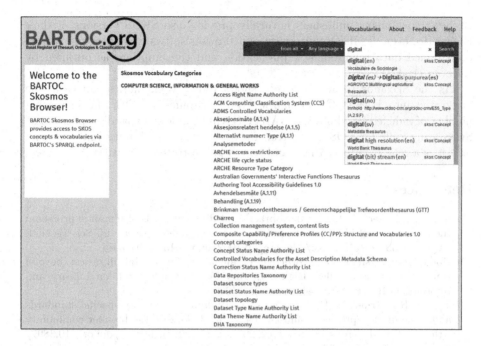

Fig. 4. BARTOC Skosmos Vocabulary Service

use in all cases. What Skosify fixes are hierarchical cycles, change duplicate skos:prefLabel to skos:altLabel, add missing language tags[35] and more. These steps ensure that most vocabularies are properly displayed by Skosmos once uploaded to Fuseki.

The last step is to upload the vocabulary to the Triple Store. This is done via the Fuseki file upload API and a simple HTTP PUT request.

With the amount of vocabularies added to the Triple Store, we found a large and diverse amount of issues. Some of these issues were resolved by the publishers of the vocabularies, after we made them aware of them. Other issues we could fix by expanding the pre-processing of the vocabularies.

4 Conclusion

This paper has argued that BARTOC could be the long anticipated terminology registry, unifying search for as well as access to KOS on the Semantic Web. The results support the idea that in a KOS community effort, not only as many vocabularies as possible should be added to the directory, but also collaborations should be set up to model even more KOS in SKOS, so that they will become open, machine readable, interoperable, and thus ready for the linked data age.

---

[35] Only if the vocabulary has a single language. But these are the only cases where language tags have been missing so far.

At best, vocabulary publishers naturally provide also SKOS versions of their KOSs. However, BARTOC directory and browser software architecture fosters both linked data requirements, publication and consumption, as outlined by Barbosa et al. [11].

As the Skosmos Browser already shows today, vocabularies can easily be integrated into BARTOC's Semantic Web environment. With the increasing number of indexed vocabularies, BARTOC will be able to expand its position as Swiss army knife for KOS, no matter if a vocabulary is still in use and evolving, or if it is a relic from past times and has to be protected as cultural heritage.

References

1. Isaac, A., Baker, T.: Linked data practice at different levels of semantic precision: the perspective of libraries, archives and museums. Bull. Assoc. Inf. Sci. Technol. **41**(4), 34–39 (2015). https://doi.org/10.1002/bult.2015.1720410411
2. Hodge, G.: Systems of knowledge organization for digital libraries: beyond traditional authority files. Digital Library Federation, Council on Library and Information Resources, Washington, DC (2000)
3. Jomier, R., Zermoglio, P., Wieczorek, J.: Building community-specific standards and vocabularies: prospects and challenges for linking to the broader community - the SINP case. Proc. TDWG **1**(e20297), 1–13 (2017). https://doi.org/10.3897/tdwgproceedings.1.20297
4. Golub, K., Tudhope, D., Zeng, M.L., Žumer, M.: Terminology registries for knowledge organization systems: functionality, use, and attributes. J. Assoc. Inf. Sci. Technol. **65**(9), 1901–1916 (2014). https://doi.org/10.1002/asi.23090
5. Suominen, O., et al.: Publishing SKOS vocabularies with Skosmos. Manuscript submitted for review (2015). http://skosmos.org/publishing-skos-vocabularies-with-skosmos.pdf
6. Sievi, O., Ledl, A., Waeber, J.: Semantische Technologien für lokale Erschliessungssysteme der Schweiz: Ein Pilotprojekt der Sportmediathek Magglingen und des Basel Register of Thesauri, Ontologies & Classifications (BARTOC.org). Informationspraxis. Manuscript submitted for publication
7. Vandenbussche, P.-Y., Atemezing, G.A., Poveda-Villalón, M., Vatant, B.: Linked open vocabularies (LOV): a gateway to reusable semantic vocabularies on the web. Semant. Web **8**(3), 437–452 (2017). http://www.semantic-web-journal.net/content/linked-open-vocabularies-lov-gateway-reusable-semantic-vocabularies-web-1
8. Baker, T., Vandenbussche, P.-Y., Vatant, B.: Requirements for vocabulary preservation and governance. Libr. Hi Tech **31**(4), 657–668 (2013). https://www.emeraldinsight.com/doi/full/10.1108/LHT-03-2013-0027
9. Nogales, A., Sicilia-Urban, M.A., García-Barriocanal, E.: Measuring vocabulary use in the linked data cloud. Online Inf. Rev. **41**(2), 252–271 (2017). https://doi.org/10.1108/OIR-06-2015-0183
10. Voss, J., et al.: Cataloging knowledge organisation systems in BARTOC - results of a student project at Hannover University of Applied Sciences and Arts. Informationspraxis **3**(2), 1–12 (2017). https://doi.org/10.11588/ip.2017.2.40335
11. Barbosa, A., Bittencourt, I.I., Siqueira, S.W.M., de Amorim Silva, R., Calado, I.: The use of software tools in linked data publication and consumption: a systematic literature review. Int. J. Semant. Web Inf. Syst. **13**(4), 68–88 (2017). https://doi.org/10.4018/IJSWIS.2017100104

Document Based RDF Storage Method for Efficient Parallel Query Processing

Eleftherios Kalogeros, Manolis Gergatsoulis$^{(\boxtimes)}$, and Matthew Damigos

Database and Information Systems Group (DBIS),
Department of Archives, Library Science and Museology, Ionian University,
Corfu, Greece
{kalogero,manolis}@ionio.gr, mgdamig@gmail.com

Abstract. In this paper, we investigate the problem of efficiently evaluating SPARQL queries, over large amount of linked data utilizing distributed NoSQL system. We propose an efficient approach for partitioning large linked data graphs using distributed frameworks (MapReduce), as well as an effective data model for storing linked data in a document database using a maximum replication factor of 2 (i.e., in the worst case scenario, the data graph will be doubled in storage size). The model proposed and the partitioning approach ensure high-performance query evaluation and horizontal scaling for the type of queries called *generalized star queries* (i.e., queries allowing both subject-object and object-subject edges from a central node), due to the fact that no joining operations over multiple datasets are required to evaluate the queries. Furthermore, we present an implementation of our approach using MongoDB and an algorithm for translating generalized star queries into MongoDB query language, based on the proposed data model.

Keywords: RDF · Linked data · Parallel processing · NoSQL ·
Document databases

1 Introduction

Web information expressed as Linked Data is rapidly growing. According to [1], the number of the datasets in the LOD cloud was doubled the years between 2011–2014, while the number of datasets belonging to the category Publications (e.g. library datasets, information about scientific publications) was the 13% of the LOD datasets. Widely used centralized RDF stores (e.g. [2,3]), usually utilize relational structures for persisting data, which however lack scalability and efficient way to process and analyze large amount of Linked Data graphs. Thus, approaches for utilizing parallel processing frameworks and distributed NoSQL databases have been investigated (e.g. [4–7]).

The last decades, where storing and efficiently querying large amount of data becomes a major challenge, databases using non-relational structures for storing data have received significant attention by the research community and been

E. Garoufallou et al. (Eds.): MTSR 2018, CCIS 846, pp. 13–25, 2019.
https://doi.org/10.1007/978-3-030-14401-2_2

getting widely used by the industry. Those types of information management systems are usually referred as NoSQL databases [8] and are characterized by their efficiency on managing complex (e.g., graph, or hierarchical) and big data (i.e., large volume of data). Representative examples of such systems include MongoDB [9], Apache HBase [10] and Neo4j [11]. NoSQL databases are classified according to the data model they use as: Key-Value stores (e.g., Redis), Columnar databases (e.g., HBase), Document databases (e.g., MongoDB) and Graph databases (e.g., Neo4j). Note that there are systems that could be classified to more than one category (e.g., Dremel [12] which uses columnar data structures to store the data, hierarchical model to conceptually structure the data and relational structure for query results). Most of the above systems support horizontal scaling and distributed query evaluation, but lack on supporting joins over the stored collections.

This paper investigates the problem of efficiently evaluating a certain type of widely-used SPARQL queries over large amount of linked data utilizing distributed NoSQL system. In particular, we propose an efficient approach for partitioning large linked data graphs using distributed frameworks (MapReduce), as well as an effective data model for storing linked data in a document databases. The partitioning approach uses a maximum replication factor of 2 (i.e., in the worst case scenario, the data graph will be doubled in storage size). The model proposed and the partitioning approach ensure high-performance query evaluation and horizontal scaling for the type of queries called *generalized star queries* (i.e., queries that allowing both subject-object and object-subject edges from the central node), due to the fact that no joining operations over multiple datasets are required to evaluate the queries. In [13] the analysis for real-world SPARQL queries show that 99.97% of them are star queries and the chain queries in 98% of them have length one. We also present an implementation of our approach using MongoDB and an algorithm for translating generalized star queries into MongoDB query language, based on the proposed data model. This paper extends our previous approach of data graph partition method, called *s-partition* [14], by getting an efficient partition method for storing data graphs into NoSQL document databases. It is important to note that, as we have proved in [14], every query can be decomposed into a set of generalized star queries [14,15], which can be used to compute the answers of the initial query. This means that, if the initial query is not in the form of a generalized star query, it can be transformed into a set of such sub-queries. These sub-queries can be evaluated in parallel, such that each sub-query can be answered locally into each document without any join. The final answers are obtained by appropriately combining the answers of the sub-queries using the algorithms presented in [14–16].

2　Related Work

During the last decade, many distributed RDF methods and systems are presented for efficient partitioning, storing and querying large amount or RDF data. SHARD [4], HadoopRDF [6], PigSPARQL [5] and EAGRE [7] use the Apache

Hadoop Distributed File System (HDFS) for storing RDF data. In SHARD all data triples having the same subject are placed in the same line of file, HadoopRDF place all data triples sharing the same predicate value in the same part of data, EAGRE uses METIS [17] graph partition tool to partition data across the cluster. PigSPARQL [5] implements a translation from SPARQL to Pig Latin [18]. Besides the use of HDFS, numerus systems use NoSQL databases to store RDF data. In H_2RDF [19] system data triples are stored in Apache HBase. Rya [20] use Apache Accumulo [21], CumullusRDF use Apache Cassandra [22] and AMADA use Amazon DynamoDB [23]. S2RDF [24] uses a novel relational schema for RDF called ExtVP (Extended Vertical Partitioning). It is implemented using the SQL interface of Apache Spark [25]. D-SPARQ [26] uses MongoDB to store data. METIS is the tool used for the partition of the data. All data triples sharing the same subject grouped in the same document.

3   Data and Query Graphs

In this section we present the basic concepts used throughout this paper. We initially consider a directed graph G with labels in edges. The set of edges of G is denoted $\mathcal{E}(G)$, while $\mathcal{N}(G)$ represents the set of nodes of G. In the following, we define two types of labeled, directed graphs, the *data graph* and the *query graph* (which equivalently represents a SPARQL query).

Definition 1. *Let U_{so} and U_p be disjoint sets of URI references and L be a set of (plain) literals.[1] An element $(s, p, o) \in U_{so} \times U_p \times (U_{so} \cup L)$ is called a **data triple**. A **data graph** is a non-empty set of data triples. A data graph G' is a **subgraph** of a data graph G if $G' \subseteq G$.*

Definition 2. *Let U_{so} and U_p be two disjoint sets of URI references, let L be a set of (plain) literals and let V and V_p be two disjoint sets of variables. An element $(s, p, o) \in (U_{so} \cup V) \times (U_p \cup V_p) \times (U_{so} \cup L \cup V)$ is called a **query triple**. A **query graph** (or simply a **query**) is a non-empty set of query triples. The **output pattern** $O(Q)$ of a query Q is the tuple $<(X_1, \ldots, X_n), (P_1, \ldots, P_m)>$, with $n, m \geq 0$, and $X_1, \ldots, X_n \in V$, and $P_1, \ldots, P_m \in V_p$ and $X_1, \ldots, X_n, P_1, \ldots, P_m$ appear[2] in Q. A query Q' is a **subquery** of a query Q if $Q' \subseteq Q$.*

In a data or a query triple $t = (s, p, o)$, s is called *subject*, p *predicate* and o *object*. t also referred as an *incoming* edge of o, as well as an *outgoing* edge of s. The nodes $\mathcal{N}(G)$ (resp. $\mathcal{N}(Q)$) of a data graph G (resp. a query Q) is the set of elements of $U_{so} \cup L$ (resp. $U_{so} \cup L \cup V$) that occur in the triples of G (resp. Q). The *edge labels* $\mathcal{L}_{\mathcal{E}}(G)$ (resp. $\mathcal{L}_{\mathcal{E}}(Q)$) of a data graph G (resp. a query Q) is the set of elements of U_p (resp. $U_p \cup V_p$) that occur in the triples of G (resp. Q). The set of literals of G is denoted as $L(G)$.

We illustrate data and query graphs as follows. A node (subject or object) which is either a URI or a variable, is represented as a rounded rectangle. An

---

[1] In this paper we do not consider typed literals.

[2] Note that not all variables of Q necessarily appear in the output pattern $O(Q)$ of Q.

object which is a literal is represented by a conventional rectangle. A triple (s, p, o) is represented by the directed edge $s \xrightarrow{p} o$, labeled by p, from s to o. Strings with initial lowercase letters represent (URIs corresponding to) predicates, while strings with initial uppercase letters denote URIs labeling graph nodes (subjects or objects). Literals are represented as strings enclosed in double quotes and variables as strings whose first symbol is the question mark (?).

We now define a class of queries called *generalized star queries*.

Definition 3. *A query Q is called a **generalized star query** if there exists a node $c \in \mathcal{N}(Q)$ such that for every triple $t \in Q$, c is either the subject or the object of t and c is not a literal. In all cases, c is called the **central node** of Q and is denoted as $C(Q)$.*

Unlike the definition of star queries in the relevant literature [27,28], where the central node is considered the subject of outgoing edges in the query graph, we use a generalized definition of star queries, where star queries may consist of both incoming and outgoing edges of the central node.

Example 1. Four generalized star queries are depicted in Fig. 1. Notice that, only the queries Q1 and Q3 are star queries as defined in [27,28]. Notice also that, query Q4 is also a chain query [27,28] of length 2.

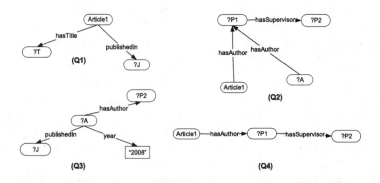

Fig. 1. s-query (Q_1), o-query (Q_2) and so-query (Q_3) examples.

To compute the answers to a query Q for a given data graph G, we consider finding an appropriate mapping from the nodes and edges of Q to the nodes and edges of G. This is formalized by the concept of *embedding*, defined as follows.

Definition 4. *An **embedding** of a query graph Q to a data graph G is a total mapping $e : \mathcal{N}(Q) \cup \mathcal{L}_{\mathcal{E}}(Q) \rightarrow \mathcal{N}(G) \cup \mathcal{L}_{\mathcal{E}}(G)$ satisfying the following conditions:*

1. *For each node $v \in \mathcal{N}(Q)$, if $v \in V$ then $e(v) \in \mathcal{N}(G)$ otherwise $e(v) = v$.*
2. *For each node $p \in \mathcal{L}_{\mathcal{E}}(Q)$, if $p \in V_p$ then $e(p) \in \mathcal{L}_{\mathcal{E}}(G)$ otherwise $e(p) = p$.*
3. *For each triple $(s, p, o) \in Q$, the triple $(e(s), e(p), e(o))$ is in G.*

We denote as $e(Q)$ the set of triples: $\{t|t = (e(s), e(p), e(o))$ and $(s, p, o) \in Q\} \subseteq G$. The **result** of Q on G, denoted as $Q(G)$, is the set $\{<(e(X_1), \ldots, e(X_n)), (e(P_1), \ldots, e(P_m))>|<(X_1, \ldots, X_n), (P_1, \ldots, P_m)>$ is the output pattern of Q, and e an embedding from Q to $G\}$. Each tuple in $Q(G)$ is an **answer** of Q.

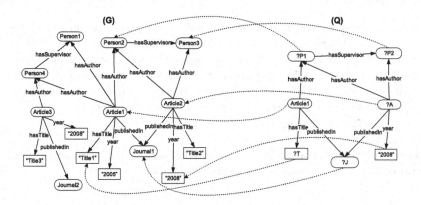

Fig. 2. A data graph G, a query Q, and an embedding of Q in G.

Example 2. A data graph G and a query graph Q is depicted in Fig. 2. The figure also depicts an embedding of the query Q in data graph G. The answer obtained by this embedding is: `<(?P1,?J,?P2,?A,?T), ()> =`
`<(Person2,Journal1,Person3,Article2,''Title1"), ()>.`

4   Data Graph Partitioning

A data graph may consist of a large volume of data triples, stored in numerous computer nodes. In this paper, we propose a method for partitioning the data graph in data graph segments in such a way that every graph segment is stored as a different document in a NoSQL/document database. In the proposed partitioning method the answers of every generalized star query can be computed in document level; avoiding, in such way, computationally expensive joins over large data tables. The proposed method offers the opportunity for horizontal scaling in a balanced manner. The definition of the partition scheme, called *node-oriented partition* (or simply *node-partition*), is given as follows.

Definition 5. *Let G be a data graph. A **node-oriented partition** (or **node-partition** for short) of G is a set of subgraphs $\mathcal{P} = \{G_{n_1}, \ldots, G_{n_m}\}$ of G, with $n_i \in (\mathcal{N}(G) - L(G))$ and $1 \leq i \leq |\mathcal{N}(G) - L(G)| = m$, such that for each $n_i \in (\mathcal{N}(G) - L(G))$, with $1 \leq i \leq m$, $G_{n_i} = \{t|t = (s, p, o) \in G$ and either $s = n_i$ or $o = n_i\}$. Subgraphs $G_1, \ldots, G_m$ are called **node-graph segments**. The node n_i node is called central node of G_i.*

The above definition implies $\bigcup_{i=1}^{m} G_{n_i} = G$; where the set-union operator is considered (i.e., duplicate triples are eliminated). By definition of node-oriented partition, we conclude that each no-literal node in the data graph is replicated at most twice, which shows that the data graph is at most doubled.

Proposition 1. *Let G be a data graph, and $\mathcal{P} = \{G_{n_1}, \ldots, G_{n_m}\}$, with $m \geq 1$, be a node-partition of G. Considering $S = \sum_{i=1}^{m} |G_{n_i}|$, we have that $S \leq 2 * |G|$.*

Example 3. Applying the node-partition method on the data graph of Fig. 2 nine different node-graph segments, one for each different URI node of the data graph, will be created. Two of them are depicted in Fig. 3 and are given below. Notice that, the triple (`Article1hasAuthorPerson2`) appears in both of them: Segment G1 (with central node *Article*1): {(`Article1 hasAuthor Person1`), (`Article1 hasAuthor Person2`), (`Article1 hasAuthor Person4`), (`Article1 hasTitle "Title1"`), (`Article1 year "2005"`), (`Article1 publishedIn Journal1`)}.
Segment G2 (with central node *Person*2): {(`Person2 hasSupervisor Person3`), (`Article1 hasAuthor Person2`), (`Article2 hasAuthor Person2`)}.

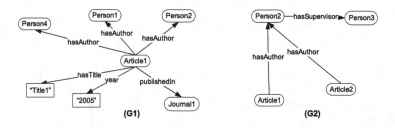

Fig. 3. Two node-partition segments (G1), (G2) obtained from the graph (G) of Fig. 2.

Theorem 1. *Let $\mathcal{P} = \{G_1, \ldots, G_m\}$, with $m \geq 1$, be a node-partition of a data graph G, and Q be a generalized star query. Then a mapping e is an embedding from Q to G if and only if there is a segment G_e in $\mathcal{P}$ such that $e(Q) \subseteq G_e$. Consequently, $Q(G) = \bigcup_{G_i \in \mathcal{P}} Q(G_i)$.*

Theorem 1 shows that the evaluation of a (generalized) star query over each segment of a node partition of a data graph is independent to the evaluation of the query over the other segments. Based on this property, we present in Sect. 6 an efficient approach for evaluating such queries over large data graphs, using a distributed document database (MongoDB).

Example 4. Applying the star query Q4 depicted in Fig. 1 to the graph segment G2 we get the answer: <(`?P1,?P2`),()> = <(`Person2,Person3`),()>.

5   The MapReduce Framework

MapReduce [29] is a programming framework, built by Google, for processing large datasets in a distributed manner. The storage layer for the Google MapReduce system is a Distributed File System (DFS). Hadoop [30] is the open source alternative system which uses the Hadoop Distributed File System (HDFS) for distributed storage. Creating a MapReduce job, the user defines two functions, *map* and *reduce* function, which run in each cluster node, in isolation. The map function is applied on one or more files, in DFS, and results <key,value> pairs. This process is called *map task*. The nodes that run the Map tasks are called *mappers*. The *master controller* directs the pairs emitted by mappers to the *reducers* (i.e., the nodes that apply the reduce function on the pairs) such that all pairs with the same key initialize a single reduce process, called *reduce task*. The reduce tasks apply the reduce function on the input pairs and also result <key,value> pairs. This procedure describes a *MapReduce phase*. Most NoSQL databases (including MongoDB) support connectors (i.e., libraries) which allow those databases to be used as either an input source, or output destination, for Hadoop MapReduce jobs. In the following, we utilize the output MongoDB connector for loading the output of a MapReduce job into MongoDB collection.

6   Document Based Graph Storage and Processing

In this section, we present an approach of utilizing the node-partition technique defined in Sect. 4, for efficiently evaluating generalized star queries over large data graphs. We focus on using the document-oriented database MongoDB [9] for storing and querying large amount of data graphs in a distributed manner; ensuring in such a way scalability, consistency and partition tolerance (CP in CAP Theorem [31]). The proposed model for storing node-partitioned data graph preserves the directed graph structure of the data into each node-graph segment. In particular, each node-graph segment is stored in hierarchical/document structure (each segment is translated to a single document). Although the proposed data model could be applied in most of the NoSQL databases that support document model for structuring the data (e.g., eXistDB [32], CouchDB [33], MongoDB [9], Dremel [12]), we focus on MongoDB, which uses JSON (JavaScript Object Notation) [34] as document format, due to proven high-performance management of large amount of hierarchical data and support of advanced indexing strategies (e.g., multikey indexes). The data model used to store each node-graph segment in a different document is defined in Fig. 4(a). In this model, each segment document/object consists of the following attributes: (1) the URI of the central node, (2) an array of subjects including all the outgoing edges, and (3) an array of objects including all the incoming edges. Note that we consider grouping of all the incoming and outgoing edges according to their predicate in order to reduce the replication of the predicate values in the edges. As an example, in Fig. 4(b), we can see the JSON document file that represents the node-graph segment $G2$ depicted in Fig. 3.

```
object node-segment {
  string "centralNode";
  object "subject" {
    string "value";
    array of objects "predicate" {
      string "value";
      array of objects "object" {
        string "value";
      }
    }
  }
  object "object" {
    string "value";
    array of objects "predicate" {
      string "value";
      array of objects "subject" {
        string "value";
      }
    }
  }
}
```

```
{
  "centralNode" : "Person2",
  "subject" : {
    "predicate" : [
      {
        "value" : "hasSupervisor",
        "object" : [
          {
            "value" : "Person3"
          }
        ]
      }
    ]
  },
  "object" : {
    "predicate" : [
      {
        "value" : "hasAuthor",
        "subject" : [
          {
            "value" : "Article1"
          },
          {
            "value" : "Article2"
          }
        ]
      }
    ]
  }
}
```

(a)   (b)

Fig. 4. (a) Document data model, (b) Segment represented by a JSON document

To ensure efficient node-partitioning of data graphs and loading the resulted segments into MongoDB, we propose the following MapReduce algorithm: The *map function* gets an input file containing data triples and for each triple outputs: (a) a pair including the subject as key and a tuple including the predicate and object as value (along with a flag specifying that the value corresponds to outgoing edge), and, (b) if the object is not literal, a pair including the predicate and subject as value (along with a flag specifying that the value corresponds to incoming edge). *Reduce function* gets all triples of a certain node-segment and distinguish them into a group of outgoing and a group of incoming edges. Within each group, it applies a secondary grouping based on the predicate values. From these groups the reduce task generates a JSON document which represents a node-segment of the data graph according to the data model presented in Fig. 4(a). Finally, the reducers upload/store the constructed documents into MongoDB.

```
mapper(key, values)
// key: data file
// values: data triples t=(s, p, o)
begin
   - for each data triple t in data file
      - Emit <s,("subject", p, o)>
      if (o ∉ L) then
         - Emit <o,("object", p, s)>
      endif
end.
reducer(key, values)
// key: s and o ∉ L of all data triples
// values: data triples t=[s,p,o]
begin
   - Group the values per "object" and "subject"
   - For each "subject" group, group the values per predicate (p) value
   - For each "object" group, group the values per predicate (p) value
   - Costruct the JSON document d based on data model shown in Fig. 4(a)
   - Load d using the corresponding MongoDB connector
end.
```

We now present an algorithm for transforming generalized star queries (given into SPARQL) into MongoDB queries:

```
generalized star query to MongoDB query transformation algorithm
// input: generalized star query Q
// output: MongoDB query
begin
  Let V the set of variables in Q and c=C(Q)
  if c ∉ V
     query +={ centralNode : e(c) }
  for each query triple tᵢ = (sᵢ,pᵢ,oᵢ) in Q do
     if sᵢ=c
       if pᵢ ∉ V and oᵢ ∉ V
          query +={subject.predicate : { $elemMatch : { value: e(pᵢ),
                  object : { $elemMatch : { value : e(oᵢ)}}}}}
       else if pᵢ ∉ V and oᵢ ∈ V
          query +={subject.predicate : { $elemMatch : { value : e(pᵢ) }}}
       else if pᵢ ∈ V and oᵢ ∉ V
          query +={subject.predicate.object : { $elemMatch : { value : e(oᵢ)}}}
     else
       if pᵢ ∉ V and sᵢ ∉ V
          query +={object.predicate : { $elemMatch : { value : e(pᵢ),
                  subject : { $elemMatch : { value : e(sᵢ) }}}}}
       else if pᵢ ∉ V and sᵢ ∈ V
          query +={object.predicate : { $elemMatch : { value : e(pᵢ)}}}
       else if pᵢ ∈ V and oᵢ ∉ V
```

```
        query +={object.predicate.subject : { $elemMatch : { value : e(sᵢ)}}}
   MongoDBQuery = { $ and : [ + query + ] }
end.
```

Example 5. The MongoDB query constructed by applying the aforementioned transformation algorithm to the generalized star query Q_2 depicted in Fig. 1 is:

```
{
  "$and" :
   [
    { "object.predicate" :
      { "$elemMatch": { "value" : "hasAuthor" ,
        "subject" : { "$elemMatch" : { "value": "Article1" } } }
      }
    },
    { "object.predicate" :
          { "$elemMatch" : { "value": "hasAuthor"} }
    },
    { "subject.predicate" :
          { "$elemMatch" : { "value": "hasSupervisor" } }
    }
   ]
}
```

7 Experimental Evaluation

We now present a set of preliminary experiments performed on a Virtual Server with the following characteristics: Intel Xeon 3.40 GHz (2 Sockets, 2 Cores) with 8 GB RAM, 100 GB HD, Ubuntu 16.04 Operating System and MongoDB version 3.2.20. We used five different datasets D1–D5 in N-Triples format obtained and adapted from the Waterloo SPARQL Diversity Test Suite (WatDiv) [27]. The number of triples of dataset, as well as the scale factors used to generate the datasets, are illustrated in Table 1. We applied the node partitioning algorithm and the data was loaded directly in MongoDB. As an indication, the dataset D4 was partitioned into 521,945 segments and the average number of data triples per segment is approximately 40 triples. We also used the generalized star queries

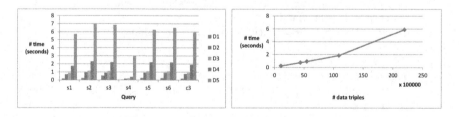

Fig. 5. Query evaluation experimental results

S1, S2, S3, S4, S5, S6 and C3 from the WatDiv Benchmark. S1 consists of nine query triples, S2–S5 four query triples, S6 three query triples and C3 six query triples. Each query was executed ten times and the average time in seconds for each query in the five datasets is depicted in Table 1. Figure 5 also illustrates a comparison of evaluation time per query, and depicts how the approach scales in terms of amount of triples in the input dataset. The right figure shows an average response time of all queries per dataset. It is important to note that the comparison of the experimental results of this method with the experimental results of the methods presented in our previous work [14–16], in which relational databases were used to store the fragments of the data graphs, shows that, the storage method (in conjuction with the node-oriented partition proposed in this paper), is more effiecient especially when the number of query triples increases.

Table 1. Comparing execution times of seven generalized star queries in five datasets.

Dataset/ query	Scale factor	Number of tuples	S1	S2	S3	S4	S5	S6	C3
D1	10	1,103,551	0.18	0.24	0.54	0.04	0.23	0.23	0.18
D2	40	4,393,717	0.70	0.93	0.88	0.15	0.88	0.88	0.75
D3	50	5,489,846	0.88	1.15	1.10	0.19	1.10	1.10	0.90
D4	100	10,916,457	1.75	2.30	2.20	0.38	2.20	2.17	1.90
D5	200	21,971,269	5.72	6.97	6.86	3.00	6.25	6.49	5.91

8   Conclusion

In this paper, we present an approach for partitioning large amount of Linked Data graphs that ensures efficient evaluation of generalized star queries in distributed manner. We also propose a document-oriented data model for storing effectively the data graph in a distributed, document database in order to utilize the distributed query processing mechanism of such systems. MongoDB is used as representative NoSQL system for implementing our approach. As future work we aim to extend our approach to more general classes of SPARQL queries.

References

1. Schmachtenberg, M., Bizer, C., Paulheim, H.: Adoption of the linked data best practices in different topical domains. In: Mika, P., et al. (eds.) ISWC 2014. LNCS, vol. 8796, pp. 245–260. Springer, Cham (2014). https://doi.org/10.1007/978-3-319-11964-9_16
2. Apache Jena. https://jena.apache.org/
3. Virtuoso Universal Server. https://virtuoso.openlinksw.com/
4. Rohloff, K., Schantz, R.E.: Clause-iteration with MapReduce to scalably query datagraphs in the SHARD graph-store. In: 4th International Workshop on Data-Intensive Distributed Computing, DIDC 2011, pp. 35–44 (2011)

5. Schätzle, A., Przyjaciel-Zablocki, M., Lausen, G.: PigSPARQL: mapping SPARQL to Pig Latin. In: SWIM 2011, pp. 4:1–4:8. ACM (2011)
6. Du, J.-H., Wang, H.-F., Ni, Y., Yu, Y.: HadoopRDF: a scalable semantic data analytical engine. In: Huang, D.-S., Ma, J., Jo, K.-H., Gromiha, M.M. (eds.) ICIC 2012. LNCS (LNAI), vol. 7390, pp. 633–641. Springer, Heidelberg (2012). https://doi.org/10.1007/978-3-642-31576-3_80
7. Zhang, X., Chen, L., Tong, Y., Wang, M.: EAGRE: towards scalable I/O efficient SPARQL query evaluation on the cloud. In: ICDE 2013, pp. 565–576. IEEE (2013)
8. Han, J., Haihong, E., Le, G., Du, J.: Survey on NoSQL database. In: ICPCA 2011, pp. 363–366. IEEE (2011)
9. MongoDB, NoSQL Document Database. https://www.mongodb.com/
10. Apache HBase. https://hbase.apache.org/
11. Neo4j Graph Platform. https://neo4j.com/
12. Melnik, S., et al.: Dremel: interactive analysis of web-scale datasets. VLDB Endow. **3**(1–2), 330–339 (2010)
13. Gallego, M.A., Fernández, J.D., Martínez-Prieto, M.A., de la Fuente, P.: An empirical study of real-world SPARQL queries. In: USEWOD Workshop (2011)
14. Kalogeros, E., Gergatsoulis, M., Damigos, M.: Redundancy in linked data partitioning for efficient query evaluation. In: FiCloud 2015, pp. 497–504. IEEE (2015)
15. Nomikos, C., Gergatsoulis, M., Kalogeros, E., Damigos, M.: A Map-Reduce algorithm for querying linked data based on query decomposition into stars. In: Workshops of EDBT/ICDT 2014, vol. 1133, pp. 224–231. CEUR-WS (2014)
16. Gergatsoulis, M., Nomikos, C., Kalogeros, E., Damigos, M.: An algorithm for querying linked data using map-reduce. In: Hameurlain, A., Rahayu, W., Taniar, D. (eds.) Globe 2013. LNCS, vol. 8059, pp. 51–62. Springer, Heidelberg (2013). https://doi.org/10.1007/978-3-642-40053-7_5
17. Karypis, G., Kumar, V.: A fast and high quality multilevel scheme for partitioning irregular graphs. SIAM J. Sci. Comput. **20**(1), 359–392 (1998)
18. Olston, C., Reed, B., Srivastava, U., Kumar, R., Tomkins, A.: Pig Latin: a not-so-foreign language for data processing. In: SIGMOD Conference 2008, pp. 1099–1110. ACM (2008)
19. Papailiou, N., Konstantinou, I., Tsoumakos, D., Karras, P., Koziris, N.: H2RDF+: high-performance distributed joins over large-scale RDF graphs. In: IEEE BigData 2013, pp. 255–263. IEEE (2013)
20. Punnoose, R., Crainiceanu, A., Rapp, D.: Rya: a scalable RDF triple store for the clouds. In: CLOUD-I (2012)
21. Apache Accumulo. https://accumulo.apache.org/
22. Apache Cassandra. http://cassandra.apache.org/
23. Amazon DynamoDB. https://aws.amazon.com/dynamodb/
24. Schätzle, A., Przyjaciel-Zablocki, M., Skilevic, S., Lausen, G.: S2RDF: RDF querying with SPARQL on spark. VLDB Endow. **9**(10), 804–815 (2016)
25. Apache Spark. http://spark.apache.org/
26. Mutharaju, R., Sakr, S., Sala, A., Hitzler, P.: D-SPARQ: distributed, scalable and efficient RDF query engine. In: ISWC-PD 2013, vol. 1035, pp. 261–264, CEUR-WS (2013)
27. Aluç, G., Hartig, O., Özsu, M.T., Daudjee, K.: Diversified stress testing of RDF data management systems. In: Mika, P., et al. (eds.) ISWC 2014. LNCS, vol. 8796, pp. 197–212. Springer, Cham (2014). https://doi.org/10.1007/978-3-319-11964-9_13
28. Wu, B., Zhou, Y., Yuan, P., Liu, L., Jin, H.: Scalable SPARQL querying using path partitioning. In: ICDE 2015, pp. 795–806. IEEE (2015)

29. Dean, J., Ghemawat, S.: MapReduce: simplified data processing on large clusters. Commun. ACM **51**(1), 107–113 (2008)
30. Apache Hadoop. http://hadoop.apache.org/
31. Fox, A., Brewer, E.A.: Harvest, yield, and scalable tolerant systems. In: 7th Workshop on Hot Topics in Operating Systems, pp. 174–178. IEEE (1999)
32. eXist-db - The Open Source Native XML Database. http://exist-db.org/
33. Apache CouchDB. http://couchdb.apache.org/
34. JSON (JavaScript Object Notation). http://www.json.org/

Legal Entity Identifier Blockchained by a Hyperledger Indy Implementation of GraphChain

Mirek Sopek[1], Przemysław Grądzki[1,2], Dominik Kuziński[1],
Rafał Trójczak[1,2], and Robert Trypuz[1,2(✉)]

[1] R&D Team, MakoLab S.A., ul. Demokratyczna 46, 93-430 Łódź, Poland
{sopek,robert.trypuz}@makolab.com
[2] Faculty of Philosophy, The John Paul II Catholic University of Lublin,
Al. Racławickie 14, 20-950 Lublin, Poland

Abstract. The main idea behind GraphChain is to use blockchain mechanisms on top of abstract RDF graphs. This paper presents an implementation of GraphChain in the Hyperledger Indy framework. The whole setting is shown to be applied to the RDF graphs containing information about Legal Entity Identifiers (LEIs). The blockchain based data management system presented in the paper preserves all the benefits of using RDF data model for the representation of LEI system reference data, including powerful querying mechanisms, explicit semantics and data model extensibility with the security and non-repudiation of LEIs as the digital identifiers for legal entities.

Keywords: Hyperledger · Hyperledger Indy · GraphChain ·
Semantic blockchain · LEI · GLEIS

1 Introduction

This paper presents the idea and proposes the implementation of blockchain based data management system that could be used for the global LEI system (GLEIS). The system preserves all the benefits of using RDF data model for the representation of LEI system reference data, including powerful querying mechanisms, explicit semantics and data model extensibility with the security and non-repudiation of LEIs as the digital identifiers for legal entities. To achieve such features we combined the solutions previously invented for the GraphChain [6] with one of the frameworks of the Hyperledger project, namely Hyperledger Indy.

The idea of combining blockchain technology with the Semantic Web principles has been proposed in [2,3,9]. An approach similar to the presented in this paper, albeit not for LEI system, can be found in [4], where Flex Ledger – a graph data model and a protocol for decentralised ledgers – was presented.

In Sect. 2, we will first introduce the basics of the Legal Entity Identifiers (LEIs), the basics of GLEIS and an ontology we have developed for the system

© Springer Nature Switzerland AG 2019
E. Garoufallou et al. (Eds.): MTSR 2018, CCIS 846, pp. 26–36, 2019.
https://doi.org/10.1007/978-3-030-14401-2_3

called GLEIO [8]. Then, after short introduction to blockchain technology in Sect. 3.1, we will explain in Sects. 3.2 and 3.3 the rationale of using it for LEI system and why the use of GraphChain is important for the goals of our work. Finally, in Sects. 3.4 and 3.5, we will present how the use Hyperledger Indy helps to achieve these goals, and present some implementation details behind our proposal.

2   Legal Entity Identifier and Its Ontology

2.1   Legal Entity Identifier

A Legal Entity Identifier, LEI in short, is a 20-digit, alpha-numeric code. It is based on the ISO 17442 standard. It is intended to be the key and unique legal entity reference number enabling straightforward identification of legal entities participating in financial transactions throughout the whole world.

Each LEI is connected to the legal entity reference information that is specified and standardised by means of Common Data File (CDF in short) formats[1]. Currently there are two levels of the LEI reference data. Level 1 provides information about the official name of a legal entity, its legal and headquarters' addresses and the LEI registration data such as LEI initial registration date, next renewal date, etc. Level 2 specifies information about relationships of a legal entity with other legal entities.

The management of the global LEI system (GLEIS) is coordinated and supported by the Global Legal Entity Identifier Foundation (GLEIF)[2]. GLEIF accredits some external organisations to operate within the GLEIS as issuers of LEIs[3]. LEI issuers are called Local Operating Units (LOUs).

For the sake of further analysis, it is important for us to understand the whole process of LEI registration and maintenance. At the beginning of the process, through self-registration, the registering legal entity supplies its reference data (such as its legal name, address or the business identifier in the jurisdiction of its legal registration). The LOU verifies the reference data with local authoritative sources and issues an LEI. Every day each LOU reports all the LEIs with their reference data to GLEIF by means of XML Concatenated Files (standardised by CDF formats as was described above). Also GLEIF publishes daily updated XML Concatenated Files including all current LEIs, their reference data and description of relationships between legal entities.

---

[1] https://www.gleif.org/en/about-lei/common-data-file-format.

[2] www.gleif.org.

[3] We shall not describe in details the whole process of accreditation by which GLEIF evaluates the suitability of organisations seeking to operate within the GLEIS as LOUs, see https://www.gleif.org/en/about-lei/gleif-accreditation-of-lei-issuers/accreditation-process.

Summarising, in the whole process of LEI registration and maintenance we may distinguish the following roles:

- users (legal entities) – requesting for LEIs and supplying their reference data
- LOUs – responsible for issuing LEIs and verifying the reference data provided by legal entities
- GLEIF – the organisation that accredits LOUs, collects and publishes all LEI reference data daily.

2.2   Global LEI Ontology

LOUs report LEIs and their reference data by means of XML files compliant with the CDF format. For instance the XML schema for LEI level 1 consists of LEI File Header and LEI Data Record as depicted in Fig. 1.

Data File		
LEI File Header		[0,1]
ContentDate	DateTime	[0,1]
Originator	LEI	[0..1]
FileContent	FileContentEnum	[0..1]
DeltaStart	DateTime	[0..1]
RecordCount	Integer	[0..1]
Extension	Extension	[0,1]
LEI Data Record		[1..*]
LEI	LEI	[0,1]
Entity	Entity	[1]
LegalName	Name	[1]
OtherEntityNames	OtherEntityName	[0..n]
LegalAddress	Address	[1]
HeadquartersAddress	Address	[1]
OtherAddresses	OtherAddresses	[0..n]
BusinessRegisterEntityID	BusinessRegisterEntityID	[0,1]
LegalJurisdiction	JurisdictionCode	[0,1]
LegalForm	Name	[0,1]
AssociatedEntity	Associated	[*]
EntityStatus	EntityStatusEnum	[1]
EntityExpirationDate	DateTime	[0,1]
EntityExpirationReason	EntityExpirationReasonEnum	[0,1]
SuccessorEntity	Successor	[0,1]
Registration	Registration	[1]
InitialRegistrationDate	DateTime	[1]
LastUpdateDate	DateTime	[1]
RegistrationStatus	RegistrationStatusEnum	[1]
NextRenewalDate	DateTime	[1]
ValidationSources	ValidationSourcesEnum	[0,1]
Extension	Extension	[0,1]

Fig. 1. Visualisation of XML schema for the CDF format of level 1

In the paper [8, Sect. 2] we have described some advantages of semantic representation of LEIs – such as precise semantics, flexible extensibility, global persistent identifiers and inference – in contrast to the current XML representation. Moreover, we have proposed Global LEI Ontology (GLEIO in short)[4] that is not only compliant with CDF Format but also allows for representation of changes

---

[4] http://lei.info/gleio/.

of LEI and related LEI reference data over time. GLEIO provided meaning for LEI data, shaped the LEI triple store and allowed for SPARQL queries[5].

The methodology and the whole process of GLEIO creation was described in [8, Sect. 2.2]. A need for expressing change of LEIs and their reference data in time was as a very important modelling requirement while creating GLEIO. The changes we had in mind considered for instance a change of LEI registration status or the change of the legal address of an entity. As described in Sect. 2.1 GLEIF publishes the XML concatenated file daily. So every day we have a new snapshot of all LEIs. GLEIO allows for explicit representation of the LEIs' snapshot changes by means of manifestations. A manifestation of an entity is a complete picture of the entity in a given time stamp (snapshot). Each LEI may have one or many (linearly ordered) manifestations.

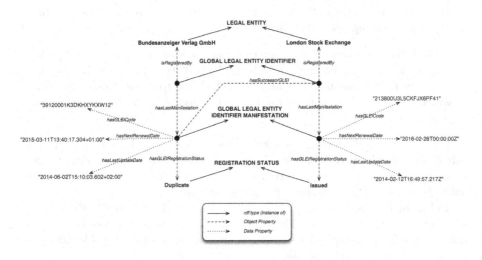

Fig. 2. Variable entity and its manifestations

GLEIO is part of SaaS (Software as a Service) application accessible at: http://lei.info – allowing for storing, displaying and integrating information about LEIs (It is also informational and educational portal about the GLEIS). Every day our LEI application reads a complete concatenated XML file and creates new manifestations for those LEIs that have changed since the last check had been performed (for instance if the status of LEI registration has changed from "Duplicate" to "Issued", then the LEI will gain a new manifestation – see Fig. 2).

Since we have eventually decided to create a chain of graphs in the blockchain spirit (our motivation is explained in the forthcoming section), manifestations have not been needed any more. Manifestations have been replaced by transactions (blocks of data). Also the linear order of manifestations has been replaced by the order of transactions in the ledger chain. A new GLEIO without manifestations can be browse here: https://lei.info/voc/.

---

[5] https://lei.info/sparql.

3   Towards Blockchained LEIs

3.1   A Short Introduction to Blockchain

The history of blockchain started ten years ago when Satoshi Nakamoto published "Bitcoin: A Peer-to-Peer Electronic Cash System" [5].

Blockchain is commonly associated with cryptocurrencies and cash transactions. But it was just the first phase of its evolution named "Blockchain 1.0" in [7]. The next blockchain evolution phase, Blockchain 2.0, proposed applications that offered smart contracts and could deal with complex financial products such as: bonds, loans or mortgages. Nowadays, we have Blockchain 3.0 offering applications going "beyond currency, finance, and markets particularly in the areas of government, health, science, literacy, culture, and art" [7].

Blockchain is usually defined by referring to its structure and function. In [1] we find the following general definition:

> A block chain is a type of database that takes a number of records and puts them in a block (...). Each block is then "chained" to the next block, using a cryptographic signature. This allows block chains to be used like a ledger, which can be shared and corroborated by anyone with the appropriate permissions.

Since we are still dealing with relatively young technology it is very difficult to classify the variety of blockchains. However there are two criteria that make it a lot clearer. These criteria are following blockchain deployment styles: public/private and permissioned/permissionless [10].

Public blockchains are open for everyone who would like to join them. They are also at least "read open". The private ones have limited access that is controlled by selected nodes. These nodes can control whether the blockchain is read-only or of read-write access.

In the permissioned blockchains there are parties that can assign different permissions/rights to the clients concerning the kinds of transactions they can carry out. Permissioned blockchains can also form "federated" or "consortium" blockchains. They may give the public right to read the blockchain. Permissionless blockchains do not have different permission levels.

Bitcoin, the first implementation of blockchain, is public and permissionless. We can observe the tendency to name only these sort of implementations "blockchains". Other ones (i.e. private or permissioned blockchains) are more commonly named "distributed ledger technologies". Sometimes "distributed ledger technology" names also public and permissionless blockchains.

In the permissionless and public blockchains the process of transaction validation is open for everyone. In the permissioned blockchains a node must satisfy certain criteria to gain permission for transaction validation. In the permissioned and private blockchain this means to become a member of the consortium.

3.2 Why Using Blockchain for LEI

From the very beginning of its existence GLEIF has not been thought of as a hub for collecting LEIs and their reference data. Its primary, and in fact only role, was management of "a network of partners, known as the LEI issuing organisations, to provide trusted services and open, reliable data for unique legal entity identification worldwide"[6].

Now keeping in mind what we have written in Sect. 2 about GLEIS, it is evident that GLEIF together with a network of LOUs and legal entities interested in getting LEIs creates a distributed system that can be adequately modelled as a permissioned (consortium) blockchain. From the high level view the proposed in this paper a new LEI system assumes the use of permissioned blockchain with three types of roles (see Fig. 3):

- Users and registars – the nodes participate in the global blockchain as passive users; they can see all the data stored in it, but can't create nor edit anything. Registars may have additional ability to "provisionally" add new LEIs to the system. However, such newly added LEIs are not visible on the system until the LOU nodes confirm them through the "Proof of Authority" mechanism.
- LOU nodes – the nodes having all the properties of the Registration nodes plus the capacity to confirm the new or modified LEIs as valid.
- GLEIF node – the node possessing all permissions

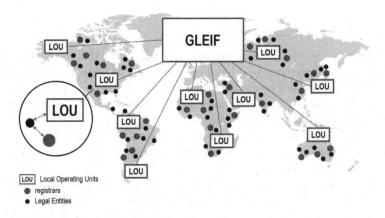

Fig. 3. GLEIS architecture

Such an architecture of the new LEI system enables thousands of registration authorities from multiple countries to participate in the new LEI creation, opening path for the true global adoption of the system.

There are many advantages of using blockchains (or distributed ledgers) in modern business applications. For the identification purposes (which is the

---

[6] See https://www.gleif.org/en/about/this-is-gleif/.

primary function of the LEI system) the most important benefits are: non-repudiation of identities and transactions, immutability of LEI data, decentralisation of LEI issuing and distribution process, lowering the LEI issuing costs, transparency to internal stakeholders and regulators, resilience to system failures, efficient replication mechanisms, far-reaching democratisation of digital identifiers generation, ability to restrict generation of identifiers to authorised agents or institutions, diversification of targets: institutions, legal and real persons, datasets and devices.

3.3   GraphChain

In [6] we presented an idea of GraphChain – a linearly ordered collection (a chain) of cryptographically secured named RDF graphs on which all nodes eventually agree. [6] describes the first preliminary (PoC) realisation of GraphChain. We described OWL-compliant GraphChain ontology that specifies all the structural, invariant elements of the GraphChain and defines their basic semantics. We have also presented some general mechanisms for calculating a digest of the named RDF graphs and some simple (naive) network mechanisms that are responsible for the distribution of the named RDF graphs among the distributed peers and for achieving the consensus.

The main idea behind GraphChain is to use blockchain mechanisms on top of an abstract RDF graph data model. In the next section we will describe how to build a distributed ledger of LEI graphs shaped by GLEIO ontology.

3.4   LEI in Hyperledger Indy

For our purposes, we have chosen Hyperledger Indy, as it is a distributed ledger built to be used for decentralised identity management[7]. The key assumption of Indy architecture is that the content (in our case LEI) data is never written to the ledger. This makes it the ideal choice for realising our idea of using blockchain mechanisms on top of triple store of LEIs.

Hyperledger Indy is a public and permissioned blockchain – Indy permits registered members to manage (write) their self-sovereign identity and everyone to read the content of the blockchain.

The ledger is maintained by the nodes, which run Plenum Byzantine Fault Tolerant Protocol, i.e. (a consensus protocol based on Redundant Byzantine Fault Tolerant) to agree on the order of transactions in the ledger. Pairwise Pseudonymous Identifiers and Decentralised Public Key Infrastructure (using asymmetric key cryptography) guarantee full privacy, prevent identity correlation and ensure that connections between the members of the system (nodes and clients) are established in secure, encrypted manner.

Another fundamental feature of Indy is using Decentralised Identifiers (DIDs)[8] – a new type of identifiers for "self-sovereign" digital identity. DIDs, as the primary keys on Indy ledger, enable long-term digital identities requiring no centralised registry services. DIDs are stored in the Indy ledger as NYM

---

[7] https://www.hyperledger.org/projects/hyperledger-indy.

[8] https://w3c-ccg.github.io/did-spec/.

records. Our first idea was to put LEI graph as attribute(s) added to NYM records corresponding to legal entities by using ATTRIB transaction. But there are a few problems related to the current implementation of Hyperledger Indy:

1. the maximum size of the data (represented as JSON) added as a attribute is limited to 5 * 1024 bytes
2. permissions assigned to roles[9] are not the same as permissions required by LEI system
3. attributes are not "searcheable" – there is no implemented request to execute full-text search based on the content of attributes.

The second idea, eventually realised by us, was to add a new transaction type: ADD_LEI. The transaction type is in fact "enhanced ATTRIB" transaction free of the limitations mentioned above. Whereas the raw data from ATTRIB transaction is stored in a separate attribute ledger—the key-value database (currently RocksDB), where the key is the hash of raw data and value is raw data[10]—our ADD_LEI transaction keeps data in the external searchable triple store (see Fig. 4). In ADD_LEI transaction, "http://lei.info/" concatenated with the hash of raw data. It forms IRI that is used as the identifier of the named graph:

$$\texttt{http://lei.info/<I-HASH>}$$

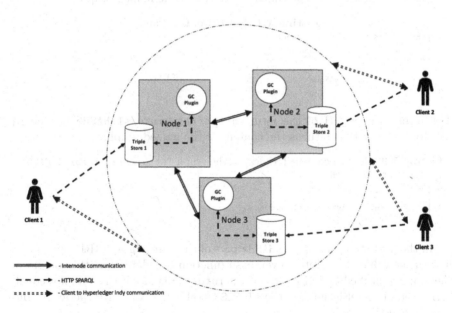

Fig. 4. The architecture of Hyperledger Indy with Triple Store

---

[9] https://docs.google.com/spreadsheets/d/1TWXF7NtBjSOaUIBeIH77SyZnawfo91c J_ns4TR-wsq4.

[10] https://github.com/hyperledger/indy-node/blob/stable/docs/transactions.md# attrib.

Functionality of the ADD_LEI transaction is implemented as "GC plugin" inside the Indy nodes (see Fig. 4). The plugin performs the following tasks:

- validates ADD_LEI transactions,
- checks users and nodes permissions to carry out transactions,
- reads and writes named graphs from/to the triple store.

Triple stores are external to the Indy nodes and allow clients to perform SPARQL queries.

3.5 Interwoven Hash Verification

In our framework, LEIs data are stored in the triple store within the named graphs. The named graphs' IRIs are made up as a concatenation of prefix "http://lei.info/" and the value of the Interwoven hash function[11] "<I-HASH>" calculated for the content of the named graph. The IRIs have the following shape: http://lei.info/<I-HASH>.

Since LEI data can be accessed directly from a triple store of a node through HTTP SPARQL query, one may wonder how to prove integrity of data in the triple store. Below we describe how to validate an LEI graph for a legal entity having legal name "EXAMPLE COMPANY LEGAL NAME".

First run SPARQL query that returns IRI of the named graph:

Listing 1.1. Get IRI of the graph

```
1  PREFIX ll:<http://lei.info/voc/ll/>
2  SELECT ?g
3  WHERE {
4      GRAPH ?g {
5          [ ll:hasLegalName "EXAMPLE COMPANY LEGAL NAME"] .
6      }
7  }
```

The result will be IRI of the form "http://lei.info/<I-HASH>". Then run SPARQL Query that returns the content of the named graph:

Listing 1.2. Get the content (triples) of the graph "http://lei.info/<I-HASH>"

```
1  CONSTRUCT { ?s ?p ?o }
2  WHERE
3  {
4    GRAPH <http://lei.info/<I-HASH>>
5    { ?s ?p ?o } .
6  }
```

In the next step, extract <I-HASH> part of the named graph IRI and compare it with the value of the Interwoven hash function calculated for (the content of) the graph identified by IRI http://lei.info/<I-HASH>. If they are not equal – verification fails, else check, if the <I-HASH> value is stored in Hyperledger Indy using request:

send GET_LEI ihash=<I-HASH>

If it's missing – verification fails. If they are equal, we have certainty of both the existence of an entity identified by such an IRI and the veracity of the retrieved data.

---

[11] The algorithm for calculating interwoven hash was described in [6, Sect. 4.3.3].

4   Conclusions

In this paper we have presented the idea and the implementation details of the proposed blockchain-based LEI system. This idea assumes the use of our GraphChain solution for the storage of LEI reference data and Hyperledger Indy framework for distributed, secured identification mechanisms and consensus about data.

As a future work we consider adding the meta-data of extracted from Indy's transactions (such as time stamp, sequence number, etc) to the triple store.

As a challenge also remains the question of storing data, which size exceeds the limit of the message size 128 *1024 (MSG_LEN_LIMIT[12]). As an option we consider cutting a line-based serialisations of RDF graphs, such as for example N-Triples, into sub-graphs that would fit the limit of size. Of course this solution would require a description of the sub-graphs in a way enabling their later "glueing" into the original graph.

Another benefit from the proposed architecture is its potential alignment to the digital identification system proposed by Sovrin Foundation[13]. The foundation's system realises the idea of Self-Sovereign Identity. The combination of such a model of digital identity and the LEI system is now being considered by us for the future of the LEI system which could enable legal entities to undeniably and uniquely identify themselves in digital space.

Acknowledgements. Our research was conducted in the project number 01.01.01-00-0982/16 funded by the National Centre for Research and Development under the Smart Growth Operational Programme.

References

1. UK Government Chief Scientific Adviser. Distributed Ledger Technology: beyond block chain. Technical report (2016)
2. English, M., Auer, S., Domingue, S.: Blockchain technologies & the semantic web: a framework for symbiotic development. In: Lehmann, J., Thakkar, H., Halilaj, L., Asmat, R. (eds.) CS Conference for University of Bonn Students, pp. 47–61 (2016)
3. García-Barriocanal, E., Sánchez-Alonso, S., Sicilia, M.-A.: Deploying metadata on blockchain technologies. In: Garoufallou, E., Virkus, S., Siatri, R., Koutsomiha, D. (eds.) MTSR 2017. CCIS, vol. 755, pp. 38–49. Springer, Cham (2017). https://doi.org/10.1007/978-3-319-70863-8_4
4. Lemieux, V.L., Sporny, M.: Preserving the archival bond in distributed ledgers: a data model and syntax. In: Proceedings of the 26th International Conference on World Wide Web Companion, Perth, Australia, 3–7 April 2017, pp. 1437–1443 (2017)
5. Nakamoto, S.: Bitcoin: A Peer-to-Peer Electronic Cash System. Technical report (2008)

---

[12] https://github.com/hyperledger/indy-plenum/blob/master/stp_core/config.py.
[13] https://sovrin.org/.

6. Sopek, M., Gradzki, P., Kosowski, W., Kuziski, D., Trójczak, R., Trypuz, R.: Graphchain: a distributed database with explicit semantics and chained RDF graphs. In: Companion Proceedings of the Web Conference 2018, WWW 2018, pp. 1171–1178, Republic and Canton of Geneva, Switzerland, International World Wide Web Conferences Steering Committee (2018)

7. Swan, M.: Blockchain: Blueprint for a New Economy, 1st edn. O'Reilly Media Inc., Sebastopol (2015)

8. Trypuz, R., Kuzinski, D., Sopek, M.: General legal entity identifier ontology. In: Kutz, O., et al. (eds.) Proceedings of the Joint Ontology Workshops 2016 Episode 2: The French Summer of Ontology Co-located with the 9th International Conference on Formal Ontology in Information Systems (FOIS 2016), CEUR Workshop Proceedings, Annecy, France, 6–9 July 2016, vol. 1660. CEUR-WS.org (2016)

9. Ugarte, H.: A more pragmatic Web 3.0: Linked Blockchain Data. Technical report, March 2017. https://www.researchgate.net/publication/315619465_A_more_pragmatic_Web_30_Linked_Blockchain_Data

10. Voshmgir, S., Kalinov, V.: Blockchain, a beginners guide. Technical report, BlockchainHub, September 2017

Query Translation for Cross-Lingual Search in the Academic Search Engine PubPsych

Cristina España-Bonet[1]([✉])(iD), Juliane Stiller[2](iD), Roland Ramthun[3](iD), Josef van Genabith[1], and Vivien Petras[2](iD)

[1] DFKI, Universität des Saarlandes, Saarbrücken, Germany
`cristinae@dfki.de`
[2] Berlin School of Library and Information Science, Humboldt-Universität zu Berlin, Berlin, Germany
[3] Leibniz-Zentrum für Psychologische Information und Dokumentation (ZPID), Trier, Germany

Abstract. We describe a lexical resource-based process for query translation of a domain-specific and multilingual academic search engine in psychology, PubPsych. PubPsych queries are diverse in language with a high amount of informational queries and technical terminology. We present an approach for translating queries into English, German, French, and Spanish. We build a quadrilingual lexicon with aligned terms in the four languages using MeSH, Wikipedia and Apertium as our main resources. Our results show that using the quadlexicon together with some simple translation rules, we can automatically translate 85% of translatable tokens in PubPsych queries with mean adequacy over all the translatable text of 1.4 when measured on a 3-point scale [0, 1, 2].

Keywords: Academic search · Psychology domain · Logfile analysis · Query languages · Query translation · Translation quality · Digital library

1 Introduction

Academic search refers to the domain of information retrieval (IR), which concerns itself with searching scientific data, mostly researching output in the form of publications [18]. Academic search is an inherent multilingual challenge. While English is considered the lingua franca of science [1], a significant portion of the world's scientific output is published in other languages [2]. The research presented here is part of the project CLuBS[1] (Cross-Lingual Bibliographic Search) with the aim to improve multilingual access to relevant material in the domain of psychology. The project works with the established academic search engine PubPsych[2] in order to test its approaches on real data and users.

---

[1] http://www.clubs-project.eu.
[2] https://www.pubpsych.eu.

© Springer Nature Switzerland AG 2019
E. Garoufallou et al. (Eds.): MTSR 2018, CCIS 846, pp. 37–49, 2019.
https://doi.org/10.1007/978-3-030-14401-2_4

PubPsych is a portal for searching a large and continuously updated database of psychological literature, treatments, tests and research data. It aggregates bibliographic metadata from various sources, mainly in English, French, German and Spanish. If the language of the source document is not one of the four, metadata in at least one of these languages is provided. Already in 2008, a survey of psychology researchers found that native language information (besides English) was considered helpful for access [29]. A survey conducted after the launch of PubPsych in 2015 confirmed this and revealed that users were satisfied with the portal, but wished for the possibility to perform multilingual search [32].

The CLuBS project develops, implements and evaluates different approaches to enable cross-lingual (CL) search such as the automatic translation of queries and the translation of metadata content, in both cases with the help of specialized multilingual dictionaries. We use MeSH, Wikipedia and Apertium as our main resources for building these dictionaries. This paper presents the results of the first query translation approach adopted by the project with the objective to provide CL search in the languages English, German, French and Spanish for the PubPsych portal. The guiding research question of the analysis is: can PubPsych queries be translated into the four target languages by mapping them to purpose-built lexical resources? Subquestions are: What proportion of queries can we cover with this approach? How good is the translation quality?

In order to answer these questions we structured the paper as follows. Section 2 discusses related work on academic search engines. In Sect. 3, we conduct a query analysis using PubPsych query logs from 2014 to 2016 to identify the prevailing query languages and their type. Section 4 describes the methodology and the resources we created for the translation of queries. We evaluate the coverage and the adequacy of the translations in Sect. 5. Finally, Sect. 6 concludes with a summary and an outlook on future work.

2   Related Work

Academic search engines (also termed bibliographic information systems or bibliographic digital libraries) are one of the oldest applications in IR (see, for example, MEDLINE[3] [21]) and were used as the first standard test collection for the Cranfield experiments [9]. The interest in these collections reawakened when digital libraries became a prominent research topic as bibliographic information systems moved to web-based user interfaces [8,26].

Academic search is studied from the user perspective with qualitative methods [25] and in recent years with large-scale logfile analyses of general academic search engines such as Elsevier's ScienceDirect [16,18] or domain-specific analyses for portals in chemistry [10], computer science [17,20], history [33], medicine [15,23,34], science and technology in general [24], or the social sciences [14]. For the psychological domain, we found one comparative analysis [33].

---

[3] https://www.nlm.nih.gov/bsd/medline.html.

These studies found significant differences between previously tested search environments—mostly for newspaper or web documents—and the academic search domain. Not only do publications or bibliographic metadata records have a particular document structure but searcher information needs and their representations in queries are different as well. The query content is adapted to the collections and document structure. While studying CiteSeer queries, Khabsa et al. [17] found searches for particular document components such as author, title, or keywords. Queries also contain more technical terms and many more entities [18], which can be mapped to controlled document keywords (such as the MeSH keywords in MEDLINE) for improved search [30].

Multilingual IR is an important research topic for academic search [11]. Qualitative studies show that switching between languages is difficult for searchers [3,22,31]. In general, the translation of queries for achieving multilinguality is performed either via dictionary-based methods or by using information extracted from parallel or comparable corpora. The first approaches show ambiguity problems due to possible multiple entries in a dictionary; the second ones limit the coverage to the domains of the corpora. As in most applications, a combination of techniques shows the best performance [28]. Few systems include multilingual functionality though. Because of their similarities with our case study, we refer here to the general domain CL retrieval systems based on machine translation Mulinex [7], MultiLexExplorer [19] and UTACLIR [13], all of them dictionary or knowledge-based engines with possible support for sense disambiguation.

3 Query Characteristics and Languages in PubPsych

We studied query logs of PubPsych to learn more about query characteristics, the potential for multilingual retrieval and how we could best adapt our strategy for query translation. We analyzed query logs ranging from 1 January 2014 to 31 December 2016 covering 154,495 sessions with 553,799 queries, of which 378,500 were unique queries.[4]

Multilingual Users and Content. As the retrieval of records in PubPsych is solely based on the bibliographic metadata, it is the language of the metadata which defines whether a record is retrievable in a given language. As for most records the metadata language is not available as separate information, it had to be inferred from the provider's language and their indexing practices. One third of the around 1 million PubPsych records came from PSYNDEX[5], which translates titles in German and/or English for records, which are not in one of these languages. Similarly, Medline contributed approximately 25% of PubPsych records, always providing an English abstract and title and keywords in English, French and German. Retrievable content in Spanish accounted for

---

[4] A median of 2 queries was issued over all sessions. PubPsych's mean query length (3.6 tokens for simple, 4.9 for advanced search) was comparable to other reported numbers (e.g. PubMed 3.5 [15], Citeseer 4.8 [17], ScienceDirect 3.8 [18]).

[5] German-speaking countries' database for psychology: https://www.psyndex.de.

Table 1. Query language categories

Annotations	Category description	Example
de, en, fr, es, other	Unique language	"Brain"
mixed	At least two languages	"schreiben older adults"
ambi	Identical in at least two languages	"Psychologie"
none	Not a specific language (e.g. ISSN)	"1869-7712"
unclear	Query language and content unclear	"ey Lim"

approximately 5%. An estimation of the content that cannot be accessed with an English query, because it has no English metadata for any field, amounts to 20%. This uneven distribution of metadata language produces result sets of varying sizes, depending on the query language. Therefore, PubPsych would benefit from CLIR solutions which enhance access to content and improve search results for users. One of these solutions is query translation.

Query Languages and Types. In order to analyze the language and the type, we took a random sample with replacement of 500 queries from our corpus. Two independent raters manually determined the query language according to the schema in Table 1.

In determining the language, raters reached an interannotator agreement (IAA) of $\pi = 0.89$ (Scott's Pi) with a percentage agreement of 92.2%. The assignment of a query to a language category follows a binomial distribution, allowing us to calculate both a point-estimator and a 95% confidence interval for the real values. In our set, we find $37.4^{+4.3}_{-4.1}$ queries for *de*, $33.4^{+4.2}_{-4.0}$ for *en*, $4.0^{+2.1}_{-1.4}$ for *es*, $3.8^{+2.1}_{-1.4}$ for *fr*, $0.4^{+1.0}_{-0.3}$ for *other*, $1.2^{+1.4}_{-0.6}$ for *mixed*, $4.0^{+2.1}_{-1.4}$ for *ambi*, $0.6^{+1.1}_{-0.4}$ for *unclear*, and $15.2^{+3.4}_{-2.9}$ for *none*. English and German queries were prevalent, with each accounting for about one third of the total queries, followed by queries with non-linguistic content (e.g. ISSN) with a share of around 15%. French, Spanish and ambivalent queries were issued with each around 5% share, while other query language categories were less common. The fact that more than half of the sessions originated from Germany suggests that German users are also searching in English or other languages. The relatively high amount of non-language-specific queries corresponds to the amount of queries dealing exclusively with named entities, which often cannot be attributed to a language.

The raters also determined whether a query is *informational*, *navigational* or *transactional* following Broder's definition [6] which was refined by Li et al. [18] for academic search engines. An informational query seeks for topics, specific authors, places or other themes. The definition of a navigational query for academic search involves publication identifiers (such as ISSN, DOIs or the use of the title field operator) to retrieve particular articles or publications. Transactional queries only play a marginal role as they seek the original resource by looking for downloadable content like PDF files. We found no transactional queries and a low number of navigational queries resulting in a Scotts's Pi[6] of

---

[6] We also calculated Krippendorff's alpha and Cohen's Kappa with the same results.

Table 2. Query types and their distribution in different domains

Query type	PubPsych (Psychology)	CiteSeer [17] (Comp. Sci.)	ScienceDirect [18] (General academic)[a]	Library [5][a]	Web search [6][a]
Informational	88.4%	87.5%	92.3%	47.85%	48.0%
Navigational	11.6%	12.5%	7.6%	50.25%	20.0%
Transactional	0.0%	n.d.	0.5% (downloads)	n.d.	30.0%

[a]Percentages do not add up to 100% but are reported as found in the papers. Whereas in [6,18] no explanation is given, [5] report on another two categories "non-classifiable" and "other" for 1,95% of their queries

0.27 for the IAA despite a high percentage agreement of 89.4%. Table 2 compares our results to other studies in different domains. Informational queries are the most frequently observed query type across all domains but are particularly high for academic search engines. With regard to query translation, informational queries need translation whereas most navigational queries do not (e.g. DOI, ISSN searches) and should not be translated. Given that the 88.4% of PubPsych queries are informational with domain specific vocabulary and there are no transactional queries, we choose to use an approach of mapping lexical resources in four languages to translate our queries.

4   Approach to Query Translation

Mapping Queries to a Multilingual Vocabulary. One approach to translate queries is to map them to a multilingual controlled vocabulary of the domain under consideration. Controlled vocabularies contain technical terminology for a domain and are used to index content in retrieval systems. A multilingual version contains precise translations of such technical terms and is therefore a useful resource. Observing a high amount of technical terminology in our queries, we tested how many queries could be translated by matching them to multilingual thesauri and implement some simple rules to maximize the matching.

This mapping approach does not require the explicit detection of the language of a query, which is considered to be a hard task [27]. We matched tokens from the query against the keys in our quadlexicon in German, English, Spanish and French, and extracted the three non-matching languages as translations. In case of multiple matches for a key, we assumed the most frequent language derived from the query language distribution in PubPsych. The following excerpt of the lexicon shows how the first field, the key, does not include any language information, only translations:[7]

```
bienestar|||en:well-being|||de:wohlbefinden|||fr:bien-etre
bien-etre|||en:well-being|||es:bienestar|||de:wohlbefinden
wohlbefinden|||en:well-being|||es:bienestar|||fr:bien-etre
wohlfuhlen|||en:well-being|||es:bienestar|||fr:bien-etre
well-being|||es:bienestar|||de:wohlbefinden|||fr:bien-etre
```

---

[7] This method additionally solves the problem of intra-query language shifts, since different tokens in the same query can be matched to different languages.

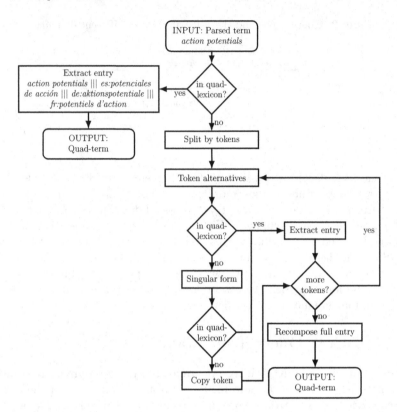

Fig. 1. Flowchart for query term translation. If a complete term cannot be matched, a token by token translation is applied

The complete methodology used to translate a query in this language-independent fashion can be seen in Fig. 1. Initially we parsed a query, removed punctuation and non-alphanumeric characters, and extracted text not belonging to a specific field (unbound text) and text for translatable fields. Examples of translatable fields[8] included titles, controlled terms and keywords. Examples of untranslatable fields[9] included years, journal titles and authors. The subset of queries with translatable text comprised 536,479 elements. These elements were mainly from informational queries—an exception were searches in the title field where one can seek an exact title (navigational search where translation is debatable) or look for keywords in title (translation is desired). Each translatable term within a query was then translated independently. A term might have more than one token. In case the full term was found in our multilingual lexicon, we extracted the translations. If not, we split the terms into single tokens, and tried to match each token individually. For those tokens still not present in the

---

[8] CM, IT, SH, CT, SW, TI and AB fields in PubPsych.

[9] AGE, EV, PLOC, AU, ISBN, ISSN, PU, SEG, CS, JT, DB, PY, LA, DT and ID.

Table 3. Aligned terms per language in the quadrilingual lexicon. Mismatches between the numbers of a row hint to the availability of synonyms for a language

	German	English	French	Spanish
MeSH	70,694	175,004	96,333	66,828
WP (titles/categories)	(81,369/38,038)			
Apertium	7,792	5,935	6,020	5,846
Manual	4,262	4,142	4,047	4,081
Total unique (QuadLex)	202,128	304,277	225,607	195,937

lexicon, we derived its possible singular form by applying simple rules of regular formation of plurals in the four languages and tried again. Finally, we copied the token as its own translation in case no match was found. Note that copying the source word into the output does not necessarily correspond to an incorrect translation because in most cases the words not contained in the lexicon were named entities. Equivalently, using the quadrilingual lexicon to translate an entry did not guarantee a correct translation, because, besides of the existing noise, the concatenation of word translations does not need to correspond to a correct term translation. Section 5 reports the evaluation of our approach.

Quadrilingual Lexicon. We created an aligned dictionary in English, Spanish, French and German for our experiments. The lexicon covered specially the domain of psychology but also contained general sources to increase the coverage:

MeSH: A common thesaurus in the bio-medical domain is the Medical Subject Headings[10] (MeSH) by the U.S. National Library of Medicine. We developed the MeSHMerger software[11] to create a multilingual MeSH version from different translations of its 2017 edition. Each of the 54,901 concepts in MeSH can have a varying number of terms, permutations of terms and synonyms attached to it in each language version. Extracting the available entries in the four languages, we obtained 175,004 concept related terms in English, 96,333 in French, 70,694 in German and 66,828 in Spanish.

Multilingual Wikipedia Entries: To increase the amount of psychological term translations, we extracted multilingual in-domain titles from Wikipedia related to psychology and health with the WikiTailor tool[12][4]. WikiTailor extracts domain articles by exploring the categories graph starting from the category describing the domain (psychology and health in our case) and identifying a subset of related categories and their associated articles[13]. Such associated articles were gathered

---

[10] https://www.nlm.nih.gov/mesh.
[11] https://github.com/clubs-project/MeSHMerger.
[12] https://github.com/cristinae/WikiTailor.
[13] We used models WT0.5-100 or WT0.5-500 depending on the language. Refer to WikiTailor manual for more details http://cristinae.github.io/WikiTailor.

independently in English, German, French and Spanish versions of Wikipedia. Afterwards, we expanded the set of articles to include all the articles identified as in-domain articles in at least one of the languages with the equivalent article in the other three languages in case they exist. With this methodology we obtained a multilingual lexicon of article names with 81,369 entries.

In a similar way, we extracted aligned category names from Wikipedia, but this time selecting all of them and not only those related to psychology. The category alignment in Wikipedia is quite clean and this allowed us to increase the coverage introducing little noise. 38,038 entries were obtained in this case.

Apertium Dictionaries: Apertium [12] is a free/open-source ruled-based translation engine that uses bilingual dictionaries for lexical transfer. We used three of their dictionaries[14] (*en-de*, *en-es* and *es-fr*) to extract a quadrilingual dictionary with the overlapping entries. Notice that different from Wikipedia entries, dictionary entries were not sense disambiguated and the union of the four languages could have introduced additional noise to the translation. The motivation was to widen the coverage of out-of-domain vocabulary also used in queries frequently. Table 3 shows the number of entries of this multilingual dictionary in comparison with the other sources.

Post-edited Automatic Translations: Finally, we selected a set of highly frequent tokens from PubPsych controlled terms which were not already covered by the previous resources. This mainly affected ∼4,000 specialized in-domain terms and expressions, which we translated with the automatic translation engine DeepL[15] and manually post-edited to improve mistranslations. Table 3 shows the exact number of entries depending on the source language in the row "Manual".

The complete multilingual lexicon, *QuadLex*, is the union of the resources in the four languages with 927,949 unique elements. Since internally terms are sent to the search engine lowercased and without diacritics, we prepared a normalized version of the lexicon with these characteristics in order to translate the queries in a realistic setting, that is, after the normalization and parsing of the query takes place. That gave a total of 927,764 entries, with 680,567 being unique. The number of elements per source language is shown in Table 3.

5   Evaluation

We evaluated our methodology to translate queries by two means. First, we studied the coverage of the quadrilingual lexicons and second, their translation quality.

Table 4 shows the coverage of the plain MeSH and extended QuadLex multilingual lexicons on the set of 536,479 queries with translatable terms. When we translated terms as a whole with the MeSH lexicon, coverage was only 7.7% of

---

[14] http://wiki.apertium.org/wiki/List_of_dictionaries.
[15] https://www.deepl.com, work took place as of 25th Jan. and 1st-2nd Feb. 2018.

Table 4. Coverage of MeSH and QuadLex on the set of 536,479 queries with translatable terms

Source	Trad. terms (%)	Untrad. terms (%)	Trad. tokens (%)	Untrad. tokens (%)
MeSH	167,152 (7.7)	2,010,469 (92.3)	2,225,598 (64.2)	1,240,800 (35.8)
QuadLex	324,033(14.9)	1,853,588 (85.1)	2,945,959 (85.0)	520,439 (15.0)

Table 5. Number of queries evaluated with a score for adequacy 0/1/2, per rater and in average, in our test set of 500 queries with 100 items per source language

	Rater A			Rater B			Rater C			Mean		
	0	1	2	0	1	2	0	1	2	0	1	2
en2de	20	34	46	0	41	59	13	41	46	11 ± 10	39 ± 4	50 ± 8
en2es	14	36	50	1	43	56	6	37	57	7 ± 7	39 ± 4	54 ± 4
en2fr	17	39	44	0	42	58	8	43	49	8 ± 8	41 ± 2	50 ± 7
de2en	36	31	33	21	40	39	23	40	37	27 ± 8	37 ± 5	36 ± 3
de2es	39	31	30	24	37	39	25	41	34	29 ± 8	36 ± 5	34 ± 4
de2fr	38	32	30	23	38	39	25	41	34	28 ± 8	37 ± 5	34 ± 5
es2en	25	46	29	3	44	53	8	39	53	12 ± 12	43 ± 4	45 ± 14
es2de	24	51	25	3	46	51	14	45	41	14 ± 11	47 ± 3	39 ± 13
es2fr	21	43	36	4	47	49	12	37	51	12 ± 9	42 ± 5	45 ± 8
fr2en	32	41	27	1	46	53	7	48	45	13 ± 16	45 ± 4	42 ± 13
fr2de	44	33	23	5	42	53	14	45	41	21 ± 20	40 ± 6	39 ± 15
fr2es	31	34	35	4	48	48	8	41	51	14 ± 15	41 ± 7	45 ± 9
none2en	10	4	86	2	11	87	7	11	82	6 ± 4	9 ± 4	85 ± 3
none2de	10	2	88	3	13	84	11	8	81	8 ± 4	8 ± 6	84 ± 4
none2es	11	0	89	4	11	85	8	9	83	8 ± 4	7 ± 6	86 ± 3
none2fr	13	1	86	5	10	85	12	7	81	10 ± 4	6 ± 5	84 ± 3
Mean	24 ± 11	29 ± 17	47 ± 25	6 ± 8	35 ± 14	59 ± 14	13 ± 6	33 ± 15	54 ± 18	14 ± 8	33 ± 15	54 ± 20

the terms. We expect this subset to have high quality translations. The inclusion of the out-of-domain resources increased the coverage to 14.9%, but the true improvement resulted from the translation at token level. In this case, we could cover up to 85.0% of the translatable tokens in PubPsych queries.

We evaluated the quality of translations for 500 queries manually. For this, we used a subset of the annotated queries described in Sect. 3 and added new manually annotated queries in order to obtain 100 queries in each language (*de*, *en*, *fr* and *es*) plus 100 queries without a definite language identification (*mixed/unclear/ambi/none*). The average length for the 100 English queries was 3.1 words, 2.2 for German, 3.5 for Spanish, 3.6 for French and only 1.7 words when no language was assigned. We evaluated the translations according to adequacy defined as how much of the meaning expressed in the source query was also expressed in the translation. Since we did not have gold translations, adequacy was defined with respect to the source and not to a gold. Given the short length of the queries, we measured the adequacy by a three-point scale: *0-None of the meaning was transfered, 1-Part of the meaning was transfered, 2-All meaning was transfered.*

Table 6. IAA (Fleiss' kappa) of three raters for different language pairs

source	2de	2en	2fr	2es
de	n/a	0.616	0.658	0.598
en	0.442	n/a	0.455	0.521
fr	0.243	0.268	n/a	0.384
es	0.422	0.354	0.472	n/a
none	0.494	0.458	0.513	0.440

Three evaluators performed the task and Table 5 shows the raw results together with average values and uncertainties given by the standard deviation. The IAA for the different languages is presented in Table 6 using Fleiss' kappa statistic for more than two raters. The main divergence among annotators was due to the fact that one of them (A) considered the meaning of non-content words to rate for adequacy while the other two did not. Despite this discrepancy, some conclusions could be gathered. We obtained an average adequacy of 1.4 on the [0, 1, 2]-scale, meaning that most of the queries had at least some of their terms properly translated. $54\% \pm 20\%$ of the queries had the maximum adequacy score when looking at the mean over languages, while only $14\% \pm 8\%$ of the queries got completely incorrect translations; the remaining $33\% \pm 15\%$ were partially well translated. The behavior per language was quite similar with two clear exceptions: *(i)* the translation of German queries had a lower quality (mean adequacy 1.1) mainly because the compound nature of German increases the number of untranslated tokens with respect to the other languages, and *(ii)* queries with undetermined language had a very high adequacy (1.8) because they are shorter and, in most of the cases, leaving the source token untranslated resulted in a good translation.

6   Conclusion

In the query analysis, we observed queries that are typical for academic search engines especially regarding the occurrence of domain-specific terminology. About 12% of the queries were navigational and contained components that should not be translated, but the remaining 88% were informational and need to be translated for CL search.

We have shown how precise term mappings could be successfully applied with the help of multilingual thesauri without the need to derive this data from general parallel corpora. We built a quadrilingual lexicon with aligned terms in German, English, French and Spanish using as main resources MeSH, Wikipedia and Apertium. After parsing the queries and extracting the translatable terms, we mapped them to the lexicon in a language-independent way to extract translations in the four languages. The design of the mapping approach was intended to maximize the retrieval recall and not translation quality by falling back to a word by word translation and generalizing for gender and number when the complete mapping was not found. With this approach, we covered 85% of the tokens in PubPsych queries and obtained an average adequacy of 1.4 on a [0, 1, 2]-scale over the full set.

The main advantage of our approach, besides simplicity, is that thesauri assure the correct translation of the domain-specific terminology and we only introduce ambiguities for the general domain vocabulary. The main disadvantage is that it does not reach a 100% of coverage as data-based systems can achieve. Our future work involves using multilingual word embeddings to increase the coverage and solve this limitation of dictionary-based methods in combination with the usage of the MeSH quadlexicon to still assure the high quality translation of the domain-specific terminology. By analyzing the translations we found several systematic errors such as those seen when trying to translate non-content words. We also detected a number of untranslated terms for German due to its compound nature. In the future, we will approach these issues to further improve the translation quality and CL retrieval performance.

Acknowledgments. This research was supported by the Leibniz-Gemeinschaft under grant SAW-2016-ZPID-2.

References

1. Alastrué, R.P., Pérez-Llantada, C.: English as a Scientific and Research Language: Debates and Discourses. de Gruyter, Berlin (2015)
2. Amano, T., González-Varo, J.P., Sutherland, W.J.: Languages are still a major barrier to global science. PLoS Biol. **14**(12), e2000933 (2016)
3. Aula, A., Kellar, M.: Multilingual search strategies. In: Conference on Human Factors in Computing Systems (CHI), pp. 3865–3870. ACM (2009)
4. Barrón-Cedeño, A., España-Bonet, C., Boldoba, J., Màrquez, L.: A factory of comparable corpora from Wikipedia. In: Proceedings of the 8th Workshop on Building and Using Comparable Corpora (BUCC), pp. 3–13, July 2015
5. Behnert, C.: Evaluation methods within the LibRank project. Working Paper, LibRank (2016)
6. Broder, A.: A taxonomy of web search. In: ACM Sigir Forum, vol. 36, pp. 3–10. ACM (2002)
7. Capstick, J., Diagne, A.K., Erbach, G., Uszkoreit, H.: MULINEX: multilingual web search and navigation. In: Proceedings of the 14th Twente Workshop on Language Technology (TWLT 14) (1998)
8. Chowdhury, G.: Introduction to Modern Information Retrieval. Facet, London (2010)
9. Cleverdon, C.: The Cranfield tests on index language devices. In: Aslib Proceedings, vol. 19, pp. 173–194. MCB UP Ltd. (1967)
10. Davis, P.M.: Information-seeking behavior of chemists: a transaction log analysis of referral URLs. J. Am. Soc. Inf. Sci. Tech. **55**(4), 326–332 (2004)
11. Diekema, A.R.: Multilinguality in the digital library: a review. Electron. Libr. **30**(2), 165–181 (2012)
12. Forcada, M.L., et al.: Apertium: a free/open-source platform for rule-based machine translation. Mach. Transl. **25**(2), 127–144 (2011)

13. Hedlund, T., Airio, E., Keskustalo, H., Lehtokangas, R., Pirkola, A., Järvelin, K.: Dictionary-based cross-language information retrieval: learning experiences from CLEF 2000–2002. Inf. Retr. **7**(1–2), 99–119 (2004)
14. Hienert, D.: User interests in German social science literature search: a large scale log analysis. In: Conference on Human Information Interaction & Retrieval (CHIIR), pp. 7–16. ACM (2017)
15. Islamaj Dogan, R., Murray, G.C., Névéol, A., Lu, Z.: Understanding PubMed®user search behavior through log analysis. Database 2009 (2009)
16. Ke, H.R., Kwakkelaar, R., Tai, Y.M., Chen, L.C.: Exploring behavior of e-journal users in science and technology: transaction log analysis of Elsevier's sciencedirect onsite in Taiwan. Libr. Inf. Sci. Res. **24**(3), 265–291 (2002)
17. Khabsa, M., Wu, Z., Giles, C.L.: Towards better understanding of academic search. In: Joint Conference on Digital Library (JCDL), pp. 111–114. ACM (2016)
18. Li, X., Schijvenaars, B.J., de Rijke, M.: Investigating queries and search failures in academic search. Inf. Process. Manag. **53**(3), 666–683 (2017)
19. Luca, E.W.D., Hauke, S., Nürnberger, A., Schlechtweg, S.: MultiLexExplorer: combining multilingual web search with multilingual lexical resources. In: Proceedings of Combined Workshop on Language-Enabled Educational Technology and Development and Evaluation of Robust Spoken Dialogue Systems, pp. 17–21 (2006)
20. Mahoui, M., Cunningham, S.J.: Search behavior in a research-oriented digital library. In: Constantopoulos, P., Sølvberg, I.T. (eds.) ECDL 2001. LNCS, vol. 2163, pp. 13–24. Springer, Heidelberg (2001). https://doi.org/10.1007/3-540-44796-2_2
21. McCarn, D.B., Leiter, J.: On-line services in medicine and beyond. Science **181**(4097), 318–324 (1973)
22. Nzomo, P., Ajiferuke, I., Vaughan, L., McKenzie, P.: Multilingual information retrieval & use: perceptions and practices amongst bi/multilingual academic users. J. Acad. Libr. **42**(5), 495–502 (2016)
23. Palotti, J., Hanbury, A., Müller, H., Kahn Jr., C.E.: How users search and what they search for in the medical domain. Inf. Ret. **19**(1–2), 189–224 (2016)
24. Park, M., Lee, T.S.: A longitudinal study of information needs and search behaviors in science and technology: a query analysis. Electron. Libr. **34**(1), 83–98 (2016)
25. Pontis, S., Blandford, A., Greifeneder, E., Attalla, H., Neal, D.: Keeping up to date: an academic researcher's information journey. J. Am. Soc. Inf. Sci. Tech. **68**(1), 22–35 (2017)
26. Ritchie, A., Teufel, S., Robertson, S.: Creating a test collection for citation-based IR experiments. In: HLT-NAACL 2006, pp. 391–398. ACL (2006)
27. Stiller, J., Gäde, M., Petras, V.: Ambiguity of queries and the challenges for query language detection. In: CLEF (2010)
28. Ture, F., Boschee, E.: Learning to translate: a query-specific combination approach for cross-lingual information retrieval. In: Proceedings of the 2014 Conference on Empirical Methods in Natural Language Processing (EMNLP), pp. 589–599. Association for Computational Linguistics, Doha (2014)
29. Uhl, M.: Survey on European psychology publication issues. Psychol. Sci. Q. **51**(1), 19 (2009)
30. Vanopstal, K., Buysschaert, J., Laureys, G., Stichele, R.V.: Lost in PubMed. Factors influencing the success of medical information retrieval. Expert Syst. Appl. **40**(10), 4106–4114 (2013)
31. Vassilakaki, E., Garoufallou, E., Johnson, F., Hartley, R.J.: An exploration of users' needs for multilingual information retrieval and access. In: Garoufallou, E., Hartley, R.J., Gaitanou, P. (eds.) MTSR 2015. CCIS, vol. 544, pp. 249–258. Springer, Cham (2015). https://doi.org/10.1007/978-3-319-24129-6_22

32. Waeldin, S.: Results from the PubPsych launch survey: short report. ZPID Sci. Inf. Online **15**(2), 3 (2015)
33. Yi, K., Beheshti, J., Cole, C., Leide, J.E., Large, A.: User search behavior of domain-specific information retrieval systems: an analysis of the query logs from PsycINFO and ABC-Clio's historical abstracts-America: history and life: research articles. J. Am. Soc. Inf. Sci. Tech. **57**(9), 1208–1220 (2006)
34. Yoo, I., Mosa, A.S.M.: Analysis of Pubmed user sessions using a full-day Pubmed query log: a comparison of experienced and nonexperienced PubMedusers. JMIR Med. Inf. **3**(3), e25 (2015)

ViziQuer: A Visual Notation for RDF Data Analysis Queries

Kārlis Čerāns[1,2(✉)], Agris Šostaks[1,2], Uldis Bojārs[1,2], Juris Bārzdiņš[3],
Jūlija Ovčiņņikova[1,2], Lelde Lāce[1,2], Mikus Grasmanis[1],
and Artūrs Sproģis[1]

[1] Institute of Mathematics and Computer Science,
University of Latvia, Riga, Latvia
`karlis.cerans@lumii.lv`
[2] Department of Computing, University of Latvia, Riga, Latvia
[3] Department of Medicine, University of Latvia, Riga, Latvia

Abstract. Visual SPARQL query notations aim at easing the RDF data
querying task. At the current state of the art there is still no generally accepted
visual graph-based notation suitable to describe RDF data analysis queries that
involve aggregation and subqueries. In this paper we present a visual diagram-
centered notation for SPARQL select query formulation, capable to handle
aggregate/statistics queries and hierarchic queries with subquery structure. The
notation is supported by a web-based prototype tool. We present the notation
examples, describe its syntax and semantics and describe studies with possible
end users, involving both IT and medicine students.

Keywords: Visual notation · Diagrammatic queries · RDF data · SPARQL ·
Ad-hoc queries · Data analysis queries

1 Introduction

SPARQL, as defined by a W3C standard [1], is the main query language over data
structured in accordance to the RDF [2] data model. This includes most of the Semantic
Web data, as well as data brought into the semantic-web formats by various mapping
approaches, as ontology-based data access (OBDA), cf. [3]. Although the semantic
RDF/SPARQL technologies offer a higher-level view on data than the classical relational databases with the SQL query language, the formal textual notation of SPARQL
queries still complicates its usage by domain experts and IT professionals alike.

A number of approaches exist to ease the SPARQL query formulation. These
include form-based interfaces as e.g. PepeSearch [4] and WYSIWYQ [5]. SPARKLIS
[6] offers faceted SPARQL query composition from natural language based snippets.
The visual/diagrammatic formalisms for SPARQL query creation apply/extend the
visual querying principles studied extensively for relational databases (cf. e.g. [7, 8]).
Most of the existing visual/diagrammatic SPARQL query builders, as SEWASIE [9],
Optique VQs [10], QueryVOWL [11], LinDA [12] or early versions of ViziQuer [13],
although efficient for visual formulation of substantial range of queries, however, are
not designed to support queries with data aggregation available in SPARQL 1.1. [1].

© Springer Nature Switzerland AG 2019
E. Garoufallou et al. (Eds.): MTSR 2018, CCIS 846, pp. 50–62, 2019.
https://doi.org/10.1007/978-3-030-14401-2_5

The UML class diagram style visual specification of SPARQL select queries with aggregation has been introduced in [14, 15] and re-formulated in a way to allow for subquery specification in [16]. In this paper we present for the first time an overall ViziQuer abstract syntax and semantics (by means of visual query translation into SPARQL), as well as describe a comparative user study showing an advantage of query over RDF data composition in ViziQuer vs. query composition in textual SPARQL notation. Should a well-established tool support be available, we would aim the ViziQuer visual notation to be useful for query over RDF data creation, presentation and sharing both for persons without specific IT training, as well. Currently there is a web-based prototype implementation available for the visual notation [17].

Onwards the Sect. 2 introduces the visual notation, Sect. 3 describes the query model and Sect. 4 outlines its semantics. Section 5 describes the user study and Sect. 6 concludes the paper. The site http://viziquer.lumii.lv/mtsr2018 contains supplementary materials for the paper, including the materials for user study reproduction.

2   Notation Examples

The visual/diagrammatic query definition is based on data model containing the vocabulary of entities, each identified by a local name and optional name prefix and providing the full entity URI, and the schema information stating the applicability, ordering and cardinalities of properties in the context of the model classes.

We shall consider example queries over a simple mini-hospital data schema, shown in Fig. 1 and adapted from [18], where it has been presented as a fragment of a realistic hospital information system. The names of properties connecting the classes, if not specified, coincide with the target class name with lowercase first letter. There is default minimum and maximum cardinality 1 assumption for properties.

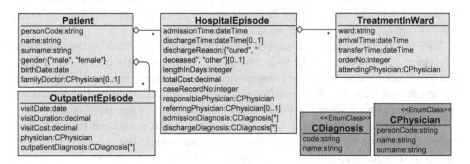

Fig. 1. Example hospital domain ontology fragment

2.1   Basic Visual Queries

A basic visual query (cf. [13, 16]) is a UML class diagram style graph with nodes describing data instances, the edges describing their connections and the fields forming the query selection list from the node instance model attributes and their expressions;

every node can specify both the instance class and additional conditions on the instance. One of the graph nodes is the main query node (shown as orange round rectangle in the concrete syntax); the structural edges (all edges except the condition ones, cf. Sect. 2.4) within the graph form its spanning tree with the main query node being its root.

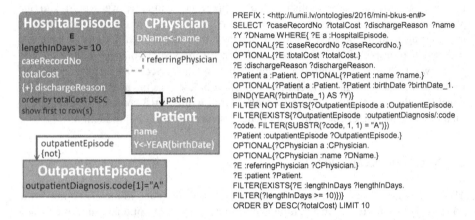

Fig. 2. An example basic visual query and its translation into SPARQL

Figure 1 shows an example basic visual query: *find 10 most expensive hospital episodes among those lasting at least for 10 days, having a discharge reason specified and having a patient that does not have any outpatient episode with an infectious disease diagnosis; list episode case record number, total cost and discharge reason, the patient name and birth year, and the name of the referring physician, if specified.*

The basic visual query links are labelled by properties (or sequences thereof) from the data model. The query in Fig. 2 illustrates the links that are required (*patient*), optional (*referringPhysician*) and negated (*outpatientEpisode*).

Each query node contains an ordered list of (instance) fields denoting the properties of instances corresponding to the node that are to be included in the query output; each field has a data expression (in the simplest case just an instance model attribute name) and an optional alias (e.g. *E*, *Y* and *DName* in Fig. 2 query). Additionally, conditions over field and other instance attribute values can be placed in the query nodes.

The presence of a node field value in the query output is optional to not bypass entire solution rows because of some missing attribute values. The *{+}* mark is used to mark a field as required (cf. *{+} dischargeReason* in Fig. 2).

The *YEAR()* function calculates the birth year from the patient's birth date that is available in the data model. The operations and functions used to construct expressions in SPARQL [1] are allowed also in ViziQuer; further operation shortcuts, such as *x[1]* standing for the first symbol in *x* are available to ease the query definition.

The *outpatientDiagnosis.code* notation in the example illustrates property chaining that is allowed both in field value expressions and in conditions.

2.2 Aggregated and Grouping Attributes

Figure 3 shows three example queries specifying the aggregated attribute computation:

(a) *Count the hospital episodes lasting for at least 10 days;*
(b) *Count the treatment cases for each ward, and*
(c) *Count the hospital instances and find their average length in days, grouped by the patient's gender and patient's age at admission time*

Fig. 3. Aggregate query examples

The principal design idea for aggregate attribute inclusion in the query, introduced in [13], is to place them in a special compartment, situated above the node class name. Should there be instance-level attributes in an aggregated query, as e.g. in Fig. 3(b) and (c) examples, these are to be regarded as grouping attributes for the aggregations.

The function *years* in Fig. 3(c) is a custom ViziQuer notation for expressing the *date* or *datetime* value difference in years (similar functions for months, days, hours, minutes and seconds are available, as well). Figure 3(c) uses also the concrete syntax option to hide the default label for links connecting the data model classes (the link name remains still present in the query abstract syntax discussed onwards in Sect. 3).

2.3 Visual Subquery Notation

The ability to create subqueries is important both for SQL queries over relational databases, and for SPARQL queries over RDF databases. Still, there is no generally accepted visual notation for definition of data queries that involve subqueries. Our proposal [13] for including subqueries in the visual query notation consists in letting certain edges in the query structure tree to be marked as subquery ones, so considering the edge together with the part of the query tree behind it as a subquery. The visual notation for the subquery edge is proposed to be a black bullet at the hosting (non-subquery) end of the edge. Figure 4 shows example queries that can be phrased, as follows:

(a) *Select all hospital episodes with at least 4 treatments in wards, show the episode case record number, treatment in ward count and list of admission diagnosis codes, order descending by treatment in ward count;*
(b) *For every physician responsible for at least one hospital episode, select the surname, as well as count and average treatment in ward count for episodes with this responsible physician.*

Intuitively, each subquery is computed in the context of a single hosting node class instance (e.g. a hospital episode, in the Fig. 4(a)). The subquery link together with its reference to the hosting node instance is considered to be a part of the subquery. The subquery results (the selection variables, as well as the references to the hosting query nodes) are projected into the hosting query, where they can be handled in a similar way as the hosting node attributes themselves (e.g. included in filters, computations, order lists and further aggregates). The subqueries can be nested, as shown in Fig. 4(b).

Fig. 4. Visual subquery examples

In the case, if a subquery does not return any result except its host node instance, it works as an existence filter, as in Fig. 5(a). In Fig. 5(c) a single-node query models the same behavior, using explicit predicate *exists* and property paths. These examples should be contrasted with a simple join query in Fig. 5(b), where the count of patients is taken over joined patient and hospital episode records.

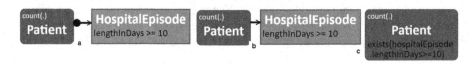

Fig. 5. Subquery as an existential quantifier

2.4   Query Structure Extensions

The visual notation considered so far is suitable for visual query specification, if the query has a tree form that is matching a data model fragment. The following more advanced notations (cf. [16]) raise the query language expressive power beyond the query tree shape and model structure matching.

Figure 6 shows two visual options for the query *"Count patients with at least 3 hospital episodes without a matching outpatient episode within the 30 day range before it"*. The query structure requires non-existence of an outpatient episode for a hospital episode, however, there is no direct link in the data model connecting these classes. To build the query structure in this case, a non-model edge (a "free" edge), marked by '++' is used (in the example it happens to be a negation link). The data connections can then be established either by extra condition links, as in Fig. 6(a), or by explicit node references (Fig. 6(b)). The condition links, drawn using a thinner line with white diamond ends, are not structure links; they are added on top of the query tree shape structure.

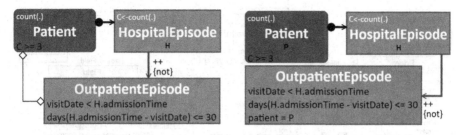

Fig. 6. Condition and non-model links

Further visual query examples, including the ones that use unit node [ ] and union node [+] for query structuring (these nodes do not correspond to data instances in the query) can be found in [13]. The ViziQuer visual notation contains counterparts of most SPARQL 1.1 select query constructs. The currently not covered constructs are named graphs, advanced property path expressions, SELECT * (in SPARQL sense) and *reduced* (cf. [16]).

3 Abstract Query Model

Figure 7 summarizes the abstract syntax of the visual queries in a UML-style model[1] that shows the query structure and is the basis of further query semantics definition.

The hierarchy of nodes (*Node*) and structure edges (*StructureEdge*) describes the query graph *G* spanning tree *T(G)*, rooted at the main query node (an edge is a *structure edge*, if it is not a condition one). Let an edge be *plain, condition, local subquery* or *global subquery* one by its *edgeType*, and *required, optional* or *negated* one by its *relationType*. A structure edge is a *union edge*, if its target is a union node (*Union-Node*), a *sub-union edge*, if its source is a union node, and a *union-free edge* otherwise. Let a structure edge characteristics apply also to the edge target node (so, there are e.g. optional local subquery nodes).

A *query fragment* is a (maximal) set of nodes in *T(G)* connected by plain required union-free edges only, together with structure edges *incoming* into fragment nodes and condition edges *outgoing* from fragment nodes. Let the fragment *head node* be the node that is above all other fragment nodes in *T(G)* and let any fragment head node attributes (e.g. optional, local subquery, union-free) extend to the fragment, as well.

We call a query or its subquery fragment *aggregated*, if it has at least one aggregated field or the distinct option (*distinct = true*) within its head node specified.

The *aggregated field* list and *distinctness* specification is allowed in the main query node and the (local and global) subquery nodes only. The ordering, limit and offset specifications are for the main query node and global subquery nodes only.

We shall assume also that there are no name coincidences among the explicit node instance names and field aliases (except for alternative union branches).

---

[1] The composition notation (a little diamond at an edge end) indicates the query item structure. For all generalization groups in the diagram the superclass is a disjoint union of subclasses.

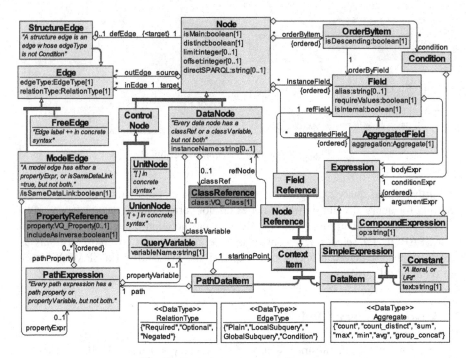

Fig. 7. Core abstract syntax of queries

The *expressions*, central both for field and condition specification, are defined on the basis of compound and simple expressions, where the operators from SPARQL expression notation [1] can be used to obtain expressions from simple expressions.

A simple expression can be a *constant* or a *data item*. A data item is either a *context item* itself (a *reference* to a node or field defined elsewhere in the query), or, most typically, it would be a *path data item* consisting of a *path* (e.g. an attribute name) starting from a context item (the context item specification is omitted in the concrete syntax in the most typical case, if it coincides with the node containing the expression's container field or condition, allowing it to become just a property name or a path expression).

For fragments X and Y let $X \rightarrow Y$ if Y is a direct child fragment of X (i.e., Y head node is a child of some X node in $T(G)$). For a fragment X we let $UC(X)$, the *upwards context* of X, to consist of all fragments reachable from X upwards in $T(G)$ (including X itself).

We allow the condition edges from a fragment X nodes to go only to nodes in $UC(X)$.

Let the *optional-closure* $o(F)$ of a fragment F be the union of F and all fragments downwards reachable from it by edges that are (i) union-free and plain, and (ii) required or optional. For a fragment F let its *selection set* $Sel(F)$ consist of all non-internal fields, all query variables, as well as all "upwards" references to nodes in $UC(F)$, found within $o(F)$. Let $SubSel(F)$ be the union of $Sel(H)$ for all subquery fragments H hosted in $o(F)$.

The node and field references in the field and condition expressions within a fragment F node n shall refer to only:

- *SubSel(F)*, the results projected out of sub-fragments;
- Nodes from *UC(F)*, the context information available for the fragment (not allowed in aggregate field expressions);
- Nodes and instance fields from *o(F)* (the field references from an instance field f body expression can go only to a n field above f; the node/field references to *o(F)*/ *F* shall not start a path expression).

The references to *UC(F)* shall allow locating the reference in the data model within F (an equality assertion with a value computed within *o(F)*, or participation in a path data item would be sufficient to allow the reference usage).

4 Query Semantics

We define the query semantics via translation into SPARQL 1.1 [1], done in three steps:

(1) providing the SPARQL query variable names for query model elements;
(2) defining local query model translations into SPARQL, and
(3) computing the SPARQL query inductively over the query fragment structure.

Let *SS* stand for all selection variables in query node direct SPARQL fragments of select query form and *SG* – for all outer scope variables in node direct SPARQL fragments of group graph pattern form.

The SPARQL query variables in a query G shall be ascribed to the following variable points: $VP(G) = DataNode \cup Field \cup DataItem \cup QueryVariable \cup SS \cup SG$. Let the SPARQL query variable name assignment $m:VP(G) \rightarrow Var$ be such that:

(1) for $x \in SS \cup SG$, $m(x) = x$ (i.e. a direct SPARQL variable is mapped onto itself);
(2) for $x \in QueryVariable$, $m(x) = x.variableName$;
(3) for $x \in DataNode$, $m(x) = x.instanceName$, if x has *instanceName* specified;
(4) for $x \in Field$, $m(x) = x.alias$, if x has *alias* specified;
(5) if $x \in DataNode$ is a node/field reference and $y \in DataNode \cup Field$ is the corresponding node/field, then $m(x) = m(y)$;
(6) $m(x) = m(y)$, if $x \in Field$ and $y = x.bodyExpression \in DataItem$ and x does not have *alias* specified (same variable for the field and the data item within it);
(7) $m(x) = m(y)$ if the nodes $x, y \in DataNode$ are connected by a same data edge;
(8) $m(x) \neq m(y)$, if the equality $m(x) = m(y)$ does not follow by the rules (1)–(7).

It is clear that an appropriate mapping m can be generated for every query G. To define $m(x)$ for $x \in PathDataItem$, a rule of thumb is to use the local name of the last property in its path component with appropriate suffix to avoid name clashes.

For a data model reference $d \in ClassReference \cup PropertyReference$ let $t(d)$ be the full IRI of the referred model entity. We extend t also to map property expressions that are sequences of property references and their inverses to SPARQL property paths concatenating the IRIs (and their inverses, as necessary) of the referred properties; let for brevity $t(p) = m(v)$ for a path expression p and query variable v, if $v = p.propertyVariable$.

Table 1 shows the definition of the "local" SPARQL-fragments $S(x)$ for x a node, an edge, a data item and a field, and filters $FL(c)$ for c a condition.

Table 1. Local SPARQL translations of query model elements

$n \in Node$	$S(x) = BGP(m(n)\ rdf{:}type\ t(n.classRef.class))$, if $n.classRef$ is defined $S(x) = BGP(m(n)\ rdf{:}type\ m(n.classVariable))$, if $n.classVariable$ is defined; otherwise $S(x)$ is empty
$e \in Edge$	$S(e) = BGP(m(e.rsc)\ t(e.propertyExpr)\ m(e.trg))$, if $e.propertyExpr$ is defined, otherwise $S(e)$ is empty
$d \in DataItem$	$S(e) = BGP(m(d.startingPoint)\ t(d.path)\ m(d))$, if d is a path data item, otherwise $S(d)$ is empty
$x \in Expression$	Let $e_1, ..., e_n$ be all (possibly none) data items contained in the expression $x = x(e_1, .., e_n)$ Let for x its **direct translation** be $T(x) = x(m(e_1), ..., m(e_n))$ and **support pattern** $Q(x)$ be the join (the concatenation) of all $S(e_i)$
$f \in Field$	Let x be f body expression Let $S_0(f) = Q(x)$, if $x \in DataItem$ and $m(x) = m(f)$, otherwise let $S_0(f)$ be $Q(x)$ extended by $BIND(T(x)\ AS\ m(f))$ Let $S(f)$ be $S_0(f)$, if $f.requireValues$, and $OPTIONAL\ \{S_0(f)\}$ otherwise
$c \in Condition$	Let x be c condition expression If $Q(x)$ is empty (there are no property references within x), let $FL(c) = T(x)$, otherwise let $FL(c) = EXISTS\{Q(x)\ FILTER\ (T(x))\}$

For $v \in VP(G)$ let its container $c(v) \in Node \cup Edge$ be the graph node or edge where v is located. Let for a fragment F the set of F variables $Vars(F)$ and the set of F external variables $Ext(F)$ be defined inductively over the fragment structure, as follows:

- $Vars(F) = \{m(x) \mid x \in VP(G) \wedge c(x) \in F\} \cup \bigcup \{Ext(F') \mid F \to F'\}$
- $Ext(F) = Vars(F)$, if F is (i) plain and (ii) either optional, union or sub-union fragment; otherwise $Ext(F) = \{m(x) \mid x \in Sel(F)\}$.

The SPARQL group graph pattern $P(F)$, its non-filtered form $P^X(F)$ and external filter $EFL(F)$ for a query fragment F is defined recursively over the query sub-fragment structure, as follows (we use the SPARQL algebra notation, as defined in [1]):

(1) If F is a **union fragment** (consisting of a single union node), let $P(F) = Union(P(F_1), ..., P(F_n))$ for $F \to \{F_1, ..., F_n\}$; for all other cases use steps (2)–(13).

(2) Consider the **raw fragment** F_0 obtained from F by replacing all node aggregate field function calls by their arguments (if F is non-aggregate, then $F_0 = F$).

(3) Join the **local SPARQL fragments** $S(x)$ for data nodes, edges and group graph pattern direct SPARQL clauses within F_0 to obtain the **initial pattern** P_0.

(4) Join to P_0 the patterns $P(H)$ of all **required subquery fragments** hosted by F_0 nodes, as well as full select direct SPARQL clauses to obtain P_1.

(5) Left join (add optional SPARQL subqueries) the patterns $P(H)$ to P_1 of all *optional subquery fragments* hosted by F_0 nodes, to obtain P_2.

(6) Extend P_2 with local SPARQL fragments for *fields* in F_0, obtaining P_3. The extension ordering has to respect the instance field ordering in all F_0/F nodes, as well as the fields not aggregated in F have to come before F aggregated fields. These conditions ensure that a node instance field body expression can refer to an earlier instance field of the same node, as well as that aggregated field body expressions can refer to instance fields within the nodes of the same fragment. The placement of subquery fragments before the fields enable the field body expressions to refer to the results projected out of the subqueries.

(7) Left join to P_3 the non-filtered patterns $P^X(H)$ of *plain optional fragments* H hosted by F_0 nodes; each fragment $P^X(H)$ is joined, taking into account the corresponding external filter expression $EFL(H)$, denote the result P_4.

(8) Subtract (using *Minus* clause) from P_4 the patterns $P(H)$ for all *negated global subquery fragments* hosted by F_0, denote the result $P*$.

(9) Collect the F_0 filter expressions specified in fragment node conditions into FL_0.

(10) Add $fn{:}not(exists(P(F_r)))$ to FL_0 for all *negated plain and local subquery fragments* F_r, hosted by F_0, (the semantics of negated plain and local subquery fragments coincide). Denote the result FL_1.

(11) The raw SPARQL pattern corresponding to F is $R(F) = Filter(FL_1, P^*)$.

(12) If F is an aggregated fragment, add over $R(F)$ the aggregation for all aggregate fields in F head node, with all non-aggregated variables in $Ext(F)$ forming the grouping set; denote the result $R'(F)$. For a non-aggregated F let $R'(F) = R(F)$.

(13) Let $R*(F)$ be obtained from $R'(F)$ by applying the order by, offset and limit operations (the offset and limit operations are allowed only for the main query and for global subquery fragments). Let $P(F) = Project(R*(F), Ext(F))$.

For a plain optional union-free F let $P^X(F) = P^*$ and $EFL(F) = FL_1$ (since F is non-aggregated, $Ext(F) = Vars(F)$). In all other cases let $P^X(F) = P(F)$ and $EFL(F) = true$.

This completes the visual query semantics description. The algorithm described here has been implemented in the ViziQuer tool, including a few adaptations required to successfully run the queries over concrete vendor-specific SPARQL endpoints (e.g. OpenLink Virtuoso).

5 User Studies

A pilot user study on visual query *readability* by domain experts without IT training has been reported in [16], indicating that most of the participants (6 out of 7) were able to correctly interpret at least 70% of visually presented queries; there has been a similar interpretation success rate both for queries that involve aggregation and those that do not, also observing that the subquery notation is not causing a particular difficulty (the success rates for 3 queries involving subqueries were 6/7, 6/7 and 4/7) [16].

A new user study was conducted to show that there is a range of data analysis queries (involving aggregation and subqueries) over RDF data that are for IT-trained users (without specific background in SPARQL) easier to compose in the visual notation and tool than to write in the textual SPARQL notation. The user study was held in conjunction with a presentation on SPARQL and RDF data querying within the Knowledge Engineering course for the Master's degree computing students at the University of Latvia. The study started with the presentation on SPARQL (including a hands-on session over the hospital data endpoint) for 90 min with half of it devoted to the general presentation of SPARQL and the other half to the usage of SPARQL in the context of the hospital data. The ViziQuer notation and tool then was presented for 25 min. The 30 students attending the class were randomly split into two groups of 15 with the groups doing SPARQL queries and the visual notation queries respectively. The students were informed about the test purpose, methodology and voluntary participation. Although the student's results shall be counted towards the credit in a course homework, a similar credit can be obtained by solving the same tasks outside the user study participation. There were two students from the SPARQL group who did not participate in the user study and chose to do visual queries instead of the assigned SPARQL queries; their results are not included in the query result analysis, so leaving 13 participants writing SPARQL queries and 15 doing queries in the visual notation.

There were 10 basic tasks given to the users corresponding to different query patterns: (1) class-attribute-condition, (2) class-attribute-links-conditions, (3) count+condition, (4) count+link+conditions, (5) statistics by attribute (with link and condition), (6) subquery (condition on linked item count), (7) count over condition on subquery results, (8) existential link and sum aggregate, (9) nested subqueries and (10) negated links. There was 70 min time limit for the query completion. Table 2 provides the success of the participants on the queries (+: success, /: notable partial success (not counted in statistics), -: not solved, a: attempted query with no submitted solution). The columns U indicate the user ID's, the columns 1–10 correspond to the tasks; the table left part shows SPARQL text writers and the right part – the visual notation users.

Table 2. Raw test results

U	1	2	3	4	5	6	7	8	9	10	U	1	2	3	4	5	6	7	8	9	10
2	+	a	/	+							1	+	/	+	+	+	−	−	−		
3	+	/	+	+	+	/	/	a			4	+	+	+	+	+	+	+	/	−	
8	+	+									5	+	+	+	+	+	+	+	−		
9	+	−	+	−	a						6	+	+	+	+	+	+	+	a		
11	+		+	+	−	−	a				7	+	a	+	+	a					
12	+	+	+	+	/	a					10	+	+	+	+	+	a				
14	+										13	+	+	+	+	+	a				
17	+	+									15	+	+	+	+	/	+	+	+	+	+
19	+	+	+	+	a						16	+	+	+	+	+	a				
22	+	+	+	+	a	/					18	+	+	+	+	+	−	−	−		
23	−	+	+	a							20	+	+	+		−	+				
24	+	+	+	+	+	/	+	+			21	+	+	+	+	a	+	a			
25	+										26	+	+	+	+	/	+	+	+	a	
											29	+	/	+	/	/	/				
											30	+	+	+	+	+	a		−		−

The rather low overall mean test results (on average 2.92 fully successful queries per participant in SPARQL query writing and 5.27 queries in visual notation) can be partly explained by the limited time the users had for a large number of query creation in a new notation. A comparative analysis of both used notations still can be performed by creating a joint rank of participants by the number of their fully successful queries, finding the rank sums A = 257.5 for SPARQL writing users and B = 148.5 for visual notation users, and calculating the test statistics Z = 3.1785 and p-value 0.0007 < 0.05 threshold for the null hypothesis that writing queries for the IT-trained users in SPARQL is easier or about as easy than composing the queries in the visual notation. The calculation details, the user tasks and the materials needed for the user study reproduction are available on paper's supplementary material site. The visual notation user difficulties with Task 8 (just 2 successful results out of 8 attempts) indicate the need for explicit existential query design pattern in the query notation presentation.

6 Conclusions

We have presented a notation for RDF data analysis query specification in the style of extended UML class diagrams; the notation is able to cover most of SPARQL 1.1 select query constructs, including basic graph patterns, as well as optional and negated blocks, aggregation, grouping and subqueries, without query nesting structure restrictions.

The query notation is meant to be used both by general IT experts who may find using the notation convenient in parallel with textual SPARQL query writing and by non-IT trained domain experts for whom the direct SPARQL query reading and writing is generally expected to be too difficult (cf. e.g. [10]).

The user studies performed so far have shown that non-IT end users shall be able mostly to read and understand the basic visual query notation (including subqueries) [16], as well as that already the current generic query creation environment shall provide an advantage over textual SPARQL query writing in RDF data query creation for general IT experts that do not have previous specific training in SPARQL.

There is web-based tool support for the introduced notation, described in [17].

References

1. SPARQL 1.1 Query Language. W3C Recommendation, 21 March 2013. http://www.w3.org/TR/2013/REC-sparql11-query-20130321/
2. Resource Description Framework (RDF). http://www.w3.org/RDF/
3. Optique. Scalable End-User Access to Big Data. http://optique-project.eu
4. Vega-Gorgojo, G., Giese, M., Heggestøyl, S., Soylu, A., Waaler, A.: PepeSearch: semantic data for the masses. PLoS ONE **11**(3), e0151573 (2016). https://doi.org/10.1371/journal.pone.0151573
5. Khalili, A., Merono-Penuela, A.: WYSIWYQ–What You See Is What You Query. In: Voila 2017, vol. 1947, pp. 123–130. CEUR Workshop Proceedings (2017). http://ceur-ws.org/Vol-1947/paper11.pdf

6. Ferré, S.: SPARKLIS: a SPARQL endpoint explorer for expressive question answering. In: Proceedings of the ISWC 2014 Posters & Demonstrations Track, vol. 1272. CEUR (2014). http://ceur-ws.org/Vol-1272/paper_39.pdf
7. Zloof, M.M.: Query by example. In: Proceedings of the National Computer Conference and Exposition, 19–22 May 1975, pp. 431–438. ACM (1975)
8. Catarci, T., Costabile, M.F., Levialdi, S., Batini, C.: Visual query systems for databases: a survey. J. Vis. Lang. Comput. **8**(2), 215–260 (1997)
9. Catarci, T., Dongilli, P., Mascio, T.D., Franconi, E., Santucci, G., Tessaris, S.: An ontology based visual tool for query formulation support. In: Proceedings of the 16th European Conference on Artificial Intelligence, pp. 308–312. IOS Press (2004)
10. Soylu, A., Giese, M., Jimenez-Ruiz, E., Vega-Gorgojo, G., Horrocks, I.: Experiencing OptiqueVQS: a multi-paradigm and ontology-based Visual Query System for end users. Univ. Access Inf. Soc. **15**(1), 129–152 (2016)
11. Haag, F., Lohmann, S., Siek, S., Ertl, T.: QueryVOWL: visual composition of SPARQL queries. In: Gandon, F., Guéret, C., Villata, S., Breslin, J., Faron-Zucker, C., Zimmermann, A. (eds.) ESWC 2015. LNCS, vol. 9341, pp. 62–66. Springer, Cham (2015). https://doi.org/10.1007/978-3-319-25639-9_12. http://vowl.visualdataweb.org/queryvowl/
12. Kapourani, B., Fotopoulou, E., Papaspyros, D., Zafeiropoulos, A., Mouzakitis, S., Koussouris, S.: Propelling SMEs business intelligence through linked data production and consumption. In: Ciuciu, I., et al. (eds.) OTM 2015. LNCS, vol. 9416, pp. 107–116. Springer, Cham (2015). https://doi.org/10.1007/978-3-319-26138-6_14
13. Zviedris, M., Barzdins, G.: ViziQuer: a tool to explore and query SPARQL endpoints. In: Antoniou, G., et al. (eds.) ESWC 2011. LNCS, vol. 6644, pp. 441–445. Springer, Heidelberg (2011). https://doi.org/10.1007/978-3-642-21064-8_31
14. Čerāns, K., Ovčiņņikova, J., Zviedris, M.: SPARQL aggregate queries made easy with diagrammatic query language ViziQuer. In: Proceedings of the ISWC 2015 Posters & Demonstrations Track, vol. 1486. CEUR (2015). http://ceur-ws.org/Vol1486/paper_68.pdf
15. Čerāns, K., Ovčiņņikova, J.: ViziQuer: notation and tool for data analysis SPARQL queries. In: VOILA 2016, vol. 1704, pp. 151–159. CEUR Workshop Proceedings (2016)
16. Čerāns, K., et al.: Extended UML class diagram constructs for visual SPARQL queries in ViziQuer/web. In: Voila 2017, vol. 1947, pp. 87–98. CEUR Workshop Proceedings (2017)
17. Čerāns, K., et al.: ViziQuer: a web-based tool for visual diagrammatic queries over RDF data. In: Gangemi, A., et al. (eds.) ESWC 2018. LNCS, vol. 11155, pp. 158–163. Springer, Cham (2018). https://doi.org/10.1007/978-3-319-98192-5_30
18. Bārzdiņš, J., Grasmanis, M., Rencis, E., Šostaks, A., Bārzdiņš, J.: Ad-hoc querying of semistar data ontologies using controlled natural language. In: Arnicans, G., Arnicane, V., Borzovs, J., Niedrite, L. (eds.) Frontiers of AI and Applications. Databases and Information Systems IX, vol. 291, pp. 3–16. IOS Press, Amsterdam (2016)

A Systematic Approach to Review Legacy Schemas Based on Ontological Analysis

Raquel Lima Façanha[1] (ID), Maria Cláudia Cavalcanti[1(✉)] (ID),
and Maria Luiza Machado Campos[2] (ID)

[1] Military Institute of Engineering, Rio de Janeiro, Brazil
rlfacanha@yahoo.com.br, yoko@ime.eb.br
[2] Federal University of Rio de Janeiro, Rio de Janeiro, Brazil
mluiza@ppgi.ufrj.br

Abstract. Usually, data schemas are the only documentation available for legacy data. Information Technology (IT) artifacts, such as conceptual schemas, if existent, are often outdated. This leads to inconsistencies and ambiguities, as well as difficulties in reusing data. This work proposes an approach for reviewing data schemas based on ontological analysis, which considers each concept according to its nature, capturing more precisely its essence and generally improving semantic richness and precision. The idea is to provide a systematic procedure to annotate legacy data, starting with its conceptual schema, and thus to contribute to generate more consistent conceptual modeling artifacts. In order to illustrate the proposed procedure, the Unified Foundational Ontology (UFO) is used as a theoretical reference for annotating a real data schema in the Legal domain.

Keywords: Ontological analysis · Conceptual modeling · Legacy data

1 Introduction

Information Technology (IT) teams make great effort on developing systems. In particular, collecting and formalizing the main concepts of the domain are not easy tasks. The interaction with business experts seems not to be enough to get IT artifacts consistently aligned to reality. In this regard, conceptual schemas are the most important IT artifacts, for their meaningful representation of business concepts, and specially because most of the other artifacts derive from them. However, it is not rare to find systems that were conceived without conceptual schemas, and even when they exist, sometimes they fail to properly reflect the business point of view. They are commonly influenced by implementation considerations from IT professionals, whose real world perspective may differ from business specialists, who deal directly with the domain. Besides, IT artifacts are usually not maintained up to date throughout the system life cycle, specially conceptual representations.

© Springer Nature Switzerland AG 2019
E. Garoufallou et al. (Eds.): MTSR 2018, CCIS 846, pp. 63–75, 2019.
https://doi.org/10.1007/978-3-030-14401-2_6

Therefore, there is a need to improve or to review such artifacts. The review of conceptual schemas usually takes place at a re-engineering effort, or because of new requirements demand. This work proposes an approach to annotate an existing conceptual schema, based on ontological analysis, which considers each concept according to its nature and semantics, usually not preserved during the development cycle. The idea is to provide a systematic procedure to annotate legacy data, and thus to contribute to review and generate more consistent conceptual modeling artifacts. In addition, such annotations bring more expressiveness to conceptual schemas. Ultimately, at the end of this process, it might indicate the need for some complimentary re-engineering effort.

There are works that propose the use of ontological analysis while conceiving a new schema [5,11,12]. However, to the best of our knowledge, no works focused on legacy schemas. Moreover, the benefit of applying ontological analysis on legacy schemas goes beyond data schema documentation. It provides an enrichment of the semantics behind the data schema, which may facilitate data reuse and interoperability. In order to illustrate the proposed procedure, the Unified Foundational Ontology (UFO) [5] was used as a theoretical reference during its execution. A real data schema in the Legal domain was chosen, and one of its main elements was analyzed in the light of UFO concepts.

2 Ontological Analysis

Conceptual modeling is a fundamental activity to capture the domain perspective and to conciliate perspectives from both the developer and the domain expert. A semantic rich conceptual model needs to provide the necessary elements to represent reality as accurate as it can be, in a way that turns to be understandable and implementation independent.

In the last decades, there has been significant advances on using ontological analysis to provide a sound foundation for conceptual models development, in order to reach better representations of computational artifacts, specially conceptual schemas [6]. Ontological analysis can be defined as "the process of eliciting and discovering relevant distinctions and relationships bound to the very nature of the entities involved in a certain domain" [4]. It is based on the use of a foundational ontology (theory), which provides a set of principles and basic categories [4], such as space, time, matter, object, event, action, etc, which are independent of any particular domain. UFO was adopted in this work, because it has been successfully used in recent years[1] to evaluate conceptual model languages and representations, applying more real world semantics to modeling elements.

UFO categories are organized in three fragments: UFO-A, UFO-B and UFO-C. UFO-A focuses on *Endurants*. Endurants and their parts are always present during existence and their identities are preserved [5]. UFO-B focuses on *Perdurants* (or *Events*), which differ from *Endurants* because of their relation with time. *Events* are individuals composed of temporal parts, such as, a conversation, a football game or a business process. An *Event* exists as long as

---

[1] http://www.menthor.net/publications.html.

its temporal parts exist. Figure 1 shows that *Events* change reality by changing the state of affairs from a previous situation (pre-state) to a posterior situation (post-state).

The main distinction in UFO-C, shown in Fig. 1, is between *Agents* and *Objects*. *Agents* are substantials that can bear intentional moments, meanwhile *Objects* are incapable to perceive events nor bear intentional moments. *Intentional Moments* are a special kind of moments that have a type: *Belief, Desire* or *Intention*; and a propositional content. *Intentional Moments* can be social or mental. *Intentions* are mental moments that represent an internal commitment of an agent; causing an agent to perform actions.

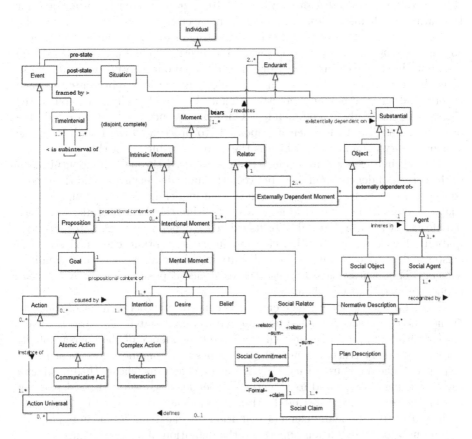

Fig. 1. UFO-B and UFO-C combined fragment. Adapted from [9]

Social Commitment is a commitment from an agent A towards an agent B; causing the creation of an *Internal Commitment* for A and a *Social Claim* from B towards A. The set of two or more pairs *Social Commitment/Social Claim* associated compose a *Social Relator*. *Actions* are intentional events that instantiate a *Plan* or an *Action Universal* that aims to satisfy some *Commitment* of an *Agent*.

3   Annotating Legacy Conceptual Schemas

This approach aims to annotate legacy database conceptual schemas towards making explicit their ontological commitment. It allows modelers to clarify the real meaning of the modeling elements (domain concepts) of the schema. The main idea is to specify a systematic way to support the commitment to a foundational ontology - ontological theory.

When all we have is a legacy database and its logical schema, additional preparation steps should be taken to obtain the conceptual schema, which will be further analyzed and committed to the selected ontological theory. These steps were described on a previous work [10]. The first step is responsible for the database schema cut-off, and focuses on selecting the core data schema elements. The next step is responsible for extracting or updating the correspondent conceptual schema, using existing reverse engineering techniques. The third step is responsible for selecting the theory (foundational ontology) to annotate with. This choice is guided by the main ontological distinctions represented in each theory, and their importance for the schema domain. Usually, a cut-off of the theory schema is also recommended. Once both conceptual schema and theory cut-offs are available, then it is possible to proceed to the fourth step, the schema-theory commitment, which is the main contribution of this work.

The schema-theory commitment can be achieved through the identification of the correspondences (matches) between the modeling elements and the theory concepts. In order to find these matches, each modeling element of the conceptual schema must be reviewed and analyzed within the domain of discourse, not only for its own nature, but also for its existence dependency (a.k.a. total participation) [2] with respect to other elements in the conceptual schema. Besides the existence dependency, each element definition and semantics must be taken into account. This is necessary because the existence dependencies are not always explicit in a conceptual schema.

Then, for each modeling element in the conceptual schema, a set of concepts of the ontological theory should be analyzed to find a match. The idea is to verify, for each candidate pair, if each existence dependency of the concept of the ontological theory (theory concept) also applies to the modeling element in the conceptual schema. During this analysis, the modeler must clarify the meaning of each modeling element and its structural dependencies, even if these dependencies are not explicitly represented. Also, the modeler must solve any ambiguity with respect to a modeling element definition, by clarifying its meaning, and by explaining how its definition adheres to the definition of a theory concept.

This matching analysis begins with the most generic concepts (top concepts) from the ontological theory. If there is a match between the modeling element and a top concept from the ontological theory, the idea is to traverse the ontological theory, searching for more specific concepts (subconcepts of that concept), to find out if there is a specific concept that also matches the modeling element. If such match is found, the previous match is replaced; otherwise the match with the top concept is maintained. In short, this is a top-down approach for matching modeling elements and theory concepts, based on the existence dependencies of the theory concepts. A procedural description of it, named Correspondence procedure, is presented as follows.

(1) Load the ontological theory T and its corresponding set of concepts $(c \mid c \in T)$;
(2) Load the set of modeling elements of the schema M $(e \mid e \in M)$;
(3) For each modeling element e, create a list of potential pairs L $(L = (e, c))$, where c are the top concepts of T;
(4) For each potential pair (e, c) of L do:
    (4.1) Check if all existence dependencies of c apply to e;
    (4.2) If not all existence dependencies of c apply to e, check the adherence of the definition of e to c;
    (4.3) If (4.1) or (4.2) are true then (e, c) is maintained in L, otherwise remove (e, c) from L and return to (4);
    (4.4) If there are immediate subconcepts of the concept c (or sc) of the pair (e, c) (or (e, sc));
        (4.4.1) Create a new list of potential pairs SL $(SL = (e, sc))$, where sc are the immediate subconcepts of concept c of the theory T;
        (4.4.2) For each pair (e, sc) of SL (or SSL) do:
            (4.4.2.1) Check if all existence dependencies of sc apply to e;
            (4.4.2.2) If not all existence dependencies of sc apply to e, check adherence of definitions;
            (4.4.2.3) If (4.4.2.1) or (4.4.2.2) are true, (e, sc) substitutes (e, c) in L and (e, sc) is added to list SSL to check for subclasses,
            (4.4.2.4) otherwise (e, sc) is removed from SL;
            (4.4.2.5) return to (4.4.2);
        (4.4.3) For each (e, sc) pair of list SSL, do (4.4) recursively

The Correspondence procedure accepts as input an ontological theory T and a list of elements that come from a legacy conceptual schema M. It begins by creating a list of the main (top) concepts, extracted from T. Then, it creates a data structure named L, which stores all pairs (e, c), where e is a modeling element of M and c is a concept of T. Then, for each pair (e, c) of L (step 4), it starts a recursive verification of existence dependencies and definition adherence. Section 4 presents an application example of the Correspondence procedure, going through each of these steps.

At the end, the output of the Correspondence procedure is a list of meta categorized pairs, i.e., for each modeling element, a theory concept is annotated. Note that although this proposal is a systematic way that leads to an ontological commitment, its output is a set of suggested matches between the elements of a schema and the concepts of the theory. The idea is to use these matches to annotate the logical schema, and the real data, with their intended meaning, as a way of clarifying the real meaning of the data.

4 Application Example in the Legal Domain

The Correspondence procedure was applied in the Procedural Law domain, which is a legal branch that studies and regulates the machinery of the courts and the methods with which the State enforces Civil and Criminal Law, solving real case situations. The key concepts of Procedural Law are: lawsuit, action and jurisdiction.

According to Liebman [8], action is the subjective right to judicial assistance. The existence of an action depends on some essential requirements termed action conditions. Jurisdiction is the right and the duty of the State to resolve actual conflicts, referring to the inherent authority of a court to hear a case and to pronounce the sentence of the law. Lawsuit is the instrument through which jurisdictional organs act to enforce the law in practical litigious cases. A lawsuit is formed by a sequence of acts that take place according to procedures imposed by law. The acts defined by law are named procedural acts. A procedural act is the smallest unit of a lawsuit and itself is a manifestation of intention from the subjects (parties) in a lawsuit. A procedural act is every human action that produces juridical effects related to the lawsuit.

The Rio de Janeiro Judicial Section (SJRJ - Seção Judiciária do Rio de Janeiro) is a trial court for cases involving a federal organ, a governmental agency or a public corporation as interested parties. SJRJ currently uses a database named SIAPRO to store information about those legal cases. SIAPRO database schema was conceived to record, distribute and classify all procedures related to lawsuits at SJRJ. It evolved and now its data are available for court servants, judges and also for citizens, legal professionals and other governmental agencies. However, there is no official documentation about SIAPRO, except for the DBMS metadata, which was automatically extracted for our study.

The SIAPRO system works as follows. When a plaintiff files a complaint or petition, a lawsuit is created in SIAPRO. After that, the court of law appreciates the complaint and a summons shall be issued under the seal of the court. After being notified, the defendant has a limited period of time to file an answer to the complaint; or in case the defendant has a claim against the plaintiff, the defendant could file a counterclaim. Until trial, both parties can make allegations and denials, including requests for production of documents, requests for admissions and depositions, presenting evidence and calling witnesses. The court deliberates about all facts and evidence to make an official announcement of the decision - judgment. Each act performed by the judge, by the parties or by the clerks of justice is a procedural act.

In order to annotate the SIAPRO legacy database schema, applying the *Correspondence* procedure presented in Sect. 3, it was necessary first to perform the preparation steps. With the help of system specialists and domain experts' knowledge, it was possible to reduce a data schema of about 600 tables to its relevant core. From this schema cut-off, the corresponding conceptual schema was derived. Three main entities were identified, together with their corresponding relationships and cardinalities, as shown in Fig. 2, the lawsuit, its development and the parties involved in it.

The *Lawsuit* entity represents all lawsuits at SJRJ. Some of its attributes are procedural class (*codclass*), which defines the court procedures, and the court of law, responsible for ruling the case (*codcourt*). Each instance of *Lawsuit* has a sequence of acts represented by the (*Development* entity). This sequence of acts takes place according to the procedures imposed by the Brazilian Code of Civil Procedural Law. Each instance of *Development* has a phase to indicate a procedural act or a set of procedural acts established by the Brazilian Code of Civil Procedural Law. *DevIntimation* represents all notifications associated to a specific development. Finally, since there is no lawsuit without parties, it is associated to at least one instance of the Person entity, which can be a physical person or a juridical person (Entity).

In order to choose the theory cut-off, it was taken into account that the legacy schema main concepts include notions of temporal relations (e.g. procedural deadlines), actions (e.g. procedural acts), and social relations and roles (e.g. lawsuit, plaintiff, defendant and judge). Due to its coverage and available usage descriptions, we chose UFO foundational ontology [5] to be our support theory, paying special attention to UFO-B and UFO-C fragments (Fig. 1).

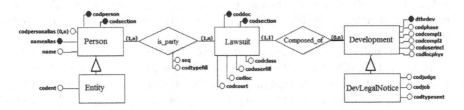

Fig. 2. SIAPRO conceptual legacy schema

Initially, the *Correspondence* procedure creates two lists (steps 1 and 2): *modelingElements (M)* and *theoryConcepts (T)*. While M contains only the *Lawsuit* element[2], T contains the top concepts of UFO-B and UFO-C schemas (Fig. 1). Then, in step (3), it pairs the *Lawsuit* modeling element with each UFO concept. These pairs are stored in the *potentialPairs (L)* list, all initialized as false. Table 1 shows this list at instant t0. In step (4), it iterates over the pairs in the *potentialPairs* list, starting with the (*Lawsuit, Endurant*) pair. First, the procedure checks for dependencies. According to UFO-C, there are no existential dependencies for *Endurant*. Then, it checks for adherence, i.e. if the *Lawsuit* modeling element is semantically similar to the *Endurant* ontological definition.

According to UFO, *Endurant* is an individual wholly present whenever it is present, maintaining its identity through all its existence. Considering that an instance of the *Lawsuit* element is a legal case formalization, when the complaint is filed, none of the courts of law are responsible for its proceedings. After random assignment, the same lawsuit is assigned to a court of law (identified by the *codcourt* attribute), which will be responsible for its proceedings. In both cases, we are dealing with the same instance of *Lawsuit*. Thus, the *Lawsuit* definition adheres to the *Endurant* definition.

Then, in step (4.4) it checks for *Endurant* subclasses: *Moment* and *Substantial*, and builds (step 4.4.1) a new list of pairs (*subClassesPairs(SL)*), as shown at instant t2 in Table 1. Again, for each pair (step 4.4.2), it verifies existential dependencies and definition adherence (steps 4.4.2.1 and 4.4.2.2). It begins with pair (*Lawsuit, Moment*). According to UFO-C, *Moment* only exists in association to other individuals named *Substantials*. *Substantials* have unique identity

---

[2] Due to space limitations, only one element was analyzed in this work. For the complete analysis please refer to [3].

and are existentially independent [9]. On the other hand, an instance of a lawsuit depends on the existence of at least one individual, since there is no lawsuit without a plaintiff. In the SIAPRO schema (Fig. 2) the relationship between *Lawsuit* and *Person* represents exactly this dependence. Since the existential dependency *existential dependence of* is represented in SIAPRO schema, the pair (*Lawsuit, Moment*) becomes a true potential pair, and substitutes the pair (*Lawsuit, Endurant*), as shown at instant t3 in Table 1 (step 4.4.2.3). Note that the pair (*Lawsuit, Endurant*) is added to the *replacedGeneralPairs* list. This happens because *Moment* is a subclass of *Endurant*, and it is conceptually closer to the *Lawsuit* modeling element than its parent. Finally, the new potential pair is added to another list (*addedPairs (SSL)*) in order to have its subclasses checked later on, recursively.

The next pair in the *subclassesPairs (SL)* list is (*Lawsuit, Substantial*). According to UFO-C, *Substantial* bears exactly one *Moment*. In the SIAPRO schema, a lawsuit does not depend on exactly one other individual to exist. Thus, the (*Lawsuit, Substantial*) pair is discarded, as shown at instant t4 (Table 1). According to step (4.4.3), if there are pairs recently added to the *addedPairs* list, then it recursively processes step (4.4). It retrieves *Moment* subclasses and builds a new *subclassesPairs* list to be processed, as shown at instant t_6. Then, it analyzes the (*Lawsuit, Intrinsic Moment*) pair. According to UFO-C, there are no existential dependencies for *Intrinsic Moment*. In [9], *Intrinsic Moments* are defined as dependent on one single individual. However, *Lawsuit* depends on more than one individual to exist. A lawsuit, as a legal protection, creates a relationship between the plaintiff and the State (court of law). A lawsuit also creates a relationship between the plaintiff and the defendant after a valid summon. Thus, the pair (*Lawsuit, Intrinsic Moment*) is discarded, at t7.

The pair (*Lawsuit, Relator*) is the next pair in the *subclassesPairs* list. Since there are existential dependencies for the *Relator* theory concept, the modeler analyzes the *Lawsuit* modeling element to determine if the *Relator* existential dependency that refers to the *Externally Dependent Moment* concept is represented in the SIAPRO schema. A *Relator* is the sum of all individuals composed of all externally dependent moments that inhere in the same individual [1]. *Externally Dependent Moments* are *Intrinsic Moments* that inhere in a single individual, but are existentially dependent on a plurality of other individuals (*Substantials*).

According to the SIAPRO schema, a legal complaint is an *Intrinsic Moment* inherent to a plaintiff (an agent). But also a legal complaint depends on the existence of a defendant and a court of law to settle the dispute. The aggregation of all externally dependent moments necessary to characterize a *Relator* is represented in the SIAPRO schema by the relationship between *Lawsuit* and *Person* and by the *codcourt* attribute, which represents the court of law responsible for ruling the legal case. Thus, the (*Lawsuit, Relator*) pair is added as a true potential pair in the *potentialPairs* list, and replaces the (*Lawsuit, Moment*) pair, which is added to the *replacedGeneralPairs* list. Since *Relator* has subclasses, it is added to the addedPairs list, as shown at instant t8. Again, it starts step 4.4 for the pairs in the addedPairs list.

Then, in step 4.4.2, the pair (*Lawsuit,Social Relator*) is analyzed. Since there are two existential dependencies for *Social Relator*: *Social Commitment* and *Social Claim*, then, the modeler has to check if both are (or should have been) also represented in the SIAPRO schema. After a plaintiff files a complaint and this complaint turns into a legal case, a lawsuit mediates a relation between the plaintiff and the State (court of law); and after valid summons a lawsuit also mediates a relation between both and the defendant. All individuals, plaintiff, defendant and State (court of law), bear commitments and claims towards each other. Deciding the legal case becomes a goal for the court of law; and as a consequence, the court has the right to enforce some duties to the plaintiff and to the defendant, such as, producing evidences (*Social Commitment/Social Claim*). Although in SIAPRO schema none of the existential dependencies mentioned above are explicitly represented, with domain and theory well-understood, we can conclude that both *Social Relator* existential dependencies (*Social Commitment/Social Claim*), pictured in our ontological theory cut-off, should have been present in SIAPRO schema. Thus, at instant t_9, the (*Lawsuit, Social Relator*) pair replaces the (*Lawsuit, Relator*) pair.

Since *Social Relator* does not have subclasses, the next pairs to be analyzed are: (*Lawsuit, Event*), (*Lawsuit, Agent*), and (*Lawsuit, Object*). They are analyzed one at a time, verifying the existential dependencies and traversing the theory concept hierarchy until finding the most specific compatible matches. Pairs (*Lawsuit, Event*) and (*Lawsuit, Agent*) are discarded before the traversing of the corresponding theory concepts. The *Lawsuit* element does not encompass the existential dependencies found for *Event* (*TimeInterval* and *Situation*) and *Agent* (*Intentional Moment*). *Lawsuit* has no date dependencies. Besides, changes in reality by changing the state of affairs from one (pre-state) situation to a (post-state) situation are not shown in the *Lawsuit* modeling element. For instance, an event like "Court of law issues a summons to a defendant" changes reality, but even after that for the *Lawsuit* nothing changes. Finally, a *Lawsuit* does not existentially depend on an *Intentional Moment*, which is defined as a mental or social state that lead an agent to perform actions. The intention belongs to an agent, in that case, intention belongs to a plaintiff, who files a complaint asking the State (court of law) to solve a dispute.

The last pair to be analyzed in the *potentialPairs* list is the (*Lawsuit, Object*) pair. There are no existential dependencies for the *Object* theory concept. Now, the modeler has to review the domain modeling elements to confirm the adherence of the *Lawsuit* modeling element, to the *Object* theory concept. *Objects* are individuals not capable of performing actions - individuals that do not bear *Intentional Moments*. In this sense, we can consider the definition of the *Lawsuit* modeling element adherent to the definition of *Object* theory concept. At this point, it checks *Object* subclasses (t10 in Table 1). Since *Social Object* has no existential dependencies, it proceeds to check definition adherence. *Social Object* is an object that depends of a social group to recognize it; and it is defined by one or more known rules that must be recognized by at least one *Social Agent*. As an instance of *Lawsuit* has its proceedings defined by norms such as the Brazilian Constitution and Brazilian Code of Civil Procedural Law, it adheres to the *Social Object* theory concept, and then the (*Lawsuit,Social Object*) pair replaces the (*Lawsuit, Object*) pair, and the replaced pair is added to the replacedGeneralPairs list, as shown in Table 1, instant t_{11}.

Table 1. Time instants for modeling element *Lawsuit*

Data Structures	t
potentialPairs = {[Lawsuit, Endurant] = false, [Lawsuit, Event] = false, [Lawsuit, Agent] = false, [Lawsuit, Object] = false}	t_0
discardedPairs = { }; replacedGeneralPairs = { }	t_1
potentialPairs = {[Lawsuit, Endurant] = false, [Lawsuit, Event] = false, [Lawsuit, Agent] = false, [Lawsuit, Object] = false}	t_1
subclasses = {Endurant = [Moment, Substantial]}	t_1
subclassesPairs = {[Lawsuit,Endurant] = [Lawsuit, Substantial], [Lawsuit, Moment]}	t_2
replacedGeneralPairs = {[Lawsuit,Endurant]}	t_3
potentialPairs = {[Lawsuit, Moment]=true, [Lawsuit, Event]=false, [Lawsuit, Agent]=false, [Lawsuit, Object]=false}	t_3
discardedPairs = {[Lawsuit,Substantial]}	t_4
replacedGeneralPairs = {[Lawsuit,Endurant]}	t_4
potentialPairs = {[Lawsuit, Moment]=true, [Lawsuit, Event]=false, [Lawsuit, Agent]=false, [Lawsuit, Object]=false}	t_4
discardedPairs = {[Lawsuit,Substantial]}	t_5
replacedGeneralPairs = {[Lawsuit,Endurant]}	t_5
potentialPairs = {[Lawsuit, Moment]=true, [Lawsuit, Event]=false, [Lawsuit, Agent]=false, [Lawsuit, Object]=false}	t_5
subclassesSub = {Moment = [Intrinsic Moment,Relator] }	t_5
subclassesPairs = {[Lawsuit,Moment] = [Lawsuit,Intrinsic Moment], [Lawsuit,Relator] }	t_6
discardedPairs = {[Lawsuit,Substantial], [Lawsuit,Intrinsic Moment]}	t_7
replacedGeneralPairs = {[Lawsuit,Endurant]}	t_7
potentialPairs = {[Lawsuit, Moment]=true, [Lawsuit,Event]=false, [Lawsuit,Agent]=false, [Lawsuit,Object]=false}	t_7
discardedPairs = {[Lawsuit,Substantial], [Lawsuit,Intrinsic Moment]}	t_8
replacedGeneralPairs = {[Lawsuit,Endurant], [Lawsuit,Moment]}	t_8
potentialPairs = {[Lawsuit,Relator]=true, [Lawsuit,Event]=false, [Lawsuit,Agent]=false, [Lawsuit,Object]=false}	t_8
subclassesSub = {Relator = [Social Relator] }	t_8
discardedPairs = {[Lawsuit,Substantial], [Lawsuit,Intrinsic Moment]}	t_9
replacedGeneralPairs = {[Lawsuit,Endurant], [Lawsuit,Moment], [Lawsuit,Relator]}	t_9
potentialPairs = {[Lawsuit, Social Relator]=true, [Lawsuit, Event]=false, [Lawsuit, Agent]=false, [Lawsuit, Object]=false}	t_9
discardedPairs = {[Lawsuit, Substantial], [Lawsuit, Intrinsic Moment], [Lawsuit, Event], [Lawsuit, Agent]}	t_{10}
replacedGeneralPairs = {[Lawsuit,Endurant], [Lawsuit,Moment], [Lawsuit,Relator]}	t_{10}
potentialPairs = {[Lawsuit,Social Relator]=true, [Lawsuit,Social Object]=true}	t_{10}
subclassesSub = {Object=[Social Object]}	t_{10}
discardedPairs = {[Lawsuit,Substantial], [Lawsuit,Intrinsic Moment], [Lawsuit,Event], [Lawsuit,Agent]}	t_{11}
replacedGeneralPairs = {[Lawsuit,Endurant], [Lawsuit,Moment], [Lawsuit,Relator], [Lawsuit,Object]}	t_{11}
potentialPairs = {[Lawsuit,Social Relator]=true, [Lawsuit,Social Object]=true}	t_{11}
subclassesSub = {Social Object=[Normative Description]}	t_{11}
discardedPairs = {[Lawsuit,Substantial], [Lawsuit,Intrinsic Moment], [Lawsuit,Event], [Lawsuit,Agent], [Lawsuit,Normative Description]}	t_{12}
replacedGeneralPairs = {[Lawsuit,Endurant], [Lawsuit,Moment], [Lawsuit,Relator], [Lawsuit,Object]}	t_{12}

The traversing of the *Object* concept hierarchy continues through the *Social Object* concept subclasses. The (*Lawsuit, Normative Description*) pair is now analyzed and discarded for not attending the existential dependency. An instance of *Lawsuit* is not recognized by a *Social Agent*. For this recognition to take place, an instance of *Lawsuit* must describe how a legal case develops itself. In fact, as previously mentioned, all rules and proceedings are established in legal norms such as the Brazilian Constitution and the Brazilian Code of Civil Procedural Law. Since there are no more potential pairs to be analyzed, we end up with two candidate metacategories for *Lawsuit*: *Social Object* and *Social Relator*.

These two candidates characterize what is called a construct overload, leading to ambiguity. With both theory concepts definitions in hands, domain experts and specialists agreed that the *Lawsuit* element corresponds to the *Social Relator* concept, taking into consideration that a lawsuit mediates relations between plaintiff, defendant and State (court of law) and has all rules and proceedings of a legal case, including parties commitments and claims, defined by the Brazilian Constitution and the Brazilian Code of Civil Procedural Law.

As mentioned before, we took into account the premise that the analysis process should start with the main ontological distinctions. Therefore, at the beginning of the analysis, we choose a set of theory concepts that represents the main distinctions in the context of the legacy schema.

Through this systematic approach it is possible to identify constructs overload, such as the one of the example, and take a decision on the real meaning of a concept, based on domain experts knowledge. It avoids a possible mistaken meta categorization. This is the main benefit of our approach, despite the manual work involved. Besides, the algorithmic specification may be used for the implementation of the proposed systematic, in order to facilitate its application.

5   Related Work

Villela [12], Tavares [11] and OntoUML [7] involve or are involved in procedures and steps to apply meta-properties and foundational ontologies meta-categories. However, these works are restricted to the validation of a schema under construction. More importantly, these approaches do not take into account that, in the context of legacy data, the schema was already conceived and represents data in use. In a previous work [10], we proposed a set of guidelines that applied to a database conceptual schema, allowing to explicit its ontological commitment and to obtain a well-founded representation. However, this approach is restricted to statical relations, using only UFO-A fragment to support the analysis of the schema. The present work extends and generalizes [10], since it includes dynamic and social relations (UFO-B and UFO-C fragments).

6   Conclusion and Future Work

IT artifacts, such as conceptual schemas, represent concepts in the business area of an organization. The alignment between business reality and IT artifacts is crucial. It is not rare for organizations to face difficulties on reusing data from legacy systems because of misconceived or unclear conceptual schemas. The main contribution of this work is to help on the revision and improvement of such conceptual schemas by proposing a systematic and well-founded procedure. It guides the modelers on establishing correspondences between modeling elements from a legacy schema and concepts from an ontological theory (foundational ontology). A case study on the Legal domain illustrated the proposed procedure.

Despite its benefits, the proposed systematic procedure has a subjective nature, thus experts and domain specialists play an essential role on clarifying the meaning of modeling elements from the legacy schema. They must have a good understanding of the foundational ontology categories. Moreover, the application of such approach is a time consuming task. Initially, it should be applied to the core of the legacy schema. Then, it can be incrementally applied to cover the whole schema. Future works include the improvement of the systematic procedure to contemplate a method to select and cut-off an ontological theory, according to a given legacy system domain. Besides, the approach can also be applied on the alignment of schemas in databases integration initiatives.

References

1. Almeida, J.P.A., Guizzardi, G.: An ontological analysis of the notion of community in the RM-ODP enterprise language. Comp. Stand. Interf. **35**(3), 257–268 (2013)
2. Elmasri, R., Navathe, S.: Fundamentals of Database Systems, 6th edn. Addison-Wesley Publishing Company, USA (2010)
3. Façanha, R.L.: Um Método para Apoiar o Resgate do Compromisso Ontológico de um Esquema de Dados Conceitual Legado (in Portuguese). Master's degree dissertation, Instituto Militar de Engenharia (IME) (2015)
4. Guarino, N.: Formal Ontology in Information Systems: Proceedings of the 1st International Conference, 1998, Trento, Italy, 1st edn. IOS Press, Amsterdam (1998)
5. Guizzardi, G.: Ontological Foundations for Structural Conceptual Models. CTIT PhD, University of Twente, Enschede (2005)
6. Guizzardi, G.: Ontological meta-properties of derived object types. In: Ralyté, J., Franch, X., Brinkkemper, S., Wrycza, S. (eds.) CAiSE 2012. LNCS, vol. 7328, pp. 318–333. Springer, Heidelberg (2012). https://doi.org/10.1007/978-3-642-31095-9_21
7. Guizzardi, G., das Graças, A.P., Guizzardi, R.S.S.: Design patterns and inductive modeling rules to support the construction of ontologically well-founded conceptual models in OntoUML. In: Salinesi, C., Pastor, O. (eds.) CAiSE 2011. LNBIP, vol. 83, pp. 402–413. Springer, Heidelberg (2011). https://doi.org/10.1007/978-3-642-22056-2_44
8. Liebman, E.T.: Manual de Direito Processual Civil, vol. 1, 3rd edn. Malheiros Ed., Rio de Janeiro (2005)
9. Nardi, J.C., et al.: Towards a commitment-based reference ontology for services. In: 17th IEEE EDOC, Vancouver, Canada, pp. 175–184 (2013)
10. Silva, A.M.F.R.: Diretrizes para o Resgate do Esquema Conceitual e seu Compromisso Ontológico a partir de um Banco de Dados (in portuguese). Master's degree dissertation, Instituto Militar de Engenharia (IME) (2012)

11. Tavares, D.B.: Procedimento de Análise para Validação de Diagrama de Classes de Domínio Baseado em Análise Ontológica (in portuguese). Master's degree dissertation, Universidade Federal de Viçosa (UFV) (2008)
12. Villela, M.L.B.: Validaçáo de Diagramas de Classe por meio de Propriedades Ontológicas (in portuguese). Master's degree dissertation, Universidade Federal de Minas Gerais (2004)

Towards a Holistic Documentation and Wider Use of Digital Cultural Heritage

Marinos Ioannides$^{(\boxtimes)}$ and Robert Davies

Cyprus University of Technology, Limassol, Cyprus
`marinos.ioannides@cut.ac.cy`

Abstract. This paper reviews work currently undertaken and planned to develop a more holistic approach to e-documentation of Cultural Heritage, thereby addressing the needs of a wider range of existing and potential audiences in the digital sphere. Building on the work of the ViMM Coordination and Support Action, funded under Horizon 2020, Digital Heritage Research Laboratory (DHRLab) at Cyprus University of Technology (CUT) has committed its research agenda for the years to come to the development these approaches, settings in train this vital process through three main mechanisms, aiming to create a holistic framework for DCH by carrying out the wide range of collaborative and multidisciplinary research needed within an overall construct of advanced documentation:

1. The Europeana Task Force on Advanced Documentation of 3D digital assets
2. The UNESCO Chair on Digital Heritage
3. The Mnemosyne European Research Area Chair on Digital Heritage (Horizon 2020).

Keywords: Digital Heritage · Holistic · e-Documentation

1 Introduction

At present, Digital Cultural Heritage (DCH) objects are not e-documented adequately to provide the knowledge and data needed by many potential target audiences. Complete knowledge and the story of the past are not available. In particular, e-documentation of monuments and/or 3D artefacts/museum objects, usually helps digitise the tangible aspects rather than the intangible. Yet in many cases, the outstanding value of cultural heritage assets is their intangible stories.

Documentation of the almost 1000-year-old Asinou church in Cyprus UNESCO, World Heritage-listed due to the outstanding artistic value of the frescos, exemplifies this [1]. This CH asset is characterized as one of the most important churches and monasteries of the former Byzantine Empire, richly decorated with murals and providing an overview of Byzantine and post-Byzantine painting in Cyprus, representing a globally unique artistic expression and technique. However, these aspects are not preserved for the generations to come, neither are the materials and structural analysis of the monument documented.

E. Garoufallou et al. (Eds.): MTSR 2018, CCIS 846, pp. 76–88, 2019.
https://doi.org/10.1007/978-3-030-14401-2_7

In general, archaeological sites are often only fully represented in a 3D geometrical record. Their story and historical value is not documented. As a result, experts, professional and others accessing major sources such as Europeana, the EU digital cultural heritage library, are not able to discover this kind of information.

The research challenges cover a lifecycle of DCH facets [2], including those concerning:

- Data acquisition (tangible and intangible/stories)
- Data processing (enrichment of metadata)
- Modelling
- Knowledge management (interpretation)
- Preservation
- Use and re-use

Obstacles which need to be overcome include:

- A lack of standards and proven approaches, particularly in areas such as 3D, intangible heritage and digital storytelling;
- The need to establish greater interoperability with developments in technical fields such as Big Data infrastructures, the use of open data and Artificial Intelligence/ Machine Learning, and innovations and advances in the state-of-the-art in VR/AR, in order to better enable their application to Cultural Heritage resources;
- Simplification of technology pipelines for end-users, including those working in local digitisation initiatives across Europe;
- Optimisation of the use of geospatial technologies in the field of Cultural Heritage to improve the impact and audience reach of projects such as Europeana;
- Scarcity of trained and qualified human resources and the resulting skills.

2   The Role of ViMM

Virtual Multimodal Museum (ViMM) is a major Coordination and Support Action (CSA), funded under the European Union (EU) Horizon 2020 programme (CULT-COOP-8-2016), with a duration of 30 months (October. 2016–March 2019) engaging a large number of key stakeholders and communities of practices on how to improve collaboration and comprehension among the entire community, in order to build up a common roadmap for future activities. ViMM brings together Europe and the world's leading public and private sector organisations working on Virtual Museums and in the wider sector of Digital Cultural Heritage (DCH), aiming to promote high quality policy development, decision making and the use of technical advances.

Major results include:

- A highly interactive and wide-reaching ViMM communication Platform[1];
- Key events at policy and practitioner/stakeholder levels and extensive use of social media;

---

[1] www.vi-mm.eu.

- A clearer, evidence-based view of the impact of Virtual Museums and Digital Cultural Heritage on society and the economy;
- A Manifesto and Roadmap for Action to be validated at the final ViMM international conference in February 2019.

In addition to its core partner consortium, an international Advisory Group of public and private sector experts has been appointed from the outset of ViMM to advise, steer and quality assure its work and to act as a vehicle for continuous communication with many of the major international bodies in the CH field, such as UNESCO, ICOMOS, ICOM, CIPA and Getty in order to maximize the value of international knowledge and work towards global consensus.

From the outset, the ViMM process envisaged, as an important underlying concept and driver of its work, moving from an open, brainstorming approach towards ever greater structuring and granularity of results, based on the achievement of wide consensus. In order to distinguish between key issues and to allow sufficient granularity and clarity of approach, the work of ViMM has been sub-divided into 7 broad Thematic Areas (TA). Each TA is the responsibility of one partner which is an experienced actor on the European scene and which is responsible for bringing together a wide community of interest in their TA. A Support Partner provides complementary expertise and back-up relevant to coordinating the agenda for each TA. All the consortium partners contribute their knowledge of each Area as appropriate. Synergies, linkages and overlaps emerging between the TA undoubtedly exist and are addressed through Action-wide coordination activities. A fuller description of the scope of each TA is available on the ViMM Platform.

The Thematic Areas are: TA1 – Definitions, TA2 – Directions, TA3 – Documentation (which focuses on emerging and future documentation needs such as those in data modelling, semantics and data acquisition and is the key focus of this paper), TA4 – Dimensions, TA5 – Demand, TA6 – Discovery, TA7 – Decisions.

Each of the Thematic Areas established three Working Groups (WG) which acted during the 9 months from March–December 2017 as the key mechanism for obtaining expert input to achieve the project's goals. The method of work was to hold a mixture of 'physical' meetings and remote discussions. The Terms of Reference, proposed outputs, Chairs and members of each Working Group are published on the ViMM Platform. More than 150 identified and invited experts participated in these Working Groups, the end product of which was a set of draft Propositions for each TA.

In April 2018, a consensus-building workshop was organised in Berlin at which over 100 participants, including members selected from the Working Groups together with additional invited experts, discussed and refined the draft Propositions with a view to their adoption or implementation by DCH stakeholders;

The Propositions were then synthesised by the ViMM project team into 10 key areas, leading to the production of a 10-point draft Manifesto, which, at the time of writing this paper is circulated for wide consultation and is receiving extensive feedback from the DCH community, which will be taken into account in producing the final version.

In the next phase, a Roadmap and Action Plan will be developed for the use of the EU, international organisations and the DCH community in developing policies and strategic investments over a 5-year period. This will likewise involve a process of extensive consultation through the ViMM platform, social media and major events, including a final 2-day international conference organised in conjunction with the European Commission in Brussels during February 2019 to seek endorsement and implementation support from the EU, international bodies and other agencies involved in DCH.

2.1   The ViMM Manifesto

Prior to the development of its Roadmap and Action Plan, the findings of ViMM are currently best embodied in its draft Manifesto. We perceive that all 10 points of the Manifesto are relevant for the participants of MTSR in one or another important sense but. We focus here on those items which are especially relevant to its themes, a number of which derive in whole or in part from TA3 -Documentation. The Manifesto is now in the final stages of consultation and subject to final modification.

Giving the Whole Picture: Data, Documentation and Semantics. Over the past two decades, digitisation of Cultural Heritage has happened in a fragmented way, following different standards. Currently, only 15% of cultural heritage resources held by CHI has been digitised and much of that which is, is not freely accessible or suitable for current re-use. The proportion of DCH items in European CHI to which descriptive metadata has been applied is around 50%.

Digitisation should scale using current standards: mass digitisation, also of 3D objects, will provide a strong basis for implementing many of the other points in this Manifesto. As a flagship EU initiative, Europeana should extend its role as the central platform for digital cultural heritage, incrementally increasing the amount and quality of 3D, interactive animations and Extended Reality (XR) content.

Increased awareness and acceptance of the "Digital Turn" and the primary importance of data, especially structured and harmonised data, is central to the future of DCH, given the heterogeneous nature of its data, contents and formats are heterogeneous (3D/2D, textual, audio, video, multilingual). Therefore, quality standards such as the FAIR (Findable, Accessible, Interoperable, and Reusable) data principles need to be prioritized in order to achieve an excellent level of integration, enrichment, retrieval and reuse of content. Standardizing DCH data and metadata will help secure interoperability and interconnection to geo-spatial, bibliographic and archival metadata thus offering a more holistic approach to cultural information, which should be supported by the opening of channels with international standards bodies.

Linked (Open) Data (LOD) performs a critical role in transforming cultural heritage collections. LOD requires semantics – ontologies, standardised controlled vocabularies, thesauri/authority files - and mapping models, and its impact is improved by contextualization of the material. There is a critical need to develop shared LOD frameworks covering the core concepts relevant to cultural heritage: people, organisations, [historical] places, events, etc. Europeana and major cultural heritage institutions can play an important role in developing and promoting such shared frameworks in collaboration with key research infrastructures such as Digital Research Infrastructure for the Arts and Humanities (DARIAH) European Research Infrastructure for Language Resources and Technology (CLARIN).

Management of cultural information is challenged by issues such as knowledge representation and information integration from different contexts. There is a need to establish and support expert-driven methodologies for managing holistic and user-oriented documentation of DCH in order to increase the scientific, economic and social potential of advanced services to users. Cultural heritage data can be an important and revealing source for big data analytics.

Many, especially older, cultural heritage objects are only partially preserved. The missing parts are then reconstructed while building 3D-objects. For scientific purposes each reconstructed part needs to be not only identifiable, but also holistically documented as to how the reconstruction was conducted and why the part has the actual dimensions, actual colour etc. This holds true especially when elements of intangible heritage are incorporated into virtual reconstructions, such as in Historic Buildings Information Modelling (HBIM) systems. There remains a need to distinguish the 'fictional' and the scientific in virtual models, drawing on principles established in the London and Seville Charters and by ICOMOS.

A vast amount of cultural assets, highly valuable for historical research, are now 'born digital'. Private born-digital archives create held by CHI create a need for further research to define authenticity and for intensive curation, quality standards, policies for long-term preservation, access rights and a code of ethics.

Personal Digital Archives represent the largest stream of born digital cultural content creation globally, through the recording activities of individuals using digital devices and social media. The management and preservation of the vast amount of all the content created by these means represents a daunting and practically impossible task. Despite this, many specific endeavours to archive, curate and make available certain types of cultural content exist, for instance through, family history projects, community photo preservation, oral history, community-based history, thematic crowdsourcing and event archiving. The dissemination of best practices in this important area can play a vital role in diffusing DCH widely and in engaging audience participation.

There is a strong argument for Europeana to extend its role as the central platform for digital cultural heritage incrementally increasing the amount and quality of 3D and XR content and improving access to intangible heritage.

Powering Contextualization. Further momentum is needed to ensure that everyone involved in creating virtual objects provides information to support contextualisation to accompany their products. Standards and methods should be followed if available and other cases addressed to provide sufficient metadata for different contextualisation scenarios.

Many 3D models created in the past have limited applicability due to a lack of associated metadata. This can make it difficult to present cultural heritage objects in the context necessary to understand their meaning and relevance or to draw scientific conclusions from them. DCH projects should emphasise the historical and cultural background of what they are presenting.

Storytelling is an important example of contextualisation. New technologies e.g. 3D and XR offer opportunities to engage, to teach, to involve and are supportive elements for CH storytelling. They will be an important part of digital/virtual exhibitions which transmit both tangible and intangible cultural heritage.

Methods of visualisation based on new technologies need to be exploited. Easy-to-use instruments should be developed to support the integration of new technologies in digital exhibitions and other storytelling applications.

Immersive storytelling through XR playful learning (learning through story, play and interaction) in cultural heritage experiences is an important objective. New areas of creating and representing meaning, in order to provide for personalised experience should be explored along with increased interaction. Presence can be defined as a psychological perception of being Immersed in the XR environment and is essential for engagement and cognitive connection to the content. This involves content which is relevant and coherent in terms of social and cultural factors, including aspects such as cultural values, recognition and significance, representation of emotional intelligence, semantic time, space, provenance and uncertainty and emotion-based user interfaces.

Simulation of 3D worlds should include multilingual interaction with people (including ancient languages) and other actors such as animals, together with integration of sensory aspects such as touch, smell and sound.

Gamification is a feedback loop that incentivises the user to progress in the experience or learning process. Care should be taken to use gamification elements judiciously so as not to overpower the story or learning objective. To sharpen their successful use, gamification techniques should be mapped to the emotional results achieved.

Frameworks and Standards: A Navigable Map. More powerful, intelligent and interconnected standards are required that can be used across domains, creating open formats, based on ontologies, that are interoperable in different systems and disciplines.

Emerging open interoperable frameworks and standards which support, create and share DCH such as the International Image Interoperability Framework (IIIF), Copernicus for Cultural Heritage and others, should be promoted and fast-tracked. However, current standards should be preserved and continuity through backward-compatibility thus sustained.

Standards need to be agreed so that digitised content (tangible and intangible) and the related metadata becomes seamlessly accessible in the long term to all. Metadata may include access to complementary material such as images, books, descriptions and drawings, illustrating the cultural and historic significance of the sites or artefacts.

A framework of 'virtual values' is needed to underpin DCH strategies and development, and to provide museum-staff with a comprehensible direction for the museum's approach to virtual and augmented content. The Virtual Values identified by ViMM include: "Virtual for all" Rule; Layered Content; Accessibility, Sustainability, Complementarity and Digital Privacy.

Driving Organisational Change. Managements of Cultural Heritage institutions should prioritise digital transformation and lead organisational change, cooperating in a shared digitisation process within a common general strategy which tackles interoperability problems, creates "economies of scale", workable frameworks for rights and strengthens the ability of museums to support new technology.

The vision for technology take-up should be mapped to the museum's mission so as not to miss out on opportunities, entailing a regular assessment of organisational 'readiness' for DCH.

In order to improve efficiency and effectiveness of the use of resources, impact assessment studies, based on mature and standardised processes and tools, are needed as a fundamental commitment of CH institutions and as part of projects funded and/or carried out by public and private institutions.

Cultural Heritage Institutions (CHI) are not working in a vacuum and should ensure openness to the outside world. For them to be able to make the most of new technology there needs to be organisational change It is important for museums to develop participatory technology strategies and to invest the needed resources in hardware and software solutions as well as training and support. Accessibility, sustainability and interoperability should be prioritised.

The Human Resources. Innovation in education and training for DCH will enhance awareness of and openness to digital initiatives. Policies should address systematic involvement and training of teachers, curators, administration and governance staff, using methodologies that promote understanding of different media paradigms.

To assure the skills and capacities of the next generation of (digital) curators and (virtual) museologists, the question 'who needs to be trained, for what purpose and at what level' should be directly addressed from a lifelong learning perspective, taking into account secondary, undergraduate, postgraduate, professional and vocational training as well as the engagement of volunteers and the public community in general. Remote and e-learning can play an important role.

Training offers, accompanied by meaningful certification, should be stimulated. These should be addressed to the different target groups involved in Cultural Heritage and their position in the 'digital workflow', broken down into different steps or stages and distinguished between technology skills, curatorial issues and decision or policy making needs. Interdisciplinary approaches are necessary to address all the needs and skills required for DCH.

Anyone involved in handling, exploitation, research and valorisation should be aware of the usefulness of XR technology to support their processes, both internal and external. This should form part of educational curricula in Cultural Heritage. Universities and schools conducting technical education should teach the relevance of cultural background information for the understanding of XR-representations of cultural heritage objects. ViMM supports the recent recommendations of the Council of Europe Strategy 21 in the areas of Knowledge and Education for Cultural Heritage [4] and proposes that the DCH sector recognises and develops them.

3   Holistic Documentation: Widening and Deepening the Approach

Building on the findings of ViMM, DHRLab at CUT has committed its research agenda for the years to come to the development of more holistic approaches to (especially digital) Cultural Heritage documentation. Currently, it sets in train this vital process through three main mechanisms, each of which is described below:

1. The Europeana Task Force on Advanced 3D Documentation
2. The UNESCO Chair on Digital Heritage
3. The European Research Area Chair on Digital Heritage (Horizon 2020).

3.1   The Europeana Task Force Group (TFG) on Advanced Documentation of 3D Digital Assets

The digital documentation of CH assets is inherently a multimedia process, addressed through the digital representation of the shape, appearance and conservation condition of the heritage/cultural object for which 3D digital model is expected to become the representation. 3D representations should progress beyond current levels to provide the necessary semantic information (knowledge/story) for in-depth studies and use by researchers and creative users, offering new perspectives and understandings. Digital surrogates can add a laboratory dimension to on-site explorations originating new avenues in the way tangible cultural heritage is addressed.

The acquisition, processing, archiving and exchange of 3D Cultural Heritage assets and information has been investigated by many projects in Europe; organizations (e.g. Getty, Europeana, the Smithsonian); Scientific Committees (e.g. ICOMOS/CIPA, ICOM/CIDOC and others) and various professionals and experts. At present, many highly elaborated theoretical approaches, principles and guidelines are proposed for data schemes and infrastructures (e.g. London and Seville Charters, CIDOC-CRM, CityGML, Web3D consortium) aiming to foster quality, compatibility and sustainability of 3D Cultural Heritage objects. On the other hand, in practice 3D reconstruction projects are often based on unique and prototypic semantics, workflows, and infrastructures and are customized for a specific purpose (e.g. the CyArk 500 project).

The generation of high-quality 3D models is still very time-consuming and expensive, not least because the modeling is carried out for individual objects rather than for entire collections and formats provided in digital reconstructions are frequently not interoperable and therefore cannot be easily accessed and/or reused or sustained.

Many projects and studies have investigated aspects related to 3D Cultural Heritage assets and highly elaborated theoretical approaches, principles and guidelines are proposed for data schemes and infrastructures. On the other hand, in practice, 3D reconstruction projects are often based on unique and prototypic semantics, workflows, and infrastructures and are customized for a specific purpose. Therefore, after an initial period, the Europeana Task Force Group (TFG), led by Marinos Ioannides, focused on user needs and requirements and on the quality of the 3D data and metadata available in different repositories in Europe and in Europeana itself, thereby providing a more holistic overview of what needs to be done in the area of 3D CH documentation.

In doing so, it paid special attention to qualitative comments on the 3D objects already in Europeana, together with suggestions for the development of standard guidelines and formats, intended for cultural heritage communities.

The multidisciplinary demands of this TFG led us to examine procedures and models on e-documentation of 3D-CH objects. However, the definition, for example, of the term '3D-CH asset' (3D object plus its memory/story) appears increasingly complex. In the field of Documentation of CH there is much misunderstanding and many misconceptions about 'what is a 3D-CH object'. Unfortunately, this also currently applies to the situation visible with the 3D objects available in Europeana. At the same time the classification of what 3D- CH assets are complicated due to the plethora of (frequently unclear) criteria used by specialists. Likewise, users and other stakeholders, together with the data itself, introduce variables that affect the decision-making procedure for e-documentation.

The experts involved in this TFG also have extensive experience in the development of tools and methodologies that engage users actively through the presentation of CH assets. During the first period of this TFG, the experts focused their work on reviewing the results of different EU projects such as CARARE, 3D ICONS, plus the current systems/repositories for 3D CH-3D assets available and a literature review.

In the second period it focused on the following:

(1) Definition and analysis of user and stakeholder needs supported by a survey.
(2) The data and metadata quality of the available 3D content in Europeana.

Following several online discussions among the TFG members, a questionnaire was developed using Google-forms. The online survey was tested by several local stakeholders in three EU countries (Cyprus, Greece and Slovenia) and then distributed to 3,500 professionals with a total of 937 survey responses. The foci included digitisation methods, metadata extraction, post-processing, modelling, harvesting, the quality of the Europeana Data Model (EDM) information and the accuracy of 3D objects (including Intangible Heritage), also covering semantically-aware 3D objects with a view to improving their archiving, retrieval, reusability and sustainability, enriching the geometrical structure(s) with related knowledge and considering the range of devices, models and software applications involved and the ongoing revolution in technology.

The following 3D objects from Europeana have been taken into consideration in the survey. This selection of objects available in Europeana give us a good overview of the current situation so far as digitisation technologies are concerned: their metadata quality, the geometrical accuracy of the 3D data, and the possibility of wide use and re-use of the data.

1. A model of Etruscan Oinochoe with small wheel-shaped handle[2]:
2. A model of statue of heroic Claudio[3]
3. Coronation medallion[4]

---

[2] https://www.europeana.eu/portal/en/record/2048703/object_HA_690.html.

[3] https://www.europeana.eu/portal/en/record/2048703/object_HA_1799.html.

[4] https://goo.gl/gNn1a5.

Table 1. Respondent's level of studies.

Level of education	% of users
a) BSc	10
b) MSc	28
c) PhD	59
d) None of the above	3

Table 2. Categorisation of users by occupation - summary

Archaeologists	13%
Engineers (all types)	12%
Architects	11.19%
Historians	9.03%
ICT specialists	7.53%
Teachers/Trainers	7.53%
Archivists/librarians/museologists	4.64%
All others	32%

4. Nuage de points de l'église de Fontains[5]
5. Saint Salvator abbey of Ename around 1595 (high res 3D)[6]

Survey Analysis. The full report of the TFG [3] is available from Europeana and provides illustrated examples of survey outcomes for each of the selected objects [1]. Taking the example was the 3D model of Coronation medallion and 37.12% were satisfied or very satisfied, 35.61% were neutral, 27.28% were adequately or not satisfied overall. In general, current satisfaction levels with 3D on Europeana at present were modest (Tables 1 and 2).

Results and Future Work. It was possible during this TFG period to provide some information on the quality of metadata and the accuracy of the corresponding 3D data. As a further step, we defined the possible group of users and their requirements and needs.

These findings have been presented to Europeana and an application is being considered to extend the work of the TFG for a second period so that new guidelines and effective methods for the processing, archiving and long-term preservation of 3D cultural heritage assets can be developed and proposed. It is proposed that this work will also promote interoperable standard formats for semantically-aware 3D modelling, analysis and representation of cultural heritage to allow easy retrieval, distribution, publishing and reuse of such models, which in turn will help ensure sustainable cross-sector collaborative work in future in both development and research. This will involve

---

[5] https://goo.gl/4GciUu.

[6] https://www.europeana.eu/portal/en/record/2048716/object_HA_2087.html?q=Enam.

suggestions for a possible modification of the EDM and improvement of the current 3D-CH assets in Europeana.

An additional outcome of the proposed second Task Force would be to gain further insight into daily practices, innovative approaches, and theoretical aspects to determine a scope of topics for further investigation.

4 Next Steps

4.1 UNESCO Chair in Digital Heritage

Dr Marinos Ioannides, Director of DHRLab, Cyprus University of Technology (CUT), was awarded the UNESCO Chair in Digital Heritage in October 2017. This UNESCO Chair will serve as a prime means of capacity building through the exchange of knowledge and sharing within the construction of the Chair's partnership, in which institutions in developing countries and countries in transition in Europe, the Balkans, Middle East and Africa join forces with developed countries. Among its wide ranging and global portfolio of activities are to:

- Introduce model Digital Heritage curricula ('cultural informatics') at vocational, undergraduate and postgraduate levels and extend course availability, teaching and study facilities to students from at least 10 countries, including 6 Developing Countries.
- Define, extend and carry out a program of research in digital heritage designed to further UNESCO's cultural heritage agenda in the region and to impact its key objectives.

4.2 ERA Chair in Digital Heritage- Mnemosyne

Cultural Heritage is a strategic resource for Europe with high cultural, social, environmental and economic value. The era of Digital Cultural Heritage (DCH) is now well underway and the European research resource for DCH has grown significantly in recent years. But the visible contribution of the Widening countries to this effort remains relatively weak. The DHRLab has been an exception in this respect, becoming a beacon in the Eastern Mediterranean and for Europe in general, in particular through its leadership of key initiatives in DCH research training[7] and in policy co-ordination and support.

The **Mnemosyne** Coordination and Support Action funded under Horizon 2020 WIDESPREAD-03-2017 - ERA Chairs, begins in January 2019. This new ERA Chair in Digital Heritage is an ideal opportunity to ensure that DHRLab strengthens its research capacity and restructures its role, by means of a well-designed and iterative process. Mnemosyne will proceed from the appointment of an outstanding researcher and research manager as ERA Chair holder in 2018 who will attract, direct and maintain high quality human resources and negotiate and implement the necessary

---

[7] https://itn-dch.net/.

structural changes to achieve excellence on a sustainable basis. The project will be carried out over a period of 5 years. Following recruitment of the ERA Chair research team, a three-phase research programme centred on holistic documentation of the DCH lifecycle in support of existing and potential user needs will be carried out and extensively evaluated, with strong attention paid to exploitation.

5 Conclusion

The work carried out by the ViMM Coordination and Support Action, carries the potential to be highly influential in supporting development of EU and international strategies for Digital Cultural Heritage in general, documentation and metadata in particular. By pointing the way to a broader concept of the role of documentation in presenting digital heritage in such a way that it tells more of the 'story' and establishes more compelling contexts in order to engage and extend knowledge to a wider audience, the prospects for DCH to play a central role in social and economic development will be significantly enhanced. The future work of the Mnemosyne UNESCO and ERA Chairs over the coming years are planned to enhance the achievement of this goal, alongside efforts to contribute to the development of Europeana as an instrument of knowledge and learning.

References

1. Carr, A., Nicolaïdès, A. (eds.): Asinou across time: studies in the architecture and murals of the Panagia Phorbiotissa, Cyprus (Dumbarton Oaks Studies 43). Dumbarton Oaks Research Library and Collection, Washington DC (2013)
2. Hayes, J., Quimet, C., Santana Quintero, M., Fai, S., Smith, L. (eds.): Digital heritage. progress in cultural heritage: documentation, preservation, and protection ICOMOS/ISPRS International Scientific Committee on Heritage Documentation (CIPA)
3. Hirst, C.S., et al.: Standardisation in 3D geometric morphometrics: ethics, ownership and methods. Archaeologies: Journal of the World Archaeological Congress (2018). https://doi.org/10.1007/s11759-018-9349-7
4. Ioannides, M., Davies, R. (eds.): Final report on advanced documentation of 3D digital assets (Europeana Task Force Group), February 2018
5. Ioannides, M., et al. (eds.): 6th International Conference, EuroMed 2016, Nicosia, Cyprus, October 31 – November 5, 2016, Proceedings, Part I & Part II (2016)
6. Ioannides, M., et al.: 3D digital libraries and their contribution in the documentation of the past. In: Ioannides, M., Magnenat-Thalmann, N., Papagiannakis, G. (eds.) Mixed reality and gamification for cultural heritage. Springer, Cham (2017). https://doi.org/10.1007/978-3-319-49607-8_6
7. Mathys, A, Lemaitre, S., Brecko, J., Semal, P.: Agora 3D: evaluating 3D imaging technology for the research, conservation and display of museum collections. Antiquity 87(336) (2013)

8. Niven, K., Richards, J. (eds.): The storage and long-term preservation of 3D data. Academic Press, London (2017)
9. Pajas, J.A., Olivam, A.S.: Assessment, dissemination and standardization of geometric data recording of archaeological heritage obtained from 3D laser scanning. Virtual respect **4**, 187–193 (2009)
10. 26th International CIPA Symposium – Digital workflows for heritage conservation (Volume IV-2/W2) 28 August–1 September 2017, Ottawa, Canada

Graph Matching Based Semantic Search Engine

Mamdouh Farouk[1(✉)], Mitsuru Ishizuka[2], and Danushka Bollegala[3]

[1] Computer Science Department, Faculty of Computers and Information,
Assiut University, Assiut, Egypt
mamfarouk@aun.edu.eg
[2] National Institute of Informatics, Tokyo, Japan
ishizuka@nii.ac.jp
[3] Department of Computer Science, University of Liverpool, Liverpool, UK
danushka.bollegala@liverpool.ac.uk

Abstract. Explosive growth of the Web has made searching Web data a challenging task for information retrieval systems. Semantic search systems that go beyond the shallow keyword matching approaches and map words to their conceptual meaning representations offer better results to the users. On the other hand, a lot of representation formats have been specified to represent Web data into a semantic format. We propose a search engine for searching Web data represented in UNL (Universal Networking Language). UNL has numerous attractive features to support semantic search. One of the main features is that UNL does not depend on domain ontology. Our proposed search engine is based on semantic graph matching. It includes semantic expansion for graph nodes and relation matching based on relation meaning. The search results are ranked depending on the semantic similarity between the user query and the retrieved documents. We developed a prototype implementing the proposed semantic search engine, and our evaluations demonstrate its effectiveness across a wide-range of semantic search tasks.

Keywords: Search engine · Semantic search · Graph matching · UNL

1 Introduction

Retrieving Web data using search engines is an integral part of all internet users. Around 85% of Internet users use search engines to find information on the web [1]. Consequently, research on information retrieval systems have received a broad attention both from academia and from the industry. Considering the fact that a user query would often return millions of results, a task of detecting relevant results to the user query has become both important and challenging.

Many approaches have been proposed to improve search results based on meaning of texts instead of direct text matching. These approaches go beyond the shallow text to mach different terms have similar meanings.

E. Garoufallou et al. (Eds.): MTSR 2018, CCIS 846, pp. 89–100, 2019.
https://doi.org/10.1007/978-3-030-14401-2_8

There are different approaches proposed for searching the web based on the meaning [17,18]. Although these approaches have the same goal, which is improving search result based on understanding user query and web data, they adopt different techniques. These approaches can be classified into two categories. The first is searching normal web pages using semantic techniques, i.e. Hakia search engine [6]. Different semantic techniques have been proposed such as handling related words, handling morphological variation, handling generalization and so on.

The second category of semantic search includes approaches that search semantic represented data such as in semantic web. Indeed, data representation plays an important role in information retrieval and search results. Knowledge must be represented in a way that facilitates storing and retrieving of meaningful data so that reasoning can be performed over this knowledge [10]. Resource Description Framework (RDF) is one of the standard data representation formats in semantic web. A huge amount of web data have been converted to RDF [2]. Searching semantic representation data such as RDF is another approach for improving query results [3]. Moreover, considering relations between RDF instances during the search process makes the results more adequate [14]. However, RDF representation is domain dependant. Different domains use different RDF ontologies to represent the data. In addition, semantic search has some limitation and restriction on user query because the user should use domain ontology concepts [8].

This work proposes a search technique, which combines two approaches of semantic search. The first one is searching depending on semantic expansion of query keywords [7]. This approach expands the user query keywords to match similar-meaning terms. The other approach is relation based searching [3]. It considers the relations between query keywords. For example, consider this query, *"river monitoring tools"*. In this query, the user asks about tools for monitoring the rivers. Finding web documents that contain these keywords, such as using Google, is not enough. Many of in-relevant documents, which talk about i.e. river monitoring in general not the tools of monitoring, will appear even in the first page of Google results. However, semantic search considers results that contain the query keywords and relations between these keywords. In addition, semantic expansion for these keywords is considered in semantic search; i.e. observation tools or watching tools can be examine in semantic search.

The proposed system merges both approaches; semantic expansion and relation-based, in one homogenous system taking data representation into consideration. This research uses Universal Networking Language (UNL), which describes the semantic/conceptual structure of content (resources). Using UNL gives a suitable environment to implement the two combined approaches in one system. UNL representation is generic and does not depend on domain ontology.

This paper is organized as follows: Sect. 2 introduces Universal Networking Language (UNL). Section 3 explains the proposed approach for searching UNL data. A proposed ranking method for search results is shown in Sect. 4. A prototype for the proposed approach and experiments are shown in Sect. 5. Section 6 discusses the results and related work. The conclusion of this work is mentioned in Sect. 7.

2   Universal Networking Language (UNL)

UNL was initiated in the Institute of Advance Studies of United Nation University in Tokyo. Its main objective is to capture the meaning of written documents. UNL is based on the representation of concepts and the relations between concepts. Moreover, UNL is used as intermediate language in some approaches of automatic machine translation [12,13]. The UNL representation of text can be used for intelligent natural language processing [11].

UNL represents a sentence as a semantic network in which notes are concepts and arcs are semantic relations between concepts. Futhermore, UNL can be used to describe all information and knowledge conveyed by natural language [11]. UNL describes the concept structure of the text based on a set of predefined semantic relations.

The design principles are different in UNL and RDF. RDF is designed to describe properties of resources, whereas UNL is designed to describe meaning of written documents regardless the used language. The main advantage of using UNL is that it does not depend on domain ontologies. However, it depends on a single ontology called Universal Words (UWs), which provides the vocabulary for UNL and the semantic background of each concept.

In UNL dictionary, a word is represented as a Universal Word in this form *headword(constraint list)*. The same word may have different constraint part according to the different meaning of this word. For example, according to UNL ontology, there are different meanings for the word *state*, such as:

state(icl > area)
state(icl > condition)
state(icl > event)
state(agt > person, obj > thing)
state(agt > person, obj > data).

According to the meaning of the sentence, one choice should be selected so that each word in the UNL statement has only one clear meaning. Consequently, there is no ambiguity in UNL representation.

Entries in UNL dictionary are organized in is-a like hierarchy in which each word is connected to a set of related words through UNL relations such as *icl* (inclusion), *iof* (instance of), *equ* (equivalent to). Some words may have more than one superclass depending on word meaning. The word is defined by a set of relations that relate the word with other words. These set of relations determine the real meaning and the behaviour of this concept. Therefore, the UNL dictionary provides enough information to understand semantic structure of a sentence.

There are two main parts of UNL semantic representation for a statement; the list of concepts and the list of relations. For example, the representation of the statement Sama drinks milk in the morning contains a list of concepts (Sama, drink, milk, morning) and a list of semantic relations among these concepts.

3   Semantic Graph Matching for UNL Data

The proposed search technique is based on inexact graph matching. The meaning of a statement in the corpus is represented by UNL semantic networks. The user query is also represented into a UNL semantic network that may contain variable/s. The problem of finding query answer is considered as a graph matching problem between a given query graph and dataset graphs.

Graph matching is the problem of finding correspondence between different graphs [5]. Moreover, there are different types for graph matching such as graph isomorphism, and sub-graph isomorphism. The proposed search process applies sub-graph isomorphism to find query results. There are many algorithms proposed for sub-graph isomorphism [15,16]. As shown in Fig. 1, there are three main steps in our graph matching: node matching, relation matching, and node ignorance. The first two steps apply inexact matching to give better results for graph matching problem.

The searching task finds a sub-graph of corpus graphs that matches the query graph. During this process, a node can be expanded to semantically equivalent concepts. Two different thesauruses is used for this expansion: Universal Word (UW) hierarchy and WordNet. Furthermore, the relation matching is not direct matching between relations' names. The proposed system allows semantic related relations to match each other with a certainty value. In addition, the proposed technique may ignore some nodes (from user query graph) that don't affect the meaning of the query. The results retrieved using ignoring process have lower rank than others.

In the adopted graph matching algorithm, an entry node is selected from query graph to start matching. The entry node is the node that has the highest degree. If the entry node does not match any node of the graph, an alternative entry node is selected because the first may be ignored. The alternative entry point has the second highest degree. After getting two matched nodes between query and statement graph, the matching algorithm starts. Algorithm 1 is an abstract of the graph matching algorithm used in the proposed technique.

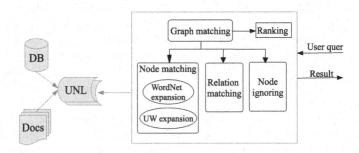

Fig. 1. System architecture

Algorithm 1 takes, as input, two matched concepts (one from query graph and the other from statement graph). The third parameter is a mapping state in which the mapped concepts and mapped relations are stored. This algorithm traverses the query graph though 'to' relation trying to find semantic corresponding nodes and relations. Moreover, the 'from' relation is checked in the same way. If there is a mapping between query graph and a sub-graph of statement graph, this statement is included into result set.

Algorithm 1. Graph Matching Algorithm

Input: two matched concept c1, c2, and mapping state Ms (*mapping state contains mapped nodes and mapped relations*).
Output: final mapping state.

1: Get list of relations Rq that their source is c1, and Rs relations that their source is c2
2: **for all** $r1 \in Rq$ **do**
3:    **if** $r1 \in Ms$ **then**
4:      continue
5:    **else**
6:      **for all** $r2 \in Rs$ **do**
7:        **if** $r2 \in Ms$ **then**
8:          continue
9:        **else**
10:          get matching value rv between $r1, r2$
11:          **if** $rv > 0$ **then**
12:            Get $E1, E2$ the destinations end of $r1$ and $r2$
13:            **if** matchConcept($E1, E2$) is true **then**
14:              addToMappingState($c1, c2, r1, r2$)
15:              **if** matchGraph($E1, E2, Ms$) is true **then**
16:                break
17:              **end if**
18:            **end if**
19:          **end if**
20:        **end if**
21:      **end for**
22:      **if** fail to map $r1$ **then**
23:        check omitting $r1$
24:        **if** omitting fail **then**
25:          return fail
26:        **end if**
27:      **end if**
28:    **end if**
29: **end for**
30: return true

3.1 Concept Matching

Node matching is based on meaning of the attached concepts. Two nodes are matched if the attached concepts are semantically matched. To achieve this goal, two different thesaurus are used; UNL Universal Words (UW) hierarchy and the well-known thesaurus WordNet. These two ontologies are used to be domain independent and to get accurate meaning-based matching. In order to facilitate using both ontologies during runtime, we connect both as a preprocessing stage; as a result, every concept in UWs is connected to a WordNet synset. Connection between UWs and WordNet is automatically created and stored. For each concept in the UWs hierarchy, the corresponding WordNet synset should be found. This process is based on hierarchical matching between UW concept and WordNet synset. For example in the UW *'process(icl > action)'*, the headword is *process* and the parent is *action*. The Wordnet synset, that contains both words as lemmas, is attached to the UW. Alternatively, a synset that has same hierarchy, which has the headword as lemma and the parent word as lemma of parent synset, is selected. In case that there is no corresponding synset the same process is repeated using the headword and its grandparent word in the UW hierarchy.

Two nodes of UNL graphs are matched if they are semantically similar. A matching value is assigned depending on similarity between nodes (concepts). Two concepts are matched in the following cases:

- If they have same UW (similarity value = 1)
- If the concept of query is related to the concept of dataset according to UW hierarchy (similarity value depending on distance between the two concepts)
- If the concept of query is related to the concept of dataset according to WordNet (similarity value depending on distance between the two concepts).

Table 1. Sample of UNL semantic relations

Relation	Meaning
agt (agent)	Thing in focus that initiate an action
cag (co-agent)	Thing not in focus that initiates an implicit event
ptn (partner)	Indispensable non focus initiator of an action
aoj (thing with attribute)	Thing that is in a state or has an attribute
plc (place)	A place where an event occurs

UW-Based Expansion. Universal Words (UW) hierarchy contains UWs in a conceptual order. It contains the relations between different words. According to UW hierarchy, a concept can be expanded to its upper level concepts. For example the word *car* can be expanded to *vehicle* because *vehicle* is upper level of *car*. The main relation in UW hierarchy is *icl* (inclusion relation equals to is-a relation). Through this relation, the parents (upper level concepts) can be retrieved from UWs.

WordNet Expansion. WordNet is a well-known thesaurus that contains English words, definitions of these words, and their relationships. Many approaches of query expansion use WordNet to expand concepts [9]. Our approach uses WordNet to expand query keyword based on meaning. The prepared links between UWs and WordNet synsetsis used to determine the correct synset directly. The proposed system exploits synonyms and hypernyms relations in WordNet to expand the query keywords.

3.2 Relation Matching

Unlike other approaches that uses exact relation matching, the proposed technique allows relation matching based on relation meaning. In UNL, 44 relations can be used to connect concepts. According to UNL specification, there is overlapping in the meaning of some relations.

In order to make semantic matching between UNL relations, a 44 × 44 matching table is constructed. This table contains matching values between every pair of relations based on UNL specification. Table 1 shows a part of UNL relations and their meaning. In the constructed matching table, for example, *agt* (agent) relation has high matching value with *cag* (co-agent) relation. Depending on the meaning of both relations in UNL specifications, the matching value is decided. At this stage of research, this table is constructed manually.

3.3 Omitting Sub-graph

In order to find the closest results to user query, the proposed Matching technique allows partial matching to query graph. The proposed technique ignores some relations and nodes from the user query graph. This looks like typical keyword search approaches that retrieve documents which contain some of the keywords. However, the proposed search engine carefully selects the nodes to be ignored from user query graph to keep the meaning of the query. The proposed technique ignores a node from query graph if the following conditions occur:

- There is no answer without ignoring this node
- The node to be ignored is a leaf node
- The relation to the ignored node should be one of these relations (pos, mod, man, aoj). These relations represent adverb or adjective.
- The number of total ignored nodes should not exceed 25% of total number of nodes in the query graph.

4 Result Ranking

The adopted ranking technique is depending on similarity between user query and resultant document. Moreover, every result in the proposed search engine is attached with a matching value. Depending on this matching value the results are ordered. The matching value is calculated based on how many nodes and relations are matched between the document graphs and the user query graph.

Semantic similarity between user query and UNL document is calculated based on the matching value between every corresponding pair of concepts and pair of relations. Equation 1 is used to calculate the matching value:

$$MV = \frac{\sum_{i=0}^{n} Ci^2 + \sum_{j=0}^{m} Rj^2}{n^2 * 10 + m^2 * 10} * \frac{n}{Qc} \tag{1}$$

MV is the matching value for a UNL result that appears in result set, n is the number of matched concepts, m is the number of matched relations, Ci is the matching value for the ith pair of matched concepts, the Rj is the matching value for the jth pair of matched relations, and Qc is number of concept in the query. The term $\frac{n}{Qc}$ is always 1 unless there are some omitted nodes.

On the other hand, the proposed search engine provides two different formats for showing results: document-based format and statement-based format. The latter shows the search results as a list of statements that matched the query statement. A matching value is attached to each statement in the result according to the previous equation. The user can select the result format. Statement-based format is usually used when the user query contains variable/s. In document-based format, the statements that belong to same document are gathered into one result titled by document name. A different equation is used to calculate the matching value for document format.

$$DMV = \sum_{i=0}^{N} MV_i^2 \tag{2}$$

The matching value for a document (DMV) is calculated according to the number of matched statement belonging to this document. In the previous equation, MV is the matching value of a statement. Therefore, DMV is the summation of squares of all MV values belong to the statements of this document.

5   Experiment

A prototype for the proposed search technique has been implemented in our lab using java. In order to test the prototyped search technique, we constructed in our lab Micro web data set. We consider this data set as a sample or simulation for the real web. A set of web pages are converted to UNL using the automatic function provided by UNL website, www.undl.org.

The final micro web data set contains around 500 documents. There are two versions of this dataset: one as a normal text and the second one converted to UNL representation. The total number of UNL statements in our micro web is around 150,000 statements. These statements stored in xml files. The search model loads the graphs from these files. The user inputs his query using Query Builder tool as a set of concepts and relations between these concepts. The Query Builder tool is easy and doesn't need any experience. The user enters natural language words and select from different meanings of this word.

In this experiment, we compare the proposed approach to Google search engine. These two search engines are directed to search same dataset. Google engine is customized to search the normal text of our corpus. However, the proposed technique searches the converted UNL corpus. Many types of queries are used to ensure diversity and to show the difference between the two search engines. Totally, 45 queries are studied in this experiment. These queries are different in length. They contain 22 queries of length 2 (2-word query), 19 of length 3-word, and 4 queries with length more than 3 words. The results of random selected queries out of the 45 queries are shown in Table 2.

Table 2. Results of sample queries using Google, and the proposed system

Query number	Query text	Google		The proposed approach	
		Number of results	Number of relevant results	Number of results	Number of relevant results
Q1	Soil salinity	10	3	3	2
Q2	Water color measurements	10	4	4	4
Q3	Biological attachment processes	10	4	10	6
Q4	Sediment removal	10	4	7	4
Q5	Sediment management measures	10	10	10	10
Q6	Soil irrigation	0	0	8	0
Q7	Types of biological filters	10	5	10	8

In order to compare results of Google search engine and the proposed technique, we calculate Mean Average Precision (MAP) for both. The following calculations are used during the experiment.

$$P@R = \frac{no.of.relevant.results}{rank} \tag{3}$$

Equation 3 is used to calculate precision at rank ($P@R$) for every document in a query's results. Equation 4 calculates average precision for query results.

$$AP = \frac{\sum_{r=0}^{n} P@R * rel(r)}{no.of.relevant.docs} \tag{4}$$

Relevance of a result, $rel(r)$, is a value that indicates the relevance of the result at rank r. There are two values for $rel(r)$: (0 irrelevant, and 1 relevant). Number of relevant documents (no.of.relevant.docs) in equation 4 is fixed as 10. This is because we don't need to calculate the absolute values. However, we just need to compare the two approaches. Finally, the mean average precision is calculated.

$$MAP = \frac{1}{N} \sum_{i=0}^{N} AP_i \qquad (5)$$

The calculated values for MAP is shown in Table 3. Table 3 includes calculated MAP for each query type. From Table 3, it is concluded that the proposed search technique has the advantages of using relations between keywords besides meaning-based expansion for the keywords. In many cases, the proposed search engine for UNL data gives better results. Moreover, T-test has been performed to check if the difference between our results and Google results is significant or not. According to the T-test the difference is considered statistically significant.

Finally, the experiments show that the proposed search technique gives better results than Google search engine especially in two cases. The first is a case when a user query needs semantic expansion for the query keywords. For example, in a query such as 'water observation', the proposed engine brings results including water monitoring. However, Google does not. Furthermore, the second is a case when the query keywords are very common in the corpus. In such cases, Google brings documents that contain these keywords even if there are no relations between these keywords.

To sum up, exploiting relations between keywords and semantic expansion for keywords has some advantages over normal search engines.

6 Related Work and Discussion

Swoogle is a search engine for semantic web [4]. It has a crawler, which crawls web pages and gets RDF documents or HTML that has RDF as meta-data. All collected documents are indexed into a DB. Swoogle provides interface for both human and web agents. A ranking algorithm is applied to arrange the search results based on popularity. Swoogle differentiates between semantic web link types. The four mentioned types of links are weighted differently in page ranking equation. This kind of page ranking is suitable for semantic web documents.

Another semantic search approach that also searches semantic RDF data and is related to ours is relation based approach. In this approach, the engine confirms the relations between query keywords. One example of this kind of search is OntoLook [3]. OntoLook has been developed in a virtual semantic web environment. It searches the web based on the relation between query keywords. The authors constructed a set of documents by annotating a set of normal web document in the field of travelling. Its crawler is based on their ontology, which are created using Protege. The user should enter his query keywords and select corresponding ontology classes to these keywords. The system detects the relations between these classes based on the defined relations in the ontology. The engine searches the annotated documents depending on the entered classes and detected relations. However, this approach is domain dependent.

Table 3. Mean Average Precision for different types of queries

	Google	Proposed
2 word query	0.241	0.322
3 word query	0.163	0.236
4 word query	0.089	0.125
All queries	0.192	0.265

Table 4. Comparison between different semantic search approaches

	Language	Query expansion	Relations	Query form	Semantic techniques	Domain ontology
Hakia	NL	–	No	NL	Yes	No
Falcons	RDF	No	No	NL	No	No
Swoogle	RDF	Limited	No	NL	No	No
Sindice	RDF	Limited	No	NL	No	No
OntoLook	RDF	No	Yes	Ontology	No	Yes
Proposed	UNL	Yes	Yes	UNL	Yes	No

On the other hand, the proposed search technique gets advantages of both categories. It searches semantic represented data using semantic technologies and considers relations between query keywords. Table 4 shows a comparison between different meaning-based search techniques. In addition, the proposed technique can search content of web DBs as well. Relational DB can be converted to UNL as reported in our previous paper [8].

7 Conclusion

The proposed search technique exploits UNL language to get results that are more relevant to user's needs. The main objective of representing web data into semantic format is to make this data machine understandable. Moreover, the proposed search technique is domain independent. It takes the advantages of searching semantic data and using semantic techniques. In addition, the proposed approach coherently combines two different techniques for semantic search: keyword semantic expansion and relation-based search. In the adopted inexact graph matching technique, concept expansion is based on UW semantic hierarchy and WordNet thesaurus. Moreover, the relation matching depends on the meaning of the relations. In addition, the proposed search engine can ignore un-necessary concept from query graph to facilitate getting results. Finally, the experiment shows that the proposed technique achieves promising results in many cases against Google search engine.

References

1. Kobayashi, M., Takeda, K.: Information retrieval on the web. ACM Comput. Surv. (CSUR) **32**(2), 144–173 (2000)
2. Blanco, R., Mika, P., Vigna, S.: Effective and efficient entity search in RDF data. In: Aroyo, L., et al. (eds.) ISWC 2011. LNCS, vol. 7031, pp. 83–97. Springer, Heidelberg (2011). https://doi.org/10.1007/978-3-642-25073-6_6
3. Li, Y., Wang, Y., Huang, X.: A relation-based search engine in semantic web. IEEE Trans. Knowl. Data Eng. **19**(2), 273–282 (2007)
4. Ding, L., et al.: Swoogle: a semantic web search and metadata engine. In: Proceedings of 13th ACM Conference on Information and Knowledge Management, November 2004
5. Caetano, T.S., Cheng, L., Le, Q.V., Smola, A.J.: Learning graph matching, pattern analysis and machine. Intelligence **31**(6), 1048–1058 (2009)
6. Tümer, D., Shah, M.A., Bitirim, Y.: An empirical evaluation on semantic search performance of keyword-based and semantic search engines: Google, Yahoo, Msn and Hakia. In: 2009 4th International Conference on Internet Monitoring and Protection (ICIMP 2009) (2009)
7. Guobing, Z., Bofeng, Z., Yanglan, G., Jianwen, Z.: An ontology-based methodology for semantic expansion search. In: Fifth International Conference on Fuzzy Systems and Knowledge Discovery, vol. 5, pp. 453–457 (2008)
8. Farouk, M., Ishizuka, M.: CDL-based semantic representation for dynamic web pages. Int. J. Semant. Comput. **6**(1), 51–65 (2012)
9. Gong, Z., Cheang, C.W., Hou U, L.: Multi-term web query expansion using wordnet. In: Bressan, S., Küng, J., Wagner, R. (eds.) DEXA 2006. LNCS, vol. 4080, pp. 379–388. Springer, Heidelberg (2006). https://doi.org/10.1007/11827405_37
10. Pfeiffer, H.D., Hartley, R.T.: A comparison of different conceptual structures projection algorithms. ICCS **2007**, 165–178 (2007)
11. Alansary, S., Nagi, M.: From language implicit structure to UNL explicit knowledge infrastructure. In: The International Symposium on Natural Language Processing SNLP 2013, Phuket, Thailand, 28–30 October 2013 (2013)
12. Alansary, S., Nagi, M., Adly, N.: Machine translation using the universal networking language (UNL). In: 8th International Conference on Language Engineering. Ain Shams University, Egypt (2008)
13. Adly, N., Al Ansary, S.: Evaluation of arabic machine translation system based on the universal networking language. In: Horacek, H., Métais, E., Muñoz, R., Wolska, M. (eds.) NLDB 2009. LNCS, vol. 5723, pp. 243–257. Springer, Heidelberg (2010). https://doi.org/10.1007/978-3-642-12550-8_20
14. Lee, J., Min, J.-K., Alice, O., Chung, C.-W.: Effective ranking and search techniques for Web resources considering semantic relationships. Inf. Process. Manag.: Int. J. **50**(1), 132–155 (2014)
15. Ullmann, J.R.: An algorithm for subgraph isomorphism. J. Assoc. Comput. Mach. **23**(I), 31–42 (1976)
16. Messmer, B.T., Bunke, H.: Efficient subgraph isomorphism detection: a decomposition approach. IEEE Trans. Knowl. Data Eng. **12**(2), 307–323 (2000)
17. Mangold, C.: A survey and classification of semantic search approaches. Int. J. Metadata Semant. Ontol. **2**(1), 23–34 (2007)
18. Ensan, F., Bagheri, E.: Document retrieval model through semantic linking. In: Proceedings of the Tenth ACM International Conference on Web Search and Data Mining, Cambridge, United Kingdom (2017)

SKOS-Based Concept Expansion
for LOD-Enabled Recommender Systems

Lisa Wenige[(✉)], Geraldine Berger, and Johannes Ruhland

Chair of Business Information Systems, Friedrich-Schiller-University Jena,
Jena, Germany
lisa.wenige@uni-jena.de

Abstract. This paper presents a concept expansion strategy for Linked
Open Data-enabled recommender systems (LDRS). This strategy is
based on annotations from Simple Knowledge Organization System
(SKOS) vocabularies. To this date, the knowledge structures of SKOS
graphs have not yet been thoroughly explored for item similarity
calculation in content-based recommender systems (RS). While some
researchers have already performed an unweighted concept expansion
on skos:broader links, the quantification of the relatedness of concepts
from SKOS graphs with quality issues, such as the DBpedia category system, should be further investigated to improve recommendation results.
For this purpose, we apply our approach in conjunction with a suitable
concept-to-concept similarity metric and test it on three different LDRS
datasets from the multimedia domain (i.e., movie, music and book RS).
The results showed that our approach has a diversifying effect on result
lists, while at least providing the same level of accuracy as a system
running in non-expansion mode.

Keywords: SKOS · Linked Open Data · Recommender systems ·
Concept expansion

1 Introduction

Content-based (CB) recommender systems (RS) generate suggestions based on
the correspondence of preferences in the user profile with the metadata descriptions of yet unseen items in the database. The more the items are similar to
previous consumption behavior, the likelier it is that a user finds these suggestions helpful [2]. However, CB engines often face the problem that data sources
are insufficient in terms of data quantity and/or quality. That is why, in recent
years, researchers have begun to harness metadata information from the Linked
Open Data (LOD) cloud to enhance content descriptions [8,12,23,32]. In this context, the subject categories from Simple Knowledge Organization System (SKOS)
vocabularies are regularly applied [8,23]. For instance, in the DBpedia repository,
an LOD resource representing a movie is characterized by SKOS-based subject
descriptors (e.g. stating the genre, topic or most important actors of the movie).

© Springer Nature Switzerland AG 2019
E. Garoufallou et al. (Eds.): MTSR 2018, CCIS 846, pp. 101–112, 2019.
https://doi.org/10.1007/978-3-030-14401-2_9

The concepts are part of the DBpedia category graph [6]. SKOS subjects are uniquely identified LOD resources. Therefore, they can be conveniently processed with the help of content-based methods [17]. In contrast to that, natural text annotations require time-consuming preprocessing operations [18]. In the LOD cloud, SKOS is a de-facto standard for expression of controlled vocabularies in machine-readable form [24]. Additionally, SKOS annotations can facilitate quick recommendation retrieval as was demonstrated by one of our previous works [29]. On top of that, SKOS systems allow for a comprehensive exploration of knowledge repositories through exploitation of their hierarchical relations. But while researchers have already successfully performed concept expansion in CB systems, these methods are limited to a simple unweighted incorporation of related subject descriptors [8]. We argue that the semantic similarity of two concepts should also be taken into account in the algorithm to improve the overall performance. Concept-to-concept similarity scores can be calculated by application of a corresponding graph-based metric on a thesaurus. But whereas most existing measures of this kind are designed to consume a directed acyclic graph (DAG) (see Sect. 2), many publicly available SKOS systems, such as the DBpedia category graph, have quality issues (e.g., cyclic hierarchical dependencies) [15,28]. Besides making thesaurus maintenance difficult [22], these issues also complicate determination of concept-to-concept similarity scores. Therefore, this paper addresses the following research gaps:

- Identification of a suitable concept-to-concept similarity metric that can be applied for recommendation retrieval on SKOS systems with quality issues (Sect. 2).
- Development of a concept expansion strategy for LOD-enabled RS that takes into account the concept-to-concept similarity scores in the recommendation model (Sect. 3).
- Evaluation of the developed concept expansion strategy in typical recommendation scenarios with realworld preference data and metadata from LOD collections to demonstrate the feasibility of the approach (Sect. 4).

2   Related Work

Automatic query expansion (AQE) in information retrieval (IR) systems dates back to the 1960s. AQE addresses the problem of brief user queries and natural language ambiguity. It is commonly applied to augment keywords with additional terms of similar meaning. Thus, document keywords that fit a user's underlying information need, but are not contained in the original query, can still be found [4]. Hence, it is no wonder that SKOS vocabularies have been recently adopted for concept expansion in RDF-based retrieval contexts as well [10,26]. Because of the similarity of IR systems and CB RS, AQE approaches can also be transferred to recommendation tasks to improve user satisfaction. The authors of [8] provide evidence for this hypothesis. In their LDRS, they enhance SKOS annotations with related concepts by following skos:broader links. In this context, the exploration of these relations is no coincidence. Concept similarity in a

SKOS graph is most effectively determined through common ancestors [13] which can be identified with the help of skos:broader links. Additionally, Ruotsalo et al. quantify relatedness of annotations with the help of a taxonomy-based similarity metric. However, they only use the concept-to-concept similarity scores to determine additional relevant concepts for retrieval but do not at all consider them in the recommendation model [23]. Therefore, it is suggested to facilitate a score-based incorporation of similar concepts into the retrieval process of LOD-enabled RS. We assume that a quantified concept-to-concept value is better suited to reflect relatedness than an exploration of direct semantic relationships on skos:broader links. This works builds on our previous research in the domain of digital library (DL) search that proved that a weighted concept expansion can enhance retrieval options [30]. However, this research was based on a high-quality SKOS graph, namely the Standard Thesaurus for Economics (STW), that resembles a DAG-like structure. On these systems, concept-to-concept similarity scores are calculated by the specificity of the to-be-compared descriptors in the graph. Determination of concept specificity requires the declaration of a root concept and transitive skos:broader relations [13,31]. However, the SKOS standard does not specify that hierarchical links necessarily have to resemble transitive relations and many SKOS vocabularies do not have a top concept [3,15,17]. Additionally, Mader et al. found out that numerous publicly available vocabularies contain cyclic dependencies. For instance, quality assessments on the DBpedia category system have shown that the graph contains more than 1,000 cycles [15]. Therefore, Stankovic et al. introduced an alternative approach that can compute concept-to-concept similarities on a cyclic non-transitive SKOS graph that does not have a root node. The corresponding metric is called *hyProximity*. It utilizes a modified path-based metric. Stankovic et al. identify similar concepts for a set of initial seed concepts by traversing chains of skos:broader links. Concepts that are found within a shorter distance of the initial seed concepts are more similar [27]. The metric can be adapted to cases with only a single initial concept. This version of the metric will be utilized for the similarity-based concept expansion method presented in this paper (see Eq. 1).

$$conceptSim_{hyP}(c, p) = \frac{pond(c, p)}{d(c, p)} \tag{1}$$

In this context, $d(c, p)$ calculates the distance between two SKOS concepts c and p by counting the links in the shortest path to their common ancestor. In order to account for the idea of concept depth in the *hyProximity* metric, the function decreases the final similarity score, the further away a common ancestor is positioned from two concepts (Eq. 2).

$$pond(c, p) = e^{-\gamma d(c, p)} \tag{2}$$

The *hyProximity* metric by Stankovic et al. has already been tested in the LDRS framework *Allied*, in which its performance was compared to other semantic similarity measures [9], such as the *Linked Data Semantic Distance* (*LDSD*) [20]. However, in our work we investigate whether the measure can be applied to improve the performance of regular concept expansion methods (i.e., on skos:broader links) in content-based RS.

3   Concept Expansion for LOD-Enabled RS

In LDRS, item similarities are usually determined by the amount of matching item features (i.e., SKOS annotations). The more annotations two LOD resources share, the more similar they are. Thereby, concepts are often assigned a weight value that increases scores for concepts that rarely occur in a LOD repository. A common weight function is the information content (IC) of a concept c (Eq. 3) [16].

$$IC(c) = -log\frac{freq(c)}{n} \tag{3}$$

It sets the frequency of a concept's occurrences in relation to the maximum frequency (n) among all relevant resources from a LOD repository. In addition to identifying all items that share annotations with a user profile item (r), a CB engine running in concept expansion mode has to determine additional concepts (i.e., proximate concepts) that are similar to the annotations of the LOD resource from the user profile. The notion of proximate concepts $(Prox(c, r))$ is specified in Definition 1.

Definition 1 (Proximate Concepts). *For a single SKOS annotation of a user profile item $(c \in Annot(r))$, proximate concepts are those that are sufficiently similar to it, i.e. the taxonomy-based concept-to-concept similarity score $(conceptSim_{hyP}(c, p))$ exceeds a specified threshold ϵ (Eq. 4).*

$$Prox(c, r) = \{ p \mid c \in Annot(r), conceptSim_{hyP}(c, p) \geq \epsilon \} \tag{4}$$

Formally, the set of all similar concepts for an input resource r from the user profile is the union of proximate concept sets of the annotations (Eq. 5).

$$Prox(r) = \bigcup_{c \in Annot(r)} Prox(c, r) \tag{5}$$

Upon having extracted suitable concepts for expansion, the retrieval process for relevant resources is started with an enhanced set of annotations. Such a process identifies relevant suggestions for a stated user preference (i.e., a LOD resource representing a movie) from a LOD repository that can be accessed through a publicly available SPARQL endpoint.

Definition 2 (Relevant resources and their annotations). *Resources that share at least an annotation with either the original SKOS annotations of the input resource (exact matches) (Ω_r) or with one of the previously identified similar concepts (proximate matches) $(\mu(?c) \in Prox(r))$. The corresponding SPARQL query evaluates the graph pattern $[[P_{exp}]]_{AD}$ over a dataset containing SKOS annotations (AD) and returns the mapping Ω_{exp} (see Eqs. 6 and 7).*

$$P_{exp} = (?q, <ANNOT.PROPERTY>, ?c) \tag{6}$$

$$\Omega_{exp} = \{ \, \mu \mid \mu \in [[P_{exp}]]_{AD}, \, \mu(?c) \in Prox(r) \, \} \cup \Omega_r \tag{7}$$

After having obtained the result set, resources $q \in \Omega_{exp}$ need to be ranked according to the score of each SKOS annotation. The notion of this score is specified in Definition 3.

Definition 3 (Annotation score). *When an annotation (c) of r is also present in the set of annotations of q, its score is represented by the IC. If this is not the case and c has proximate concepts that are present in the annotation set of q (S(c,r,q), Definition 4, Eq. 9); the maximum concept-to-concept similarity score among these values (sim(c,r,q), Definition 4, Eq. 10) is utilized to decrease the information content. Hence, the respective annotation is contributing slightly less to the final similarity score of the two resources. When an annotation neither appears in the set of annotations of q nor has similar concepts that are present in the annotation set of q, the score is set to 0 (Eq. 8).*

$$annotScore(c,r,q) = \begin{cases} IC(c), & c \in Annot(q) \\ sim(c,r,q) \times IC(c), & c \notin Annot(q), S(c,r,q) = \emptyset \\ 0, & otherwise \end{cases} \tag{8}$$

The specification of the maximum concept-to-concept similarity score $(sim(c,r,q))$ that is needed for the annotation score is given in Definition 4.

Definition 4 (Concept-to-concept similarity score). *The engine identifies expansion candidates for an annotation (c ∈ Annot(r)) by looking at the annotations of a resource q, whose recommendation score with r needs to be determined. When a concept p appears in the set of similar concepts of the input annotation (Prox(r)) as well as in the annotations of q (Annot(q)), its concept-to-concept similarity score is added to the set of relevant values (Eq. 9). From these values, the maximum similarity score is selected (Eq. 10).*

$$S(c,r,q) = \{ \, conceptSim_{hyP}(c,p) \mid p \in Prox(c,r) \cap Annot(q)\} \tag{9}$$

$$sim(c,r,q) = max(S(c,r,q)) \tag{10}$$

Based on the annotation score, the recommendation score of two items r and q can be determined. This is specified in Definition 5.

Definition 5 (Recommendation score). *The scores of each concept of the annotation set of r are aggregated by summation to determine the final similarity value of two resources r and q.*

$$recScore(r,q) = \sum_{c \in Annot(r)} annotScore(c,r,q) \tag{11}$$

By application of the presented concept expansion method, it may be possible to change the composition of result lists thus enabling users to receive better recommendations.

4 Experiments

4.1 Evaluation Metrics and Experimental Setup

A sound evaluation of the presented recommendation approach should measure suitable quality dimensions, such as the *accuracy* of recommendations. For this purpose, *precision* and *recall* are frequently applied [1,2,11,21,25]. The two measures are often combined in a single metric, called *f-measure* ($f1$ score). It is the harmonic mean of *precision* (*prec*) and *recall* (*rec*) [11].

Aside from *accuracy*, other quality dimensions were considered in our evaluation. For instance, relevant suggestions may not be helpful, if they are already familiar to the user [25]. Castells proposes to calculate the likelihood of the user to choose a certain item i (i.e., the number of occurrences of the item in the profiles of the entire database) to determine *novelty* scores that are based on the notion of popularity. These scores are then averaged for the set of recommendations a user receives (Eq. 12).

$$nov_{pop} = \sum_{i=1}^{k} \frac{-log_2 p(i)}{k} \qquad (12)$$

It can also be beneficial, when result lists are topically diversified [33]. Therefore, this evaluation applied a diversity metric as well. It determines item-to-item similarity values with the cosine similarity metric. Scores are then converted to distance values (Eq. 13) and averaged for the recommendation list (Eq. 14) [5].

$$dist(i_l, i_m) = 1 - cos(i_l, i_m) \qquad (13)$$

$$div = \frac{2}{k(k-1)} \sum_{l<m} dist(i_l, i_m) \qquad (14)$$

The presented concept expansion method was evaluated with historical data. For this purpose, we utilized a collection of DBpedia-mapped RS data. The collection comprises the MovieLens1M (movie domain), the LastFM (music domain) and the LibraryThing (book domain) dataset [14]. We applied the LOD-enabled RS datasets in offline simulation runs to test our novel concept expansion method. First, the datasets were prepared for a 5-fold cross-validation. From each dataset, the 100 first listed users were selected. The preference data of users was divided into 5 equally large subsets. In each run, one fifth of the preference information from a user was applied as test and four fifths as training data. The subsets of preferences were utilized to identify the 20 most similar resources from DBpedia as recommendations. These suggestions were determined by calculating recommendation scores (see Definition 5) for each potentially relevant

LOD resource that was similar to a single user profile item and then by finally summating the scores for the entire profile. The sum-based aggregation was performed, because it was often the case that a to-be-recommended LOD resource was similar to more than one item in the user profile. The simulations were implemented in Java code. The application processed user profiles, generated suggestions and compared the predicted values with the actual feedback data stated in the test set thereby determining the degree of concordance between the engine's predictions and the user's true preferences. By this means, accuracy (*prec*, *rec*) values were calculated. Additionally, the test measured the diversity (*div*) of recommendation lists and calculated novelty scores (nov_{pop}).

We applied the $conceptSim_{hyP}$ metric by Stankovic et al. to determine recommendation scores. As has been mentioned before, this metric relies on a pondering function that decreases the similarity value the further away the concept is located from the initial concept [27]. However, the researchers do not specify the exact value for the parameter γ, which regulates how strongly the similarity decreases with an increasing shortest path distance between two concepts. Since the authors do not provide any empirical evidence regarding the best parameter, preliminary simulations had to be run to identify the optimal configuration. Figure 1 shows the $f1$ scores indicating recommendation quality for different γ values in each domain. After determination of the optimal γ parameter, we tested configurations with varying shortest path distances from the respective seed annotation. Thus, aside from evaluating similarity-based concept expansion, when adjacent concepts ($d(c, p) = 1$) were incorporated, the wider neighbourhood of an annotated seed concept ($d(c, p) = 2$) was also taken into account. The simulations did not include longer path distances, because with each increment of the distance value, the amount of data rose by a multitude, due to the cyclic dependencies of the SKOS graph. Two-step distances were deemed to be manageable in the context of a real-world recommendation scenario. Figure 2 shows the results of the preliminary distance-based simulations runs. It can be

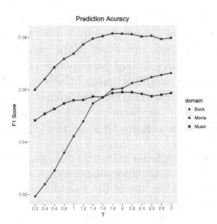

Fig. 1. Results of the experiments on parameter configuration

seen that the incorporation of a wider concept neighborhood ($d(c, p) = 2$) only increased performance results in the music domain. These pretests identified the best parameters for the $conceptSim_{hyP}$ metric to be used in the simulation runs.

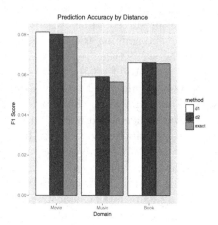

Fig. 2. Results of the experiments on distance-based similarity

4.2   Results

Table 1 shows the main results of the computational experiments.[1,2] Comparisons were made between exact concept matching, a `skos:broader` concept expansion (i.e., baseline methods) and the similarity-based concept expansion approach proposed by this paper. For the baseline methods, the annotation score was determined by only considering the information content ($IC(c)$) of matching item features or - in case of the simple `skos:broader` concept expansion method - of related categories.

It appears that the similarity-based concept expansion method does, in fact, improve *accuracy* values. This approach almost always achieved the best *precision* and *recall* scores. The sole exception is the *precision* value in the book domain which indicates a slightly weaker performance of the method in comparison to the approach of exact concept matchings. One can further draw the conclusion that a concept expansion on `skos:broader` links is not well suited for LOD-enabled recommendation scenarios operating on the DBpedia category graph. The scores of the `skos:broader` approach are far lower than the scores of the other two

---

[1] Unless otherwise indicated, significant statistical tests reached the level of $p < 0.001$. In case of significant differences, the performance scores of the best performing approach are marked in bold, the figures of the second best method in solid and the results of the worst approach are marked in dashed lines.

[2] M stands for the mean, SD for the standard deviation and N for the number of users for whom recommendations could be generated in the 5-fold cross-validation setting.

approaches. Additionally, we conducted FDR-adjusted Friedman tests for *accuracy* values in each subdomain. Friedman tests provide lower statistical power than a repeated measures ANOVA. But according to Demšar et al., nonparametric tests should be applied for cross-validated data [7].

Table 1. Performance results of the simulation runs

Dimension (metric)	Domain	broader		exact		sim		N	Sig.
		M	SD	M	SD	M	SD		
Accuracy (*rec*)	Movie	0.0694	0.0581	0.0866	0.0576	**0.0870**	**0.0638**	100	✓
	Music	0.0466	0.0445	0.0552	0.0529	**0.0588**	**0.0445**	95	✓
	Book	0.0334	0.0458	0.0663	0.0750	**0.0673**	**0.0765**	100	✓
Accuracy (*prec*)	Movie	0.0960	0.1084	0.1120	0.1046	**0.1269**	**0.1267**	100	✓
	Music	0.0552	0.0566	0.0597	0.0587	0.0607	0.0581	95	x
	Book	0.0410	0.0456	**0.0854**	**0.1060**	0.0835	0.1021	100	✓
Novelty (*nov_pop*)	Movie	**9.9085**	**1.1475**	9.5948	0.8020	9.0511	2.2065	100	✓
	Music	11.0932	3.0087	10.7295	3.7810	10.7076	3.7469	71	x
	Book	12.0522	2.1212	11.9175	2.5186	11.8663	2.4642	69	x
Diversity (*div*)	Movie	**0.8907**	**0.0533**	0.8550	0.0533	0.8817	0.0526	100	✓
	Music	**0.8912**	**0.0450**	0.8693	0.1036	0.8902	0.0371	94	✓
	Book	**0.8843**	**0.1013**	0.8437	0.1329	0.8592	0.1291	100	✓

In terms of *precision*, Friedman tests confirmed significant differences in the movie and the book domain. In the movie domain, additional Wilcoxon pairwise post-hoc tests (FDR-adjusted) verified the superiority of the similarity-based concept expansion method over the other approaches (sim vs. exact: $p < 0.01$), whereas in the book domain post-hoc tests only confirmed, that `skos:broader` concept expansion performs worse than the other retrieval strategies.

For the performance metric of recall (*rec*), Friedman tests confirmed significant differences in each multimedia domain. Respective subsequent post-hoc analyses revealed a comparably weaker performance of the `skos:broader` concept expansion method in comparison to the other two recommendation approaches (music domain - exact vs. broader: $p < 0.01$). In the domains of movie and book recommendations, no significant differences could be identified between exact concept matching and similarity-based concept expansion. On the Lastfm dataset (music domain), however, the similarity-based concept expansion method performed significantly better than the other two approaches in terms of *recall* (sim vs. exact: $p < 0.05$).

In summary, these findings indicate a poor performance of the `skos:broader` concept expansion method with regard to *accuracy* values, whereas the other two approaches mostly performed equally well. Additionally, in some domains (movie and music) significance tests even confirmed the superiority of the novel concept expansion method with regard to either *precision* or *recall*.

In terms of *novelty* almost no meaningful differences were identified between the three retrieval approaches. Despite the small variations in this regard, Friedman tests confirmed their significance only for the movie domain dataset, where Wilcoxon post-hoc tests revealed that `skos:broader` concept expansion, on average, produced the most novel recommendations, followed by the approach of exact concept matching (sim vs. exact: $p < 0.05$). Here, the similarity-based concept expansion method, while generating highly precise results, often recommended rather popular items.

For *diversity* scores, Friedman tests confirmed significant differences in each multimedia domain. The ranking of *div* scores was confirmed by the Wilcoxon tests in the movie and in the book domain. In the music domain, post-hoc analyses only confirmed the superiority of the concept expansion methods (i.e, `skos:broader` and similarity-based concept expansion) over regular retrieval.

5   Conclusion

In this paper, we have presented a strategy of SKOS-based concept expansion for LOD-enabled RS which relies on taxonomy-based similarity calculation. Our experiments have shown that our method still works well, even if a SKOS vocabulary with quality issues, such as the DBpedia category graph, is applied. We evaluated the approach in offline tests against two baseline approaches (i.e., exact concept matching and `skos:broader` expansion). The results of the simulation runs showed that the similarity-based concept expansion method has a positive effect on recommendation quality. In some cases, the method proved to be significantly better regarding *accuracy* and/or *diversity* scores. Concept expansion on `skos:broader` links seemed to have had the same positive impact on *diversity* scores, but at the same time led to significantly worse results in terms of *accuracy*. Hence, in summary, it can be stated that similarity-based concept expansion offers an interesting additional retrieval strategy for LOD-enabled recommendation tasks.

References

1. Adomavicius, G., Tuzhilin, A.: Toward the next generation of recommender systems: a survey of the state-of-the-art and possible extensions. IEEE Trans. Knowl. Data Eng. **17**(6), 734–749 (2005)
2. Aggarwal, C.: Recommender Systems: The Textbook. Springer, Heidelberg (2016). https://doi.org/10.1007/978-3-319-29659-3
3. Baker, T., Bechhofer, S., Isaac, A., Miles, A., Schreiber, G., Summers, E.: Key choices in the design of Simple Knowledge Organization System (SKOS). Web Semant.: Sci. Serv. Agents World Wide Web **20**, 35–49 (2013)
4. Carpineto, C., Romano, G.: A survey of automatic query expansion in information retrieval. In: ACM Computing Surveys (CSUR), vol. 44, no. 1 (2012)
5. Castells, P., Vargas, S., Wang, J.: Novelty and diversity metrics for recommender systems: choice, discovery and relevance. In: International Workshop on Diversity in Document Retrieval (DDR 2011) at the 33rd European Conference on Information Retrieval (ECIR 2011) (2011)

6. DBpedia (2017). https://wiki.dbpedia.org/
7. Demšar, J.: Statistical comparisons of classifiers over multiple data sets. J. Mach. Learn. Res. **7**(1), 1–30 (2006)
8. Di Noia, T., Mirizzi, R., Ostuni, V.C., Romito, D., Zanker, M.: Linked Open Data to support content-based recommender systems. In: Proceedings of the 8th International Conference on Semantic Systems, pp. 1–8 (2012)
9. Figueroa, C., et al.: Allied: a framework for executing Linked Data-based recommendation algorithms. Int. J. Semant. Web Inf. Syst. (IJSWIS) **13**(4), 134–154 (2017)
10. Hajra, A., Latif, A., Tochtermann, K.: Retrieving and ranking scientific publications from Linked Open Data repositories. In: Proceedings of the 14th International Conference on Knowledge Technologies and Data-Driven Business (2014)
11. Herlocker, J., Konstan, J., Terveen, L., Riedl, J.: Evaluating collaborative filtering recommender systems. ACM Trans. Inf. Syst. (TOIS) **22**(1), 5–53 (2004)
12. Khrouf, H., Troncy, R.: Hybrid event recommendation using Linked Data and user diversity. In: Proceedings of the 7th ACM Conference on Recommender Systems, pp. 185–192 (2013)
13. Lin, D.: An information-theoretic definition of similarity. ICML **98**, 296–304 (1998)
14. LODrecsys-datasets (2017). https://github.com/sisinflab/LODrecsys-datasets
15. Mader, C., Haslhofer, B., Isaac, A.: Finding quality issues in SKOS vocabularies. In: Zaphiris, P., Buchanan, G., Rasmussen, E., Loizides, F. (eds.) TPDL 2012. LNCS, vol. 7489, pp. 222–233. Springer, Heidelberg (2012). https://doi.org/10.1007/978-3-642-33290-6_25
16. Meymandpour, R., Davis, J.: Recommendations using Linked Data. In: Proceedings of the 5th Ph.D. Workshop on Information and Knowledge, pp. 75–82 (2013)
17. Miles, A., Bechhofer, S.: SKOS simple knowledge organization system reference. In: W3C Recommendation (2009)
18. Mobasher, B., Jin, X., Zhou, Y.: Semantically enhanced collaborative filtering on the web. In: Berendt, B., Hotho, A., Mladenič, D., van Someren, M., Spiliopoulou, M., Stumme, G. (eds.) EWMF 2003. LNCS (LNAI), vol. 3209, pp. 57–76. Springer, Heidelberg (2004). https://doi.org/10.1007/978-3-540-30123-3_4
19. Ostuni, V., Di Noia, T., Di Sciascio, E., Mirizzi, R.: Top-n recommendations from implicit feedback leveraging Linked Open Data. In: Proceedings of the 7th ACM Conference on Recommender Systems (RecSys 2013), pp. 85–92 (2013)
20. Passant, A.: dbrec — music recommendations using DBpedia. In: Patel-Schneider, P.F., et al. (eds.) ISWC 2010. LNCS, vol. 6497, pp. 209–224. Springer, Heidelberg (2010). https://doi.org/10.1007/978-3-642-17749-1_14
21. Pu, P., Chen, L., Hu, R.: A user-centric evaluation framework for recommender systems. In: Proceedings of the 5th ACM Conference on Recommender Systems (RecSys 2011), pp. 157–164 (2011)
22. Quarati, A., Albertoni, R., De Martino, M.: Overall quality assessment of SKOS thesauri: an AHP-based approach. J. Inf. Sci. **43**(6), 816–834 (2017)
23. Ruotsalo, T., et al.: SMARTMUSEUM: a mobile recommender system for the web of data. Web Semant.: Sci. Serv. Agents World Wide Web **20**, 50–67 (2013)
24. Schmachtenberg, M., Bizer, C., Paulheim, H.: Adoption of the Linked Data best practices in different topical domains. In: Mika, P., et al. (eds.) ISWC 2014. LNCS, vol. 8796, pp. 245–260. Springer, Cham (2014). https://doi.org/10.1007/978-3-319-11964-9_16
25. Shani, G., Gunawardana, A.: Evaluating recommendation systems (2011)

26. Shekarpour, S., Hoffner, K., Lehmann, J., Auer, S.: Keyword query expansion on Linked Data using linguistic and semantic features. In: IEEE 7th International Conference on Semantic Computing (ICSC), pp. 191–197 (2013)

27. Stankovic, M., Breitfuss, W., Laublet, P.: Discovering relevant topics using DBPedia: providing non-obvious recommendations. In: IEEE/WIC/ACM International Conferences on Web Intelligence and Intelligent Agent Technology, pp. 219–222 (2011)

28. Suominen, O., Mader, C.: Assessing and improving the quality of SKOS vocabularies. J. Data Semant. **3**(1), 47–73 (2014)

29. Wenige, L., Ruhland, J.: Flexible on-the-fly recommendations from linked open data repositories. In: Abramowicz, W., Alt, R., Franczyk, B. (eds.) BIS 2016. LNBIP, vol. 255, pp. 43–54. Springer, Cham (2016). https://doi.org/10.1007/978-3-319-39426-8_4

30. Wenige, L., Ruhland, J.: Retrieval by recommendation: using LOD technologies to improve digital library search. Int. J. Digit. Libr. **19**(2/3), 253–269 (2018)

31. Wu, Z., Palmer, M.: Verbs semantics and lexical selection. In: Proceedings of the 32nd Annual Meeting on Association for Computational Linguistics, pp. 133–138 (1994)

32. Zarrinkalam, F., Kahani, M.: A multi-criteria hybrid citation recommendation system based on Linked Data. In: 2nd International eConference on Computer and Knowledge Engineering (ICCKE), pp. 283–288 (2012)

33. Ziegler, C., McNee, S., Konstan, J., Lausen, G.: Improving recommendation lists through topic diversification. In: Proceedings of the 14th ACM International Conference on World Wide Web, pp. 22–32 (2005)

Navigating OWL 2 Ontologies Through Graph Projection

Ahmet Soylu[1,2(✉)] and Evgeny Kharlamov[3]

[1] Norwegian University of Science and Technology, Gjøvik, Norway
ahmet.soylu@ntnu.no
[2] SINTEF Digital, Oslo, Norway
[3] University of Oxford, Oxford, UK
evgeny.kharlamov@cs.ox.ac.uk

Abstract. Ontologies are powerful, yet often complex, assets for representing, exchanging, and reasoning over data. Particularly, OWL 2 ontologies have been key for constructing semantic knowledge graphs. Ability to navigate ontologies is essential for supporting various knowledge engineering tasks such as querying and domain exploration. To this end, in this short paper, we describe an approach for projecting the non-hierarchical topology of an OWL 2 ontology into a graph. The approach has been implemented in two tools, one for visual query formulation and one for faceted search, and evaluated under different use cases.

Keywords: OWL 2 · Ontologies · Graph navigation ·
Knowledge graphs

1 Introduction

Ontologies are powerful, yet often complex, assets for representing, exchanging, and reasoning over data. Particularly, OWL 2 ontologies [4] have been key for constructing semantic knowledge graphs (e.g., [7,8]). A knowledge graph describes real world entities and their interrelations [17]. They have been used both in academia, such as Yago [3] and DBpedia [9], and in industry such as Google's Knowledge Graph, Facebook's Graph Search, and Microsoft's Satori. Semantic knowledge graphs are typically stored or exported as RDF datasets, which allow for storing sparse and diverse data in an extensible and adaptable way [16]. Semantics of such datasets are typically encoded in OWL 2 ontologies.

Ability to navigate ontologies is essential for understanding the domain of interest (e.g., visual exploration) [6,10], its representation, and underlying data; and for supporting various other knowledge engineering tasks such as querying (e.g., query by navigation) [12,14]. However, it is not straight forward to explore implicit and explicit connections between the classes of an OWL 2 ontology, which is basically a collection of logical axioms. To this end, in this short paper,

Funded by EU H2020 TheyBuyForYou (780247) and FP7 Optique (318338) projects.

E. Garoufallou et al. (Eds.): MTSR 2018, CCIS 846, pp. 113–119, 2019.
https://doi.org/10.1007/978-3-030-14401-2_10

we describe an approach for projecting the non-hierarchical class topology of an OWL 2 ontology into a graph. This approach has been implemented in two semantic tools, namely OptiqueVQS [11] for visual query formulation and Sem-Facet [1] for faceted search and evaluated under different use cases.

The rest of the paper is structured as follows. Section 2 presents our graph projection approach from ontologies, while Sect. 3 presents the tools using our approach. Finally, Sect. 4 concludes the paper.

2 Graph Projection

Our goal for graph projection is, given an ontology, to create a directed labelled graph, called navigation graph [1], whose nodes correspond to the named classes and datatypes in the ontology and edges between nodes to the object properties and datatype properties. Let C_1, C_2, and C_3 be classes, r_1, r_2, and r_3 object properties, d_1 a datatype property, i_1 and i_2 individuals, and dt_1 a data type. First, each class and datatype in the ontology is translated to a node in the navigation graph. Then we add edges of the form $r_1(C_1, C_2)$ and $d_1(C_1, dt_1)$ derived from the axioms of the ontology. The types of axioms resulting in an edge are presented with examples in the followings using description logic (DL) [2].

Ontologies have a propagative effect on the amount of information to be presented. This case is considered in two forms, namely the top-down and bottom-up propagation of property restrictions [5,14]. The first form emerges from the fact that, in an ontology, explicit restrictions attached to a class are inherited by its subclasses. The second form is rooted from the fact that the interpretation of an OWL class also includes the interpretations of all its subclasses. Therefore, for a given class, it may also make sense to derive edges from the (potential) object and datatype properties of its subclasses and superclasses.

2.1 Edges Through Object Properties

Domains and Ranges: Domain and range axioms using named classes are translated to an edge. For example, axioms given in Eq. 1 map to edge $r_1(C_1, C_2)$.

$$\exists r_1.\top \sqsubseteq C_1 \text{ and } \top \sqsubseteq \forall r_1.C_2 \tag{1}$$

$$\exists r_1.\top \sqsubseteq C_1 \text{ and } \top \sqsubseteq \forall r_1.(C_2 \sqcup C_3) \tag{2}$$

If a complex class expression, formed through intersection ($\sqcap$) or union ($\sqcup$), appears as a domain and/or range, then an edge is created for each pair of domain and range classes. For example, axioms given in Eq. 2 map to edges $r_1(C_1, C_2)$ and $r_1(C_1, C_3)$.

Object Property Restrictions: Object property restrictions used in class descriptions, formed through existential quantification ($\exists$), universal quantification ($\forall$), individual value restriction, max ($\geq$), min ($\leq$), and exactly ($=$), are mapped to edges. For example, axioms given in Eqs. 3 to 5 map to $r_1(C_1, C_2)$. Note that in Eq. 5, there is a complex class expression on the left-hand-side.

$$C_1 \sqsubseteq \exists r_1.C_2 \tag{3}$$

$$C_1 \equiv \leq_n r_1.C_2 \tag{4}$$

$$\forall r_1.C_1 \sqsubseteq C_2 \tag{5}$$

Axioms given in Eq. 6 include an individual value restriction and an edge is created with the type of individual, that is $r_1(C_1, C_2)$.

$$C_1 \sqsubseteq \exists r_1.\{i_1\}, \text{ and } i_1 : C_2 \tag{6}$$

Axiom given in Eq. 7 includes a complex class expression. In this case, an edge is created for each named class, that is $r_1(C_1, C_2)$ and $r_1(C_1, C_3)$.

$$C_1 \sqsubseteq \exists r_1.(C_2 \sqcup C_3) \tag{7}$$

Given an enumeration of individuals, an edge is created for each individual's type. For example, axioms given in Eq. 8 map to two edges, that is $r_1(C_1, C_2)$ and $r_1(C_1, C_3)$.

$$C_1 \sqsubseteq \exists r_1.\{i_1\} \sqcup \{i_2\}, \ i_1 : C_2, \text{ and } i_2 : C_3 \tag{8}$$

Inverse Properties: Given an edge in the navigation graph such as $r_1(C_1, C_2)$ and an inverse property axiom for the corresponding object property such as given in Eq. 9, a new edge is created for the inverse property, that is $r_{\bar{1}}(C_2, C_1)$.

$$r_1 \equiv r_{\bar{1}} \tag{9}$$

Role Chains: Given two edges $r_1(C_1, C_2)$ and $r_2(C_2, C_3)$ in the navigation graph, and a role chain axiom between r_1, r_2, r_3 such as given in Eq. 10, a new edge is created for $r3$, that is $r_3(C_1, C_3)$.

$$r_1 \circ r_2 \sqsubseteq r_3 \tag{10}$$

Top-Down Propagation: Given an edge $r_1(C_1, C_2)$ in the navigation graph and a subclass axiom such as as given in Eq. 11, a new edge is added to the graph, that is $r_1(C_3, C_2)$. Similar edges could be created for subproperties.

$$C_3 \sqsubseteq C_1 \tag{11}$$

Bottom-Up Propagation: Given an edge $r_1(C_1, C_2)$ in the navigation graph and a subclass class axiom such as given in Eq. 12, a new edge is added to the graph, that is $r_1(C_3, C_2)$. Similar edges could be created for superproperties.

$$C_1 \sqsubseteq C_3 \qquad (12)$$

2.2   Edges Through Datatype Properties

Domains and Ranges: Domain and range axioms using datatype properties are translated to an edge. For example, axioms given in Eq. 13 map to an edge, that is $d_1(C_1, dt_1)$.

$$\exists d_1.DatatypeLiteral \sqsubseteq C_1 \text{ and } \top \sqsubseteq \forall r_1.dt_1 \qquad (13)$$

Datatype Property Restrictions: Datatype property restrictions, formed through existential quantification ($\exists$), universal quantification ($\forall$), max ($\geq$), min ($\leq$), exactly ($=$), and value are mapped to edges. For example, axiom given in Eq. 14 maps to $d_1(C_1, dt_1)$.

$$C_1 \sqsubseteq \exists d_1.dt_1 \qquad (14)$$

Top-Down Propagation: Given an edge $d_1(C_1, dt_1)$ in the navigation graph and a subclass axiom such as as given in Eq. 15, a new edge is added to the graph, that is $d_1(C_2, dt_1)$. Similar edges could be created for subproperties.

$$C_2 \sqsubseteq C_1 \qquad (15)$$

Bottom-Up Propagation: Given an edge $d_1(C_1, dt_1)$ in the navigation graph and a subclass class axiom such as given in Eq. 16, a new edge is added to the graph, that is $d_1(C_3, dt_1)$. Similar edges could be created for superproperties.

$$C_1 \sqsubseteq C_3 \qquad (16)$$

3   Applications

Variants of this approach have been implemented and evaluated in OptiqueVQS [11], a visual query formulation tool, and SemFacet [1], a faceted search tool. Both interfaces support tree-shaped conjunctive queries.

OptiqueVQS (see Fig. 1) is a visual query system. It allows users to navigate the conceptual space and each traversal from a class to another adds a typed variable-node and object property connecting it to the query graph. OptiqueVQS was deployed and evaluated in different use cases, including Siemens' case for sensor data [15], Statoil's case for oil and gas [11], and on generic datasets [13]. SemFacet (see Fig. 2) is full-fledged general-purpose faceted search interface.

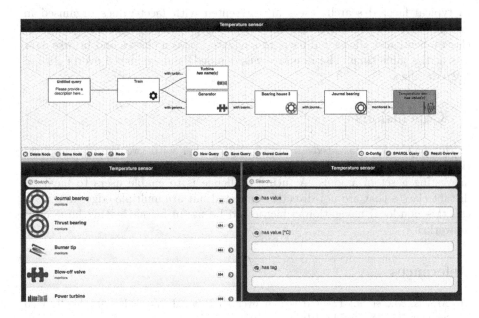

Fig. 1. OptiqueVQS over a use case provided by Siemens.

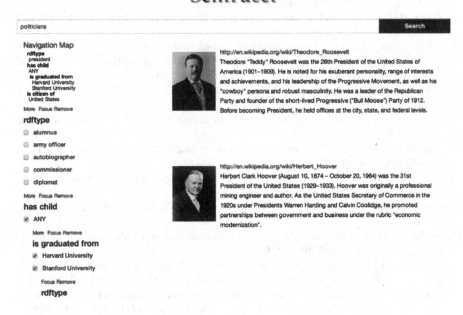

Fig. 2. SemFacet over Yago database.

In typical faceted search, users are presented with facet-values organised in groups according to facet-names and it is often not allowed to navigate between classes. SemFacet allows end users to navigate between classes and browse data sets at the same time. The interface was deployed and evaluated over a slice of Yago database [1].

4   Conclusions

In this paper, we presented an approach, together with two example applications, for navigating OWL 2 ontologies by projecting them into graphs through harvesting a set of axioms. A future challenge is to enable users to navigate distant classes that are not directly connected but are multiple edges away. We call this non-local navigation, which could be useful for navigating large class networks.

References

1. Arenas, M., et al.: Faceted search over RDF-based knowledge graphs. J. Web Semant. **37–38**, 55–74 (2016)
2. Baader, F., et al. (eds.): The Description Logic Handbook: Theory, Implementation, and Applications. Cambridge University Press, New York (2003)
3. Biega, J., et al.: Inside YAGO2s: a transparent information extraction architecture. In: Proceedings of the 22nd International Conference on World Wide Web (WWW 2013), pp. 325–328. ACM, New York (2013)
4. Grau, B.C., et al.: OWL 2: the next step for OWL. J. Web Semant. **6**(4), 309–322 (2008)
5. Cuenca Grau, B., et al.: Towards query formulation, query-driven ontology extensions in OBDA systems. In: Proceedings of the 10th International Workshop on OWL: Experiences and Directions (OWLED 2013) (2013)
6. Katifori, A., et al.: Ontology visualization methods - a survey. ACM Comput. Surv. **39**(4), 10 (2007)
7. Kharlamov, E., et al.: Ontology based data access in statoil. J. Web Seman. **44**, 3–36 (2017)
8. Kharlamov, E., et al.: Semantic access to streaming and static data at Siemens. J. Web Seman. **44**, 54–74 (2017)
9. Lehmann, J., et al.: DBpedia - a large-scale, multilingual knowledge base extracted from wikipedia. Seman. Web **6**(2), 167–195 (2015)
10. Lohmann, S., et al.: Visualizing ontologies with VOWL. Seman. Web **7**(4), 399–419 (2016)
11. Soylu, A., et al.: OptiqueVQS: a visual query system over ontologies for industry. Semantic Web **9**(5), 627–660 (2018)
12. Soylu, A., et al.: Ubiquitous web navigation through harvesting embedded semantic data: a mobile scenario. Integr. Comput.-Aided Eng. **19**(1), 93–109 (2012)
13. Soylu, A., et al.: Experiencing optiqueVQS: a multi-paradigm and ontology-based visual query system for end users. Univ. Access Inf. Soc. **15**(1), 129–152 (2016)
14. Soylu, A., et al.: Ontology-based end-user visual query formulation: why, what, who, how, and which? Univ. Access Inf. Soc. **16**(2), 435–467 (2017)

15. Soylu, A., et al.: Querying industrial stream-temporal data: an ontology-based visual approach. J. Ambient Intell. Smart Environ. **9**(1), 77–95 (2017)
16. Suchanek, F.M., et al.: Knowledge bases in the age of big data analytics. Proc. VLDB Endowment **7**(13), 1713–1714 (2014)
17. Yan, J., et al.: A retrospective of knowledge graphs. Front. Comput. Sci. **12**(1), 55–74 (2018)

Linked Data Live Exploration with Complete Results

Samita Bai$^{(\boxtimes)}$ ⓘ, Sharaf Hussainⓘ, and Shakeel Khojaⓘ

Institute of Business Administration (IBA), Garden Road, Karachi 74400, Pakistan
{sbai,shussain,skhoja}@iba.edu.pk

Abstract. Linked Data is one of the emerging ways to publish and link structured and machine-processable data on the Web, however, the existing techniques to perform live query Linked Data are based on recursive URI look-up process. These techniques contain a limitation for the query patterns having subject unbound and object containing a foreign URI. In such cases, the live query does not produce any answers to the query as the querying process could not be initiated due to unavailability of subject field in the triple pattern. In this paper, we make use of backlinking to extract and store foreign URIs and using this information for executing the queries live where the subject is unbound.

Keywords: Linked Data · Live querying · Backlinking

1 Introduction

The Linked Data is different from the typical unstructured data on the Web and is more dynamic in nature, hence efficient techniques are required to query this data. The use of centralized approaches for copying Web contents and searching those contents using optimized indexes is not a feasible solution for Linked Data. To cater the dynamic nature of Linked Data, more emphasis is given towards the query processing approaches for querying the Linked Data sources live. Such approaches provide slow but fresh results. The basic strategy is to 'follow-your-nose', the URI's are looked-up at the time of query execution process itself and the results are obtained by following more related URI's. However, these strategies have a major drawback as they fail to answer the queries where subject is unbound e.g. (?s foaf:knows #o)[1] with predicate and object bound. This problem persists since definition-wise the Linked Data sources are subject-centric [12] and require an index for query evaluation. The same problem is termed as Inverse Linked Traversal [7] where authors claim that the query patterns with subject unbound and rdf:type predicate (e.g. ?s rdf:type #o) cannot be answered with Linked Traversal strategies and hence require Inverse Linked Traversal.

---

[1] '#' indicates that the specific entity is given and the '?' denotes that the respective entity is variable or unbound.

© Springer Nature Switzerland AG 2019
E. Garoufallou et al. (Eds.): MTSR 2018, CCIS 846, pp. 120–126, 2019.
https://doi.org/10.1007/978-3-030-14401-2_11

A SPARQL query can comprise of 8 query patterns i.e. (?s ?p ?o) (#s ?p ?o) (?s #p ?o) (?s ?p #o) (#s #p ?o) (#s ?p #o) (?s #p #o) & (#s #p #o) where s, p and o denotes subject, predicate and object respectively. Out of 8 query patterns live querying is capable of answering the 3 query patterns i.e. (#s ?p ?o), (#s #p ?o), (#s #p #o) [11], where subject is necessarily required for queries to be answered. The subject serves as starting point for the recursive URI look-up process.

In this paper, we propose the use of backlinking the Linked Data instead of indexing the whole Linked Open Data (LOD) Cloud and then executing queries live using this information can help to answer the query patterns such as (?s ?p #o) and (?s #p #o).

The remaining paper is organized as follows, in Sect. 2 the existing work on backlinking the LD is discussed, in Sect. 3 an analysis of real-world SPARQL query logs is made to assess the importance of query patterns under research, in Sect. 4 live querying is performed using information of backlinks, finally in the last Section conclusion and future work are provided.

2 Related Work

Currently, most of the data sources in LOD cloud are not appropriately inter-linked, with over 50% of them being interlinked with only one or two other data sources. Nearly, two-thirds of the data sources are not linked back to the data sources they are linked from. This results in a loosely interlinked and generally unidirectional graph of the Linked Data which hinders applications relying on link traversal [1]. However, the level of interlinking could be drastically improved by identifying and managing the backlinks between the Linked Data sources [4]. This can be done with the help of backlinking which can be defined as:

"Backlinking is the process of consistent management of the references (back-links) that are made to a resource within the Linked Data repository from other repositories through their triples."

There are few research initiatives done for backlinking of Linked Data. In [4] the local RDF data sources are parsed to locate triples containing the foreign URI's. The foreign entity references are the URIs belonging to the different triple stores for the triples contained in a triplestore. The foreign URIs can be defined as follows:

Definition 1: (Foreign URI) "In an RDF graph G, a URI Ux is assumed as foreign, if $\exists tds(s; p; Ux)(G(tds) \wedge domain(Ux) <> domain(G))$" [6].

The foreign URIs cause hindrances in navigating WoD and this is a very frequent pattern since the number of statements with foreign URIs is quite large and are created using join point data sets [6].

Approaches like [6], discovers foreign URIs and eliminates the missing back-links by asserting rdfs:seeAlso statement into the 4store[2] knowledge base. The rdfs:seeAlso triple refers to the actual URI for the reverse navigation.

---

[2] https://github.com/4store/4store.

Another approach [4] falls in this category. It is an auto-suggest application based on Linked Open Data backlinks.

The Semantic Pingback [10] approach is an addition to the conventional Pingback [3] process with the aim of providing a social dimension to the Linked Data.

In another approach [1], "Referer" request header (as defined by the HTTP protocol specification) is used to determine remote resource which contains Linked Data resources linking to local resources. The type of backlinks depends on the type of forward links which are typed RDF links.

One more approach [9], that allows bidirectional interlinking between Linked Data resources in remote repositories in a distributed manner. Unlike Semantic Pingback [10] approach, it does not rely on pingbacks or trackbacks.

All the discussed approaches make use of backlinking for different purposes but none of them uses it for adding to the query results of live exploration of SPARQL queries. In the next Section, we will discuss the analysis of real world SPARQL query logs.

3   Analysis of Real World SPARQL Query Logs

An analysis of real world SPARQL query logs is performed to identify the significance of backlinking to perform the live exploration of SPARQL queries, this is done by finding the ratio of the queries with subject unbound. Such research was also made previously by different researchers, the details can be found in [7]. Nonetheless, we conducted the analysis using USEWOD2015[3] to assess the query trends of all the queries with subject unbound. It consists of 14 log files from DBPedia-3.9 dataset. To analyze these logs, firstly we RDFsized them with the help of LSQ system [5]. Secondly, we loaded these RDFsized logs in Apache TDB. Finally, SPARQL queries are executed over these logs to find out the total number of SELECT queries with subject unbound as shown in the Table 1. There is a visible variation in the percentages of the queries under focus but promising enough to carry out this research work.

4   Live Querying Linked Data Using Backlinking

The SWDF dataset is selected for the creation of backlinks. The backlinks are created by identifying the foreign URIs and storing them as rdfs:seeAlso links. These links are used for re-directing queries with subject unbound. The backlinks are published as Linked Data and are stored in RDF/XML format. The relationship between the number of triples in the dataset and discovered backlinks is depicted in Fig. 1. The correlation coefficient is computed between the two said variables is 0.950. This value indicates a strong positive correlation between the two variables. The ratio between no. of triples and no. of backlinks is around 10%. Hence, the presence of backlinks cannot be ignored for the link

---

[3]   https://github.com/Samita53/USEWOOD2015Queries.

Table 1. Analysis of USEWOD2015 SPARQL Query Logs.

USEWOD2015 DBPedia log files	Total number of queries	SELECT queries	SELECT queries with subject unbound
Log_ File_ 1	261570	83%	72%
Log_ File_ 2	227756	89%	62%
Log_ File_ 3	385925	95%	36%
Log_ File_ 4	657777	70%	49%
Log_ File_ 5	2110432	95%	10%
Log_ File_ 6	1692412	97%	5%
Log_ File_ 7	191753	87%	4%
Log_ File_ 8	1223589	96%	4%
Log_ File_ 9	1204096	98%	20%
Log_ File_ 10	1374034	96%	15%
Log_ File_ 11	586037	93%	33%
Log_ File_ 12	881554	73%	37%
Log_ File_13	343895	91%	35%
Log_ File_ 14	497059	91%	32%

traversal of query execution, otherwise a significant number of queries will go unanswered. The regression line in Fig. 2 clearly shows that there exists statistical relationship between no. of triples (i.e. predictor variable) and the no. of backlinks (i.e. response variable) created. The equation can be given as:

$$NoB = 145.5 + (0.1476 \times NoT) \tag{1}$$

Where, NoB = No. of backlinks, NoT = No. of triples, β_o is a y-intercept and the value of $\beta_o = 145.5$, \$$\beta_1$ is a coefficient of no. of triples and the value of $\beta_1 = 0.1476$.

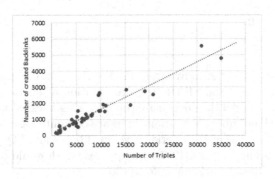

Fig. 1. Relationship between no. of triples and no. of backlinks

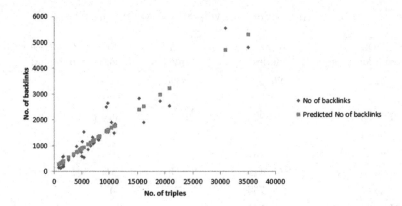

Fig. 2. Comparison between actual and predicted backlinks

Table 2. No. of solutions retrieved and execution times of queries.

Query	No. of solutions retrieved	Time taken by each query (in secs)
BQ1	292	38.369
BQ2	25	48.274
BQ3	3092	852.628
BQ4	4	31.856
BQ5	39	28.799
BQ6	9921	3215.931
BQ7	3	32.433
BQ8	305	91.877
BQ9	1044	114.513
BQ10	10693	3299.593
FQ1	828	87.357
FQ2	119	34.924
FQ3	858	97.370
FQ4	48	244.135
FQ5	0	62.667

We have selected 15 queries five from FedBench [8] and 10 manually crafted queries. The description and SPARQL representation of queries is available at Github [add footnote]. All the queries are run live using backlinks, the number of solutions retrieved and query execution times are computed as shown in Table 2 where BQ1–BQ10 represent the queries developed by us and FQ1–FQ14 are the FedBench queries. The BQ1–BQ10 are the queries which would otherwise could not be answered without backlinks information.

In the next Section, we discuss conclusion and future work.

5   Conclusion and Future Work

This research focuses on a new direction to provide required information for source selection to live exploration strategies than existing indexing mechanisms i.e. use of backlinking. As discussed in the previous section that ratio between no. of triples in the dataset to the number of created backlinks is 10% which means we need to store only 10% of the data which makes the maintenance of the local backlinks easier. Also, we achieve results for the queries which were otherwise returning empty results. In future, we plan to store this backlinks information in HDT format [2] for efficient storage for much bigger dataset i.e. DBPedia. Also, we wish to improve backlinking algorithm by analyzing most popular predicates and then creating the backlinks instead of finding foreign URIs. This will reduce the time taken to for backlink generation to a significant level. Currently the query execution times are quite high, for improving these we aim to make use of parametrized SPARQL queries for identifying the queries with subject unbound and splitting them into two so that the part of query which requires look-up from local backlink storage should be executed individually then second part of query should be executed live, this will surely improve query execution times. An empirical investigation of the proposed approach to compare it other approaches quantitatively is also one of the goals of future work.

References

1. Augmenting the Web of Data using Referers, April 2011
2. Fernandez, J., Martínez-Prieto, M.A., Gutierrez, C., Polleres, A., Arias, M.: Binary RDF representation for publication and exchange (HDT). Web Semant. Sci. Serv. Agents World Wide Web **19**, 22–41 (2013)
3. Langridge, S., Hickson, I.: Pingback 1.0 (2016)
4. Papadakis, I., Stefanidakis, M.: An autosuggest service based on lod backlinks, p. 8, June 2018
5. Saleem, M., Ali, M.I., Hogan, A., Mehmood, Q., Ngomo, A.-C.N.: LSQ: the linked SPARQL queries dataset. In: Arenas, M., et al. (eds.) ISWC 2015. LNCS, vol. 9367, pp. 261–269. Springer, Cham (2015). https://doi.org/10.1007/978-3-319-25010-6_15
6. Salvadores, M., et al.: Domain-specific backlinking services in the web of data. In: Main Conference Proceedings of 2010 IEEE/WIC/ACM International Conference on Web Intelligence, WI 2010, Toronto, Canada, 31 August-3 September 2010, pp. 318–323 (2010)
7. Scheglmann, S., Scherp, A.: Will linked data benefit from inverse link traversal? In: Proceedings of the Workshop on Linked Data on the Web Co-located with the 23rd International World Wide Web Conference (WWW 2014), Seoul, Korea, 8 April 2014 (2014)
8. Schmidt, M., Görlitz, O., Haase, P., Ladwig, G., Schwarte, A., Tran, T.: FedBench: a benchmark suite for federated semantic data query processing. In: Aroyo, L., et al. (eds.) ISWC 2011. LNCS, vol. 7031, pp. 585–600. Springer, Heidelberg (2011). https://doi.org/10.1007/978-3-642-25073-6_37

9. Stefanidakis, M., Papadakis, I.: Linking the (un)linked data through backlinks. In: Proceedings of the International Conference on Web Intelligence, Mining and Semantics, WIMS 2011, Sogndal, Norway, 25–27 May 2011, p. 61 (2011)
10. Tramp, S., Frischmuth, P., Ermilov, T., Auer, S.: Weaving a social data web with semantic pingback. In: Cimiano, P., Pinto, H.S. (eds.) EKAW 2010. LNCS (LNAI), vol. 6317, pp. 135–149. Springer, Heidelberg (2010). https://doi.org/10.1007/978-3-642-16438-5_10
11. Umbrich, J.: A hybrid framework for querying linked data dynamically. Ph.D. thesis, National University of Ireland, Galway Ollscoil na hEireann, Gaillimh (2012)
12. Verborgh, R., et al.: Triple pattern fragments: a low-cost knowledge graph interface for the web. J. Web Semant. **37–38**, 184–206 (2016)

The Genesis of EngMeta - A Metadata Model for Research Data in Computational Engineering

Björn Schembera[1][(✉)] and Dorothea Iglezakis[2]

[1] High Performance Computing Center, Nobelstr. 19, 70569 Stuttgart, Germany
schembera@hlrs.de
[2] University Library Stuttgart, Holzgartenstr. 16, 70174 Stuttgart, Germany
dorothea.iglezakis@ub.uni-stuttgart.de

Abstract. In computational engineering, numerical simulations produce huge amounts of data. To keep this research data findable, accessible, inter-operable and reusable, a structured description of the data is indispensable. This paper outlines the genesis of EngMeta – a metadata model designed to describe engineering simulation data with a focus on thermodynamics and aerodynamics. The metadata model, developed in close collaboration with engineers, is based on existing standards and adds discipline-specific information as the main contribution. Characteristics of the observed system offer researchers important search criteria. Information on the hardware and software used and the processing steps involved helps to understand and replicate the data. Such metadata are crucial to keeping the data FAIR and bridging the gap to a sustainable research data management in computational engineering.

Keywords: Research data management · Metadata · Big data · High performance computing · Simulation · Computational engineering

1 Introduction

Data-intensive science, and computational engineering in particular, are largely driven by computer simulations, that make use of high performance computing (HPC) systems to create, analyze and visualize TeraBytes of data per single simulation project. But despite the importance of research data as the source of scientific reasoning in engineering, this field suffers from a lack of reliable, scalable methods for research data management. Besides organizational and technical challenges like missing incentives and the volume and variety of the data [9], one of the main issues is a lack of a structured description of the data. Typically, no explicit metadata are attached, leaving characterization of the files limited to file names and directory structures [1]. Even though metadata plays a crucial role for keeping the data FAIR (Findable, Accessible, Inter-operable, Reusable) [10], metadata annotation, metadata models[1] and -workflows are rare in HPC and in

---

[1] See Metadata Directory of the RDA, http://rd-alliance.github.io/metadata-directory/standards/, last checked on June, 4th, 2018.

© Springer Nature Switzerland AG 2019
E. Garoufallou et al. (Eds.): MTSR 2018, CCIS 846, pp. 127–132, 2019.
https://doi.org/10.1007/978-3-030-14401-2_12

the field of engineering applications.[2] To enable better data organization, the following work introduces a metadata model for engineering sciences with a focus on thermodynamics and aerodynamics. The metadata model is a joint effort involving the University of Stuttgart Library and the High Performance Computing Center Stuttgart together with the Institute of Thermodynamics and Thermal Process Engineering and the Institute of Aerodynamics and Gas Dynamics of the University of Stuttgart. It is being developed within the project DIPL-ING, focused on research data management concepts for engineering applications.[3]

2   The Genesis of the Metadata Model

Our process of deriving the metadata model started with consideration of the requirements of engineering researchers [6]: What information is important when trying to find, understand and replicate engineering data? In the next steps, we built an object model that complements existing standards and ontologies by including new fields to represent this information.

2.1   Requirements for a Metadata Model for Engineering Applications

In the scientific workflows we identified in the requirement analysis, we found that a description of the data must address three requirements: to find the data, to understand the data and to replicate the data.

To find the data, structured metadata has to cover discipline-specific criteria beyond standard metadata such as author, year, or title. Discipline-specific search criteria include the observed and controlled variables, methods used, parameters of the observed system, and the spatial or temporal resolution of the observation.

To understand the data, there has to be information about the methods and software used, about the computing environment, and about encoding and formats. To document negative results as well, the data should be describable as successful or failed.

To replicate the data in later simulation runs, a detailed description of the data provenance has to include information about every processing step (who did what with which method and which software on which hardware) that was executed to obtain the data. This also implies the necessity of including technical metadata like file formats.

---

[2] In contrast, climate sciences offer much more advanced research data management possibilities making use of well-established metadata models [8].

[3] The project DIPL-ING (http://www.ub.uni-stuttgart.de/dipling) is funded by the Federal Ministry of Education and Research (BMBF) under grant no 16FMD008.

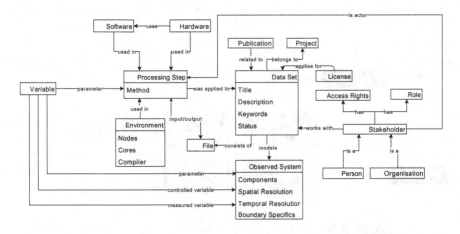

Fig. 1. Object model with inflated domain-specific characteristics for engineering

2.2 Object Model

Based on the requirements in the previous subsection, we created an object model that is depicted in Fig. 1. In the center is a *Data Set* that consists of one or several *Files*, described by technical information like file size, file type or checksum to make preservation possible. Generic descriptive metadata like a description, keywords or subject characterizes the data set from a general point of view – for example to which *Project* and *Publication* it belongs or which *Stakeholders* are involved. Besides these general entities (which are collapsed in Fig. 1), the focus of our model is on the domain-specific metadata categories. The entity *Processing Step* delivers methodological information about the research and describes the creation process of the data. Not only the methods applied, but also the hardware and software components used together with the computing environment can be documented in detail. Because the specific hardware platform (for example the HPC system specifics) has severe implications for understanding the data, it is described by the *Environment* entity. A respective *Software* entity describes the software that was used for data creation and its details (such as the version of Gromacs used for thermodynamics). With the *Hardware* entity any instruments that were used can be characterized. The *Observed System* entity makes it possible to document the object of the research, a central factor in all engineering simulations in thermo- and aerodynamics. This entity describes the components and boundary specifics of the simulated system together with their parameters. The entity also includes spatial resolution (often referred to as grid or mesh) and the temporal resolution of the simulation, characteristics that are fundamental for engineering science. The *Variables* entity represents the observed and controlled variables of the simulation (referred to as ensemble in thermodynamics), their values and their encoding.

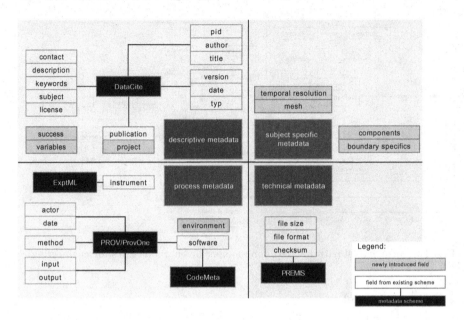

Fig. 2. Components and fields of the EngMeta metadata model

2.3 The Metadata Core

No existing metadata standard covers all of this information, although some contain parts of our model. For this reason we included the following: DataCite [5] provides metadata fields for citation and general descriptive metadata; PROV [2] and its extension ProvOne [4] cover provenance information to document the scientific workflow; CodeMeta [7] describes software; and, parts of ExptML [3] are suitable to describe experimental hardware. Figure 2 shows all metadata fields contained in our model, along with their origin and their classification. Our main contribution consists of introducing new fields that are mainly specific for computational engineering; these fields together with their semantics are summarized in Table 1.

The whole model is implemented as an XML schema[4], having the advantage of a strict structure that can be verified against. To use the metadata in repositories or search indices, the metadata can be easily transformed into other formats like JSON-LD. To embed metadata in container formats like NetCDF or HDF5, a flattened subset of the metadata model can be generated.

2.4 Evaluation

We have discussed the first version of the metadata model with several researchers in the field of aero- and thermodynamics who were not involved

---

[4] The full XSD file as well as an example can be found online: http://www.ub.uni-stuttgart.de/engmeta, last checked on Aug, 16th, 2018.

Table 1. Introduced metadata elements and their semantics

Metadata element	Semantics
Success	Flag and explanation for success, used to document negative results
Variables	Captured and controlled variables (ensemble), usable as search criteria
Project	Related (sub-)project, usable as search criteria
Environment	Description of the computational environment, includes fields such as *compiler* and *nodes* used to estimate the complexity of the simulation
Mesh	Spatial resolution of observation
TemporalResolution	describes the number of time steps and intervals
Component	Description of the components of the simulated system, and their parameters like the *forceField*, important for thermodynamic simulations
Boundary specifics	Specifics for thermodynamics of liquids
Method	Describes the specific method of the simulation, such as numerical simulation

in the creation of the model, resulting in an enhanced version of the model. To test the applicability of the model in other engineering disciplines, we presented the model to researchers from environmental engineering and civil engineering.

3   Conclusions and Future Work

During our research, we developed a discipline-specific metadata model for HPC-based computational engineering. This was forced by the needs of engineers and due to the fact that – to the best of our knowledge – no such model yet exists. Besides generic metadata, our data-centric model emphasizes discipline-specific metadata for computational engineering, making it possible to document the creation process of the data and to describe the characteristics of the observed system. Still ongoing is the evaluation of our model: Even though it was developed in collaboration with engineers, an evaluation "in the field" remains to be conducted. Moreover, we intend to incorporate our metadata model into an infrastructure to manage engineering research data during the whole data life cycle. To accomplish this, we will work further on a deep integration of new metadata fields with existing standards, vocabularies and ontologies and on modularizing the metadata information to extract search criteria in a flattened structure to comply with existing interfaces and protocols. As the next step, the model will be tested for practical use in local management, sharing and publishing of engineering data of three different institutes in a data repository based on the open source software dataverse.[5] An automatic harvester, yet to be developed,

---

[5] https://dataverse.org/, last checked on August, 16th, 2018.

will parse existing process-information from input and log files of simulations to automate parts of the metadata generation. With structured metadata already attached to the data at an early stage, and based on our discipline-specific metadata model, we hope to facilitate sharing, publishing and reuse of research data in engineering.

References

1. Arora, R.: Data management: state-of-the-practice at open-science data centers. In: Khan, S.U., Zomaya, A.Y. (eds.) Handbook on Data Centers, pp. 1095–1108. Springer, New York (2015). https://doi.org/10.1007/978-1-4939-2092-1_37
2. Belhajjame, K., et al.: PROV-DM: the PROV data model (2013). w3C Recommendation http://www.w3.org/TR/2013/REC-prov-dm-20130430/. Accessed 6 June 2018
3. Chalk, S.: The experiment markup language (2014). http://exptml.sourceforge.net/. Accessed 16 Aug 2018
4. Cuevas-Vicenttín, V., et al.: ProvOne: a PROV extension data model for scientific workflow provenance (2016). http://vcvcomputing.com/provone/provone.html. Accessed 16 Aug 16 2018
5. DataCite: DataCite metadata schema for the publication and citation of research data, version 4.1. (2017). https://doi.org/10.5438/0015. Accessed 6 June 2018
6. Iglezakis, D., Schembera, B.: Anforderungen der Ingenieurwissenschaften an das Forschungsdatenmanagement der Universität Stuttgart - Ergebnisse der Bedarfsanalyse des Projektes DIPL-ING. o-bib. Das offene Bibliotheksjournal 5(3), 46–60 (2018). https://doi.org/10.5282/o-bib/2018H3S46-60
7. Jones, M.B., et al.: CodeMeta: an exchange schema for software metadata, version 2.0. (2017). https://doi.org/10.5063/schema/codemeta-2.0
8. Lautenschlager, M., Toussaint, F., Thiemann, H., Reinke, M.: The CERA-2 data model (1998). https://www.pik-potsdam.de/cera/Descriptions/Publications/Papers/9807_DKRZ_TechRep15/cera2.pdf
9. Schembera, B., Bönisch, T.: Challenges of research data management for high performance computing. In: Kamps, J., Tsakonas, G., Manolopoulos, Y., Iliadis, L., Karydis, I. (eds.) TPDL 2017. LNCS, vol. 10450, pp. 140–151. Springer, Cham (2017). https://doi.org/10.1007/978-3-319-67008-9_12
10. Wilkinson, M.D., et al.: The fair guiding principles for scientific data management and stewardship. Sci. Data 3 (2016). https://doi.org/10.1038/sdata.2016.18. Article no. 160018

Digital Libraries, Information Retrieval, Big, Linked, Social and Open Data

Analysing and Visualising Open Data Within the Data and Analytics Framework

Francesca Fallucchi[1,2(✉)] ⓘ, Michele Petito[3] ⓘ,
and Ernesto William De Luca[1,2] ⓘ

[1] DIII, Guglielmo Marconi University, Rome, Italy
{f.fallucchi,ew.deluca}@unimarconi.it
[2] DIFI, Georg Eckert Institute, Brunswick, Germany
{fallucchi,deluca}@gei.de
[3] Università di Pisa, Pisa, Italy
michele.petito@unipi.it

Abstract. The principles of open data and the five-star model allow companies to develop low-cost services and Public Administrations (PA) to improve efficiency. However, the process of implementing open data models and principles is not easy unless it is supported by an appropriate technology platform. Today there is a huge number of technological platforms which each promise to be the ideal solution for opening data. Current solutions (commercial or free) do not provide users with easy access to data, nor tools for analysing and displaying data. In this paper, we discuss the potential of the DAF (Data Analytics Framework), a project based on big data, which was created by the Italian government in 2017 and which fosters the integration and standardisation of data, as well as providing three powerful tools for analysis and data visualisation. The paper will then illustrate a concrete case of dashboard development within the DAF, released at an important hackathon organised by the Italian PA sector in October 2017. The project serves as a use case in DAF implementation, where its analytical tools are used for data analysis & visualisation. They also translate a large amount of data into simple representations and use clear and effective language.

Keywords: Big data · DAF · Data & analytics framework ·
Data visualisation · Dashboard · Open data · Linked open data

1 Introduction

The availability and release of open data is a valuable asset for society and for businesses, but in order to fully exploit the information it is necessary to make open data self-describing and to infer knowledge from aggregation and from the correlation of different datasets. For example, Linked Open Data (LOD) certainly allows the normal limits of open data to be exceeded, as it provides an identity and make it interoperable allowing the connection of information from different sources. This process semantically enriches the information making it more useful and easier to read.

Some challenges of the last years have slowed the spread of LOD and of open data quality in general (4 or 5 stars). This phenomenon can be ascribed to the large number

© Springer Nature Switzerland AG 2019
E. Garoufallou et al. (Eds.): MTSR 2018, CCIS 846, pp. 135–146, 2019.
https://doi.org/10.1007/978-3-030-14401-2_13

of databases and open data portals designed silos in the various PAs, so non-interoperable between them. Furthermore, very few companies have adopted standardised production, analysis or data storage. However, no Public Administration (PA) has ever designed a user experience/user interface (UX/UI) for data use and the transmission of information between PAs, companies and citizens. Data needs to be correlated with a team of data scientists and engineers using automatic tools within a big data platform and legislative framework to make the much-discussed data-driven decision making' actually possible.

In this scenario, the Data & Analytics Framework (DAF) [1] project by the Digital Transformation Team [2] represents Italy's latest effort to valorise public information assets, which started in 2010–2011 with the realisation of the first Italian open data portals (data.piemonte.it and dati.gov.it). They continued with the publication of the European and national metadata profile (DCAT-AP_IT) [3] defined within the framework of the European Interoperability Framework (EIF) [4] and the ISA2 programme. The aim of the project was to create an Italian data lake, an enormous pool of data in which anyone has had the opportunity, for their own field of expertise, to analyse data and interpret social and economic phenomena, make decisions, improve services to citizens and compete on the international scene [5]. The framework foresees the presence of a team of experts and competent governance that coordinates the generation, integration and standardisation of data. Data visualisation enables the real value of big data to be exploited, thus accelerating the understanding of data and allowing decision makers to act quickly; thanks to open source business intelligence tools integrated in DAF, you can generate excellent quality dashboards. This allows us to evaluate the real value of big data, accelerating the understanding of data [6].

Within the currently evolving DAF framework, we present a use case scenario for the creation of a complex dashboard, whose modules are highly integrable, scalable and powerful (see below). The immediacy of the instrument has no equal on the market: other systems either do not have tools for creating dashboards or those that exist are not perfectly integrated with the open data portal. Without such a tool, the user must download one or more datasets, create a dashboard on his/her machine using external software (e.g. Microsoft Excel) and then publish it on the open data portal. The process of development and publication in such cases is not yet fully automated or integrated. Therefore, the availability of two data visualisation tools (Metabase and Superset) in the DAF, enables simpler and faster sharing and reuse of dashboards as well as the dissemination of skills. Given the huge amount of data that the PA has available, the DAF is certainly an exceptionally important digital transformation project that could bring many benefits to the Italian PA, citizens and businesses. In this paper, we describe a real use case featuring the first ever dashboards created within the DAF, at the 'hack developers' event on October 30, 2017. The power and simplicity of the dashboards overcame the limitations many open data portals had encountered through *data visualization*.

The rest of the paper is organised as follows. Section 2 shows the most recent solutions for the development of existing dashboards. In Sect. 3 we describe the DAF in terms of its role as a big data platform and present a legislative framework for data-driven decisions to be applied in the PA. In Sect. 4 we describe the experimental framework used for dashboard development and the related results. Section 5 concludes the paper.

2   Related Works

Knowledge organisation systems are present in different fields from cultural heritage [7–10] to the PA domain [11, 12] or humanitarian assistance and disaster relief [13–15] as well as new challenges in health [16–18] and industry 4.0 [19, 20]. There are several solutions for dashboard development, but often these are proprietary software platforms on the cloud that are difficult to integrate with open data portals without paying a subscription. Some examples are Tableau [21], Google Data Studio [22] e Plot.ly [23]. These products provide aggregate functions such as: average, count, minimum, maximum and count distinct. Tableau allows the creation of complex dashboards with great flexibility that do not require in-depth technical knowledge, but do require an application to be installed on the PCs [24]. There is also a free version (Public Tableau) [25] for non-commercial use. Google Data Studio is a web service, but it does not allow the use of more than one dataset within the same dashboard. Plot.ly allows the creation and sharing of quick interactive dashboards. But it only accepts datasets with a maximum size of 5 MB and the published graphics must be public (for them to be private it is necessary to pay a subscription).

More integrated solutions also provide data catalogue functionality, such as Socrata [26], a platform used by the open data portal of the Lombardy Region [27]. In addition to the classic catalogues, with which users can navigate the various categories (security, health, taxes, etc.), the Socrata portal also provides an advanced tool for data visualisation, within which users can 'build' and save their dashboard (upon registration). The Socrata platform (on which the Lombardy data portal is based) is not open source and licenses are expensive. The DAF solution is an open source framework that would allow the Lombardy Region, for example, and in general the Italian state, to save public money in their PA. Another possible solution is Yucca [28], an open source project written in the Python programming language and freely downloadable from GitHub [29]. This platform makes it possible to implement application solutions based on the Internet of Things (IoT) and Big Data and provides a public data catalogue (Userportal) [30] as well as a tool for dashboard development: Yucca Dashboard [31]. The latter has many limitations in comparison to the power offered by the DAF data visualisation tools. To create a slice in Yucca it is necessary to explore the dataset through the Userportal, note the dataset code and the column names and then insert these parameters in the Yucca widget (the equivalent of the Superset slice). This process is transparent in the DAF, as Superset and Metabase provide access to the data sets on the big data platform and allow, through an exceptionally intuitive interface, the creation of complex dashboards with a much higher number of charts (47 in Superset compared to the 13 in Yucca) that are also of higher quality.

From a recent study [32] which analysed 1,104 open data portals and 1,921,636 datasets worldwide, it appears that CKAN [33] is the most widespread platform in the world (95.8%) followed by Socrata (1.6%). CKAN was developed in 2007 and, due to its free software license, (AGPL [34]) has been adopted by many organisations that aim to promote the accessibility of data, including the US federal government which in 2013 transferred approximately 73,000 datasets [35] to this format. At the time of writing (June 2018), the US open data portal reached 283,522 datasets. A further study

[36] states that CKAN is among the top four platforms in that it supports at least 9 of the 12 evaluation criteria. The same study highlights the deficiencies in CKAN with regards to data analysis and visualisation tools.

From the point of view of linked data [37], the main platforms currently on the market allow the metadata to be extracted from the dataset and allow for a description of its structure, but lack a guided process for the association of data to semantic concepts present in ontologies and vocabularies. The DAF, being connected to the repository of Onto-PiA [38], the network of Italian controlled ontologies and vocabularies, guides the user in a simplified way and allows an association between datasets, ontologies and controlled vocabularies, thus facilitating the standardisation process and the normalisation and integration of datasets from different sources.

Unfortunately, no data platform, including the DAF, provides a simple and user-friendly interface to allow RDF resources to be visualised or navigated [39]. The LodLive project [40] provides a demonstration of how simple it is to browse RDF resources. The software only works at the client level and executes calls on specific SPARQL endpoints [41] and retrieves serialised results in the JSON format, then analyses them in JavaScript and displays the resources and their properties in an HTML5 web page. The integration of LodLive into the DAF would allow the visualisation of an ontology in the form of a semantic chart that could be understood by anyone. It should be pointed out that none of the solutions described so far have a distributed processing capacity in which to apply machine learning models. The DAF, in addition to meeting the four requirements that a good data visualisation tool should have [24], provides Notebook Jupyter [42] a software that can perform complex analysis and visualisations, exploiting the processing power of the distributed calculation of Apache Spark [43], through languages such as Python, R [44], Julia [45] and Scala [46].

3   Data and Analytics Framework

The goal of the *Data & Analytics Framework* (DAF) [5] is to improve and simplify the interoperability and exchange of data between PAs; promoting and improving the management and usage of open data and optimising analysis and knowledge generation activities. The idea is to open the world of PA to the benefits offered by modern big data management and analysis platforms. The *DAF* is not simply a piece of software; it also includes the following components:

1. **a regulatory framework**: this is a normative component that institutionalises data and analytics activity at government level (art. 50-ter of the Code for Digital Administration)[1]. It provides the mandate for the PA that will manage the DAF, in compliance with privacy policy.
2. **the National Digital Data Platform**: which stores, integrates and standardises the data from each PA, implements machine learning mechanisms, redistributes data

---

[1] https://cad.readthedocs.io/it/v2017-12-13/_rst/capo5_sezione1_art50-ter.html.

via APIs and displays it (data portal). The system's flat design is divided into a back-end and a front-end:

a. *a big data platform* (back end), consisting of a data lake, a big data engine, tools for data lake data analysis and for the realisation of machine-learning models;

b. *a data portal* (front end), that is the user interface for the functionalities implemented in the DAF, which consists of a CKAN-based dataset catalogue and user interfaces to access the analysis and data visualisation tools;

3. **A big data team**, a team of data experts, composed of data scientists, data engineers and big data architects who provide the design and conceptual evolution of the big data platform, the construction of inter-connection models of the various sources data, data analysis, the development of machine learning models and the coordination of data application development.

The DAF was designed with the aim of collecting data from the various Italian PAs. As a result, it provides simple and powerful mechanisms for data ingestion (open and closed, structured and non-structured) to the big data platform with minimal human intervention. Storing a large amount of data within a single infrastructure has several advantages: the possibility of analysis, standardisation and exchange of public data; ease of retrieval and use of data; immediate sharing; the correlation between datasets; quality control; definition and monitoring of data-driven policies; and, the enhancement of information assets, valuable for civil society and businesses.

The DAF is a centralised environment that acquires public data of interest and makes it more usable. It improves and simplifies the interoperability and exchange of data between PAs, promoting the management and usage of open data, optimising analysis and knowledge generation activities. It allows the development of *data applications:* software applications that perform complex or simple operations, from simple *data retrieval* to *machine learning* techniques, and puts the analyses generated at the disposal of an end user or another application.

3.1 DAF Architecture

The DAF is based on a **big data platform**, composed of: a *data lake,* a set of *data engines* and tools for data communication. For data integration, the DAF has been designed with a 'silo-based' architecture; that is, components that are well separated and isolated but that interact through common interfaces, realised through the well-established mechanism of RESTful web services [47].

The DAF platform integrates a series of open source technologies and software, including:

- open source front-end platforms (Metabase [48], Superset [49], Jupyter Notebook [42], CKAN);
- open source back-end platforms and big data technologies (OpenTsdb [50], Livy [51], Nifi [52], etc.);
- software components developed by the Digital Transformation team to manage all the mechanisms underlying the DAF (for example, the Catalog Manager, the Ingestion Manager, etc.) [53].

3.2   Semantic Microservices

The DAF uses semantic web technologies, in particular those for LOD, which allow the current limitations of open data to be overcome, providing identity and interoperability not only between data but also between heterogeneous systems and infrastructures. Interoperability, in addition to being a necessary condition to provide high quality, safe, low cost and on schedule public services, allows better sharing of knowledge between countries and the achievement of common objectives.

The DAF is designed with a microservice infrastructure. In addition to the services for the management of the basic functions of the platform (core microservices), the DAF provides the semantic microservices that allow the implementation of semantic technologies, namely the standardisation, production, and publication of LOD. The architecture is internally split into different microservices [54]. The semantic microservices realised can be illustrated in 4 different areas (see Fig. 1): (1) catalogue front end, (2) standardised data ingestion in DAF, (3) RDF/linked data and triplestore, and (4) metadata validation and production.

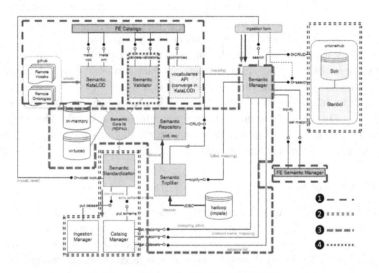

Fig. 1.   Semantic microservice DAF

3.3   Data Visualisation Tools

The use of semantic technologies certainly provides added value for the enhancement of public information assets, but it is not sufficient to make the large amount of PA data comprehensible to non-mathematicians or non-statisticians. Nowadays, data visualisation plays a fundamental role: good visualisation of data in fact allows information to be communicated clearly and efficiently. Effective visualisation helps users analyse and interpret data and evidence. It represents the core of business analytics: it is the way in which a large amount of complex data is transformed into easy-to-understand communication that is also rich in insight and accessible. Selected analytical and data visualisation tools make the process of transforming information an operation that can be performed by those with little or no data science expertise. In this context the choice of the appropriate data visualisation tool becomes significant.

The DAF provides data visualisation functionality through two docker containers:

1. *Metabase-PostgreSQL* [55] *-MongoDB* [56], this docker container is constructed using the data visualisation application Metabase and two databases: a relational database PostgreSQL and one called MongoDB (also known as NoSQL [57]);
2. *Superset-PostgreSQL-Redis* [58], this docker container encapsulates the Apache Superset open source software that, similarly to Metabase, allows data visualisation and business intelligence operations, all via the web. This product also uses PostgreSQL for the storage of relational data, while Redis is preferred for NoSQL-type data.

The DAF, through its 'DataPortal' component, offers citizens the opportunity to explore and discover data, make it available to communities and understand it more easily through user interfaces known as 'dashboards'. The dashboard allows data to be visualised in a creative and useful way for users, using the tools available to the DAF (Metabase, Superset and Notebook Jupyter).

3.4   Dashboard Design With Superset

For the implementation of some dashboards in DAF, we used Apache Superset, one of its integrated data visualisation tools. In Superset, slices are the basic blocks with which to build dashboards. The slices are based on D3.js [59] and can be reused on one or more dashboards. One slice is associated with one of the many Superset views but also with some parameters and filters. Firstly, to create visualisations a data source must be provided. Superset allows multiple data sources to be integrated. After the addition of a data source you should add tables from that DB and specify field properties. You can specify whether a field is groupable, filterable, temporal and so on. It is also possible to add custom metrics (in addition to default ones such as SUM, COUNT, COUNT DISTINCT, MEDIA, etc.). The metrics can be assigned one or more different values in the graphic display phase. To accomplish this, you need to follow the following procedure: in sources > tables select the table, then click on 'edit' to edit the table. In 'list columns' modify the fields that enable the dimensions to be altered: for example, the groupable option allows, during the creation of slices, rows to be grouped or filtered. You then create slices. A slice is a single plot based on your data. Note that although you can only build slices for one table at a time you can always create a new view by joining as many tables as needed. Depending on the type of graph used, it is possible to create different slices. For example, the 'tree map' slice is a quantitative representation of hierarchical data in a limited space such as a computer screen. The data is displayed as rectangles of various sizes and colours, which contain other smaller rectangles (lower-level elements derived from the upper layer). A 'tree map' can be extended to hierarchies of any depth, number of levels and components, because the dynamic view ranges from the general to the most minute details. Another example of a graph is the 'Sunburst': a visualisation similar to the pie-chart but hierarchical. It is ideal for showing both proportions and hierarchies within a single data series. DAF, as data visualisation tool, offers evident benefits. Below we describe its first use in developing dashboards using its integrated data visualisation tools (see Sect. 4).

4 Case Study

At the Italy Hack.Developers [60] event, a code sprint for programmers and IT professionals with the aim of contributing to the open source projects of the Italian PA, the participants experimented with DAF (alpha version) for the first time. The objective was to develop a number of dashboards using Apache Superset, one of the data visualisation tools integrated into DAF.

The following four dashboards, created during the hackathon, were announced on 21 November 2017 in Rome, in the presence of Diego Piacentini, Government Commissioner for the implementation of the Italian Digital Agenda.

The first dashboard was related to a dataset related to Italian parapharmacies and consisted of two slices. One of the slices of this dashboard was created using 'map box', a map based on OpenStreetMap, to provide a geolocalised display of parapharmacies. This was possible thanks to the presence in the open dataset of the longitude and latitude fields.

The second dashboard concerned a dataset from the municipality of Roma Capitale concerning disinfestation activities against the tiger mosquito. The dashboard was created using three 'distribution - bar chart' slices. The three slices were substantially the same, but each of them was associated with a dataset from a different year (2014, 2015 and 2016).

The third dashboard was created thanks to an open dataset from the Ministry of Economic Development (MISE) containing a geolocalised list of fuel distributors. To make the reading of the dataset clearer, five slices were used, they were: two 'pie charts', a 'map box', a 'filter box' and a 'table view'. In this way it was possible to immediately and easily communicate the geographical distribution and types of fuel distributors.

The fourth dashboard was the most complex and represented a dataset owned by the Ministry of Economy and Finance (MEF) related to the income of Italians to 2015. The dataset, in CSV format, had 47 columns, each representing a type of income. We analysed only those considered most significant. We created several slices in order to realise the dashboard: see examples below.

The 'country map' (left in Fig. 2) shows the reference nation (in this case Italy) divided according to provinces. Through the use of colours, it is possible to identify at a glance the richest and poorest areas of Italy. The map shows a gap between the incomes of the central-northern regions compared to that of the southern regions. The value shown is the income of the individual provinces. An ISO standard that defines geographical codes was used to identify the provinces, in the case of Italy this is 3166-2: IT [61].

The 'table view' (right in Fig. 2) is a tabular representation of the numerical data from certain income categories, such as income from a building, a pension or that of an employee. The data can be arranged by clicking on any of the 4 columns: in this way it is possible to find out the amount of gross income for each province. Milan is the

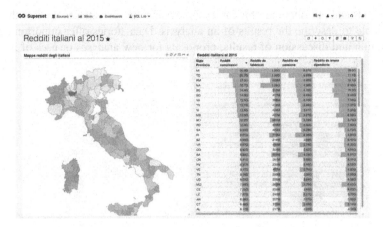

Fig. 2. The first two slices of the 'Italian income' dashboard

province with the highest taxable income, while Trieste has the lowest. However, it must be emphasised that these indices are absolute. A statistical analysis published by the MEF[2] considers the average income, calculated according to the number of tax payers per region: this analysis shows that the region with the highest overall average income is Lombardy (24,520 euro) followed by the province of Bolzano (22,860 euros), while Calabria has the lowest average income (14,780 euros). The study by the MEF provides a great deal of other interesting data: for example, it shows that the total Italian income of 2,015 amounts to about 833 billion euros for an average value of 20,690 euros per person (an increase of 1.9% compared to 2014). With regard to types of income; that of employees and retirees represented approximately 82% of total declared income, while retirement income represented about 30%.

In the 'pie chart' representation (see Fig. 3), Italian pension earnings were compared with income from employment. From the analysis it is possible to detect a close correlation between the two types of income. The region with the highest income (both pension and employee) is Lombardy, followed by the

Veneto and Emilia. Moreover we could use the 'filter' function to redraw all the graphs, recalculated according to the selected provinces, thus allowing more focused analyses to be conducted.

These graphs represent only a small example of what can be achieved with open data on the MEF website. As mentioned at the beginning, only a few columns were selected from the original dataset, thus excluding some important income categories such as self-employed workers and companies. Moreover, as already mentioned above, the incomes are represented by absolute values, as opposed to more informative average values. Despite these limitations it was possible to show how simple it is to create dashboards with the DAF and to obtain information potentially useful for growth from the perspective of PAs, businesses and citizens. The heart of the DAF is in fact the ability to

---

[2] http://www1.finanze.gov.it/finanze2/analisi_stat/v_4_0_0/contenuti/analisi_dati_2015_irpef.pdf?d= 1494338400.

share insights and information. This can be done using the 'data stories' tool, with which it is possible to describe the results of an analysis. Data stories offer opportunities for collaboration and discussion of results, proposals for new analyses or uses of insights.

Fig. 3. Comparison between pension income and employee income.

5   Conclusion

In this paper we presented the shortcomings of the main data platforms and highlighted the differences with the new DAF project. In particular, we focused on its architecture and its semantic microservices that allow the implementation of the linked open data paradigm, which is often disregarded by the competing platforms. Finally, we presented and discussed real examples of a visual representation of the income data of Italian citizens created with Apache Superset.

The DAF is a very important project for growth in Italy because it helps to improve the quality of open data and therefore improves the services offered to citizens and businesses. The data portal is not simply a catalogue of open data, but a platform that helps to disseminate the insights contained in the data and to stimulate the participation and collaboration of citizens. Given the nature of the project (open source) we expect many developers, companies and PAs will contribute further through a pull request on GitHub. Moreover, this platform can be used and adapted by public administrations in other countries or even by private companies for data analysis (e.g. in the IoT domain).

References

1. Lillo, R., et al.: Data & Analytics Framework. https://developers.italia.it/en/daf/
2. Government Digital Service, Digital Transf. (2014). https://www.gov.uk/transformation
3. DCAT-AP_IT v1.0 – Profilo italiano di DCAT-AP | Dati.gov.it. https://www.dati.gov.it/content/dcat-ap-it-v10-profilo-italiano-dcat-ap-0
4. EIF, European Interoperability Framework, White Pages (2004). https://ec.europa.eu/isa2/eif_en
5. Lillo, R.: Data and Analytics Framework. How Public Sector Can Profit from Its Immense Asset, Data, pp. 3–9 (2018)
6. Sedkaoui, S., Monino, J.L.: Big Data, Open Data and Data Development. ISTE-Wiley, New York (2016). https://books.google.it/books?id=IfpRCgAAQBAJ. ISBN 9781848218802

7. Beccaceci, R., et al.: Education with 'living artworks' in museums. In: CSEDU 2009 - Proceedings of the 1st Inter. Conference on Computer Supported Education, vol. 1 (2009)
8. Arcidiacono, G., et al.: The use of lean six sigma methodology in digital curation. In: CEUR Workshop Proceedings, no. 2014 (2016)
9. Fallucchi, F., et al.: Connecting and mapping LOD and CMDI through knowledge organization. In: Track Digital Humanities and Digital Curation of the 12th Metadata and Semantics Research Conference, 23–26 October 2018, Limassol, Cyprus (2018)
10. Fallucchi, F. et al.: Creating CMDI-profiles for textbook resources. In: Track Digital Humanities and Digital Curation of the 12th Metadata and Semantics Research Conference, 23–26 October 2018, Limassol, Cyprus (2018)
11. Fallucchi, F., Alfonsi, E., Ligi, A., Tarquini, M.: Ontology-driven public administration web hosting monitoring system. In: Meersman, R., et al. (eds.) On the Move to Meaningful Internet Systems: OTM 2014. LNCS, vol. 8842, pp. 618–625. Springer, Heidelberg (2014). https://doi.org/10.1007/978-3-662-45550-0_63
12. Bianchi, M., et al.: Service level agreement constraints into processes for document classification. In: Proceedings of 16th International Conference on Enterprise Information Systems vol. 1 (2014)
13. Zhang, D., et al.: A knowledge management framework for the support of decision making in humanitarian assistance/disaster relief. Knowl. Inf. Syst. 4(3), 370–385 (2002)
14. Fallucchi, F., et al.: Supporting humanitarian logistics with intelligent applications for disaster management. In: INTELLI 2016, p. 64 (2016)
15. Fallucchi, F., Tarquini, M., De Luca, E.W.: Knowledge Management for the Support of Logistics During Humanitarian Assistance and Disaster Relief (HADR). In: Díaz, P., Bellamine Ben Saoud, N., Dugdale, J., Hanachi, C. (eds.) ISCRAM-med 2016. LNBIP, vol. 265, pp. 226–233. Springer, Cham (2016). https://doi.org/10.1007/978-3-319-47093-1_19
16. Ferroni, P., et al.: Risk assessment for venous thromboembolism in chemotherapy-treated ambulatory cancer patients. Med. Decis. Mak. 37(2), 234–242 (2017)
17. Ferroni, P., et al.: Validation of a machine learning approach for venous thromboembolism risk prediction in oncology. Dis. Markers 2017, 1–7 (2017)
18. Scarpato, N., Pieroni, A., Di Nunzio, L., Fallucchi, F.: E-health-IoT universe: a review. Int. J. Adv. Sci. Eng. Inf. Technol. 7(6), 2328–2336 (2017)
19. Pieroni, A., Scarpato, N., Brilli, M:. Industry 4.0 revolution in autonomous and connected vehicle a non-conventional approach to manage big data. J. Theor. Appl. Inf. Technol. 96(1), 10–18 (2018)
20. Pieroni, A., Scarpato, N., Di Nunzio, L., Fallucchi, F., Raso, M.: Smarter City: smart energy grid based on blockchain technology. Int. J. Adv. Sci. Eng. Inf. Technol. 8(1), 298–306 (2018)
21. Tableau, Business Intelligence and Analytics (2016). https://www.tableau.com/
22. Google Data Board. http://think.withgoogle.com/databoard/#lang=en-us&study=23&topic=59
23. Modern Visualization for the Data Era - Plotly. https://plot.ly/
24. Alvaro Graves, J.H.: Visualization tools for open government data (2013)
25. Tableau, Free Data Visualization Software, Tableau Public (2011). http://www.tableausoftware.com/public
26. Socrata: Data-Driven Innovation of Government Programs. https://socrata.com/
27. Open Data Regione Lombardia. https://www.dati.lombardia.it/
28. Presentation - Smartdatanet. http://www.smartdatanet.it/presentation.html
29. The world's leading software development platform GitHub. https://github.com/
30. Yucca - Cerca Dati. https://userportal.smartdatanet.it/userportal/#/dataexplorer/search
31. Dashboard - Smartdatanet. http://www.smartdatanet.it/yuccadashboard/dashboard.html

32. Correa, A.S., et al.: Investigating open data portals automatically. In: Proceedings of 19th Annual International Conference on Digital Government Research Governance in the Data Age, pp. 1–10 (2018)
33. CKAN. https://ckan.org/
34. affero.org: affero general public license faqs. http://www.affero.org/oagf.html
35. U.S. government's data portal Data.gov relaunched on CKAN – ckan. https://ckan.org/2013/05/23/data-gov-relaunch-on-ckan/
36. Deliverable 2.1 now available | ROUTE-TO-PA. https://routetopa.eu/deliverable-2-1-state-of-the-art-report-and-evaluation-of-existing-open-data-platforms-now-available/
37. Linked Data - Design Issues. https://www.w3.org/DesignIssues/LinkedData.html
38. GitHub - italia/daf-ontologie-vocabolari-controllati: Elenco di ontologie e vocabolari controllati. https://github.com/italia/daf-ontologie-vocabolari-controllati
39. RDF - Semantic Web Standards. https://www.w3.org/RDF/
40. Camarda, D.V., et al.: LodLive, exploring the web of data. In: Proceedings of the 8th International Conference on Semantic Systems - I-SEMANTICS 2012, p. 197 (2012)
41. Aliprand, J., Unicode Consortium: The Unicode standard. Addison-Wesley, Reading (2003)
42. Project Jupyter, Project Jupyter | Home (2017). http://jupyter.org/
43. Apache SparkTM - Unified Analytics Engine for Big Data. https://spark.apache.org/
44. R. C. Team: The R Project for Statistical Computing, Http://Www.R-Project.Org/ (2013). https://www.r-project.org/
45. Edelman, A.: The Julia Language (2013). http://julialang.org/
46. Scala, The Scala Programming Language (2011). http://www.scala-lang.org/
47. R. T. Fielding: Architectural Styles and the Design of Network-based Software Architectures (2000)
48. Metabase https://www.metabase.com/
49. Apache Superset (incubating) (2016). https://superset.incubator.apache.org/index.html
50. StumbleUpon, OpenTSDB - A Distributed, Scalable Monitoring System (2012). http://opentsdb.net/
51. Apache Livy. https://livy.incubator.apache.org/
52. The Apache Software Foundation, Apache NiFi, Website (2017). https://nifi.apache.org/
53. GitHub - italia/daf: Data Analytics Framework (DAF). https://github.com/italia/daf
54. Daf Semantics repository. https://github.com/italia/daf-semantics/
55. PostgreSQL, PostgreSQL: The world's most advanced open source database, Http://Www.Postgresql.Org/ (2014). http://www.postgresql.org/. Accessed 07 June 2018
56. MongoDB, MongoDB for GIANT Ideas | MongoDB, MongoDB (2018). https://www.mongodb.com/
57. Adhikari, M., Kar, S.: NoSQL databases, Handbook of Research on Securing Cloud-Based Databases with Biometric Applications (2014). https://www.scopus.com/inward/record.uri?eid=2-s2.0-84945404497&doi=10.4018%2F978-1-4666-65590.ch006&partnerID=40&md5=227b5b6488851b9879d98ddc127ab017
58. Redis. https://redis.io/
59. D3.js - Data-Driven Documents. https://d3js.org/
60. Hack.Developers - Cambia la PA, Riavvia il sistema Operativo del Paese. https://hack.developers.italia.it/
61. ISO 3166-2:IT - Wikipedia. https://it.wikipedia.org/wiki/ISO_3166-2:IT

Formalizing Enrichment Mechanisms
for Bibliographic Ontologies
in the Semantic Web

Helena Simões Patrício[1,2]([⊠]) (iD), Maria Inês Cordeiro[1]([⊠]) (iD),
and Pedro Nogueira Ramos[2,3]([⊠]) (iD)

[1] Biblioteca Nacional de Portugal, Lisbon, Portugal
{hpatricio, icordeiro}@bnportugal.pt
[2] Information Sciences, Technologies and Architecture Research Center
(ISTAR-IUL), Lisbon, Portugal
[3] University Institute of Lisbon (ISCTE-IUL), Lisbon, Portugal
pedro.ramos@iscte-iul.pt

Abstract. This paper presents an analysis of current limitations to the reuse of
bibliographic data in the Semantic Web and a research proposal towards solutions to overcome them. The limitations identified derive from the insufficient
convergence between existing bibliographic ontologies and the principles and
techniques of linked open data (LOD); lack of a common conceptual framework
for a diversity of standards often used together; reduced use of links to external
vocabularies and absence of Semantic Web mechanisms to formalize relationships between vocabularies, as well as limitations of Semantic Web languages
for the requirements of bibliographic data interoperability. A proposal is
advanced to investigate the hypothesis of creating a reference model and
specifying a superontology to overcome the misalignments found, as well as the
use of SHACL (Shapes Constraint Language) to solve current limitations of
RDF languages.

Keywords: Linked open data · Bibliographic data · Semantic Web · SHACL ·
LOD validation · Ontologies · Reference model · Bibliographic standards

1 Introduction

The principles of the Semantic Web and the new data structures emerging from RDF
languages have raised the need for new models of bibliographic description. On this
matter Godby, Wang and Mixter [1] acknowledge that there is already a critical mass of
bibliographic data available as linked data, yet no corresponding evolution of the
underlying standards did occur, thus calling for a reflection on the modeling of bibliographic data in the context of the Semantic Web.

From the most recent literature on the subject it is possible to identify a set of
limitations to a full convergence of the bibliographic ontologies with the principles and
techniques of the Semantic Web. Moreover, the RDF language does not provide means
for the needs of validation, quality and consistency control of ontologies.

© Springer Nature Switzerland AG 2019
E. Garoufallou et al. (Eds.): MTSR 2018, CCIS 846, pp. 147–158, 2019.
https://doi.org/10.1007/978-3-030-14401-2_14

In the following sections the limitations and inadequacies of bibliographic ontologies and RDF languages are analyzed and the possibilities to overcome them through solutions based on semantic enrichment and validation of their vocabularies are explored.

2 Limitations at the Conceptual Level

Taking into account that modelling languages are built with a particular paradigm in mind, which constrains its applicability [2] and the profound impact of the new Semantic Web paradigm, it is important to understand to what extent the conceptual models created in recent years for bibliographic information translate such new paradigm and ensure the subsequent alignment. At this level, we refer to two types of limitations: first, the inadequacy for the Semantic Web of both the FRBR (Functional Requirements for Bibliographic Records) model[1] and its representations in RDF; and second, the absence of a framing reference model.

2.1 Shortcomings of the FRBR Model

Despite being the first conceptual model explicitly defined for bibliographic data and resulting from the emergence of Internet and World Wide Web technologies, FRBR is not aligned with the Semantic Web paradigm. In fact, one of the criticisms about FRBR is that its elements have derived from standards of a paradigm prior to the Semantic Web. For Willer and Dunsire [3], this reinforces the need to rethink the more abstract models, rather than just define a new framework for old data elements. In the same line, Murray [4] identifies several issues from the fact that the model is based on requirements defined for functions and data structures characteristic of legacy systems such as card catalogues or MARC (Machine Readable Cataloging) formats, resulting in the creation of entities, attributes and relationships derived from pre-existing standards. Besides, the FRBR model does not provide context for its elements that allow them to be understood in wider environments, whether bibliographic or other domains. This makes it difficult for FRBR descriptions to co-exist with descriptions produced by different organizations and make FRBR entities to be seen as purely theoretical and not as data structures designed to be connected [4].

As for FRBR representations in Semantic Web languages, such as FRBRer[2], FRBR Core[3] and FRBRoo[4] ontologies, some authors [5, 6, e.g.] point out that generally these models are not well aligned with the principles and techniques of linked data because they do not allow for class hierarchy, thus not enabling transitivity and basic mechanisms of inference. Consequently, the entities below the WEMI (Work, Expression, Manifestation, Item) sequence are unable to use the attributes of the higher entities.

---

[1] https://www.ifla.org/publications/functional-requirements-for-bibliographic-records.

[2] http://iflastandards.info/ns/fr/frbr/frbrer/.

[3] http://vocab.org/frbr/core.rdf.

[4] https://www.ifla.org/files/assets/cataloguing/FRBRoo/frbroo_v_2.4.pdf.

For Coyle [6], this intransitivity derives from the ER (Entity-Relationship) model, which does not support hierarchies.

Zapounidou, Sfakakis and Papatheodorou [7] claim that there is no hierarchy in WEMI entities because they have been modelled as disjoint classes and implemented with cardinality constraints that do not determine the transitivity of a hierarchy, but rather a sequence of WEMI entities' instantiations. In fact, the WEMI class disjunction prevents the sharing of properties or relationships and the connection to similar data [8] and determines that each instance can only belong to one of the WEMI classes, while in the actual world resources can be instances of more than one class [9].

Clearly, divergences most evident between FRBR and the Semantic Web result from ER model being natural to the "closed world" of databases [8], which may explain the fact that in many cases the representation of FRBR for the Semantic Web have been a mere "syntactic transcription" in RDF [3]. Baker, Coyle and Petiya [9] point out that the application of ER in FRBR has determined that WEMI entities have certain attributes (domain and range constraints) and are linked together by dependency relationships (cardinality restrictions). Therefore, according to the ER model, it should be possible to validate data against these constraints. It happens, however, that these ER concepts do not fit the Semantic Web, since neither the RDF domain constraints nor the cardinality of OWL (Ontology Web Language)[5] axioms can validate data. In both cases, they are constraints that just allow to infer new information, which may be wrong. This is a problem of Semantic Web languages, to be discussed later, that also translates in the superficial nature of FRBR publications in RDFS (Resource Description Framework Schema)[6]/OWL. For example, in the FRBRer ontology a cardinality constraint has been specified which determines that an *expression* can only be an execution of one single *work*. In this case, if an *expression* is related to more than one *work*, semantic reasoners will not mark these statements as error; instead, they will infer that both works are the same with different URIs and this new inferred information may not be correct [9].

As a "multi-entity" model, FRBR has changed the focus from the record as a whole to its disaggregated data components where elements and attributes are not seen as parts of a record but become linked to specific entities [9]. This model is perfectly suited to the rules underlying linked data, because data being freed from the record unit can more easily be linked to other information, allowing the expression of multiple points of view about a given resource [1]. In this respect, Murray and Tillet [10] even argue that each FRBR entity is not properly an autonomous entity, but rather a point of view about a resource which in a multi-entity perspective can be expressed in bibliographic data graphs that bring together multiple statements or points of view on a given resource. Therefore, it can be concluded that the objective of having a single bibliographic model, as in the creation of FRBR in the 1990s, is outdated, since RDF is prepared to optimize the fusion of data from multiple sources through graph structures which group together multiple descriptions or points of view [9, 11].

---

[5] https://www.w3.org/TR/owl2-primer/.

[6] https://www.w3.org/TR/rdf-schema/.

The criticism about FRBR arises precisely from the fact that the model neither establishes the creation of a "super-entity" that could group WEMI entities nor assigns them properties to allow them to be treated as a whole. On the other hand, FRBR does not appear as the model most appropriate to the perspective of entities as points of view because it makes a strict demarcation of WEMI entities and specifies with little clarity the relations between them. For these reasons, some authors refer to the need of rethinking FRBR [9, 11] and consider the possibility of creating a multi-entity model different from FRBR, as the distinction between WEMI entities cannot be so rigid because such distinction is not universal and varies culturally [10].

In August 2017, a new model, named IFLA Library Reference Model (IFLA-LRM) was approved [12], envisaging not only the editorial consolidation of the various models of the FRBR family, but also the construction of a single and coherent model capable of structuring the bibliographic data more clearly and better adapted to the Semantic Web [13] and of combining the different analysis' standpoints of the various FRBR models by using a common model and terminology [14]. IFLA-LRM maintains the ER framework, therefore the above-mentioned criticisms in this respect still apply. As for the remaining issues inherent to FRBR, with the new model all seems to be overcome [13]. However, as we are not aware of initiatives to represent IFLA-LRM in RDFS or OWL and previous FRBR representations are still valid, it seems relevant to ask whether convergence with the Semantic Web has improved with the new model and to analyze the transformation initiatives that, meanwhile, will appear.

2.2 Absence of a Conceptual Framework for Bibliographic Standards

The scattered nature of existing bibliographic standards has been replicated in the respective representations in RDF languages, with no guarantee of the consistency and quality of their inter-relationship. The need for a common conceptual model is revealed, first and foremost, in the relationship between standards because the multiplicity of them in the bibliographic field can easily lead to contradiction and difficulties in their combined application [15]. Sprochi [16] points out the need for a reference model to frame the different levels of bibliographic standards, such as FRBR, RDA and BIBFRAME, because they are closely related and strongly dependent on one another for implementation.

In what concerns ISBD (International Standard Bibliographic Description), the main criticisms of its representation as LOD are the lack of a model based on entities and relationships, as it is typical of the Semantic Web, in contrast with its underlying flat model of the bibliographic record as a text [17], with some authors suggesting that ISBD should be replaced by another language of description more adequate to the new paradigms [3].

RDA (Resource Description and Access), in turn, is a standard already born in the generation of FRBR that is, according to most authors [6, 18, e.g.], completely compatible with the Semantic Web because it implements FRBR as a multi-entity conceptual model and, in its RDF representation[7], is connected to DCMI Metadata Terms[8]

---

[7] http://www.rdaregistry.info/.

[8] http://dublincore.org/documents/dcmi-terms/.

by subclass relationships with its elements, which facilitates understanding the more than 900 RDA elements and prevents them to get stuck in bibliographic data silos [6]. However, some authors [14, e.g.] point out significant differences between the FRBR model and RDA which may justify a deeper analysis of this bibliographic standard.

At the level of data coding standards, the introduction of conceptual models based on graphs and tree models, such as FRBR, made MARC formats unsuitable because of their "record model" structure of "flat" files originally thought to be sequentially accessed. This not only implies a considerable duplication of metadata but also relies on textual data (textual values) instead of Uniform Resource Identifiers (URI). Although having representations in RDF, MARC formats have structural limitations to adapt to the Web environment because they are based on coding standards older than 40 years and originally designed to automate the creation and printing of catalogue cards [18].

These limitations motivated, in 2008, the beginning of a transition process towards a new bibliographic format aligned with the Semantic Web, BIBFRAME[9]. BIB-FRAME appears among the ontologies most compatible with the open Web because, unlike FRBR, it uses the class hierarchy and does not define disjunctions between classes [6].

With regard to local initiatives for the publication of LOD datasets by libraries, the lack of a comprehensive bibliographic standard results in the proliferation of ontologies developed locally as "proving ground" for the experimentation of models of data transformation [19]. The absence of a common conceptual framework is evident from the combined application of standards with different levels of abstraction and developed upon very different conceptual models. Suominen and Hyvonen [20] argue that libraries are risking to abandon "silos" of MARC data to adopt "silos" of linked data, since the models being adopted may be incompatible.

3 Limitations in Semantic Interoperability

RDF is a data language that relies on the use of triples to declare facts about resources. In the Semantic Web, aggregation of data from multiple sources is achieved through URIs that identify the component parts (classes and properties) of RDF triples and allow pointing to vocabularies or ontologies that contain the definitions of such classes and properties. Ontologies are, thus, fundamental to the Semantic Web, as vocabularies of elements that provide the correct interpretation of the linked data, making them self-descriptive [21].

An ontology is the explicit and shared formal representation of a conceptualization, defining a set of representation primitives for modeling a domain of knowledge or discourse [22]. In the context of the Semantic Web, ontologies are used to specify conceptual vocabularies for information sharing between systems, providing services that facilitate interoperability between multiple and diverse systems [22].

In this context, it is important to analyze the level of semantic interoperability of bibliographic ontologies. From the main bibliography and a first analysis of

---

[9] https://www.loc.gov/bibframe/.

bibliographic ontologies, the most frequent and transversal aspects are highlighted: underuse of semantic mechanisms; reduced number of links to other vocabularies; and point-to-point mappings.

3.1   Underuse of the Semantic Mechanisms of Classification and Hierarchy

Not making use in bibliographic vocabularies of basic mechanisms of the Semantic Web, such as class hierarchy or other class-level relationships, prevents the bibliographic domain from taking advantage of all the potentialities of linked data technologies. For example, not using classification, which relates all instances of a given class to the instances of another class, prevents inference inherent to classification, with relationships having to be at the individual level, i.e., at the level of data and not at that of vocabulary.

Another example is the non-use of hierarchies or relationships between classes: the addition of a new class obliges to define relationships at the instance level because it is not possible to infer new relationships from already established relationships with any superclass to which the new class would belong. In fact, the implementation of RDA in RDF makes little use of class hierarchy and shows few relationships between terms, which is probably a remnant of its origins as a list of terms [6].

Another aspect is data constraints which, most often, in bibliographic standards are not formalized with inference languages, rather consisting of textual notes only.

3.2   Reduced Linking to Other Vocabularies

Linking to URIs of elements from external ontologies is an essential component of the linked data technique. However, in the development of bibliographic ontologies a cherry-picking methodology [19] has been followed, meaning the use of elements from external vocabularies without a semantic link to elements of the ontology that instantiates external elements, not allowing these to benefit from the advantages of the semantic integration of vocabularies, also called LOV - Linked Open Vocabularies.

For example, if a particular element of a local ontology would be linked to a subclass of an ontology element such as schema.org, any instance of the local class would be, by the semantic mechanism of inheritance, an instance of the superclass of schema.org, thus making it possible to be directly "consumed" by search engines of a general scope. That is, domain-specific vocabularies, such as those of the bibliographic domain, would become visible to general search engines [19].

In fact, a preliminary analysis of bibliographic standards published in the linked data cloud shows that, in general, there are few links to data elements of other ontologies or little use of elements from external vocabularies. For example, FRBRer, representing the FRBR conceptual model, makes use of elements from two external ontologies only: FOAF (Friend of a Friend) and DCMES, applying them just to identify administrative data about the ontology itself, such as the FRBR *title* and *creator* of the ontology homepage.

On the other hand, despite most standard ontologies being based on the FRBR model, the formal use of elements from FRBR ontologies is not much representative.

According to information on the LOV website, only the ISBD ontology makes use of the official IFLA representation of FRBRer. Often the replication of external vocabulary elements happens because, at the moment the ontology is developed, there is still no RDF representation of such external vocabularies, as it happened, for example, with the creation of FRBR classes in RDA that adopts FRBR as a conceptual model but did not choose to follow any of the vocabularies that express FRBR in RDF, establishing instead its own FRBR classes [6, 9].

As for initiatives of publishing bibliographic datasets as LOD, libraries have preferentially chosen to mix elements from external ontologies with locally developed ontologies of data elements. It happens, however, that local elements are created without any link to standard bibliographic vocabularies (for example, the National Library of Spain data is based on FRBR but created its own representation of elements); other issues are limitations arising from the application of standard ontology elements at the level of data instantiation only, where they appear mixed with the local elements. Finally, the formalization of elements taken from different bibliographic standards is often absent, occurring in a combination of standards with different levels of abstraction and different conceptual models. These issues may be caused by the experimental nature of many bibliographic data transformation initiatives or even, as Godby [19] points out, by the lack of time for discussion and integration of elements of pre-existing ontologies.

3.3   Proliferation of Vocabularies

The dispersion of bibliographic standards was replicated in their publication as RDF ontologies, with no guarantee of consistency and quality of their interrelationship. According to Zapounidou, Sfakakis and Papatheodorou [7] the structural heterogeneity of bibliographic standards can lead to incompatibilities between standards of different levels of abstraction. For example, the implementation of FRBRer or FRBRoo in BIBFRAME is impossible, because in BIBFRAME there is a 1:1 relationship between *Work* and *Item* classes, whereas in FRBR ontologies the relation between these classes is 1:*. The same authors also raise other structural problems such as conflicts between the primitives of different models and different modeling solutions for the same entities of the real world. Besides the already mentioned standards, other ontologies and models with bibliographic components will be considered in our research, such as BIBO[10], VIVO[11] and the CERIF model[12].

In the process of transforming bibliographic data into LOD, libraries define the vocabularies or ontologies to be used for publishing datasets. It may happen that this mixture of ontologies and creation of new elements/properties does not fit the data to be modeled [23].

---

[10] BIBO – The Bibliographic Ontology - http://bibliontology.com.

[11] VIVO Ontology for Researcher Discovery - http://purl.bioontology.org/ontology/VIVO.

[12] CERIF - The Common European Research Information Format - https://www.eurocris.org/cerif/main-features-cerif.

In addition to the fragmentation of standard ontologies used by libraries, each library develops its own ontology, both standard and local ontologies can be based in very different conceptual models. In fact, as Suominen and Hyvonen [20] point out, bibliographic data expressed in different vocabularies can be very difficult to combine and use together; and, although small differences in vocabulary can be solved using mappings, it is not clear if this can suffice to guarantee the interoperability of bibliographic data in the Semantic Web.

The main problems encountered in library LOD transformation initiatives are the proliferation of vocabularies for the same data, coupled with the lack of good practice in vocabulary development and management. This is leading to truly chaotic situations [20, 23–25]. Thus, it is urgent to find common strategies for the publication, discovery, evaluation and mapping of vocabularies of bibliographic elements [24].

The absence of a common conceptual model and methodology for the creation or mapping of linked data in the library field has led to the proliferation of multiple independent efforts to map and combine data, which makes initiatives difficult to sustain [26]. The excessive number of vocabularies used in the publication of bibliographic data as linked data impairs the reusability of such data. This diversity is well demonstrated in Willer and Dunsire [3] analysis of vocabulary and ontology diversity.

3.4   Point-to-Point Mappings

As mentioned in Sect. 3.2, links to external vocabularies are rarely used in bibliographic ontologies; it is therefore important to know if there are mappings between elements of different ontologies made by "third party" ontologies. Although there are several alignments and mappings between bibliographic ontologies, we are not aware of any standard ontology created at a higher level to express semantic relations between vocabularies.

Indeed, existing mappings have been developed in a distributed manner, making point-to-point connections between ontology elements. The best-known example are the alignments made by the IFLA ISBD Working Group, relating not only IFLA standards to each other (FRBR, UNIMARC and ISBD), but also ISBD with the external vocabulary RDA. As the alignments are made unidirectionally from ISBD to RDA, it is necessary to have the reverse mapping from RDA to ISBD [27]. This would not be needed if there was a central ontology for representing, at a higher level of abstraction, the semantic connections between these vocabularies.

Current mappings between bibliographic ontologies are being carried out as "crosswalks" or schema-to-schema mappings, characteristic of XML. This type of relationship between elements of different vocabularies ensures a "mapping interoperability" that facilitates the exchange of data between different schemas but does not solve semantic compatibility issues [28]. In fact, this type of mapping works for 1:1 relationships, but does not ensure semantic interoperability in 1:* or *:1 relationships and does not solve situations of mismatch as well. For these cases, one must consider the use of mechanisms of semantic linking between the elements, attributes, entities and relationships of different ontologies [29].

Regarding technologies feasibility assessment, the Systematic Literature Review of linked data software tools undertaken by Barbosa [30] will be considered in our research.

4   RDF/RDFS/OWL Limitations

As already mentioned in previous parts of this paper, there are also issues with the use of Semantic Web languages of the RDF family for the representation of bibliographic data. In this section, they are reviewed and synthesized in two main aspects: (i) the missing capability for data structures validation; and (ii) the poor adequacy for the purposes and characteristics of bibliographic data, especially given the granularity and atomization of its elements.

In the first aspect, we should remind that FRBR applies the ER model, establishing for each entity its own attributes or properties. However, in RDF the use of a certain property cannot be limited to a certain class, due to the Semantic Web "AAA Principle" that states that *Anyone can say Anything about Anything*. In fact, the use of RDF restrictions such as "range" and "domain" to constrain the use of a property to a certain class allows the inference of new information only, not its validation. The specification of data structures that can be validated against certain constraints is a requirement of multi-entity models such as FRBR, but this will have to be done with languages other than those of the RDF family [9].

The same limitation applies to hierarchy: RDF expresses transitive properties and classes, but for inference only. It is not possible to use RDF to "impose" a given hierarchy. That is, RDF does not solve the historical problems of lack of transitivity of bibliographic data models, since it allows to connect WEMI entities, for example, but not in a hierarchical way. RDF has a graph rather than a hierarchical or tree structure, so it can connect virtually everything in any direction [15].

The specification of many constraints in RDF, which occur in most bibliographic ontologies, is also not very adequate from the point of view of the graph structure itself. In fact, vocabularies in RDF are as more reusable as they have fewer data constraints. Constraints greatly isolate the ontologies and should be expressed in "profiles" for data quality control, independently of the ontologies to which they apply [9].

In the second aspect, the adequacy for the purposes and characteristics of bibliographic data, Yee [15] argues that RDF is not suitable for bibliographic data because of its excessive atomization, reflected in standards such RDA.

5   Exploring New Interoperability Solutions: A Reference Model and a SHACL-Based Superontology

With RDF providing mechanisms to combine multiple data sources in an "open world" where bibliographic description can be an aggregation of multiple viewpoints about a resource, the claim for a single common bibliographic model to overcome the limitations in the interoperability of bibliographic standards and ontologies, suggested by some authors [17, e.g.] is no longer justified [9]. However, as explained in the previous sections, simply translating existing ontologies into RDF is not enough and RDF languages have limitations that make them inadequate for certain interoperability requirements.

In this context, it seems relevant to investigate the possibility of higher abstraction mechanisms to potentiate semantic interoperability, at two levels:

(i) the creation of a reference model capable of encompassing the different existing models in the bibliographic and similar domains; and

(ii) the specification of a superontology based on the reference model, i.e., a reference ontology of a higher level of abstraction than existing standard and local ontologies, in the sense defined by Brinkley [31], that would be an instrument for relating semantically the elements of standard bibliographic vocabularies and for specifying mechanisms for restricting or constraining bibliographic data.

Despite the multiplicity of points of view of an "open world" for the bibliographic field, the need still remains for a solution to control the quality and consistency of bibliographic data, that is, to "close the world" when necessary through the specification of constraints to validate data structures. As stated above, this would be a requirement of the superontology that RDF languages cannot meet, given its limitations already explained in the previous section of this paper.

The lack of standards to express data constraints led to the creation of Shapes Constraint Language (SHACL)[13], a schema language for RDF that allows the specification of constraints (called "shapes") for the validation of RDF graphs [32]. SHACL is also more powerful than OWL in the inference mechanisms because it can be used for rule-based inferences [33]. In this sense, it is worth investigating the hypothesis of using SHACL, a high-level vocabulary for the expression of data constraints which is simultaneously a language for ontologies, approved as a W3C Recommendation in July 2017.

Although constraints for validation of bibliographic data should be expressed separately from the vocabularies to which they apply [9], in our research we will not consider the use of application profiles, extension vocabularies or other mechanisms specific to languages of metadata schemas, since they do not have validation effects in the Semantic Web. Indeed, such extension profiles or ontologies need to be formally recognized by the entities that manage the base-ontologies, while AAA and OWA (Open World Assumption) principles allow that inconsistent or non-formally recognized profiles or extensions can exist and be applied. For this reason, we will instead explore the possibility of using SHACL as a language to validate data from the "open world" of the Semantic Web with "closed world" constraints [9].

6   Conclusions

This paper has provided a review of current limitations to the convergence between existing bibliographic ontologies and the Semantic Web that impair the potential of reuse of bibliographic data in that context. The review provides an analysis of the

---

[13] https://www.w3.org/TR/shacl/.

issues deriving from the use of a variety of different bibliographic standards and vocabularies separately conceived and managed, insufficiencies of their expression in Semantic Web languages and limitations of practical experiences in bibliographic LOD data transformation as well.

In order to improve bibliographic data interoperability in the Semantic Web, a research proposal is put forward to investigate new means to enrich and integrate the semantics of ontologies already in use by libraries, through the creation of a reference model and the formalization of a higher level ontology making use of SHACL to overcome limitations identified in the RDF family of languages, especially in what concerns the enabling of constraint mechanisms, capable of ensuring the semantic validity and quality of data.

Acknowledgments. This project was partially funded by the Fundação para a Ciência e Tecnologia (ISTAR UID/Multi/4466/2016).

References

1. Godby, C.J., Wang, S., Mixter, J.K.: Library Linked Data in the Cloud: OCLC's Experiments with New Models of Resource Description. Morgan & Claypool, San Rafael (2015). https://doi.org/10.2200/s00620ed1v01y201412wbe012
2. Cordeiro, M.I.: Information technology frameworks in LIS: exploring IT constructs as sources of conceptual alignment. Thesis submitted for the Degree of Doctor of Philosophy at the University of London (UCL) (2005)
3. Willer, M., Dunsire, G.: Bibliographic Information Organization in the Semantic Web. Chandos, Oxford (2013)
4. Murray, R.J.: The FRBR-Theoretic library: the role of conceptual data modeling in cultural heritage information system design. In: iPRES 2008: Proceedings of the Fifth International Conference on Preservation of Digital Objects, British Library, London, pp. 163–168 (2008)
5. Peponakis, M.: Conceptualizations of the cataloging object: a critique on current perceptions of FRBR Group 1 entities. Cataloging Classif. Q. **50**(5–7), 587–602 (2012)
6. Coyle, K.: FRBR, Before and After: A Look at Our Bibliographic Models. American Library Association, Chicago (2016)
7. Zapounidou, S., Sfakakis, M., Papatheodorou, C.: Representing and integrating bibliographic information into the Semantic Web: a comparison of four conceptual models. J. Inf. Sci., 1–29 (2016)
8. Coyle, K.: FRBR, twenty years on. Cataloging Classif. Q. **53**(3–4), 265–285 (2015). https://doi.org/10.1080/01639374.2014.943446
9. Baker, T., Coyle, K., Petiya, S.: Multi-entity models of resource description in the Semantic Web: a comparison of FRBR, RDA and BIBFRAME. Libr. Hi Tech **32**(4), 562–582 (2014). https://doi.org/10.1108/LHT-08-2014-0081
10. Murray, R.J., Tillett, B.: Cataloging theory in search of graph theory and other ivory towers. Inf. Technol. Libr. **30**(4), 170–184 (2011)
11. Martin, K.E., Mundle, K.: Positioning libraries for a new bibliographic Universe: a review of cataloging and classification literature 2011–12. Libr. Resour. Tech. Serv. **58**(4), 233–249 (2014)
12. Riva, P., Le Boeuf, P., Zumer, M.: IFLA Library Reference Model: A Conceptual Model for Bibliographic Information. IFLA, Den Haag (2017)

13. Riva, P.: Il nuovo modello concettualle dell' universo bibliografico: FRBR Library Reference Model. AIB Studi **56**(2), 265–275 (2016)
14. Peponakis, M.: In the name of the name: RDF literals, ER attributes, and the potential to rethink the structures and visualizations of catalogs. Inf. Technol. Libr. **35**(2), 19–38 (2016)
15. Yee, M.M.: Can bibliographic data be put directly onto the Semantic Web? Inf. Technol. Libr. **28**(2), 55–80 (2009)
16. Sprochi, A.: Where are we headed? Resource description and access, bibliographic framework, and the functional requirements for bibliographic records library reference model. Int. Inf. Libr. Rev. **48**(2), 129–136 (2016). https://doi.org/10.1080/10572317.2016.1176455
17. Svensson, L.G.: Are current bibliographic models suitable for integration with the Web? Inf. Stand. Q. **25**(4), 7–13 (2013)
18. Szeto, K.: Positioning library data for the Semantic Web: recent developments in resource description. J. Web Librarianship **7**(3), 305–321 (2013). https://doi.org/10.1080/19322909.2013.802584
19. Godby, C.J.: A division of labor: the role of Schema.org in a Semantic Web model of library resources. In: Seikel, J., Seikel, M. (eds.) Linked Data for the Cultural Heritage, pp. 73–101. ALCTS, Chicago (2016)
20. Suominen, O., Hyvonen, N.: From MARC silos to Linked Data silos? o-bib. Das offene Bibliotheksjournal **4**(2) (2017)
21. Hawtin, R., et al.: Review of the evidence for the value of the "linked data" approach: final report to JISC. JISC, Curtis+Cartwright (2011)
22. Gruber, T.: Ontology. In: Liu, L., Özsu, M.T. (eds.) Encyclopedia of Database Systems. Springer, Boston (2009). https://doi.org/10.1007/978-0-387-39940-9_1318
23. Hanneman, J., Kett, J.: Linked data for libraries. In: World Library and Information Congress: 76th IFLA General Conference, Gothenburg, 10–15 August 2010
24. Dunsire, G., et al.: Linked data vocabulary management: infrastructure, data integration, and interoperability. Inf. Stand. Q. **24**(2–3), 4–13 (2012)
25. Hallo, M., et al.: Current state of linked data in digital libraries. J. Inform. Sci. **42**(2), 117–127 (2016). https://doi.org/10.1177/0165551515594729
26. Coyle, K., Silvello, G., Tammaro, A.M.: Comparing methodologies: Linked Open Data and Digital Libraries. In: AIUCD 2014 - Proceedings of the Third AIUCD Annual Conference - Humanities and Their Methods in the Digital Ecosystem, article no. 3. ACM Digital Library (2014). https://doi.org/10.1145/2802612.2802615
27. Escolano Rodriguez, E.: RDA and ISBD: history of a relationship. JLIS.it **7**(2), 49–81 (2016)
28. Howarth, L.C.: FRBR and linked data: connecting FRBR and linked data. Cataloging Classif. Q. **50**(5–7), 763–776 (2012). https://doi.org/10.1080/01639374.2012.680835
29. Doerr, M., Riva, P., Zumer, M.: FRBR entities: identity and identification. Cataloging Classif. Q. **50**(5–7), 517–541 (2012). https://doi.org/10.1080/01639374.2012.681252
30. Barbosa, A., et al.: The use of software tools in linked data publication and consumption: a Systematic Literature Review. Int. J. Seman. Web Inf. Syst. **13**(4), 68–88 (2017)
31. Brinkley, J.F., et al.: A framework for using reference ontologies as a foundation for the semantic web. In: AMYA Symposium Proceedings 2006, pp. 96–100 (2006)
32. Knublauch, H., Kontokostas, D. (eds.): Shapes Constraint Language (SHACL). W3C Recommendation 20 July 2017. W3C (2017)
33. Knublauch, H.: SHACL and OWL compared (2017). spinrdf.org

GLOBDEF: A Framework for Dynamic Pipelines of Semantic Data Enrichment Tools

Maria Nisheva-Pavlova[⊠] and Asen Alexandrov[⊠]

Faculty of Mathematics and Informatics,
Sofia University "St. Kliment Ohridski", Sofia, Bulgaria
{marian, asenaleksandrov}@fmi.uni-sofia.bg

Abstract. Semantic data enrichment adds information to raw data to allow computational reasoning based on the meaning of data. With the introduction of Linked Data a lot of work is spent on combining existing tools for specific enhancement needs into multi-domain reusable enhancement pipeline.

As part of the GloBIG project, we are working on the development of a framework for data enhancement, which attempts to be domain-agnostic and dynamically configurable. It works with pluggable enhancement modules, which are dynamically activated to create on-the-fly pipelines for data enhancement.

Our research goal is to find a way for processing large amounts of data and automatically enhancing it while leveraging variety of domain knowledge sources and tools by selecting and using the most suitable ones according to the data.

In this paper we present our proof-of-concept implementation of the so called GLOBDEF framework and discuss the challenges and next steps on its development.

Keywords: Linked Open Data · Semantic annotation ·
Semantic enhancement · Metadata · Ontology

1 Introduction

In the modern inter-connected world computational activities often have to process huge amounts of data coming from various sources and in various formats. This creates the need for more agile data processing methodologies that can adapt to different kinds of data, learn to understand the data's broader semantic context and focus only on the parts of data most relevant to the purpose of the particular data processing task.

1.1 Semantic Enhancement

The main idea of the so-called semantic utilization or semantic enrichment of data is to position the data in some broad semantic context by annotating it with concepts from a proper domain of knowledge. An annotation is a form of metadata attached to a dataset or a specific part of it, like a database field or document, or a document section. Compared to tagging, which speeds up searching and helps one to find relevant and precise information, a semantic annotation goes one level deeper: It enriches the

© Springer Nature Switzerland AG 2019
E. Garoufallou et al. (Eds.): MTSR 2018, CCIS 846, pp. 159–168, 2019.
https://doi.org/10.1007/978-3-030-14401-2_15

unstructured or semi-structured data with a context that is further linked to the available structured domain knowledge and makes it possible to process complex filter and search operations expecting results that are not explicitly related to the original search queries.

Ontologies are a standard way for describing domain knowledge and as such provide semantic enhancement of data with suitable interoperable vocabulary for annotations. This kind of semantic enhancement may be characterized as an "arm's length approach" [1] – it presumes no change of data but association of each piece of data with an entire knowledge base. Data should be left as it is but incrementally tagged with terms from a consistent set of ontologies. In this way it is enriched with appropriate open, sharable and reusable knowledge that allows automatic interpretation and reasoning.

1.2   The GloBIG Project

The research presented in this paper is part of the project entitled "GloBIG: A Model of Integration of Cloud Framework for Hybrid Massive Parallelism and its Application for Analysis and Automated Semantic Enhancement of Big Heterogeneous Data Collections" funded by the National Science Fund of Bulgaria. The GloBIG project is aimed at development and evaluation of a model for implementation of open science frameworks. The main subjects of the planned study are a number of issues concerning the deployment of one of the latest models of processing research data, which requires open access to data services in the context of open science.

The term "open science" [2] summarizes the very fast changes in the way research is carried out; in the way that researchers collaborate; in the way knowledge is shared and the way science is organized. These changes are made possible by information technologies and are driven by the exponential growth of data available for the scientific community. A major aspect of the open science is the practice of open access to research results funded by public sources, e.g. scientific publications and research data. The GloBIG project will develop a model for practical implementation of a processing platform for open science purposes. Such type of platform should provide means to ensure semantic scalability, semantic interoperability and re-usability of datasets as well as tools for their automatic interpretation and reasoning on them.

Therefore, one of the main objectives of GloBIG is to elaborate efficient methods for automated semantic enhancement of heterogeneous datasets, including: selection of appropriate ontologies to be used as sources of conceptual knowledge about the corresponding domain; building semantic annotations of data; extraction and preservation of various types of metadata.

Another objective of the GloBIG project is to address the ascertainment that the developed models and frameworks should be scalable and applicable to unforeseeably large datasets. This dictates that any chosen techniques or tools for semantic enhancement in particular should be architectured to work well as distributed or parallelized systems in order to optimize the used computational resources.

This paper discusses some initial results of an activity within the GloBIG project aimed at development of an experimental framework for semantic enhancement of data by use of a dynamically constructed pipeline of enhancement tools.

2 GloBIG Data Enhancement Framework

There are many tools and frameworks that provide annotation capabilities. Researchers have made several surveys outlining the current state of the art over the years [3, 4]. With regards to data content, much of the focus in the field is on annotating textual data, with some tools providing extended ability for semantic annotation of multimedia. The generally adopted approach for storage of annotation metadata is in a centralized data repository or as embedded content in the original data, but in some cases annotations are stored as sidecar files that accompany the data files. All modern tools offer some ways for automation of the annotation process and are focused around a specific domain ontology (or manually extendable set of ontologies). The typical final product of processes using annotation tools is a continuously growing semantically rich, searchable index.

The concept of Linked Data [5] and the continuous growth of the Linked Open Data Cloud [6] has allowed researchers to work towards cross-domain enhancement frameworks, which combine multiple enhancement engines and domain knowledge sources into pipelines for data enhancement. There is a trend with time for frameworks to become more and more flexible. For example, Apache STANBOL[1] supports usage with configurable chains of enhancement engines while latest developments like FREME[2], are designed as a set of reusable services that can be chained to create enhancement pipelines from different components. The authors of FREME have provided a short discussion of similar frameworks and the benefits of the flexibility of using multiple independent services [7].

2.1 Our Goals

As part of the GloBIG project we are attempting to extend the above picture by providing a framework that could be used to integrate various data enhancement tools and frameworks in one place. We have called it GLOBDEF as a short from GloBIG Data Enhancement Framework. Like FREME, the framework should serve as a combinator of different enhancement engines or services, with the addition of automated intelligent mechanism for selection of the proper enhancement tools based on the processed data and the enhancement needs specified by a user.

To achieve this, we are aiming to provide:

- support for easy integration of already existing enhancement engines,
- support for dynamic, automatic intelligent creation of enhancement pipelines based on the processed data or some specific enhancement needs,
- support for provenance to allow for future auditing and estimation of veracity of the enhancing annotations,
- scalability that allows handling of large volumes of data, coming at huge velocity.

---

[1] https://stanbol.apache.org.

[2] http://www.freme-project.eu/.

The first goal expresses the desire for cross-domain annotation capabilities and ability to quickly expand data research experiments by leveraging pre-existing engines, while the second aims to solve the problem of handling heterogenous big data – by automating the decision making for its enhancement. The third goal ensures that there is a way to measure the accuracy of the annotation process, which is an implicit requirement in any scientific research. The fourth comes from a main focus of the GloBIG project - handling of Big Data and parallelism.

2.2   Design Overview

The overall design of GLOBDEF is shown on Fig. 1. In Phase 1 data enters the process of semantic enhancement and receives a small sidecar metamodel that will grow to comprehend all the semantic annotations, which will enrich the original data. Additionally, a user of the system (human or automated process) can add auxiliary metadata to that metamodel, to describe specific enhancement needs or provide configuration for enhancement engines. We call this couple of data and metadata a *data bundle*.

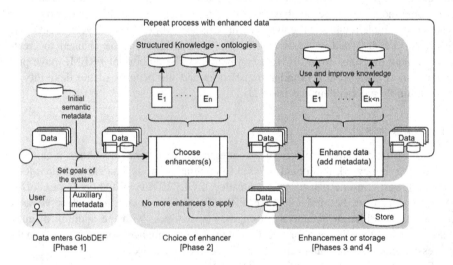

Fig. 1.   Overview of GLOBDEF's design

In Phase 2 the *data bundle* enters the enhancement process. As can be seen on Fig. 1 this is a cyclic process, through which the bundle can go multiple times. First, an appropriate enhancement engine (or enhancer for short) is chosen from a pool of available enhancers, depending on the current information in the metamodel.

In Phase 3 the chosen enhancer processes the *data bundle* and adds enhancement annotations to the metamodel. Then the *data bundle* goes back to the pipeline and can be picked by another enhancer, chosen as most suitable for the updated metamodel. This process continues until no more enhancers from the ones available are applicable. Then in Phase 4 the *data bundle* is taken out of the pipeline and stored for future use.

With this design each data bundle can be processed by a different enhancement pipeline, created dynamically based on the data and its metamodel.

2.3   The Data Bundle

The *data bundle* is the atomic data entity that can be handled by the framework. It represents the minimal chunk of data and all the metadata pertaining to that data. In our initial implementation we have postulated that data chunks are at a file level and the metadata is stored as a sidecar file, thus the data bundle becomes a couple of files.

The benefits of this non-centralized approach for representation of the semantic metadata are: it is easy to implement, allowing us to focus on other parts of the framework; the access to the metadata is fast, because we don't have to wait for queries from a central repository.

The major disadvantages are: there is no central entry point for generic access to the metadata for all enhanced data; there is heavy dependency on the implementation and performance of the file system used for storage; the framework is unable to handle streaming data, as is, because it requires that data comes in whole files.

Considering the pros and cons, we took the distributed approach since GLOBDEF is working with data and metadata only during the enhancement process and is not concerned by how this metadata is used afterwards. However, if needed, a user of the framework may gather all metadata in a centralized repository after a bundle exits the GLOBDEF pipeline.

2.4   Representing the Sidecar Metamodel

The sidecar metamodel contains annotations added by enhancers and auxiliary metadata added by the framework during the enhancement process. The metadata enhancing the original data is expected to follow the Linked Data principles [5] and provide references to domain specific ontologies used by the various enhancers. The auxiliary metadata is based on a minimalistic set of classes and properties described in our own GLOBDEF metadata ontology [8].

In our initial implementation, the metamodel is represented in RDF [9]. This format is universal enough to allow for easier integration of different enhancement engines, while providing a unified approach for querying of and reasoning on semantic information. It further allows enhancers to use more complex languages that can be represented with RDF such as OWL[3], if an enhancer's purpose is to add annotations that allow advanced reasoning; or NIF [10], if an enhancer works with linguistic data.

Combining RDF triples from different sources into the same model is not an easy task, especially when these sources are pluggable and unknown in advance. Therefore, we impose a limitation on all enhancer implementations that the annotation metadata should not contain definitions of RDF classes or properties but should refer to such via URIs. In this way the annotations added by each enhancer to a metamodel contain only instances with all their relations.

---

[3] https://www.w3.org/TR/owl-ref/.

An excerpt from a sample metamodel can be seen on Fig. 2. It shows the result of selection of a *DataFormatEnhancer* (which recognizes the format of the data stored in a file) and the enhancements that it has added to the metamodel. The grey background marks auxiliary metadata entities, described in the GLOBDEF ontology, while the bold italic font marks the entities from the external domains referred to by the enhancer.

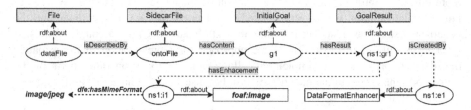

Fig. 2. Sample contents of a meta model

The data file and the sidecar metadata are described by individuals of the classes *globdef:File* and *globdef:SidecarFile* respectively. Goals are auxiliary constructs used to describe and control the dynamic selection of enhancers as the data bundle goes through the pipeline. In Fig. 2, the *DataFormatEnhancer* instance *e1* was activated by the presence of *g1* (instance of InitialGoal) in the metamodel. As result of this activation the auxiliary instance *gr1* links to the annotation *i1* generated by the enhancer. This annotation marks the dataFile's type as a jpeg image. Note that the diagram has been simplified for illustrative purposes. The full example can be found in the examples folder in the globdef-py repository[4].

2.5   Enhancers

Enhancers in GLOBDEF are plugins wrapping around enhancement engines (services, tools, algorithms) that provide some domain-specific data enhancement. To integrate with GLOBDEF an enhancer plugin must:

- provide a semantic description of itself;
- be able to determine if it can be activated to enhance a given data bundle;
- be able to translate between data bundles and the wrapped enhancement engine.

The enhancer's description is provided in an RDF model that describes the enhancer as individual of the *globdef:Enhancer* class. All properties of the enhancer instance from this model are appended to the metamodels of each enhanced data bundle.

The second requirement is the main building block of the dynamic pipeline creation. By analyzing the current content of the metamodel for a bundle, an enhancer plugin can determine if the enhancer is a match for this data. The framework uses this in Phase 2 (on Fig. 1), to select the correct enhancer. For example, the

---

[4] https://github.com/globdef/globdef-py/tree/master/examples.

DataFormatEnhancer from Fig. 2 will always match for a bundle with *InitialGoal* instance that does not already have an enhancement result from this enhancer.

The third requirement hides the technical details for each enhancer implementation. It may vary from mere transfer of data and metamodel to complex data transformations, in order to utilize a specific enhancement engine.

2.6   Dynamic Pipelines

In our initial research we use forward chaining to create dynamic pipelines. Enhancers get selected for some current contents of the metamodel and produce new data in the metamodel that causes selection of other enhancers. We have chosen this approach as it is easier to implement and to later experiment with new types of data and new types of enhancers. After we have gathered information from such experiments we shall attempt to implement a backward-chaining approach where enhancers specify their dependencies and outputs upfront, and the framework uses this information to create a plot for a pipeline with a specific outcome in mind.

3   Current Progress and Future Work

Our initial focus is on creating a proof of concept implementation that satisfies our initial goals, for variety of enhancement domains, scalability, provenance awareness and dynamic creation of the enhancement pipeline.

3.1   A Proof of Concept

The first version of GLOBDEF can be found in the globdef-py repository[5]. We have chosen Python as the main programming language due to its readability, vast toolset of libraries and ease of integration with other tools and technologies. The globdef-py prototype implements the design from Fig. 1 with sidecar metamodel and dynamic iterative selection of enhancers, which uses forward-chains to construct a pipeline.

Variety of Domains. This is achieved with the way of construction of the metamodel, as it is co-created iteratively by enhancers, which add only new individuals of classes from external ontologies. This ensures no conflicts between different enhancers. We have experimented with DBPedia Spotlight[6] and Apache STANBOL[7] and while the second is a framework that also wraps the first, we can get both sets of enhancement annotations to co-exist in the meta model (more on handling duplication below).

Scalability. The choice to store metadata in sidecar files proves effective when used with file systems optimized for distributed usage. Experiments with LucidLink[8] show

---

[5] https://github.com/globdef/globdef-py.

[6] https://www.dbpedia-spotlight.org/.

[7] https://stanbol.apache.org.

[8] https://www.lucidlink.com/.

that an enhancement engine running on one machine retrieves (to that machine) only the file data of the bundles that it is enhancing. With this approach enhancers scale horizontally quite easy.

Provenance. The unified metamodel stores all information about the enhancer that added each annotation and when that annotation was added. Additionally, enhancement engines with provenance support add necessary information to their output, which is also incorporated in the metamodel.

Dynamic Pipelines. We use only forward chaining for the dynamic pipeline construction in our proof-of-concept, with naïve conflict resolution of choosing only the first enhancer that matches. This approach has been enough to demonstrate that a pipeline can be created dynamically based on the data and backward chaining as well as better conflict resolution strategies are on the far roadmap for now.

3.2 Challenges

Related work. The biggest challenge that we face is validating the research and business need for yet another data enhancement framework. A quick overview of the semantic enhancement scenery showed us only separate tools and domain specific endpoints (e.g. like DBPedia). However, as we searched more we found other enhancement pipeline frameworks like the one in Open Semantic ETL toolkit [11], the SAPP framework [12], Apache STANBOL, FREME [7] and others. They all offer modularized approach to the creation of data enhancement pipelines and can be extended by custom-build pluggable modules. Also, they have been around for a while and one can see multiple real-life use cases that validate their existence. However, we have not found any framework that offers the dynamic on-the-fly pipelining from our initial goals. Thus, dynamic pipelining has become the feature on which we will be putting most of our efforts.

The meta model. The biggest technical challenge is ensuring a consistent and optimized meta model. From what we have observed it can grow unnecessarily in size due to the already mentioned duplication or due to the addition of annotations irrelevant to the general topic of the data (e.g. geographical locations in a text describing mathematical formulas).

3.3 Experimentation Results

Using the MASC dataset[9] and a python wrapper for libmagic[10] we have successfully managed to observe a dynamic pipeline of two enhancers, the first recognizing the type of the data (text) and the second selected for that specific type of data and running the STANBOL engine on it. The produced metamodels were valid RDF graphs and contained all annotations added by the two enhancers. In terms of performance we observed that a bigger data bundle could spend quite some time within the queue of a

---

[9] http://www.anc.org/data/masc/downloads/data-download/.

[10] https://github.com/ahupp/python-magic.

complex enhancer like one based on STANBOL. We alleviate that by using several STANBOL instances to allow for parallel processing of multiple data bundles.

4   Conclusion

GLOBDEF follows the Blackboard System approach [13], with multiple enhancers working together each adding its own expertise to the shared metamodel to achieve an overall enhancement of the data. The flexibility of this approach provides a good platform for initial research on some unknown dataset. A researcher can just add pre-existing enhancement engines to the framework and GLOBDEF will integrate them in a dynamic pipeline and produce results for interpretation, without the need for any advanced preliminary configuration.

While the current state of GLOBDEF is far from perfect, with a lot of infrastructural improvements on the roadmap we have shown that implementation of our initial goals is possible. The framework's usability depends on the variety of enhancement engines, which can be leveraged for research on any data. Thus, our next research target is the integration of annotation engines that work not only on textual but also visual and audial data. This shall validate our research goals and confirm the usefulness of the GLOBDEF approach.

Acknowledgements. This work has been partially supported by the National Science Fund of Bulgaria within the "GloBIG: A Model of Integration of Cloud Framework for Hybrid Massive Parallelism and its Application for Analysis and Automated Semantic Enhancement of Big Heterogeneous Data Collections" project, contract DN02/9/2016.

References

1. Salmen, D., Malyuta, T., Hansen, A., Cronen, S., Smith, B.: Integration of intelligence data through semantic enhancement. In: Proceedings of the Sixth International Conference on Semantic Technologies for Intelligence, Defense, and Security, Fairfax, VA, USA, November 16–17, 2011 (2011)
2. H. 2. European Commission: The EU framework Programme for Research and Innovation: Open Science (Open Access) (2013). https://ec.europa.eu/programmes/horizon2020/en/h2020-section/open-science-open-access
3. Uren, V., et al.: Semantic annotation for knowledge management: requirements and a survey of the state of the art. Web Semant. **4**, 14–28 (2006)
4. Oliveira, P., Rocha, J.: Semantic annotation tools survey. In: 2013 IEEE Symposium on Computational Intelligence and Data Mining (CIDM) (2013)
5. Berners-Lee, T.: Linked Data - Design Issues (2006). http://www.w3.org/DesignIssues/LinkedData.html
6. McCrae, J.P.: The Linked Open Data Cloud (2018). http://lod-cloud.net/#about
7. Sasaki, F., Dojchinovski, M., Nehring, J.: Chainable and extendable knowledge integration web services. In: Knowledge Graphs and Language Technology, Kobe (2017)
8. Nisheva-Pavlova, M., Alexandrov, A.: GLOBDEF Ontology for sidecar metadata description (2018). https://globdef.github.io/ontology/globdef-meta.owl
9. W3C: RDF 1.1 Concepts and Abstract Syntax (2014)

10. Hellmann, S., Lehmann, J., Auer, S., Brümmer, M.: Integrating NLP using linked data. In: in International Semantic Web Conference (2) (2013)
11. Search, O.S.: Open Semantic ETL toolkit for data integration, data analysis, document analysis, information extraction and data enrichment. https://www.opensemanticsearch. org/etl
12. Koehorst, J.J., Dam, J.C.J., Saccenti, E., Martins dos Santos V.A.P., Suarez-Diez, M., Schaap, P.J.: SAPP: functional genome annotation and analysis through a semantic framework using FAIR principles," Bioinformatics, p. btx767 (2017)
13. Corkill, D.D.: Blackboard systems. AI expert (1991)

Ontologies for Data Science: On Its Application to Data Pipelines

Miguel-Ángel Sicilia$^{(\boxtimes)}$, Elena García-Barriocanal, Salvador Sánchez-Alonso,
Marçal Mora-Cantallops, and Juan-José Cuadrado

Computer Science Department, University of Alcalá, Polytechnic Building. Ctra.
Barcelona km. 33.6, 28871 Alcalá de Henares (Madrid), Spain
{msicilia,elena.garciab,salvador.sanchez,marcal.mora,jjcg}@uah.es

Abstract. Ontologies are usually applied to drive intelligent applications and also as a resource for integrating or extracting information, as in the case of Natural Language Processing (NLP) tasks. Further, ontologies as the Gene Ontology (GO) are used as an artifact for very specific research aims. However, the value of ontologies for data analysis tasks may also go beyond these uses and span supporting the reuse and composition of data acquisition, integration and fusion code. This requires that both data and code artifacts support meta-descriptions using shared conceptualizations. In this paper, we discuss the different concerns in semantically describing *data pipelines* as a key reusable artifact that could be retrieved, compared and reused with a degree of automation if semantically consistent descriptions are provided. Concretely, we propose attaching semantic descriptions for data and analytic transformations to current backend-independent distributed processing frameworks as *Apache Beam*, as these already abstract out the specificity of supporting execution engines.

Keywords: Data science · Ontologies · Data pipelines · Apache Beam

1 Introduction

Data science is a concept that has emerged to describe a set of interdisciplinary skills that apply scientific methods and processes together with algorithms and systems to extract knowledge and insights from structured and unstructured data. This requires a set of abilities from data scientists that include those of domain expert, data engineer, statistician, computer scientist, communicator and team leader [3]. Processing data thus requires a methodical approach, resulting in the specification of series of steps that may be executed in parallel or in sequence, locally or in a cluster of computers, forming computational graphs usually called *data pipelines*. These apply different types of filters and transformations on datasets that, in turn, may be bounded or represent streams of continuously updating data.

© Springer Nature Switzerland AG 2019
E. Garoufallou et al. (Eds.): MTSR 2018, CCIS 846, pp. 169–180, 2019.
https://doi.org/10.1007/978-3-030-14401-2_16

The current proliferation of platforms and languages supporting data analysis entails that data wrangling and analytic tasks are often executed in heterogeneous environments, which has raised the need to separate the specification of the pipeline and its actual deployment details. That has led first to proposals of abstractions for distributed processing as the *Dataflow* model [1], resulting in programming models that are able to run on different platforms. An example is Apache Beam[1], a model in which pipelines written once can be executed in different and diverse distributed execution backends as Apache Apex[2], Apache Flink[3] or Apache Spark[4] to name a few.

While current high-level pipeline frameworks successfully abstract out the distinction of batch, micro-batch and streaming (and also other system-specific constructs), they are still not sufficient for other requirements that are in the horizon of reproducible and abstract, platform and backend independent, data analysis. These include the comparability and retrieval of data analysis pipelines, and the possibilities for composing or reusing pipeline steps based on semantic descriptions. The former has been addressed for example in [17] with the proposal of a "data science" ontology representing "semantic flow graphs" in which annotations can be used for finding semantic equivalences between program fragments. The latter may be achieved using existing ontologies and schemas that describe datasets as a basis. Some of them are formal ontologies, as in the case of the Extensible Observation Ontology (OBOE), a generic conceptual framework for describing the semantics of data sets consisting of observations and measurements [15], and others are schemas that can also be modeled formally as the case of the Statistical Data and Metadata eXchange (SDMX) format for interchange of statistical data [7].

The use of ontologies and, more broadly, of semantic technologies to support data science processes can be approached from different viewpoints. We have identified at least three dimensions in which ontologies can be used. First, as *data artifacts* themselves, that can be used as input for data analysis, as in the case of the *Gene Ontology*. Second, ontologies can be used as a *mediating artifact* that is used for the fusion or integration of data, or as part of elaborating data, as it is the case of their use in Natural Language Processing (NLP). Third, they can be used to model data science processes themselves, i.e. as a *process artifact*. We are focusing here on that third aspect, and concretely we describe how semantic models for describing data and analytic transformations can be integrated with data pipeline code (in contrast to other approaches that consider semantic metadata as an asset created during separate processes, e.g. [11]), opening possibilities to add support for comparing, reusing and composing code to the backend-independence that data pipeline frameworks as Beam already provide.

---

[1] https://beam.apache.org/.

[2] https://apex.apache.org/.

[3] https://flink.apache.org/.

[4] https://spark.apache.org/.

The rest of this paper is structured as follows. Section 2 briefly refers to previous work on data pipelines and ontologies that is relevant to the description of data and analytic transformations. Then, Sect. 3 discusses the issues in the reuse of existing ontologies for the purpose of representing datasets and transformations. In Sect. 4, the case of integrating those semantic descriptions with pipeline models is illustrated with an example using Apache Beam. Finally, conclusions and outlook are provided in Sect. 5.

2 Background

Data and transformations are the core building blocks of actual processing tasks in data science, and its combination is captured in the notion of a *pipeline* that is common also in programming interface design in machine learning libraries [6]. Current distributed processing engines as Apache Spark include support for them, in this case using the *Pipeline API* [16]. Apache Beam attempts to provide a pipeline framework that unifies batch and streaming (being the latter a common scenario nowadays [12]), and provides a higher-level abstraction that is portable across run-times. *Pipeline61* [23] is another attempt to provide execution management to data transformation pipelines combining steps executed on Spark, map-reduce and simple shell scripts. However, these platforms do not provide semantic descriptions of their code artifacts and do not attempt to process them, not even to the checking of input and output semantic matching across the steps in the pipelines.

Ontologies in a broad sense are shared conceptualizations of a specific domain. In some narrower sense, they are formal representations that use logic-based languages for describing those domains and enable reasoning. While there is not a single "data science" ontology in widespread use, previous work on describing scientific data (e.g. the OBOE ontology [15]) is applicable to this domain, as well as terminologies for statistical transformations as OBCS [25]. There are also schemas that are useful as widely adopted, non-formal terminologies. Notable examples are SDMX [7] for statistical data and PMML [9] for machine learning models.

Scientific workflow systems [2] provide also a notion of pipeline, in this case mainly aimed at provenance and reproducibility. Structural and semantic compatibility of services in workflows has been used as the basis for models composing services, e.g. [5], but as a separate layer in which actual computational steps are only defined by inputs and outputs. In our approach, the description is embedded in code and the services themselves are also part of the artifact to be reused (as opposed to frameworks as Apache Taverna[5] in which code is assumed to be services, i.e. "àctivities" as Web services or local processes). The requirements for scientific workflows as proposed by McPhilips et al. [14] include well-formedness, clarity, predictability, recordability, reportability, reusability, scientific data modeling, and automatic optimization. Nowadays, however, these

---

[5] https://taverna.incubator.apache.org/.

requirements need to be formulated in terms of the new data processing infrastructure. As that infrastructure provides built-in pipeline models already supporting some of them, one should ideally focus on the non-supported features.

Patterson et al. [18] have reported a first preliminary attempt to semantically model data science flows from actual code. In their approach, concepts formalize the abstract ideas of machine learning, statistics, and computing on data, and then map actual software artifacts to them. The main benefit pointed out by the authors is that formal representation provides a way to map semantically equivalence between software artifacts, e.g. that two pieces of code perform the same kind of analysis step, e.g. an application of clustering. However, their model is not reusing previous ontologies, and in its current description is aimed at the aspects more closely related to code equivalence but not to a full description of the semantics of data.

3 Representing Datasets and Transformations

The representation of the elements of pipelines entails describing both datasets and transformations. Here we describe how current data science practices may adopt the description of data and code artifacts with existing semantic models.

3.1 Datasets and Domains

There are different proposals for describing the semantics of datasets, and they may differ from the typical representation using data tables similar to a relational database. For example, the following SDMX fragment[6] illustrates rich descriptions of data, including units and description of the series globally in a separate DSD (*Data Structure Definition*):

```
<data:Series FREQ="M" indic_bt="TOVT" nace_r2="MIG_DCOG"
unit="I2015_SCA" geo="DE" TIME_FORMAT="P1M">
<data:Obs TIME_PERIOD="2017-08" OBS_VALUE="111.0" />
<data:Obs TIME_PERIOD="2017-09" OBS_VALUE="109.4" />
<data:Obs TIME_PERIOD="2017-10" OBS_VALUE="109.5" />
...
<data:Series FREQ="M" indic_bt="TOVT" nace_r2="MIG_DCOG"
unit="I2015_SCA" geo="DK" TIME_FORMAT="P1M">
<data:Obs TIME_PERIOD="2017-08" OBS_VALUE="106.2" />
...
```

In the above example, the semantics of the entities observed are described using labels in different languages provided in the DSD, e.g.: `<struct:Description xml:lang="en">MIG-durable consumer goods</struct:Description>`. In this

---

[6] Turnover in industry - consumer durables, available at https://data.europa.eu/euodp/es/data/dataset/Z3YE842s0KutFv7stmNmDw/resource/51c01810-f40a-48d6-b178-c7701a01f821.

case, the code is referring to the *Statistical Classification of Economic Activities in the European Community*, revision 2. The type of indicator `indic_bt` is a reference to the EIONET vocabulary[7]. These references provide the semantic hooks for comparing data, including the entity, the measurement, units and format.

The semantics in SDMX are specified by referencing shared vocabularies. Other observation models provide formal semantics for the description of data. The OBOE ontology[8] specifies the entity being measured, and the measurement of different characteristics, along with the units of measurement and the protocol used for acquiring the datum. While the ontology was devised for scientific observations, it is generic enough to be applied to other cases, and as a simple case, for factual data as customer information, demographic or economic indicators or the like. OBOE provides a model for units of measurement, that may be complemented with other models available [24]. This is important for checking and automation, and this again is not a common requirement in the description of data pipeline transformations in platforms as Beam.

Another important element of these models is that of referring to entity classes and properties that of which data is collected. Many domain-specific ontologies and terminologies exist for that, and also sources as Wikipedia may provide a common ground for this, provided that there is a selection of articles that are meaningful. For example, scientific domains can be identified to create lists of articles [8]. Following the example above, the entity measured are countries, which in this case is implicit in the description of the series.

In any case, the description of the data should be attached and built-in with existing code artifacts. Typically, data science languages provide a *dataframe* abstraction (a table) or simpler *key-value* data structures (as in column-family databases like HBASE). An example as the above should embed metadata in a dataframe object at two levels:

- Dataframe or whole dataset level. It should be noted that some transformations may not change this metadata, e.g. converting or normalizing the scale of a column.
- Column or series level. Also, there are transformations not affecting this kind of metadata, e.g. filtering may produce a new dataset with the same column schema.

It should be noted that the mapping of the description to the actual shape of the data may not be straightforward. In the SDMX example, the hierarchical structure of the XML should be flattened if the target is a dataframe. These are transformations that change the structure of the data itself (e.g. the aggregation by country might end up in a new column de-aggregating data), of a different nature than the rest of them, and are thus responsible of some kind of *source* transformations that deal with the specificity of the input format.

---

[7] "Index of turnover-Total", http://dd.eionet.europa.eu/vocabulary/eurostat/indic_bt/TOVT.

[8] https://github.com/NCEAS/oboe.

Following the above discussion, what is needed for modeling datasets is: (a) a way of mapping ontology elements to program elements, and (b) a flexible description of metadata at dataset and column levels. Mapping (a) in its simplest form may be a set of tuples $(oent, pend, kind)$, where $oent$ could be an ontology element IRI, and $pend$ a symbol in program's code. Qualifiers may account for exact (logical equivalence), approximate or other kinds of mappings. Descriptions for (b) could reuse models from OBOE or other similar schemas.

3.2   Models of Transformations

The model for transformations need to differentiate among algorithms (which are intellectual work descriptions) from actual software implementations that realize them in a concrete language and/or platform, and are subject to versioning and release control. That modelling can be found in commonsense ontologies and in Software Engineering ontologies [22]. In some cases, the application of a data transformation operation is straightforward and should produce same results across implementations (with a margin of difference due to floating point arithmetic). Examples are bucketization, which requires computing quantiles, or in general normalization operations. The Ontology of Biological and Clinical Statistics (OBCS) [25] is an example of terminology for algorithms.

Algorithms that produce models as machine learning ones are a different case, as they are usually based on a high-level description of an algorithm, and there are many implementation variants and a number of hyperparameters that modify the behaviour of the algorithm significantly. These along with transformations and the model themselves have been modeled in the PMML schema, and utility packages exist to export PMML from different platforms, for example, the R package pmml [9]. However, for the sake of clarity, here we restrict the discussion to data transformations that are typical of the steps previous and posterior to the training of machine learning models, since in these, the transformations are primitive and easily traceable from input-output specification of the different steps in the pipeline.

However, the most important aspect of modeling transformations is the actual definition of concrete input-output transformations in a declarative and concise form. Known transformations as statistical operations appearing in OBCS or algorithms in PMML vocabularies should be considered primitive in that expressions. However, other operations not included on those terminologies still need to be expressed in terms of arithmetic (e.g. particular re-scaling) or predicate expressions (e.g. filtering). To account for the diversity and flexibility of current storage NoSQL engines, languages as NotaQL [21] provide a starting point.

4   Integrating with Dataflow Frameworks: An Example

We discuss here the integration of the ideas discussed in previous sections into abstract pipelines. In particular, we use Apache Beam as the case[9]. In Beam, a `Pipeline` applies a set of `PTransforms` to bounded or unbounded (stream) datasets (`PCollections`). Some of the transforms are used for input and output using supported formats, and others take functions as parameters. Those functions use the conventions of an SDK (Java, Python or others) and perform analytic tasks, including filtering, grouping, aggregating or predicting to name a few. The distributed computation is defined, according to the documentation as a DAG of `PValues` and their `PTransforms`. Conceptually the values are the nodes and the transforms are the edges.

The following code fragment shows a typical pipeline[10] where Beam transforms have been substituted by subclasses (prefixed with `A`) that support metadata annotations carrying the semantics of the data:

```
p = beam.Pipeline(options=PipelineOptions())
m, n = (100, -100)
sdmx= ann.FileBasedSDMXSource('teiis180.sdmx.xml', 'teiis180.dsd.xml')
series = p | 'read series' >> ann.ARead(sdmx)
series_filtered = series | 'filter' >>
        ann.AParDo(FilterOutliersFn(m, n))
series_normalized = series_filtered | 'change scale' >>
        ann.AParDo(RescaleFn(min_value))
series_keyed = series_normalized | 'index by (country, year)'>>
        ann.AParDo(KeyRecordsFn())
series_combined = series_keyed | 'mean of groups'>>
        ann.ACombinePerKey(beam.combiners.MeanCombineFn())
series_combined| beam.io.WriteToText('series_final.txt')
p.run()
```

Functions that are passed to transforms follow a set of conventions, e.g. implementing `DoFn` for transform `ParDo`. Those functions can be augmented with additional information on input and output, and also referring to the semantic description of the algorithm itself, with the simple subclassing mechanism that allows for attaching metadata to Python objects. These meta-descriptions could be extracted from the code and aggregated in some kind of repository or database to implement retrieval of pipelines or its fragments, as the basis for composition and reuse. The individual meta-information of the different `PTransforms` can then be accessed via augmentation of a the class `beam.Pipeline` using the series of transformations.

---

[9] At the time of this writing, Bean is mainly used as a data transformation framework not including distributed machine learning algorithms, for example, TensorFlow Extended (TFX) [4] is built on top of Beam but there are not algorithms available as aggregate transformations.

[10] The transformations are just examples, they are not intended as analytics with real practical value.

Dataset-level metadata should be attached as a dictionary with the main elements. Descriptors may include references to existing ontologies; in the example, a reference to a term in SUMO [19] is used for the entity (mappings shown below). Observation types determine the context of the observations, in one or several dimensions, demanding particular types of data columns (later marked with kind). In our case, we assume a single characteristic is measured for the sake of simplicity. The following is an example of dataset-level metadata associated to the original collection read from the SDMX mentioned in Sect. 3.

```
{'entity': 'DurableConsumerGoodsProduction',
 'mapping' : 'production',
 'observation-type': ['timed', 'geographic-bounded']
 'measurements':[{'characteristic':'Turnover in industry',
                  'standard':'TOVT',
                  'freq': 'month'
                  'unit':'EUR;INDEX[base=2015]'
            }]}
```

Note that mapping defines a symbol that can be used in other parts of the descriptions and mapped to ontologies as described later. Column-level metadata describes the mappings of each of the columns in the dataset to symbols (that are then used to specify the transformations), and associated information on its type. The following example shows how these could be described.

```
{'OBS_VALUE':  {'mapping': 'obs', 'type': 'float'},
 'TIME_PERIOD':{'mapping': 'period', 'unit':'month', kind: 'period'},
 'GEO':{'mapping': 'geo', 'vocab': 'iso-alpha-2', 'kind':'country'}}
```

The types associated to the columns may in turn be mapped to ontology elements, as in the example of country provided below.

Following the example, Table 1 describes the transformations applied to metadata in the different steps of the pipeline. The transformations should ideally be expressed in a formal language that is concise and schema-independent. We have use a syntax similar to NotaQL [21] that was proposed for schema-less data transformations independent of particular NoSQL database engines[11].

The filter transformation is just expressed as a condition on the inputs, then the row ids are equal at input and output after the application of the filter. The change of scale leaves the same all the columns that are not obs and applies a transformation only to that column, but it changes the unit of measurement. Finally, aggregation is changing the row identifier space, which now is defined by tuples (country, year), and the groups of previous observations are aggregated using the mean.

Filter and changing scale transformations maintain the overall description of the dataset but aggregation result in a different type of magnitude that should

---

[11] This would require integrating a parser of that language for checking and manipulation, that could include exploiting semantic mappings.

Table 1. Metadata transformation across pipeline transformations

Step	Transformation
Read	Elements mapped from the definitions above: **obs, period, geo**
| Filter | ```
IN-FILTER: obs>-100 AND obs<100
OUT._r <- IN._r,
OUT.$(IN._c) <- IN._v
``` |
| Change scale | ```
OUT._r <- IN._r,
OUT.$(IN._c?()!=obs) <- IN._v
OUT.obs <- log(IN.obs + min_value)
OUT._characteristic.unit <-
    log(IN._characteristic.unit + min_value)
``` |
| Aggregation | ```
OUT.r <- (IN.geo, year(IN.period))
OUT.avg_tov <- mean(IN.obs)
OUT._characteristic.freq <- year
``` |

be considered different from the original indicator value. In those cases, the metadata for the overall entity should also be changed, as the dataset rows have changed the dimension, this is denoted by referring to the elements in the metadata as _characteristic.

Mapping to ontologies can be added with maximum flexibility by mapping the symbols used to refer to the global or column-related entities. The following are examples.

```
{'ont': 'sumo', 'term':'Making',
'mapping': 'production', kind:'related'}
{'ont': 'OBCS', 'term':'http://purl.obolibrary.org/obo/OBI_0200094'
        'mapping':'log', 'kind': 'exact'}
{'ont': 'OBCS', 'term':'http://purl.obolibrary.org/obo/OBI_0200079'
        'mapping':'mean', 'kind': 'exact'}
{'ont': 'DBPedia', 'term':'http://dbpedia.org/page/Country'
        'mapping':'country', 'kind': 'exact'}
...
```

The first mapping is a non-exact mapping to a term in the SUMO ontology [19] for the entity being measured in the original dataset. The second and third are examples of mapping to OBCS classes logarithmic transformation and arithmetic mean calculation, so that the terms used in the descriptions in Table 4 are semantically interpretable. It should be noted that the introduction of
```

terms for known transformations makes the expression more concise. For example, a term representing the K-Means algorithm could be used for descriptions in PMML and also as a primitive in transforms, hiding the details of the internals of the algorithm that is treated as a single symbol in declarative descriptions. If interoperability is required, terminologies need to be public, shared and to some extent accepted, but a different use case is that of a private, organization-wide repository, in which the term mappings are to transformations that are common for the particular domain, typical cases or customers of the organization.

The descriptions as described so far can be used beyond documentation purposes in combination with query engines for a number of retrieval tasks. An example would be that of finding pipelines dealing with some particular kind of data, or finding structurally equivalent fragments of pipelines. As both datasets descriptions and mappings and transformations are provided as code artifacts, they can be extracted programmatically as a derived description that can be updated with the updates in the code itself, just as *docstrings* in many programming languages.

5   Conclusions and Outlook

Data science is moving to higher degrees of automation and portability across computing engines, with pipeline frameworks being one of the approaches for decoupling the definition from the deployment of data transformations. Recent advances on dataflow models are able to unify batch and stream processing around some processing abstractions. However, the actual processing code in each of the steps is still opaque to external observation. The use cases of reproducibility and also others as finding semantic equivalences require that pipelines are annotated semantically.

We have identified some existing ontologies and schemas that can be used for describing graphs of computation, with detailed observational ontologies as OBOE used for data artifact description, complemented with transform terminologies as OBCS for classifying algorithmic transformations. These can be reused for the semantic description of data transformations.

The embedding of these semantic descriptions into current code can be done using different approaches. Here we proposed the use of augmentation via subclassing that attach meta-information to particular elements of the data pipeline interfaces, but other techniques may be used instead, for example, code metadata attached to symbols or collections in homoiconic languages as Clojure. In any case, those descriptions could subsequently be used for reasoning, checking or other tasks, using, for example, embedded logic programming domain specific languages (DSL) as MiniKanren.

We have discussed the basics of semantic annotation of code taking Apache Beam as an example, since Beam is intended to be computing-engine independent and thus is highly abstract. Unlike previous approaches to scientific workflows, here we emphasize that semantic descriptions become a part of code artifacts (and not a separate summary of text [10] or services), which entails that they are documented, reused and exploited as part of the same processes that data scientists or data engineers tackle with in their daily work.

Future work can be organized in three main directions. First, there is a need to assess, map and eventually combine existing ontologies that are adequate for this concrete use (as the ones mentioned in the paper) eventually coming up with a comprehensive schema tailored to different kinds of data and commonly applied transformations. Second, the addition and eventual synthesis [17] of meta-descriptions using these ontologies should be addressed to ease annotation as much as possible, as a way to match infrastructure with human understanding [13], possibly with visualization of linked descriptions as clues for graphical interfaces [20]. And last but not least, tools exploiting the meta-descriptions for different purposes need to be devised and developed.

References

1. Akidau, T., et al.: The dataflow model. Proc. VLDB Endow. 8(12), 1792–1803 (2015)
2. Barker, A., van Hemert, J.: Scientific workflow: a survey and research directions. In: Wyrzykowski, R., Dongarra, J., Karczewski, K., Wasniewski, J. (eds.) PPAM 2007. LNCS, vol. 4967, pp. 746–753. Springer, Berlin, Heidelberg (2008). https://doi.org/10.1007/978-3-540-68111-3_78
3. Baškarada, S., Koronios, A.: Unicorn data scientist: the rarest of breeds. Program 51(1), 65–74 (2017)
4. Baylor, D., Breck, E., Cheng, H.T., et al.: TFX: a tensorflow-based production-scale machine learning platform. In: Proceedings of the 23rd ACM SIGKDD International Conference on Knowledge Discovery and Data Mining, pp. 1387–1395. ACM (2017)
5. Bowers, S., Ludäscher, B.: An ontology-driven framework for data transformation in scientific workflows. In: Rahm, E. (ed.) DILS. LNCS, vol. 2994, pp. 1–16. Springer, Berlin, Heidelberg (2004). https://doi.org/10.1007/978-3-540-24745-6_1
6. Buitinck, L., Louppe, G., Blondel, M., et al.: API design for machine learning software: experiences from the scikit-learn project. arXiv preprint arXiv:1309.0238 (2013)
7. Capadisli, S., Auer, S., Ngonga Ngomo, A.C.: Linked SDMX data. Semantic Web 6(2), 105–112 (2015)
8. Figuerola, C.G., Groves, T.: Analysing the potential of Wikipedia for science education using automatic organization of knowledge. Program 51(4), 373–386 (2017)
9. Guazzelli, A., Zeller, M., Lin, W.C., Williams, G.: PMML: an open standard for sharing models. R J. 1(1), 60–65 (2009)
10. Hajra, A., Tochtermann, K.: Linking science: approaches for linking scientific publications across different LOD repositories. Int. J. Metadata Semant. Ontol. 12(2–3), 124–141 (2017)
11. Karimova, Y., Castro, J.A., Silva, J.R.D., Pereira, N., Rodrigues, J., Ribeiro, C.: Description+ annotation: semantic data publication workflow with Dendro and B2NOTE. Int. J. Metadata Semant. Ontol. 12(4), 182–194 (2017)
12. Lanza, J., et al.: Managing large amounts of data generated by a smart city internet of things deployment. Int. J. Semantic Web Inf. Syst. (IJSWIS) 12(4), 22–42 (2016)

13. Lytras, M.D., Raghavan, V., Damiani, E.: Big data and data analytics research: from metaphors to value space for collective wisdom in human decision making and smart machines. Int. J. Semant. Web Inf. Syst. (IJSWIS) **13**(1), 1–10 (2017)
14. McPhillips, T., Bowers, S., Zinn, D., Ludäscher, B.: Scientific workflow design for mere mortals. Future Gener. Comput. Syst. **25**(5), 541–551 (2009)
15. Madin, J., Bowers, S., Schildhauer, M., Krivov, S., Pennington, D., Villa, F.: An ontology for describing and synthesizing ecological observation data. Ecol. Inform. **2**(3), 279–296 (2007)
16. Meng, X., Bradley, J., Yavuz, B., et al.: MLlib: machine learning in Apache Spark. J. Mach. Learn. Res. **17**(1), 1235–1241 (2016)
17. Patterson, E., Baldini, I., Mojsilovic, A., Varshney, K.R.: Semantic representation of data science programs. In: Proceedings of the Twenty-Seventh International Joint Conference on Artificial Intelligence (IJCAI-18), pp. 5847–5849 (2018)
18. Patterson, E., Baldini, I., Mojsilovic, A., Varshney, K.R.: Teaching machines to understand data science code by semantic enrichment of dataflow graphs. arXiv preprint arXiv:1807.05691 (2018)
19. Pease, A., Niles, I., Li, J.: The suggested upper merged ontology: a large ontology for the semantic web and its applications. In: Working Notes of the AAAI-2002 Workshop on Ontologies and the Semantic Web, vol. 28, pp. 7–10 (2002)
20. Peña, O., Aguilera, U., López-de-Ipiña, D.: Exploring LOD through metadata extraction and data-driven visualizations. Program **50**(3), 270–287 (2016)
21. Schildgen, J., Deßloch, S.: NotaQL is not a query language! it's for data transformation on wide-column stores. In: Maneth, S. (ed.) BICOD 2015. LNCS, vol. 9147, pp. 139–151. Springer, Cham (2015). https://doi.org/10.1007/978-3-319-20424-6_14
22. Sicilia, M.A., García-Barriocanal, E., Sánchez-Alonso, S., Rodríguez-García, D.: Ontologies of engineering knowledge: general structure and the case of software engineering. Knowl. Eng. Rev. **24**(3), 309–326 (2009)
23. Wu, D., Zhu, L., Xu, X., Sakr, S., Lu, Q., Sun, D.: A pipeline framework for heterogeneous execution environment of big data processing. IEEE Softw. **33**(2), 60–67 (2016)
24. Zhang, X., Li, K., Zhao, C., Pan, D.: A survey on units ontologies: architecture, comparison and reuse. Program **51**(2), 193–213 (2017)
25. Zheng, J., et al.: The Ontology of Biological and Clinical Statistics (OBCS) for standardized and reproducible statistical analysis. J. Biomed. Semant. **7**(1), 53 (2016)

Relating Legal Entities via Open Information Extraction

Giovanni Siragusa[1]([✉]), Rohan Nanda[1], Valeria De Paiva[2], and Luigi Di Caro[1]

[1] Department of Computer Science, University of Turin,
Corso Svizzera 185, Turin, Italy
{siragusa,nanda,dicaro}@di.unito.it
[2] Nuance Communication Inc., Sunnyvale, CA, USA
Valeria.dePaiva@nuance.com

Abstract. Concepts and relations within existing ontologies usually represent limited subjective and application-oriented views of a domain of interest. However, reusing resources and fine-grained conceptualizations is often challenging and requires significant manual efforts of adaptation to fit with unprecedented usages. In this paper, we present a system that makes use of recent Open Information Extraction technologies to unravel and explore corpus-centered unknown relations in the legal domain.

Keywords: Open Information Extraction ·
Natural language processing · Ontologies · Legal concepts · Legal text ·
IATE

1 Introduction

The Semantic Web research community needs tools for enriching and adapting existing semantic resources as well as for exploring relations within a given semantic resource and within a specific corpus. If we use such tools, extracted relations can be made then accessible to automatic systems or to domain experts in order to improve or support some particular work load. In this context, Open Information Extraction (OIE) systems [1] can be adopted to extract sets of triples of the form (*argument1*; *relational phrase*; *argument2*), where *argument1* and *argument2* are words (or multi-word expressions) and *relational phrase* is a phrase excerpt that describes the semantic relation between the two arguments.

In this paper, we present an OIE system, dubbed *LegOIE*, that automatically discovers concepts and relations in legal documents given a specific input ontology. The purpose of LegOIE is to enrich and adapt semantic resources, dynamically contextualizing concepts, browsing and providing other interactive facilities. Thus, we developed an OIE system that uses IATE, an European Union inter-institutional terminology database, to discover legal terms in the text and extract the phrase excerpt that connects two entities. Using a dictionary of legal

© Springer Nature Switzerland AG 2019
E. Garoufallou et al. (Eds.): MTSR 2018, CCIS 846, pp. 181–187, 2019.
https://doi.org/10.1007/978-3-030-14401-2_17

terms improves the performance of the system since it will focus on specific entities, the legal ones. To prove this, we will compare LegOIE system with three state-of-the-art ones: Ollie [10], Reverb [6] and ClausIE [4].

2   Related Works

Open Information Extraction (OIE) was conceived to solve the problems of *Information Extraction*, which does not scale well in large corpora, where a huge set of relation is present. OIE have reached notable results in extracting relational phrases in large corpora such as Wikipedia and the Web [1,12]. To the best of our knowledge, such systems are based on two steps: a tagging step where a Part-Of-Speech tagger or a dependency parser is applied to the sentence, and an extraction step that unravels the relational phrases. However, those systems can suffer from uninformative (relations which omit relevant information - for example, the triple (faust; made; a deal with the devil)) and incoherent (relations with no meaningful interpretation) extractions. Some research works have tried to solve this issue using heuristics. For instance, Reverb [6] uses syntactical constraints to filter relations, while Moro et al. [8] use a dependency parser and check if one of the arguments is marked as subject or object of a word in the relational phrase.

Differently from the previous systems, DefIE [5] constructs a syntactic-semantic graph by merging the output of the dependency parser with a Word Sense Disambiguation system. It extracts the relational phrases only between disambiguated words.

Other works used OIE systems to create or to populate ontologies and taxonomies. Nakashole et al. [9] applied OIE to automatically build a taxonomy, while Carlson et al. [3] and Speer and Havasi [11] used OIE to extend an existing ontology.

3   Resource, OIE System and Evaluation

In this section, we introduce the dictionary called IATE to label legal entities in running text and an Open Information Extraction (OIE) systems that use those tagged elements to extract triples. We will evaluate our system with three existing ones: Reverb, Ollie and ClausIE. Our evaluation seems to indicate that a system that uses a dictionary of legal terms can perform better than one that does not have such knowledge.

3.1   IATE Dictionary

The Inter-Active Terminology for Europe[1] (IATE), is the EU's inter-institutional terminology database, to discover concepts in the text. IATE consists of 1.3 million entries in English. Every entry (concept) in IATE is mapped to a subject

---

[1] See http://iate.europa.eu/about_IATE.html for further details.

domain. However, since some entities are wrong while others are entire sentences, we decided to filter some of these. First, we filtered out stopwords and concepts mapped to the *"NO DOMAIN"* label. Then, to find if a concept is related to a domain, we trained a word embedding using 2884 European Directives documents and 2884 Statutory Instruments documents. As word embedding model, we used *fasttext*[2] [2] with an embedding size of 128 and default hyperparameters. This filtering phase was conducted using cosine similarity: we filtered all <term, domain> pairs that have a similarity lower then a given threshold. To choose the right threshold value, we manually constructed a developer set composed of 60 <term, domain> pairs manually extracted from IATE, equally divided in 30 pairs labelled as *incorrect* and 30 pairs labelled as *correct*. Then, we computed the cosine similarity between the embedding of the term[3] and the embedding of the domain, labelling as incorrect those entries that have a score lower than the threshold. Figure 1 shows the number of elements correctly recognized using different thresholds[4]. From the figure, we chose a 0.5 threshold (which is frequently used for this kind of tasks). After the cleaning, we obtained a dictionary composed of 37,158 entries.

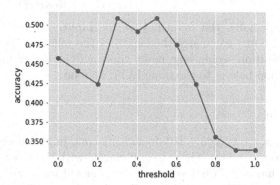

Fig. 1. The figure shows the accuracy for each threshold value. We experimented with a threshold in the range [0, 1], with a 0.2 step.

3.2 The OIE System

LegOIE takes as input a sentence and the IATE concepts that appear in the text, and returns a phrase excerpt for each possible pair of concepts. First, it processes the sentences through two steps: a Dependency Parser step and a Merging step. In the first step, Stanford CoreNLP [7] parser is applied on the

---

[2] Fasttext, like Word2Vec, has both CBOW and SkipGram models. We used the CBOW since it performed well compared to the other one.

[3] In case that the term (or domain) is a multi-word expression, we represented it as the average of its word embedding.

[4] We recognized as correct an element that has a score lower than the threshold and that is labelled with *incorrect*.

sentences to generate a dependency graph. The graph is passed as input to the second phase, where words that form a single IATE concept are merged together. This steps allow to extract better relations that do not contain entity words. Finally, LegOIE uses the list of entities in input to extract the shortest path that connects them in the undirected version of the graph. The output of the system is a set of triples of the form *(argument1, shortest path, argument2)* in which *argument1* and *argument2* are two IATE concepts. The extracted relations are then checked to see if they contain a verb (those not satisfying such condition are removed).

The extracted triples are then ordered according to their score. We computed the score of a triple using its frequency in the extraction and the length of the relation (number of words). Our intuition is to promote frequent triples with a short relation, while penalizing those that have a long relation name. Experience shows that long relations do not contain relevant verbal phrases that express a semantic relation (e.g., *made of* is a relevant relation). Our score formula is represented in Eq. 1:

$$score(arg1, rel, arg2) = \frac{freq(arg1, rel, arg2)}{(H(rel) + 1)len(rel)} \tag{1}$$

where $freq(\cdot)$ calculates the frequency of the input, $H(\cdot)$ is the entropy of the relation, and $len(\cdot)$ calculates the length of the relation. We computed the entropy of the relation seeing how many times all the arguments that appear within that relation belong to the same IATE domain.

3.3 Evaluation

For the extraction, we tagged 4,310 documents containing European Directives (laws that all European States have to implement) with the filtered IATE dictionary. We found that only 77,507 sentences contained at least two IATE concepts. Then, we applied LegOIE to extract triples, obtaining 2,267 such ones. We also extracted triples using Ollie, Reverb and ClausIE on the corpus. Those systems extracted[5] 3,060, 297,306, and 969 triples respectively.

Once we completed the extraction phase, we evaluated those systems on the base of their extracted triples: if the Open Information Extraction system could extract an informative triple where the two arguments are multi-word expression. In details, we randomly sampled 100 triples for each systems and we manually annotated them to check accuracy. Thus, we compute an accuracy score, calculating how many triples are labelled as correct. Table 1 shows the results of the evaluation, where we can see that LegOIE performed best, followed by Reverb. Furthermore, we can see that all OIE systems have a low accuracy, meaning that the task of extracting legal triples is challenging for automated systems.

---

[5] ClausIE and Ollie stopped without completing the extraction due to an exception.

Table 1. The table shows the four Open Information Extraction systems and their accuracy on 100 randomly sampled triples.

OIE system	Ollie	Reverb	ClausIE	LegOIE
Accuracy	0.17	0.21	0.13	0.32

4 Visualization

We decided to visualize the extracted triples in order to explore the relations extracted from the European Directives and how the concepts interact each other. From the sorted triples, we selected the first 200 ones (those ones with a score equal or greater than 500). Then, we manually revised them, removing wrong ones. After this phase, we obtained 108 triples. We inserted those triples into GraphDB[6] to visually-explore them. GraphDB allows to search a relation, a domain or a an argument. Then, it is possible to expand a node to visualize its relations, navigating the graph and unveiling unknown semantic OIE-based interactions between concepts. This knowledge may be used to enrich the original resources. Figure 2 shows on the left the expanded graph created by clicking on the *animal* concept.

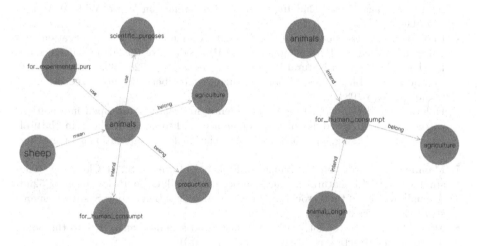

Fig. 2. The figure shows the entity *animal* and its relations with other entities. Each relation is represented by a labelled arrow. The label describes the relation type. The right graph reports the relations of the entity *for_human_consumption*.

---

[6] https://ontotext.com/products/graphdb/.

5 Conclusion

We presented an Open Information Extraction-based system able to extract triples from a corpus containing concepts belonging to an existing input legal ontology. The triples found by the system can be explored, discovering unprecedented interactions between the concepts. We compared our system with three existing OIE systems, founding that our performed well. As future work, we want to improve the Open Information Extraction system as well as the integrated visualization module, directing the investigation towards questions posed by subject experts interested in the contents of the European directives.

References

1. Banko, M., Cafarella, M.J., Soderland, S., Broadhead, M., Etzioni, O.: Open information extraction from the web. In: IJCAI, vol. 7, pp. 2670–2676 (2007)
2. Bojanowski, P., Grave, E., Joulin, A., Mikolov, T.: Enriching word vectors with subword information. arXiv preprint arXiv:1607.04606 (2016)
3. Carlson, A., Betteridge, J., Kisiel, B., Settles, B., Hruschka Jr, E.R., Mitchell, T.M.: Toward an architecture for never-ending language learning. In: AAAI, vol. 5, p. 3 (2010)
4. Del Corro, L., Gemulla, R.: ClausIE: clause-based open information extraction. In: Proceedings of the 22nd International Conference on World Wide Web, pp. 355–366. ACM (2013)
5. Delli Bovi, C., Espinosa Anke, L., Navigli, R.: Knowledge base unification via sense embeddings and disambiguation. In: Proceedings of the 2015 Conference on Empirical Methods in Natural Language Processing, pp. 726–736. Association for Computational Linguistics, Lisbon, Portugal, September 2015. http://aclweb.org/anthology/D15-1084
6. Fader, A., Soderland, S., Etzioni, O.: Identifying relations for open information extraction. In: Proceedings of the Conference on Empirical Methods in Natural Language Processing, pp. 1535–1545. Association for Computational Linguistics (2011)
7. Manning, C., Surdeanu, M., Bauer, J., Finkel, J., Bethard, S., McClosky, D.: The stanford coreNLP natural language processing toolkit. In: Proceedings of 52nd Annual Meeting of the Association for Computational Linguistics: System Demonstrations, pp. 55–60 (2014)
8. Moro, A., Navigli, R.: Integrating syntactic and semantic analysis into the open information extraction paradigm. In: IJCAI (2013)
9. Nakashole, N., Weikum, G., Suchanek, F.: PATTY: a taxonomy of relational patterns with semantic types. In: Proceedings of the 2012 Joint Conference on Empirical Methods in Natural Language Processing and Computational Natural Language Learning, pp. 1135–1145. Association for Computational Linguistics (2012)
10. Schmitz, M., Bart, R., Soderland, S., Etzioni, O., et al.: Open language learning for information extraction. In: Proceedings of the 2012 Joint Conference on Empirical Methods in Natural Language Processing and Computational Natural Language Learning, pp. 523–534. Association for Computational Linguistics (2012)

11. Speer, R., Havasi, C.: Representing general relational knowledge in conceptNet 5. In: LREC, pp. 3679–3686 (2012)
12. Wu, F., Weld, D.S.: Open information extraction using Wikipedia. In: Proceedings of the 48th Annual Meeting of the Association for Computational Linguistics, pp. 118–127. Association for Computational Linguistics (2010)

Ontology-Based Information Retrieval: Development of a Semantic-Based Tool for the Media Industry

Ricardo Eito-Brun[✉]

Universidad Carlos III de Madrid, c/Madrid, Getafe, Madrid, Spain
reito@bib.uc3m.es

Abstract. This paper describes the creation of an RDF ontology designed to support information retrieval needs of journalists and media professionals.

The purpose of the ontology is to complete the automated extensions of query terms by using the relationships between the concepts and terms registered in the ontology. By using this ontology, end-users can identify additional concepts that are related to the selected topic, and incorporate new terms to the query that will be later launched against a full-text indexer based on SOLR.

The ontology focuses on politics, and has been successfully tested with the collaboration of a large Spanish media company. The ontology contributes to a better recall of the search results.

Keywords: Human computer interaction ·
Ontologies and controlled vocabularies · Semantic technologies in industry

1 Introduction

This paper describes the development of a RDF-based ontology to support end-users in the construction of complex queries. The development of this ontology has been done for a Spanish TV and communication company. This company has an internal department of searchers with around fifty employees, who are in charge of searching for information and data to support the preparation of the TV programs and scripts. The information they search is kept in an Oracle/Open Text based database that store the transcriptions of the video files, interviews, etc.

Searchers searching for information in this database must figure out the terms that can be useful to build complex queries and ensure the relevance and recall of the search results. They have also developed lists of terms and thesauri that can be manually searched to identify similar, equivalent and related terms that can be incorporated to their queries.

With the aim of improving the recall of the current system, the development of an ontology was proposed to store and keep complex relationships between concepts and entities. In particular, it was relevant to keep the information about the relations between persons and entities and the different designations that can be used to refer to them.

© Springer Nature Switzerland AG 2019
E. Garoufallou et al. (Eds.): MTSR 2018, CCIS 846, pp. 188–195, 2019.
https://doi.org/10.1007/978-3-030-14401-2_18

The typical use case that represents a common query in the daily activity of searchers refers to finding members of an organization – e.g., members of a political party, national, regional or local government – talking about a particular topic. These queries are complex to build, as searchers should identify in advance all the persons who are members of that particular entity in order to build an exhaustive query.

With the help of the ontology, searchers will be able of expressing their information need (finding any of the members of a target institution or entity) without worrying in advance who are those persons and without worrying about their current membership to the target entity or institution. All these relations are stored in the ontology, and the system will use it to automatically expand the query adding all the alternative designations available for the persons who match those criteria.

The ontology sits in the middle, between the searchers building the queries and the information retrieval system. The ontology keeps the names and terms that can be incorporated to complex queries in order to improve the recall of the search results. Query expansion is a field where research efforts have been made based on traditional knowledge organization tools [1, 2]. Today, ontologies and semantic data based language offer additional possibilities to leverage current information retrieval systems and to improve recall [3–5].

The proposed solution supports two methods of interaction between the user and the ontology:

The module used to build the queries shows to the searcher the terms and names – extracted from the ontology – that represent the different designations for the entities and persons matching the end-user's interests. The searchers can then select the terms/designations they want to add to the query.

The module used to build the query expands automatically the query by adding those terms extracted from the ontology that match the users' interests.

In both cases, this module will build the query by combining the names and designations using the OR operator, and will run the query against the full-text index.

The activities completed for the development of this solution included:

Semantic modeling and creation of the ontology. The initial scope of the ontology was limited to politics and sports, although it was later expanded to include additional entities for arts, enterprises, geographic locations, celebrities, etc.

Assessment, selection and deployment of tools to maintain the ontologies. This phase was relevant, as one of the objectives of the project was to change the focus of the searcher work from building complex queries to maintain and evolve the ontology.

The final objective is that any user working for the company could work autonomously with the information retrieval system taking the advantage of the assistance provided by the query builder and the ontology files.

2 Technical Approach

The proposed technical approach was based on the following principles:

– Descoping the ontology and the information retrieval tool.

The tool used for keeping the content and searching used full-text capabilities were not modified, and an additional layer was built to assists the end-users build complex queries with the help of the ontologies. By keeping the ontology data in separate files, using the W3C standards, the capability of reusing the ontology data in other projects beyond their initial purpose was ensured.

- Descoping the data from their exploitation and visualization in the Web.

The use of W3C standards for ontology modeling (RDF/XML, RDFS) ensures the independence of the data with respect to their exploitation and visualization in the web. The use of XML technologies allows building different user interfaces to explore the ontology contents.

3   Content of the Ontology

3.1   Competence Queries

As previously stated, the purpose of the ontology is to support the expansion of query terms starting with the information or concept initially provided by the searcher.

The first step in the development of the ontology (following the recommendations of the popular methodologies like Methontology [6], Ontology 101 [7], etc.), was the identification of the typical information needs of the future ontology users. These competence questions were identified by means of interviews kept with a set of user representatives. Examples of these competence questions are listed below:

- Leaders of a political party talking about a merge of two companies.
- People involved in specific events, including judiciary cases.
- Leaders of a regional government talking about a natural disaster.
- Celebrities giving their opinion about a politician.
- Spanish football players playing in the Premier League.
- Politicians involved in corruption cases.
- Sportsmen and sportswomen who have been involved in doping/drug consumption.
- Celebrities who have divorced due to infidelity.
- Artists talking about budget cuts made by the government.
- Etc.

The analysis of these competence questions led to the identification of the main entities or classes in the ontology, and their relationships. Once the entity types were identified, the project team – with the collaboration of the end-users representatives – identified the data sources where the different data (that is to say, the ontology individuals) could be identified to feed the RDF files. Data sources included different public, open sites, and some information was extracted from Dbpedia and national initiatives for publishing linked, open data.

Ontology modeling was done using the RDFS and OWL languages. The creation of classes and properties was done incrementally, as additional data was identified and added in response to the information needs stated by the end-user representatives.

In general terms, the ontology distinguishes two types of data:

– Those relative to entities, persons and organizations.
– Those relatives to "topics". These topics were identified in response to the competence questions with the form: "people talking about that topic", and their structure is similar to a classical thesaurus. Alternative, more generic and more specific terms used to refer to topics were added to this section of the ontology to expand the queries.

Regarding the first section of the ontology, it includes data about:

– People, organizations and groups.
– Relationships between people, organizations and groups.
– Events in which people or organizations have participated.

3.2   Identification of the Main Classes and Properties

The ontology establish an initial division between Agents and Events. These classes are further divided into subclasses. For example, the Agents class includes subclasses for Persons, Families and Organizations. The Organizations class is further divided into different subclasses: political parties, companies, trade unions, sport clubs, governments, public administration entities, etc.

The Events class also includes different subclasses like judiciary cases, war conflicts, political conflicts, sport competitions, etc., which are also further subdivided.

The names used for classes, properties and individuals were taken – in some cases – from existing namespaces (e.g. Dbpedia). In those cases where it was not possible to identify reusable classes or properties, as well as individuals -, a specific namespace was used to group the ontology terms. The set of reused terms include some class and property names taken from the SKOS vocabulary (prefLabel, altLabel), FOAF or DBPEDIA (dbpprop:firstName, dbpprop:genre, dbprop:lastName, etc.).

3.3   Individuals

The individuals in the ontology were identified by URIs (Uniform Resource Identifiers), according to Semantic Web standard practices. In the case of entities that are part of another entity (e.g. administrative divisions or departments), a naming convention was applied to reflect this dependencies (the identifier of the dependent department was preceded by the name of the upper-level entity, and both names were separated by the ._ characters).

Individuals' data also included a set of alternative designations used to refer to the entity. This information was relevant for the purpose of the ontology, as the query expansion requirements request the inclusion of alternative designations used to refer to a person or entity, in order to ensure the appropriate recall in the query results. For example, the alternative designations for an individual can include variants like "Mariano Rajoy Brey", "Mariano Rajoy", or "Presidente Rajoy".

The ontology needs to represent the activity, profession or dedication of the individuals (sportsmen, politicians, etc.) This can be done using a hierarchically arranged set of classes to which the individuals belong (having different classes for each profession), or by means of a property that stores the relation between the individuals and the different professions.

The first alternative offers a greater flexibility for query expansion. Having a hierarchy of classes based on professions allows representing facts like "a singer is a kind of artist", and when an individual is assigned to a class (e.g. Antonio López is a painter) then he is automatically related to the ancestor classes (in this case, Artists).

Another aspect represented in the ontology is the fact that one person belongs to a specific group, institution or organization. RDF restrictions – where triples are composed of a subject, predicate and object -, make difficult the representation of these relationships, as an RDF statement only permits the representation of relationships between two individuals (the one used as subject and the one used as object). This restriction makes difficult to represent facts that involve more than one individuals or entities, e.g., expressing that one person plays a specific role in an entity, or that one person played a specific role in an institution for a specific time period.

To represent these facts, the team decided to represent them by means of classes acting as domains for several properties that associate these classes with individuals, roles or time periods. The ontology incorporated a Memberships class, which was the domain of several properties, for example:

- Member – the range of this property is the Person class and any of its subclasses.
- Organization – the range of this property is the Organization class or any of its subclasses.
- Role – this property is used to indicate the role of the person in the entity. Roles are identified by two sub-properties:
    role – this property has as a range a subclass, to support taking its value from a predefined list.
    roleDesc – this property has as a range a string, to complete its value using free text with no restriction.
- dateIn and dateEx – these properties are used to indicate the time period when the relationship was active.
- Season – this property is used for sport competitions, to indicate the season when the sportsman was a member of a club or team.

Individuals of the Membership class could be created as anonym nodes, but instead of that, automatically generated IDs have been assigned and used as part of its URI. This approach gives the possibility of referring to those individuals from other sections of the ontology in case it is needed.

The next fragments show the RDF/XML code used to represent the relations of membership. The example indicates that the politician José Luis Ábalos belongs to a specific political party, and that the Abdoulaye_Doucouré football player played for the team "Granada C.F." in the 2015–16 season:

```
<org:Membership rdf:about="http://www.uc3m.com/onto/Mem-
bership_78">
<org:dateIn>2011-12-15</org:dateIn>
  <org:organization rdf:resource="
PP._Grupo_Parlamentario"/>
  <org:member rdf:resource="
José_Luis_Ábalos_Meco"/> </org:Membership>

<org:organization rdf:re-
source="http://www.uc3m.com/onto/Gra-
nada_Club_de_Fútbol"/>
  <org:member rdf:re-
source="http://www.uc3m.com/onto/Abdoulaye_Doucouré"/>
<org:season>2015-2016</org:season>
</org:Membership>
```

Another aspect that was necessary to represent was the whole-part relationships. This was important to represent that one organization is made up of different areas, departments or dependent units. A specific property – isPartOf -, was added to the ontology to represent these relationships.

4 Validation of the Ontology

The validation of the ontology was done by answering to the competence questions identified in the initial step of the project. The data were loaded into an RDF repository tool supporting the SPARQL query language.

The next examples shows some of the SPARQL queries used to validate the ontology, giving answer to the specified user needs:

- List of the presidents of regional governments that belong to a specific political party:

```
SELECT ?name ?region
WHERE
{
   ?subject skos:prefLabel ?name .
   ?subject rdf:type <http://www.uc3m.com/onto/Politic> .
   ?subject org:memberOf <http://www.uc3m.com/onto/PP> .
   ?subject org:hasMembership ?member .
   ?member org:role <http://www.uc3m.com/onto/Presi-
dente_Gobierno_Autonómico> .
   ?member org:organization ?regionID .
   ?regionID skos:prefLabel ?region .
}
```

– People involved in a corruption case:

```
SELECT ?name
WHERE
{
  ?subject skos:prefLabel ?name .
  ?subject rdf:type <http://www.uc3m.com/onto/Person> .
  ?subject :isImputedIn* <http://www.uc3m.com/onto/Gur-
tel> .
}
```

– Relatives of the people involved in a corruption case:

```
SELECT ?imputado ?pareja
WHERE
{
  ?subject skos:prefLabel ?imputado .
  ?subject :isImputedIn*
<http://www.uc3m.com/onto/Gur-tel> .
  ?relative :marriedWith ?subject .
  ?relative skos:prefLabel ?familiar .
}
```

– Politicians who have joined the national parliament after January1st 2015:

```
SELECT ?diputado ?ini
WHERE
{
  ?subject skos:prefLabel ?diputado .
  ?subject org:hasMembership ?membership .
  ?membership org:organization
<http://www.uc3m.com/onto/PSOE_._Grupo_Parlamentario> .
  ?membership org:dateIn ?ini .
FILTER (?ini > "2015-01-01"^^xsd:date)
}
```

In order to make the creation of SPARQL queries easier – avoiding end-users the need of knowing this language's syntax, a user interface was created. The user interface in-corporates a set of drop-down lists that are completed with the main elements of the ontology (classes and properties). These values (the list of classes and properties) are dynamically loaded as the end-user interacts with the user interface.

As a first step, the users must load the entity type or the class of the individuals they want to incorporate to the query. For example, if they are interested in getting a list of politicians, they should select the corresponding class in the first drop-down list. The system will load automatically – in a separate drop-down list -, the list of properties that are related to the chosen class. The query-builder allows the combination of several criteria used to create the SPARQL query, and incorporates information on the ontology structure to let the users know the meaning and semantic of the different classes and properties.

References

1. Qiu, Y., Frei, H.P.: Concept based query expansion. In: Proceedings of the 16th Annual International ACM SIGIR Conference on Research and Development in Information retrieval, pp. 160–169. ACM, July 1993
2. Sihvonen, A., Vakkari, P.: Subject knowledge improves interactive query expansion assisted by a thesaurus. J. Doc. **60**(6), 673–690 (2004)
3. Chauhan, R., Goudar, R., Sharma, R., Chauhan, A.: Domain ontology based semantic search for efficient information retrieval through automatic query expansion. In: 2013 International Conference on Intelligent Systems and Signal Processing (ISSP), pp. 397–402. IEEE, March 2013
4. Bhogal, J., MacFarlane, A., Smith, P.: A review of ontology based query expansion. Inf. Process. Manag. **43**(4), 866–886 (2007)
5. Fu, G., Jones, C.B., Abdelmoty, A.I.: Ontology-based spatial query expansion in information retrieval. In: Meersman, R., Tari, Z. (eds.) OTM 2005, Part II. LNCS, vol. 3761, pp. 1466–1482. Springer, Heidelberg (2005). https://doi.org/10.1007/11575801_33
6. Corcho, O., Fernández-López, M., Gómez-Pérez, A., López-Cima, A.: Building legal ontologies with METHONTOLOGY and WebODE. In: Benjamins, V.R., Casanovas, P., Breuker, J., Gangemi, A. (eds.) Law and the Semantic Web. LNCS (LNAI), vol. 3369, pp. 142–157. Springer, Heidelberg (2005). https://doi.org/10.1007/978-3-540-32253-5_9
7. Noy, N.F., McGuinness, D.L.: Ontology development 101: a guide to creating your first ontology (2001). http://liris.cnrs.fr/alain.mille/enseignements/Ecole_Cen-trale/What%20is%20an%20ontology%20and%20why%20we%20need%20it.htm

Cultural Collections and Applications

Evaluating Data Quality in Europeana: Metrics for Multilinguality

Péter Király[1], Juliane Stiller[2](✉), Valentine Charles[3], Werner Bailer[4],
and Nuno Freire[5]

[1] Gesellschaft für wissenschaftliche Datenverarbeitung mbH, Göttingen, Germany
peter.kiraly@gwdg.de
[2] Humboldt-Universität zu Berlin, Berlin, Germany
juliane.stiller@ibi.hu-berlin.de
[3] Europeana Foundation, The Hague, Netherlands
valentine.charles@europeana.eu
[4] Joanneum Research, Graz, Austria
werner.bailer@joanneum.at
[5] INESC-ID, Lisboa, Portugal
nuno.freire@tecnico.ulisboa.pt

Abstract. Europeana.eu aggregates metadata describing more than 50 million cultural heritage objects from libraries, museums, archives and audiovisual archives across Europe. The need for quality of metadata is particularly motivated by its impact on user experience, information retrieval and data re-use in other contexts. One of the key goals of Europeana is to enable users to retrieve cultural heritage resources irrespective of their origin and the material's metadata language. The presence of multilingual metadata descriptions is therefore essential for successful cross-language retrieval. Quantitatively determining Europeana's cross-lingual reach is a prerequisite for enhancing the quality of metadata in various languages. Capturing multilingual aspects of the data requires us to take into account the full lifecycle of data aggregation including data enhancement processes such as automatic data enrichment. The paper presents an approach for assessing multilinguality as part of data quality dimensions, namely completeness, consistency, conformity and accessibility. We describe the measures defined and implemented, and provide initial results and recommendations.

Keywords: Metadata quality · Multilinguality ·
Digital cultural heritage · Europeana · Data quality dimensions

1 Introduction

Europeana.eu[1] is Europe's digital platform for cultural heritage. It aggregates metadata describing more than 50 million cultural heritage objects from a wide

---

[1] http://www.europeana.eu/.

variety of institutions (libraries, museums, archives and audiovisual archives) across Europe. The need for high-quality metadata is particularly motivated by its impact on search, the overall Europeana user experience, and on data re-use in other contexts such as the creative industries, education and research. One of the key goals of Europeana is to enable users to find the cultural heritage objects that are relevant to their information needs irrespective of their national or institutional origin and the material's metadata language.

As highlighted in the White Paper on Best Practices for Multilingual Access to Digital Libraries [13], most digital cultural heritage objects do not have a specific language, i.e., as they are not in textual form, and can only be searched through their metadata, which is text in a particular language. The presence of multilingual metadata descriptions is therefore essential for improving the retrieval of these objects across language spaces. Quantitatively determining Europeana's cross-lingual reach is a prerequisite for enhancing the quality of metadata in various languages.

In this paper, we present multilinguality as a measurable component of different data quality dimensions: completeness, consistency, conformity and accessibility. We capture data quality by defining and implementing quality measures along the full data-aggregation lifecycle, taking also into account the impact of data enhancement processes such as semantic enrichment. The model the data is represented in, namely the Europeana Data Model (EDM)[2], is also a key element of our work.

In the next section, we present data quality frameworks, dimensions and criteria that are commonly referred to in the context of data quality measurement. Section 3 describes how multilingual metadata is presented in Europeana's data model and the data quality dimensions we use are also introduced. In Sect. 4, we describe the implementation of the different measures as well as the calculation of the scores. Section 5 describes first results and measures that were taken to improve metadata along the different quality dimensions and the first recommendations we have been able to identify based on the results from the metrics. We conclude this paper with an outline of future work.

2   State of the Art

Addressing data quality requires the identification of the data features that need to be improved and this is closely linked to the purpose the metadata is serving. Libraries have always highlighted that bibliographic metadata enables users to find material, to identify an item and to select and obtain an entity [6]. Based on this, Park [10] expands functional requirements of bibliographic data to discovery, use, provenance, currency, authentication and administration, and related quality dimensions. The approach to metadata assessment for cultural heritage repositories presented in [2] also starts from use for a specific purpose. While the work mentions the issue of multilinguality, it does not propose specific metrics to measure it.

---

[2] http://pro.europeana.eu/edm-documentation.

Different sets of dimensions have been proposed for classifying metadata quality measures. Bruce and Hillmann [3] define the following measures for quality: completeness, accuracy, provenance, conformance, logical consistency and coherence, timeliness and accessibility, multilinguality is not addressed in this work. The existing works that consider multilinguality assign it to different quality dimensions, depending on the purpose of the measurement. Zaveri et al. [16] propose dimensions for quality assessment for linked data. Completeness is listed as an intrinsic criterion, while multilinguality is covered by versatility, which is considered a representational criterion. The ISO/IEC 25012 standard [8] defines a data quality model with 15 characteristics, discriminating between inherent and system-dependent ones, but putting many of the criteria in the overlap between the two classes. Completeness is defined as an inherent criterion, while accessibility and compliance (conformity) are in the overlapping area. Multilinguality could be seen as being compliant to providing a certain number of elements in a certain number of languages, and as enabling access to users who are able to search and understand results in certain languages. Radulović et al. [11] propose a metadata quality model for linked data, and define multiple languages as an indicator for the quality dimension availability, i.e., can it be accessed by users with the requirement to get the data in a specific language. Ellefi et al. [5] propose a taxonomy of features for profiling RDF datasets, of which one part discusses quality. They define representativity as one dimension of quality in their model, under which they see versatility (including multilinguality) as one measure. To the best of the authors' knowledge, the only resource which actually measured multilingual features in metadata is [14], cited in [9]. Albertoni et al. [1] also include multilinguality in a scoring function, although in the context of importing other linked data vocabularies.

It becomes apparent that while multilinguality is considered in some works, it is usually not treated as a separate quality dimension, but rather as part of other criteria or dimensions existing at quite different levels in different quality models. We use the measures based on the frequency of language tags described in [14] as a basis, and following the conclusion from the literature, consider multilinguality in the context of different quality dimensions. Our work started with the development of metrics to measure the multilingual quality of metadata in Europeana within the EU-funded project Europeana DSI-2[3]. A first iteration of a multilingual saturation score that counted language tags across metadata fields in the Europeana collections as well as the existence of links to multilingual vocabularies was introduced by Stiller and Király [12]. The score was extended in [4] by including measures that define multilinguality as part of different quality dimensions.

3   Approach

Firstly, to determine the multilingual degree of metadata across several quality dimensions, we have to understand the different ways multilingual information

---

[3] https://pro.europeana.eu/project/europeana-dsi-2.

is expressed in Europeana's data model. Secondly, the structure of multilingual data informs the criteria and metrics that enable us to measure multilinguality across several metadata quality dimensions.

3.1 Multilingual Information in Europeana's Metadata

Multilinguality in Europeana's metadata has two perspectives: concerning the language of the object itself, and the language of the metadata that describes this object. First, the described cultural object, insofar as it is textual, audiovisual or in any other way a linguistic artefact, has a language. The data providers are urged to indicate the language of the object in the *dc:language* field in the Europeana Data Model (EDM) in this way: `<dc:language>de</dc:language>`. If used consistently and in accordance with standards for language codes, this information could then be used to populate a language facet allowing users to filter result-sets by language of objects. The language information is essential for users who want to use objects in their preferred language. Second, the language of metadata is essential for retrieving items and determining their relevance. Metadata descriptions are textual and therefore have a language. Each value in the metadata fields can be provided with a language tag (or language attribute). Ideally, the language is known and indicated by this tag for every literal in each field. If several language tags in different languages exist, the multilingual value can be considered to be higher. For instance, consider as an example this data provided by an institution:

```
<#example> a ore:Proxy ;  # data from provider
  dc:subject "Ballet",    # literal
  dc:subject "Opera"@en . # literal with language tag
```

The first *dc:subject* statement is without language information, whereas the second tells us that the literal is in English. Multilingual information is not only provided by the institutions but can also be introduced by Europeana. Europeana assesses metadata in particular fields to enrich it automatically with controlled and multilingual vocabularies as defined in the Europeana Semantic Enrichment Framework.[4] As shown in the following example, the dereferencing of the link (i.e., retrieving all the multilingual data attached to concepts defined in a linked data service) allows Europeana to add the language variants for this particular keyword to its search index.

```
<#example> a ore:Proxy ; edm:europeanaProxy true ;
  # enrichment by Europeana with multilingual vocabulary
  dc:subject <http://data.europeana.eu/concept/base/264> .

<http://data.europeana.eu/concept/base/264> a skos:Concept ;
  # language variants are added to index
  skos:prefLabel "Ballett"@no, "Ballett"@de, "Balé"@pt,
                 "Baletas"@lt, "Balet"@hr, "Balets"@lv .
```

---

[4] https://docs.google.com/document/d/1JvjrWMTpMIH7WnuieNqcT0zpJAXUPo6 x4uMBj1pEx0Y/edit.

The record now has more multilingual information than at the time of ingestion into Europeana. The labels are added to the search index and this particular record can be retrieved with various language variants of the term *ballet*. The different language versions from multilingual vocabularies are likely to be translation variants. This distinction between the provided metadata and the metadata created by Europeana needs to be taken into account for measuring multilinguality as defined in Sect. 4.

3.2 Multilinguality as a Facet of Quality Dimensions

For measuring multilinguality, we identify four quality dimensions: completeness, consistency, conformity and accessibility. Each of these dimensions assesses multilinguality from a different perspective.

Completeness. Completeness is a basic quality measure, expressing the number (proportion) of fields present in a dataset, and identifying non-empty values in a record or (sub-)collection. For a fixed set of fields, completeness is thus straightforward to measure, and can be expressed as the absolute number or fraction of the fields present and not empty. However, the measure becomes non-trivial when data is represented using a data model with optional fields (that may e.g. only be applicable for certain types of objects), or with certain fields for which the cardinality is unlimited (e.g., allowing zero to many subjects or keywords). These characteristics apply to EDM. In such cases the measure becomes unbounded, and a few fields with high cardinality may outweigh or swamp other fields.

In the context of measuring multilingual completeness, the metric is two-fold. First, the concept of completeness can be applied to measuring the presence of fields with language tags. This measure of multilinguality must be seen in relation to the results of measuring completeness. Only fields both present and non-empty can be said to have or lack language tags and translations. A record which is 80% complete can still reach 100% multilingual completeness if all present and non-empty fields have a language tag. Second, the completeness measure can reflect the presence of the *dc:language* field that identifies the language of the described object.

Consistency. Consistency describes the logical coherence of the metadata across fields and within a collection. With regard to multilinguality, the dimension assesses the variety of language values in the *dc:language* field and the language tags that specify the language in a given field. Consistent values should be used to describe the same language.

In Europeana, the consistency measure for the *dc:language* field is mainly relevant for the language facet. The more consistent languages are expressed, the more useful language facets become. Ideally, inconsistencies in expressing languages through language codes should be fixed through normalization (see Sect. 5).

Conformity. Conformity refers to the accordance with values to a given standard or a set of rules. Here, the language values in the *dc:language* field and the language tags in any given field can be assessed with regard to their conformity to a given standard such as ISO-639-2[5]. The conformity measure for the *dc:language* field influences the usefulness of a language facet.

Table 1. Dimensions, criteria and measures for assessing multilinguality in metadata.

Dimension	Criteria	Measures
Completeness	Presence or absence of values in fields relating to the language of the object or the metadata	• Share of multilingual fields to overall fields • Presence or absence of *dc:language* field
Consistency	Variance in language notation	• Distinct language notations
Conformity	Compliance to ISO-639-2	• Binary or share of values that comply or not comply
Accessibility	Multilingual saturation	• Numbers of distinct languages • Number of language tagged literals • Tagged literals per language

Accessibility. Accessibility describes the degree to which multilingual information is present in the data, and allows us to understand how easy or hard it is for users with different language backgrounds to access information. So far, Europeana has little knowledge about the distribution of linguistic information in its metadata – especially within single records. To quantify the multilingual degree of data and measure cross-lingual accessibility, the language tag is crucial. The more language tags representing different languages are present, the higher is the multilingual reach. Resulting metrics can be scaled to the field, record and collection levels. In practical terms, the accessibility measure serves to gauge cross-language recall and entity-based facet performance. To summarize: with regard to multilinguality, we identified the dimensions, quality criteria and measures presented in Table 1.

4   Operationalizing the Metrics for Multilinguality

The different metrics for the assessment of multilinguality in metadata are implemented in the metadata quality assurance framework of Europeana.[6] Implementation of the metrics requires a good understanding of the data aggregation workflows which can contribute to the increase of multilingual labels (such as machine learning and natural language processing techniques for language detection, automatic tagging, or semantic enrichment) in the metadata. Before

---

[5] https://www.loc.gov/standards/iso639-2/php/code_list.php.
[6] http://144.76.218.178/europeana-qa/multilinguality.php?id=all.

being displayed in Europeana, the source data goes through several levels of data aggregation. EDM doesn't represent the different data processes that take place at each of these levels but captures the different data outputs. EDM allows us to distinguish between (a) values provided by the data provider(s) and (b) information (automatically) added by Europeana (for instance by semantic enrichment) by leveraging on the proxy mechanism from the Object Re-use and Exchange (ORE) model. The metadata provided to Europeana are captured under a `ore:Proxy` while the metadata created by Europeana are captured under a `edm:EuropeanaProxy`. The examples in Sect. 3.1 demonstrate how the mechanism enables the representation of resources in the context of different aggregations of the same resource [7]. Any implementation of quality measures, and in particular of multilingual ones, needs to take into account this distinction. For instance, the score for accessibility might be higher if we only consider the Europeana proxy where a value was enriched with a multilingual vocabulary (e.g. DBpedia) leading to more language tags than initially provided by an institution.

4.1   Measurement Workflow

The process for assessing the multilinguality of metadata is based on the metadata quality assurance framework, which has four phases:

1. Data collection and preparation: the EDM records are collected via Europeana's OAI-PMH service[7], transformed to JSON where each record is stored in a separate line, and stored in Hadoop Distributed File System[8].
2. Record-level measurement: the Java applications[9] measuring different features of the records run as Apache Spark jobs, allowing them to scale readily. The process generates CSV files which record the results of the measurements such as the number of field instances, or complex multilingual metrics.
3. Statistical analysis: the CSV files are analyzed using statistical methods implemented in R and Scala. The purpose of this phase is to calculate statistical tendencies on the dataset level and create graphical representations (histograms, boxplots). The results are stored in JSON and PNG files.
4. User interface: interactive HTML and SVG representations of the results such as tables, heat maps, and spider charts. We use PHP, jQuery, d3.js and highchart.js to generate them.

---

[7] https://pro.europeana.eu/resources/apis/oai-pmh-service.   Our   client   library: https://github.com/pkiraly/europeana-oai-pmh-client/.

[8] We made two data snapshots available: 2015 December (46 million records, 392 GB): https://hdl.handle.net/21.11101/EAEA0-826A-2D06-1569-0, 2018 March (55 million records, 1,1 TB): http://hdl.handle.net/21.11101/e7cf0a0-1922-401b-a1ae-6ec9261484c0.

[9] Source code and binaries: http://pkiraly.github.io/about/#source-code.

Since we intend to measure multilingual saturation of the provided and enriched metadata separately, we perform measurements for the following objects: the provider (source) created proxy S, the Europeana created proxy E (containing enrichments) and the whole EDM record O. Each proxy has several properties, such as *dc:title*, *dc:subject*, etc. These properties might have multiple instances. Each instance might have either a string only, a tagged literal or a URI. We suppose that if the URI is resolvable then a contextual object was created, so we check only whether a contextual entity exists within the same object. If we found one, we use its *skos:prefLabel* property to check whether it is a string or tagged literal.

For each property we define the following quantities: nt_p, the number of tagged literals of a property p, l_p, the list of language tags of p and d_p, the set of distinct language tags of p, thus $|d_p| \leq |l_p|$.

We calculate the basic scores for both proxies. We denote the four resulting values for the proxies as tp_S, tp_E, the number of tagged properties in provider and Europeana proxies, tl_S, tl_E, the number of tagged literals, dl_S, dl_E, the set of distinct language tags, and nl, the number of distinct languages.

On object level, these values are aggregated from the proxies by summation/union, i.e., $tp_O = tp_S + tp_E$, $tl_O = tl_S + tl_E$, $dl_O = dl_S \cup dl_E$, and $nl_O = |dl_O|$. Note that $l_O \leq (l_S + l_E)$, as the provider and Europeana proxy typically contain overlapping languages. In many practical cases, it is likely that $l_O = \max(l_S, l_E)$.

4.2 Deriving Metrics from Basic Scores

In this section, we discuss how we derive metrics from these scores that relate to the different quality dimensions concerning multilingual saturation.

Completeness. The number of languages present can be used to measure completeness, in particular, when the resulting score is also checked against a target value. A basic metric is the fraction of properties and literals that have language tags, i.e., $fp_S = \frac{tp_S}{|p \in S|}$ and $fl_S = \frac{tl_S}{\sum_{p \in S} l_p}$, where $p \in S$ is the set of properties of S. The same calculation can be applied to E and O. The languages per property for the proxies and the object are defined as the normalized number of languages, i.e., $lpp_S = \frac{l_S}{tp_S}$ (and analogously for E and O).

Consistency. We assess consistency of the language tags used throughout the dataset, such as standard vs. non-standard codes, two vs. three letter codes for the same language, short vs. extended language tags, etc. In order to determine a metric for consistency of language tags, we need external information that groups synonymous language identifications. The Languages Name Authority List (NAL) published in the European Union Open Data Portal[10] provides synonyms for languages. This vocabulary was used for language normalization as reported in Sect. 5.

---

[10] https://open-data.europa.eu/en/data/dataset/language.

We denote the set of languages as $L = \{l_1, \ldots, l_n\}$, and the language tag for language l_i in vocabulary v as $t_{l_i}^v$. Examples for v could be the two letter tags from ISO-639-1 or the different three letter tags from ISO-639-2/T and ISO-639-2/B. For each of the languages l_i we can thus define a set of tags T_i. For the standards, it is well defined which tags denote the same language, and using the syntactic rules of extended language tags those can be included as well (e.g., associate "en-gb" with "en"). In addition there may be custom tags, (e.g., "british english").

We can then determine the consistency as

$$cs_S = \frac{1}{l_S} \sum_{l_i \in dl_S} 1 - \frac{|\{t_{Sj}|j = 1, \ldots, tl_S\} \cup T_i| - 1}{\sum_{k=1}^{|T_i|} |\{t_{Sj}|j = 1, \ldots, tl_S\} \cup t_i^k|}, \tag{1}$$

where t_{Sj} is the language tag of literal j in S, and $\{t_{Sj}|j = 1, \ldots, tl_S\}$ is the set of language tags of the literals. This score is 1 if a single language tag is used for all literals, and close to 0 if each literal uses a different language tag. For E and O the score can be determined analogously.

Table 2. Results for the measures in the different dimensions.

Dimension	Measures	Results
Completeness	• Share of multilingual fields to overall fields • Presence or absence of *dc:language* field	• Measureable for each field per dataset • 25.5% of datasets (35.14% of records) have no *dc:language* field
Consistency	• Distinct language notations	• Over 400 distinct language notation across all fields
Conformity	• Binary or share of values that comply or not comply	• See Table 3 for statistics on conformity with ISO-639
Accessibility	• Numbers of distinct languages • Number of language tagged literals • Tagged literals per language	• Median of 6.0 (mean 41.2±53.65) per object • Median of 15.0 (mean 73.3±111.17) per object • Median of 1.6 (mean 2.3±3.46) per object

Conformity. We assess whether the language tags used are from a standard set of tags, such as one of the parts of ISO-639. Similar as for consistency, we define a set of possible standard tags of a language l_i, denoted as T_i'. We determine a conformity metric as the fraction of language tags from this set.

$$cf_S = \frac{1}{l_S} \sum_{l_i \in dl_S} \frac{\sum_{j=1}^{tl_S} |t_{Sj} \cup T_i'|}{tl_S}, \tag{2}$$

where t_{Sj} is the language tag of literal j in S. For E and O the score can be determined analogously.

Accessibility. The richness of metadata in a particular language is a metric for how easily the object can be found and interpreted in that language. Next to the number of distinct languages and the number of language tagged literals, we use the average number of tagged literals per language as a metric, and determine it as $tll_S = \frac{tl_S}{l_S}$ (an analogously for E and O).

5   Results

The metrics are implemented in the metadata quality assurance framework using a snapshot of the data from March 2018. In Table 2, we report on some of the results from various dimensions and describe some of the developments they initiated. The data quality issues observed in the results lead to a series of best practices beneficial for further improvement.

Completeness. With regard to the presence of the *dc:language* field, the measure indicates that 905 out of 3,548 datasets have no value in the *dc:language* field, which shows the field is missing. On a record level, 64.86% of the records have a *dc:language* field.[11] Furthermore, we can determine the share of multilingual fields across all records for given fields. For example, 97.05% of all records have a *dc:title* field. The great majority of these fields have no language indicated for their values. Approximately a fourth of the *dc:title* fields have values with a language. Titles in German, English, Dutch, Polish and Italian contribute to more than half of the *dc:title* values that have a language tag. The metric allows to investigate the share of fields with multilingual tags across specific datasets or Europeana as a whole. It is also possible to compare different versions of the Europeana dataset to track progress and improvements. In a multilingual context, the completeness of the metadata is improved by the presence of languages for metadata elements supporting literals (*dc:subject, dc:description, dc:title*), or by the presence of links to contextual entities with multilingual features.

Table 3. Presence of ISO-639 codes in the values of the dc:language field.

Total values in the Europeana dataset	33,070,941
Total values already normalized (ISO-639-1, 2 letter codes)	23,634,661
Total values already normalized (ISO-639-3, three letter codes)	4,831,534

Consistency. Next to measuring the consistency in the language tag notation, we specifically measured the consistency in the *dc:language* field. This revealed

---

[11] http://144.76.218.178/europeana-qa/frequency.php.

that over 400 different language variants are present in the field. To ensure consistent use of language codes over the whole collection, they need to be normalized and standards applied within the *dc:language* field. This element must be provided when a resource is of *edm:type* TEXT and should be provided for these other types (AUDIO, IMAGE, VIDEO, 3D). Identifying the absence of language is also needed to properly assess the degree of multilinguality. We therefore recommend the use of the ISO 639-2 code for non-linguistic content (i.e. "zxx").

Conformity. After determining the heterogeneity of values in *dc:language* (dimension: consistency), we normalize the values in this field. *Dc:language* values are predominantly normalized in ISO-639-1 or ISO-639-3, but, in contrast, values nevertheless sometimes occur in natural language sentences that cannot be processed automatically. We also find language ISO codes without their reference to the ISO standard in use, or references to languages by their name. A language normalization operation was implemented consisting of a mix of operations, comprising cleaning, normalization and enrichment of data. Table 3 presents some general statistics about the presence of ISO-639 codes in the values of *dc:language* in the Europeana dataset. The metric helps us to design further language normalization rules which in turn can be used to improve the results of the quality measures. Tackling the heterogeneity of languages tags in other fields is still an open issue that needs to be tackled in future.

Accessibility. As noted earlier, our approach to measuring multilingual saturation in metadata allows us not only to measure the data's quality as it is provided by contributing institutions, but also provides us with insight into the effectiveness of Europeana's data enhancement processes, such as semantic enrichment. The measures for accessibility allow us to determine the number of distinct language tags per dataset or specific fields revealing which languages are covered and can be exploited for display and retrieval. For example, the Europeana collection after applying its automatic data enhancement workflow to its datasets has a median of 6 distinct languages per object where the maximum of distinct languages in an object is 182. Per object, there are 15 language tagged literals (median) with 14.5% or the records do not have any tagged literals and one object having as many as 62,997 tagged literals. Delving into datasets, we can determine the amount of objects with particular language tags per field, as well as whether these language tags were coming from providers' data or are added by Europeana automatically. The results enable metadata experts to determine the multilingual reach of a dataset on field level and allow them to develop strategies for increasing the multilingual saturation. Being able to track progression over time by comparing different snapshots of the data is another valuable asset of the framework.

In summary, the results obtained for the dimensions above focus on the multilingual quality of the metadata with the sole objective to improve the accessibility of the cultural heritage objects available in Europeana.

6   Conclusion and Future Work

In this paper we present our approach for assessing the multilingual quality of data in the context of Europeana. This approach is the result of a long term research activity of Europeana, providing essential conclusions for the establishment of a reliable multilingual quality measurement for its services and data providers. The measures for multilinguality are embedded into the data dimensions of completeness, consistency, conformity, and accessibility. Results of these measures allow Europeana to define and implement language normalization rules and several recommendations for data providers.

We identify several potential improvements on the quality measures, which should be further elaborated in future iterations of this activity at Europeana. We also conclude that improvements of the metrics can be achieved if they consider more the needs of users providing data to Europeana or re-using it for building their own applications. Refining visualization reports will help interpreting the measurements and to adjust our metrics. For instance, in order to get a comprehensive view of the quality of data, the different metrics will need to be presented together (e.g. multilinguality on top of completeness) so that the interrelation between the different metrics is made visible.

The metrics proposed in this paper are potentially applicable to a wider range of applications, beyond providing multilingual access to cultural assets, as stated in the Strategic Research Agenda for Multilingual Europe 2020[12]. One other important application is research data, for which multilinguality may also be relevant. The FAIR principles [15] include findability and accessibility by both humans and machines — for which multilinguality is one component. We intend to publish the metrics in a way that can be consumed by third parties interested in the Europeana data, as well as applying them to their data. The recently published W3C Data Quality vocabulary[13] is a good candidate for a machine-readable representation of our metrics and the measurement results.

Acknowledgments. This work was partially supported by Portuguese national funds through Fundaç ão para a Ciência e a Tecnologia (FCT) with reference UID/CEC/50021/2013.

References

1. Albertoni, R., De Martino, M., Podesta, P.: A linkset quality metric measuring multilingual gain in SKOS thesauri. In: LDQ@ ESWC (2015)
2. Bellini, E., Nesi, P.: Metadata quality assessment tool for open access cultural heritage institutional repositories. In: Nesi, P., Santucci, R. (eds.) ECLAP 2013. LNCS, vol. 7990, pp. 90–103. Springer, Heidelberg (2013). https://doi.org/10.1007/978-3-642-40050-6_9

---

[12] http://www.meta-net.eu/sra/.
[13] https://www.w3.org/TR/vocab-dqv/.

3. Bruce, T.R., Hillmann, D.I.: The continuum of metadata quality: defining, expressing, exploiting. In: Hillmann, D., Westbrooks, E. (eds.) Metadata in Practice, pp. 238–256. ALA Editions, Chicago (2004)
4. Charles, V., Stiller, J., Király, P., Bailer, W., Freire, N.: Data quality assessment in Europeana: metrics for multilinguality. In: Annalina, C., et al. (eds.) Joint Proceedings of the 1st Workshop on Temporal Dynamics in Digital Libraries (TDDL 2017), the (Meta)-Data Quality Workshop (MDQual 2017) and the Workshop on Modeling Societal Future (Futurity 2017) (TDDL_MDQual_Futurity 2017) co-located with 21st International Conference on Theory and Practice of Digital Libraries (TPLD 2017), Grand Hotel Palace, Thessaloniki, Greece, 21 September 2017. CEUR Workshop Proceedings, vol. 2038 (2017). http://ceur-ws.org/Vol-2038
5. Ellefi, M.B., et al.: RDF dataset profiling-a survey of features, methods, vocabularies and applications. Semantic Web 9, 677–705 (2017)
6. IFLA: Functional requirements for Bibliographic records: final report/IFLA Study Group on the Functional Requirements for Bibliographic Records. No. vol. 19 in UBCIM publications; new series, K.G. Saur, München (1998)
7. Isaac, A.: Europeana data model primer. Technical report (2013)
8. ISO: ISO/IEC 25012, Software engineering - Software product Quality Requirements and Evaluation (SQuaRE) - Data quality model (2000)
9. Palavitsinis, N.: Metadata Quality Issues in Learning Repositories. Ph.D. thesis, Alcala de Henares, Spain, February 2014
10. Park, J.r.: Metadata quality in digital repositories: a survey of the current state of the art. Cataloging Classif. Q. 47(3–4), 213–228 (2009)
11. Radulovic, F., Mihindukulasooriya, N., García-Castro, R., Gómez-Pérez, A.: A comprehensive quality model for linked data. Semantic Web 9, 1–22 (2017). (Preprint)
12. Stiller, J., Király, P.: Multilinguality of metadata. Measuring the multilingual degree of Europeana's metadata. In: Proceedings of 15th International Symposium of Information Science (ISI), pp. 164–176 (2017)
13. Stiller, J. (ed.): White Paper on Best Practices for Multilingual Access to Digital Libraries. Technical report, Europeana (2016)
14. Vogias, K., Hatzakis, I., Manouselis, N., Szegedi, P.: Extraction and Visualization of Metadata Analytics for Multimedia Learning Object Repositories: The case of TERENA TF-media network (2013)
15. Wilkinson, M.D., et al.: The FAIR guiding principles for scientific data management and stewardship. Sci. Data 3 (2016)
16. Zaveri, A., Rula, A., Maurino, A., Pietrobon, R., Lehmann, J., Auer, S.: Quality assessment for linked data: a survey. Semantic Web 7(1), 63–93 (2016)

The Benefits of Linking Metadata for Internal and External Users of an Audiovisual Archive

Victor de Boer[1,2(✉)], Tim de Bruyn[1,2], John Brooks[1,2],
and Jesse de Vos[2]

[1] Vrije Universiteit Amsterdam, Amsterdam, The Netherlands
v.de.boer@vu.nl
[2] Netherlands Institute for Sound and Vision, Hilversum, The Netherlands

Abstract. Like other heritage institutions, audiovisual archives adopt structured vocabularies for their metadata management. With Semantic Web and Linked Data now becoming more and more stable and commonplace technologies, organizations are looking now at linking these vocabularies to external sources, for example those of Wikidata, DBPedia or GeoNames. However, the benefits of such endeavors to the organizations are generally underexplored. In this paper, we present an in-depth case study into the benefits of linking the "Common Thesaurus for Audiovisual Archives" (or GTAA) and the general-purpose dataset Wikidata. We do this by identifying various use cases for user groups that are both internal as well as external to the organization. We describe the use cases and various proofs-of-concept prototypes that address these use cases.

Keywords: Audiovisual metadata · Wikidata · Case study

1 Introduction

The Netherlands Institute for Sound and Vision (NISV)[1] is an audio-visual archive located in Hilversum, the Netherlands. This cultural historic institute manages over 70% of all material relating to Dutch AV heritage including Dutch radio programs, television programs, documentaries and music. Together with several other Dutch organisations who manage Dutch audio-visual heritage, NISV have developed the GTAA, the Common Thesaurus for Audio-visual Archives[2]. This thesaurus provides the terms used in part of the metadata for the audio-visual material. The GTAA includes person names, objects, subjects, genres, geographical data, concepts, company names and so on. It also contains synonyms, quasi-synonyms, homonyms and different spellings for these terms.

With the help of linked data, connections can be made between the own collection and other data sources [1]. Cultural heritage institutes like NISV are looking for new ways to manage their cultural heritage collections and are exploring the possibilities of

---

[1] http://beeldengeluid.nl.

[2] http://gtaa.beeldengeluid.nl.

© Springer Nature Switzerland AG 2019
E. Garoufallou et al. (Eds.): MTSR 2018, CCIS 846, pp. 212–223, 2019.
https://doi.org/10.1007/978-3-030-14401-2_20

using Linked Data to add value to their collections [2]. Cross-linking between organization- or domain-specific vocabularies and more general purpose linked data sets allows institutions to enhance their collection with a vast amount of additional data. This promise of Linked Data, coupled with the maturity and uptake of the technology has convinced many organizations of the potential added value of linked data. However, in many cases, the actual benefits to end-users remain unclear and underexplored. In this paper, we investigate the added value using four very specific use cases. We specifically do this for internal users and external users of the metadata. Internal users include employees and researchers inside the NISV organization, while external parties are heritage professionals, media professionals, teachers, students and researchers, each with their own information needs.

In each case, we start with a use case elicitation process based on interviews with the stakeholders. This process then results in a specified use case, where links between GTAA and the general-purpose knowledge base Wikidata [3] are exploited for a specific (information retrieval) task. We then develop a proof-of-concept tool or mockup that matches the use case and finally perform a limited evaluation to show the added value and receive additional feedback on the case. This work is limited to the part of GTAA describing persons, but similar cases can be constructed for other parts of GTAA.

In Sect. 3, we provide a brief analysis of GTAA, Wikidata and existing links for the person concept scheme. Then, in Sects. 4 and 5 we describe use cases for internal and external users respectively. In each section, we describe the elicitation method, the use cases themselves as well as the proof-of-concept end-user applications. We close this paper with a short discussion on generalized findings. In the next section, we first discuss related work.

2   Related Work

Vrandečić and Krötzsch state that Wikidata's goal is to allow its data to be used both internally and in external applications, such as the external thesauri [3]. Erxleben et al. have conducted research on Wikidata and its possibilities for being connected to the linked data [4]. They describe how Wikidata is linked to multiple external datasets. These existing links range from the ISSN dataset, which identifies all journals and magazines etcetera, to more highly specialized databases, such as the database of North Atlantic hurricanes. Färber et al. looked specifically into the quality of the most noteworthy large knowledge databases including Wikidata [5]. This extensive research show that multiple quality aspects of the data contained within Wikidata were the highest of any of the noteworthy knowledge graphs. This research provides motivation for our own research to investigate links to Wikidata.

Thornton et al. also conducted research on Wikidata's possible role to serve as repository for international organizations concerned with digital preservation [6]. They concluded that Wikidata had the advantage of being structured, query-able and computable. Another advantage Wikidata has is that it's multilingual. Since Wikidata also had a Dutch version it supports alignments to the GTAA better.

Debevere et al. conducted research into linked data to improve the metadata of thesauri. This improved metadata allows better retrieval of information on search queries. To this end, they developed an alignment algorithm that automatically linked data categories of DBpedia to another media thesaurus used to annotate archived media items at the Flemish public service broadcaster (VRT). It returned acceptable results, specifically for the Person category [7].

Tordai et al. provide a systematic approach to build a large semantic culture web [8]. They did so by making clear to heritage institutions what they need to do to make their collections fit for becoming a part of this semantic culture web. They advise to use the paradigm of open access, open data and open standards. They conclude that collection owners should be provided with the necessary support facilities.

A similar case study approach as ours was described in [9]. This paper describes the linking of a thesaurus for economics to DBpedia and other large thesauri using SKOS/RDF methods. In the end the linking to DBpedia returned a high number of unsuccessful matches. These unsuccessful matches are contributed to simple derivations in the compared strings and the fact that a significant number of economic concepts did not exist in DBpedia yet.

3   Analysis of Linked GTAA and Wikidata

GTAA. The Common Thesaurus for Audiovisual Archives (GTAA) is used by NISV to annotate the different collections. It follows the ISO-2788 standard for thesaurus structures and consists of several *concept schemes* the media objects: subjects, people, entities, locations, etc. The GTAA, available as SKOS, contains approximately 180,000 terms and is actively maintained, being updated as new concepts emerge on television. It includes about 90,000 scope notes.

Wikidata. Wikidata is continuous crowd-sourced concept where Wikipedia's data is cleaned and integrated to make it machine-readable as well as human-readable [3]. It is available in RDF and can be queried using the SPARQL query language. Each term or object within Wikidata has a unique identifier (URI), and several other identifiers from different sources. Each term has its own label, aliases and description, including property-value pairs and qualifiers, which includes contextual information.

Alignment Between GTAA and Wikidata Persons. A partial alignment between Wikidata and GTAA was established by the Wikidata community using the "Mix 'n' Match" tool[3]. This tool was used to automatically match person entities based on first and last names. In total, 10,350 GTAA person concepts are linked to Wikidata entries. Even though this is only a small percentage of the total number of person names in GTAA (8.4%), this includes the most well-known people. An example of a linked person concept is found at https://www.wikidata.org/wiki/Q37079, which shows the Wikidata information for actor Tom Cruise, including the link to the matching GTAA concept http://data.beeldengeluid.nl/gtaa/86659. If we can identify enough added

---

[3] https://tools.wmflabs.org/mix-n-match/#/catalog/34.

benefits, the scope of the alignment can be increased through further alignment initiatives. To identify the added value of these Wikidata links, we determine statistics on a number of biographical properties found in Wikidata. Table 1 shows the coverage for each of these properties. This shows that basic information is generally available, although in some cases, potentially interesting properties are missing. In accordance with [10], we found that generally, popular entries have a high completeness whereas less popular entries have a low completeness.

Table 1. Coverage for selected biographical properties for linked GTAA concepts in Wikidata

Property	Occurrences	% of total
Name	10,350	100.00%
Gender	10,294	99.46%
Date of birth	10,040	97.00%
Occupation	9,988	96.50%
Country of citizenship	9,976	96.39%
Place of birth	7,390	71.40%
Date of death	3,644	35.21%
Place of death	2,776	26.82%
Birth name	839	8.11%
Pseudonym	124	1.20%

4   Use Cases for Internal Users

4.1   Elicitation

A series of interviews with stakeholders of different departments of NISV was conducted. These departments deal with media (1) intake, (2) information management and (3) research and development respectively. The goal of these interviews was to result in use cases for the linked data. The interviewee is shown the extra data contained within Wikidata. The interviewee is also shown the results of the earlier analysis. After, the interviewee is asked if he/she based on this data sees any concrete use cases for when more data gets linked. This resulted in three use cases which we further explore in subsequent sections. In Sect. 4.5, we describe the evaluation of the three use cases.

4.2   UC-I-1: Receiving an Alert When the Copyright on a Person's Work Expires

This use case was identified by interviewees of all departments and represented a suggested use of the links that was earlier discussed within the organization. This use case is that of a copyright expiration alert on the work of persons in the GTAA came forward. In Dutch copyright law, works enter the public domain 70 years after a maker's death. On the basis of alignments between the GTAA and Wikidata, using the date of death can be retrieved for specific persons. The use case involves for information management and other stakeholders to get an alert on first day of a year, 70 years after a person's death. The user can then review the information and determine whether works by that person can be made openly accessible to the public [11].

Table 1 shows that 35.21% of the investigated subset have indeed a date of death available in Wikidata. Based on these statistics, we can determine that we should at maximum expect a return of 3,644 people for the alert. This number was further reduced by explicitly focusing on people that worked as producers/creators rather than other people in the thesaurus (for example politicians or sports persons who *appear* in programs). To this end, we filter on occupations. In total we found that there were 798 different occupations in Wikidata and selected manually those that are related to the fields of television, movies, radio, theater and music. This results in a reduced set of 1,626 persons.

To receive alerts, a simple proof-of-concept application was developed which generates calendar events for each of the potential out-of-copyright dates. Stakeholders can consult this calendar or subscribe to it. Specifically, as NISV uses Google for their email, calendar and daily activities and therefore a Google Calendar was created. Figure 1 shows an example of a copyright expiration notice for January 2030.

Fig. 1. Example of a copyright expiration notice for January 2030 in Dutch.

4.3   UC-I-2: Provide More Information on a Person Appearing in Online Story

The second use case that came forward during the interviews was the ability to provide extra information on persons mentioned in the new story platform currently under construction: https://www.beeldengeluid.nl/verhalen. This platform is a news platform maintained by the institute and contains multiple stories (blog posts). In the current version, the author of the story is already displayed in a sidebar. Using the data in Wikidata it is possible to present quick background information on the persons mentioned in the story.

Figure 2 shows a screenshot of the mockup we created, where mentioned persons are displayed in the story are now added to that sidebar. When someone clicks on one of the persons on the bottom of the story he/she will be redirected to a separate

DE KONING GAAT MET ZIJN TIJD MEE

Met Willem-Alexander als koning lijkt er een nieuw tijdperk aangebroken voor de relatie tussen het Koningshuis en de media. De koning schuwt grote interviews niet en op Dumpert is zelfs een 'dab' van hem terug te vinden. Zijn moeder en oma hadden er destijds wat meer moeite mee. Jeroen Snel, koningshuisverslaggever en presentator Blauw Bloed, legt uit hoe de relatie tussen het Koningshuis en de media in elkaar zit.

Verhaal

Jeroen Snel
Verslaggever Koninklijk Huis

Personen

Willem-Alexander der Nederlanden
Koning der Nederlanden

Beatrix der Nederlanden
Koningin der Nederlanden

Juliana der Nederlanden
Koningin der Nederlanden

DELEN

Fig. 2. Screenshot of the mockup made for use case 2. This shows persons mentioned in an example article on the NISV story platform.

webpage generated from Wikidata containing extra information on said person as well as other stories the person is mentioned in.

In a finalized version of the tool, story authors can be suggested persons to be displayed based on Entity resolution results and select relevant person entities as a fully automatic tool could potentially display information on many persons that are not relevant to the story.

4.4 UC-I-3: Using Wikidata for Story Recommendation

This third use case also involves the story platform of the previous case. When persons are mentioned in the story this can be used to generate "Stories you might also like" links. Such recommendation can be done on the basis of structural properties retrieved from Wikidata. An example could be about a story about US news anchor Walter Cronkite[4]. Where Wikidata includes many properties that can be used for such recommendation (for similar linked data based recommendation strategies see [12]).

At the same time, many properties are less relevant for such recommendation. We manually identified a number of properties after further interviews with participants. Relevant properties for Walter Cronkite (Wikidata entity *Q31073*) would be: country of citizenship, award received, date of birth, child, religion, occupation and date of death. These fields can be used to retrieve other stories that are linked through these properties and present them to the users as recommendations. There can be multiple strategies to ensure relevancy of these stories, for example by using semantic distance measures based on the number of matching property-values (a user can be recommended other stories mentioning US-born journalists born in the 1910s).

---

[4] https://www.beeldengeluid.nl/verhalen/hoe-cronkite-de-kijk-op-de-vietnamoorlog-veranderde.

4.5   Evaluation of Internal Cases

We evaluated the use cases and mockups in two evaluation rounds. In the first round, internal users of the R&D department were shown paper prototypes in short focus group sessions during which they were asked to reflect on the cases and prototypes. A proposed change for UC-I-1 was to further focus on people with a media background. For UC-I-2 the proposed change was to include possible archive material on the extra information page for a person mentioned in a story. It was also proposed to move extra information button from the top right to the bottom of the page as it could prove too distracting. UC-I-3 did not receive proposed changes at this stage.

The changes were implemented and presented for second round of evaluation in informal focus groups. These conversations allowed us to get in insight into the projected usefulness of the use cases. The updated UC-I-1 was evaluated as a useful tool for keeping track of copyright expirations. Further alignments between the GTAA and Wikidata are still needed to tackle the problem of incompleteness of the data. UC-I-2 and UC-I-3 were evaluated as interesting assets for the new story platform but further evaluations would need to be done on the basis of prototypes with higher fidelity.

5   Use Case for External Users

There are many external users of the archive, including creative (media) professionals, students, and interested laypeople. We here focus on (humanities) researchers that seek access to media resources, knowledge and use technical tools to support their research. Within this group, there are still different types of researchers with their own information needs. In the context of the CLARIAH project[5], in which NISV is a partner, a digital research environment is being developed and this provided us with opportunities to engage with external users.

5.1   The CLARIAH Media Suite

The CLARIAH Media Suite [13] is an environment designed for media researchers and humanities scientists. It allows the user to explore, select and analyze audio-visual and textual material. It offers various tools to aid the user in their research. These tools allow the user to select the dataset that they are interested and carry out their research on it. In this research, we focus only on the "Search" Tool which allows the user to explore a dataset through textual keyword queries.

5.2   Elicitation Method

To identify specifically relevant exploratory suggestions, five scholars were interviewed. The participants ranged from media studies scholars to digital historians, cultural heritage professionals and humanitarians. Each of these participants was a potential user of the Media Suite. They had different areas of research they focus on,

---

[5] http://www.clariah.nl.

specifically: (1) Drugs, (2) Sports, (3) Occupations, (4) History and (5) Disruptive media events. The semi-structured interview included questions about their area of expertise and type of research. The interviews aimed to find out how the participants used the CLARIAH Media Suite and to identify possible improvements. In order to give the participants an idea of the data a Wikidata page contains, several examples of Wikidata pages were shown. In order to see how Wikidata could play a role in the CLARIAH Media Suite, researchers were asked to share their thoughts.

5.3   UC-E-1: Exploratory Extension of the CLARIAH Media Suite

The elicited use case focus on providing opportunities for advanced retrieval beyond this keyword search. Specifically, we focus supporting scholars in the *exploratory* research phase [14], where they do not yet know exactly the content and scope of the dataset nor their exact information need (no known item search).

In such an information retrieval scenario, researchers have a general idea of what they are interested in but do not know the specifics of their interest. For example, a researcher might be interested in all members who belong or have belonged to a certain political party. Such data is available in structured datasets (in our case in Wikidata) and therefore the proposed extension is to include additional results in an improved interface of the Media Suite.

5.4   Proof of Concept

A proof-of-concept prototype was designed and implemented as an extension of the CLARIAH Media Suite. This "Wikidata retrieval service" is a look-up service that allows the user to set parameters to retrieve lists of matching *persons*. Figure 3 displays a prototype mock-up of the CLARIAH Media Suite with the additional functionality of Wikidata. The user can select a single property from this list and then search for entities belonging to that property.

Next to the retrieved person names, two buttons are depicted for GTAA and Wikidata, which redirect the user to the respective external web page. On mouseover, a small infobox with relevant information is displayed next to the cursor. The GTAA box contains information such as *skos:prefLabel, skos:scopeNote*, whereas the Wikidata box contains all known statements about the selected person (Fig. 4).

This additional information assists the user in exploring possible follow-up queries around persons in the CLARIAH Media Suite Search Tool.

Finally, the user can select one or multiple persons by clicking on the desired person names. The selected persons are highlighted and once selected, are used as a filter for the CLARIAH Media Suite Search Tool. Once the selection has been confirmed, the user can use the existing search box to search for other terms and keywords.

This functionality allows the researcher in his or her exploratory phase to identify more specific information needs. The added functionality allows the user to retrieve a list of associated persons from Wikidata, and be able to filter by selecting the people who are displayed in the list. An additional benefit is to have a quick and easy overview of all facts belonging to a person The Wikidata Retrieval Service uses SPARQL queries in the background to retrieve properties and values from Wikidata, but hides the

Fig. 3. Wikidata Retrieval Service - dropdown property list

Fig. 4. Wikidata Retrieval Service: Wikidata (Left) and GTAA hover functions (Right)

complexity of the query language for the user. The queries are generated on the fly according to the set parameters and sent live to the Wikidata Query Service[6].

5.5   Qualitative Evaluation

Setup. Several participants from the first interviews were asked to participate in an evaluation session to gather feedback and see if the proposed improvements add value. The participants were asked to sit in front of a computer which displayed the mock-up prototype and were asked to complete three tasks, which were based on realistic research tasks as identified in the earlier interview:

1. Assume you are a researcher interested in sports; in particular female sport participation in association football. Use the Wikidata Retrieval Service to retrieve a list of all female football players.

---

[6] https://query.Wikidata.org/.

2. Assume you are a researcher interested in politics; in particular the political party "VVD". Use the Wikidata Retrieval Service to retrieve a list of all members of the VVD who died before the year 2000.

3. Assume you are a researcher interested in disruptive media events; in particular, the death of Pim Fortuyn. You know that Pim Fortuyn died of a homicide, you decide to research whether there were any other related deaths by homicide during a time period of 2 years before and after his death (06-05-2002). Use the Wikidata Retrieval Service to retrieve a list of people who died of a homicide during a period of 2 years before and after Pim Fortuyn's death. Unfortunately, you find no correlation between the retrieved persons. You decide to look up all people who died of the same cause of death: ballistic trauma. Use the Wikidata Retrieval Service to retrieve a list of people who died of a ballistic trauma.

After the participants had completed the tasks, they were asked questions relating to the Wikidata Retrieval Service about the added value to their research, what its drawbacks were and if they could think of any improvements.

Results. All three participants were able to complete the aforementioned tasks with relative ease. One stated that they felt it added value to a researcher, as researchers generally work in concepts and it is difficult to search for a list of individual persons. The participants raised questions of completeness of the data shown and stated that the data as of now is still lacking. User of the tool would have to be informed of the data incompleteness and be aware that the tool serves as an exploratory search, filling in missing knowledge. A suggested improvement would be to order the ontology in a useful way for researchers and to make the connections between entities clear; i.e.: where do they overlap? However, the participant also raised the issue of data completeness and questioned when it would be possible to say the data is complete enough to indeed add value. Another suggestion made by the participants is to cluster properties into categories in the user interface, as the current -complete- list of properties displayed was perceived to result in an information overload, causing the user to spend too much time searching for a specific property.

The third participant had an extensive knowledge of Wikidata and had worked on projects with Linked Open Data and the CLARIAH Media Suite. As such, they stated that integration with Wikidata can be very beneficial, especially for media researchers as it provides context for the user. This was seen as the most important enrichment as it serves as a support for exploration. Furthermore, they added that most users would not know about Wikidata's data (in)completeness and would have to be made aware of that before using the tool, perhaps in a tutorial beforehand.

6 Discussion

With the adoption of Linked Data by cultural heritage organizations, opportunities of reusing external general purpose datasets arise. However, in many cases, such opportunities stem from a 'technology push'. In this paper, we aim to identify these opportunities from the perspective of the heritage organization itself, more specifically from the perspective of internal and external users. We describe a user-centric method using interviews with different stakeholders to identify possibilities for using links from an organization-specific structured vocabulary to a general purpose knowledge base. The case study at NISV explores the possibilities that the links between GTAA and Wikidata provide for three types of internal users and for external users. The proofs of concepts indeed show added benefits to these users.

The method of iterative design of use cases and focus group discussions was shown to be a useful way of determining the added value of linked metadata. This research aimed to find answers to the questions of what use cases can be formed by an enriched GTAA and the differences in wishes between internal and external users are. This research also showed that when giving users insight in all the raw data and its properties, new ideas about the usefulness of said linked data can be identified. We show that focus on different properties within the data lead to completely different and independent use cases. The use cases that came forward in this research were connected to a specific focused group of properties. For UC-I-1 the focus lied on the "date of death" property. For UC-I-2 the focus lied on properties with a high occurrence rate. For UC-I-3 the focus lied on very specific properties that were handpicked for relevancy. For UC-E-1, all properties are used.

Differences between internal and external users include the access to and familiarity with backend tooling. Where to internal users, many tools are already available, for external users this might not be the case. There are differences in the wishes of the two groups of users. Internal users want to mainly use an enriched GTAA to set up further project or create new tools. Whereas the external users mainly want to use an enriched GTAA to receive as much extra information as possible as well as add some functionality to their search behavior. The similarities in the wishes mainly lie in the background information and added functionality to specific aspects of their workload.

A common comment in both user groups is that data completeness and quality are both crucial and unclear with respect to the external data. Even though Wikidata contains a significant amount of information and it is being updated daily by an active community of ~ 19.000 users it is far from complete. Researchers cannot be assured of the retrieved data to be complete as there is always a possibility data is not available or incorrect. One way to mitigate this is to use the external data mostly to provide *extra* information and to use it in exploratory search activities.

Another potential downside of using external services such as the Wikidata SPARQL endpoint is that it relies on external servers and such servers might be down, unavailable or data might be changed without the user's knowing.

However, as a net result, both internal and external users are enthusiastic about the affordances that metadata and vocabularies linked to general purpose knowledge base give. Therefore, we expect further uptake of Linked Data at not only this organization, but others like it.

References

1. Bizer, C., Heath, T., Berners-Lee, T.: Linked data-the story so far. In: Semantic Services, Interoperability and Web Applications: Emerging Concepts, pp. 205–227 (2009)
2. Hyvönen, E.: Publishing and using cultural heritage linked data on the semantic web. Synth. Lect. Semant. Web Theor. Technol. **2**(1), 1–159 (2012)
3. Vrandečić, D., Krötzsch, M.: Wikidata: a free collaborative knowledgebase. Commun. ACM **57**(10), 78–85 (2014)
4. Erxleben, F., Günther, M., Krötzsch, M., Mendez, J., Vrandečić, D.: Introducing Wikidata to the linked data web. In: Mika, P., et al. (eds.) ISWC 2014. LNCS, vol. 8796, pp. 50–65. Springer, Cham (2014). https://doi.org/10.1007/978-3-319-11964-9_4
5. Färber, M., Bartscherer, F., Menne, C., Rettinger, A.: Linked data quality of dbpedia, freebase, opencyc, wikidata, and yago. Semant. Web **9**(1), 77–129 (2018)
6. Thornton, K., Cochrane, E., Ledoux, T., Caron, B., Wilson, C.: Modeling the domain of digital preservation in Wikidata. IPress Technical Document (2017). https://ipres2017.jp/wp-content/uploads/7.pdf
7. Debevere, P., et al.: Linking thesauri to the Linked Open Data cloud for improved media retrieval. In: 12th International Workshop on Image Analysis for Multimedia Interactive Services (WIAMIS-2011) (2011)
8. Tordai, A., Omelayenko, B., Schreiber, G.: Thesaurus and metadata alignment for a semantic E-culture application. In: Proceedings of the 4th International Conference on Knowledge Capture, pp. 199–200. ACM (2007)
9. Neubert, J.: Bringing the "Thesaurus for Economics" on to the web of linked data. In: LDOW, 25964 (2009)
10. Ahmeti, A., Razniewski, S., Polleres, A.: Assessing the completeness of entities in knowledge bases. In: Blomqvist, E., Hose, K., Paulheim, H., Ławrynowicz, A., Ciravegna, F., Hartig, O. (eds.) ESWC 2017. LNCS, vol. 10577, pp. 7–11. Springer, Cham (2017). https://doi.org/10.1007/978-3-319-70407-4_2
11. Brinkerink, M.: Open images: towards an audiovisual commons. In: OKCon (2011)
12. Maccatrozzo, V.: Burst the filter bubble: using semantic web to enable serendipity. In: Cudré-Mauroux, P., et al. (eds.) ISWC 2012. LNCS, vol. 7650, pp. 391–398. Springer, Heidelberg (2012). https://doi.org/10.1007/978-3-642-35173-0_28
13. Martinez-Ortiz, C., et al.: CLARIAH media suite: enabling scholarly research for distributed audiovisual and mixed media data sets in a sustainable infrastructure. In: Proceedings of DHBenelux 2018, Amsterdam (2018)
14. Boer, D., et al.: DIVE into the event-based browsing of linked historical media. Web Semant. Sci. Serv. Agents World Wide Web **35**, 152–158 (2015)

Authify: The Reconciliation of Entities at Scale

Philip E. Schreur[1]([⊠]) and Tiziana Possemato[2,3]

[1] Stanford University, Stanford, CA, USA
pschreur@stanford.edu
[2] @Cult, Rome, Italy
[3] Casalini Libri, Fiesole, Italy

Abstract. Libraries' shift to the semantic web has been underway for a number of years. Mellon funded projects such as Linked Data for Production (LD4P) [1] or the BIBFRAME European Workshop 2018 in Florence [2] show the commitment of national, public, and academic libraries, as well as vendors, to this transition. Libraries worldwide, however, are enmeshed in hundreds of millions of metadata records communicated through flat files (the MARC formats) [3]. The shift to linked data will require the conversion of these flat files to a semantically expressive model such as the Resource Description Framework (RDF) [4]. The conversion of such large amounts of semantically inexpressive data to semantically rich data will require automated enhancements in the conversion process. Data hidden within the flat files, such as role (author, illustrator, composer, etc.), can greatly aid with the reconciliation of entities within those files. Authify is one of the first tools available to libraries to both convert their metadata to linked data, but also enrich the reconciliation process with semantic data hidden within the MARC fields. As libraries look to convert their legacy data to linked data, Authify can help them move their data to the Web in as a semantically rich way as possible.

Keywords: Linked data · Reconciliation · MARC formats · Authify · Libraries · Semantic web

1 Introduction

There has been tremendous interest in moving towards linked data as a means of discovery across the library, museum, and archives space for many years now. In 2011, Stanford held a linked data workshop with representatives from major information providers across North America and Europe [5]. One of the outcomes of that meeting was a "Manifesto for Linked Libraries (And Museums And Archives And …)" [6].

Although the practices enumerated there are stated simply, their implementation is difficult. Of particular interest is structuring data semantically. The Resource Description Framework (RDF), established by the W3C, has been widely adopted as a model for expressing data semantically on the Web. But even if the data is recorded semantically, entities will not "link" unless the same identifier has been used. Libraries have approached this issue in the past by creating authority records for entities they wish to establish so that references to the same entity can be linked by a unique text string. These authority records can be converted to identifiers representing the real world object they

© Springer Nature Switzerland AG 2019
E. Garoufallou et al. (Eds.): MTSR 2018, CCIS 846, pp. 224–229, 2019.
https://doi.org/10.1007/978-3-030-14401-2_21

describe and so may be used to link matching entities on the Web. As library metadata is converted to linked data, however, the appropriate authority record or identifier can easily be missed, especially if the text string varies from that used in the authority record. And in addition, there are many entities for which no authority record was ever created, making conversion of this metadata to linked data problematic. The process of reconciliation, or the linking of identifiers for matching entities, becomes a critical step in the conversion of library metadata to linked data.

2 Current Services

The need for reconciliation is widespread. Organizations such as the Bibliothèque nationale de France (BnF) have incorporated reconciliation into their digital services platform. As a national library, data they produce is of high quality and much reconciliation can be resolved through the use of authority files. Works, however, are a particularly difficult problem as authority records are infrequently produced for them. The BnF is currently working on algorithms for the extraction of work identifiers from bibliographic data.

Culturegraph [7], a platform for services around data networking for cultural entities, has taken another approach. Projects such as their resolution and look-up service make available an open, central infrastructure for, among other things, the identification of equivalent records through a common URI.

Europeana [8] has a more complex task. The data they work with has neither the uniform quality of the BnF nor the more limited scope of the Culturegraph resolution and look up service. The heterogeneous nature of their data, along with varying standards of construction and supporting authority files, makes reconciliation of the data very complex.

Similar to Europeana, Linked Data for Production [9], or LD4P, must work with data from a mix of institutions with varying quality standards. Many headings lack authority records making their reconciliation dependent upon clues in the bibliographic data. Authify, in part, exploits this information in an attempt to reconcile entities when standard authority records or identifiers are lacking.

3 Authify

The Authify reconciliation service represents the heart of an ecosystem developed by @Cult and Casalini Libri called the SHARE-Virtual Discovery Environment or SHARE-VDE [10]. It offers several search and detection services with the scope of creating a 'cluster' of variant name forms coming from different sources but referring to the same entity. The process will produce an Authority Knowledge Base (AKB) composed of entity clusters that are continuously increased as new sources are encountered and ingested. The idea of Authify started at the beginning of the SHARE-VDE project as a way of overcoming some limitations of the public Virtual International Authority File (VIAF) Web APIs. VIAF [11], being a public project, does not allow a massive call on its APIs. For those use cases where such a requirement is needed, the project provides a download of the whole dataset. Authify indexes and stores the VIAF clusters dataset and provides powerful full-text and bibliographic search services built upon them.

VIAF was the first of the sources to be added to Authify. Other sources, not only in the Resource Description Framework (RDF), but also in other formats, are now also considered by Authify for inclusion in the AKB. Thanks to this broadening of sources, the module is even more effective and is able to fulfill the requirement expressed by libraries for external datasets to be used in the detection and clusterization processes. Examples of these sources are: the Library of Congress Name Authority File (LC NAF) [12], Library of Congress Subject Headings (LCSH) [13], Faceted Application of Subject Terminology (FAST) [14], Gemeinsame Normdatei (GND1) [15], and ISNI [16].

Authify uses these different sources applying different strategies, depending on the availability of data from the source:

- if the source is available as a dump db (in different formats, such as MARC, xml, RDF) the data are indexed into a SOLR component or in a RDF triple store in order to be used for queries;
- if the source is not available as a dump db, but offers APIs and web services to be queried, Authify uses these tools to interrogate the source and retrieve the useful information.

Different sources are queried and each source endpoint declares in the URL the related source (e.g./viaf/names, /fast/subjects).

The ability to search and retrieve data from different sources enhances the project 'clusters' that represent entities in the real world (so, each cluster is considered a Real-World-Object entity, with all the necessary attributes to identify it). The detection and clusterization processes mentioned above, makes possible the identification of an entity (as a person, as a work, as a subject etc.), the identification of the role the entity has in relationship to a resource, and the creation of a 'cluster' that identifies it with an ID and that gathers together the different attributes useful for identification.

The logic of creating a new cluster begins with the search of an entity within the databases used in the project (a Postgres relational database used to register the clusters upon creation before they are added to the AKB or the Authify SOLR database built with data from external sources used in the project (VIAF, NAF, etc.)). Data extracted from library records are used to query these databases to ascertain whether a cluster already exists, a VIAF ID exists, the form used by the library exists as a preferred form or as a variant form, etc. Both the normalized forms used for queries and the responses received from Authify are registered to the Postgres database in order to be used for the creation (or feeding) of the AKB. But before being used in queries, the library authority and bibliographic records need to be passed through two preliminary processes of normalization that eliminates the sub-field separators and any non-standard punctuation, and the creation of a sort-form that transforms the original string in uppercase and removes diacritics, accents and special characters. In the construction of the normalized string and the sort-form, the tags and sub-fields coming from the authority and bibliographic records are used, depending on the type of tag.

If the search result gives a positive answer (a cluster for this entity already exists), the existing cluster will be expanded to include a new variant form. If the variant form is already present, no action will be made on the cluster. If the search result gives a negative answer, a new cluster will be created in the Postgres database and in the AKB.

All variants retrieved by external sources are grouped by source (e.g. VIAF, ISNI etc.) and all variants belonging to a given source are associated with the same URI. The final SHARE-VDE cluster will be composed of a cluster ID (the SHARE-VDE URI) that includes all variant forms from local authority files that inherit the same SHARE-VDE URI and that are brought together with the SameAs relationship; all forms from external sources (each one having a preferred form and variant forms), all with the same source URI, and brought together with the SameAs relationship; all variant forms from bibliographic records that do not match authoritative forms but that inherit the same SHARE-VDE URI and are brought together with the SomeAs relationship; additional information (such as Authority notes); and operational data such as the cluster creation date, the update date, the cluster type, etc.

One of the most relevant function in Authify is the cluster search service. As the name suggests, this provides a full-text search service that queries names, works, and other entities available from different sources. All search services are made available as HTTP endpoints. The parameter used to start a search is the name form (or title, or subject) used in the project's original data source (a heading, in the case of biblio-graphic or authority data). The search Web API uses an "invisible queries" approach in order to find as precise a match as possible for the search parameter among the forms already present in the external sources, or in the AKB.

The invisible queries approach makes everything transparent to the user. Following a single search request, the system executes a chain of different searches with different priorities. The first match that produces a result that will populate the response returned. Each new response will progressively populate the new (or already existent) cluster that has been created in the AKB. For debugging purposes, the response will also include the search that produced the results. The goal of each search strategy is to return as precise a result as possible with the minimum recall possible.

Query responses are used in a series of data analysis logics that are part of a process called 'Similarity score'. This process assigns a weight to the various results in order to identify the elements (for example the variants forms of a name) to be assigned to the same cluster. The Similarity score allows the system to decide if and when to feed an already existing cluster or to create a new cluster. At the end of the search process, the heading either is assigned to an already existent cluster in the AKB or it produces a new cluster if one does not already exist. Each cluster, for each entity type, is marked with an identifier (the cluster ID) used to produce the URI that will identify the entity in the RDF conversion process. At the end of each process, the AKB will have a name form marked as 'preferred' and a number of other forms marked as variant that are useful to create 'sameAs' relationships. Additional attributes are available to enrich the AKB, such as the original source of each variant/preferred form and the URIs/ID for each form.

One of the most delicate processes in the handling of bibliographic data is 'Entity recognition' or entity detection. In some cases, this step is crucial to the identification of an entity and relates to the identification of the role that a person has had in the creation or production of a resource. In the bibliographic world, the identification of a person is usually realized through the relationship with his/her work and, vice-versa, the identification of a work is realized through the association with its creator.

Authify uses the "Relator term detection" service to identify these relationships. Starting from a MARC record, the system analyses all (configured) tags that contain a name and tries to determine the corresponding role within the work represented by the given record using the statements of responsibility and other note fields.

To identify the role that an Agent has in relation to a resource, the 'Relator term detection' service uses a 'Roles Knowledge Base' that is progressively fed (with text analysis processes, automatically and manually) with all possible expressions useful to identify a role. As an example, two main roles may be detected, for instance, author and an unclassified role (other). The "other" role is a catch-all role used when no valuable information can be gathered from the analysis. At the end of each entity detection process, the system produces a report of non-matching role-expressions associated with the bibliographic records identifiers. This report enables the library cataloguers to check the record and to add the specific role term or code in the appropriate subfield. Behind a simple token matching analysis, there is a more complicated logic that tries (using, among other things, the search services described in the previous point) to find the role of each name found using its variant forms or using a set of tokens that could identify such role (e.g. edited by, by, illustrated by). At the end of this process, a certain number of records are enriched with roles and a related report with 'undefined' roles is made available to allow for manual checks by professional users. This added element of human curation can help resolve issues that an automated process would find too difficult at present.

4 Conclusion

Libraries' shift to the semantic web through the conversion of their MARC data has been underway for a number of years. However, millions of headings within libraries MARC metadata are uncontrolled, that is, have no matching authority record. On conversion to RDF, each heading will receive a unique identifier even if that heading may already exist in another bibliographic record within the library's holdings, or in another library's holdings worldwide. This proliferation of multiple identifiers for the same entity makes the linking of these entities problematic.

Authify is one of the first tools available to libraries to both convert their metadata to linked data, but also enrich the reconciliation process with semantic data hidden within the MARC fields. By making use of additional data points, such as role, contained in free text within the MARC record, services such as Authify can match related entities even if the text strings for those entities do not match. As libraries worldwide will need to convert hundreds of millions of MARC records in their library systems to RDF, sophisticated, automated services for the conversion and reconciliation of their data will be critical for their transition to the semantic web.

References

1. LD4P Homepage. https://wiki.duraspace.org/pages/viewpage.action?pageId=74515029. Accessed 14 June 2018
2. European BIBFRAME Workshop Homepage. http://www.casalini.it/EBW2018/. Accessed 14 June 2018
3. MARC Standards Homepage. https://www.loc.gov/marc/. Accessed 14 June 2018
4. RDF Homepage. https://www.w3.org/RDF/. Accessed 14 June 2018
5. Report of the Stanford Linked Data Workshop. http://www.clir.org/wp-content/uploads/sites/6/LinkedDataWorkshop.pdf. Accessed 14 June 2018
6. Report of the Stanford Linked Data Workshop, p. 22. http://www.clir.org/wp-content/uploads/sites/6/LinkedDataWorkshop.pdf. Accessed 14 June 2018
7. Culturegraph Homepage. http://www.culturegraph.org/Subsites/culturegraph/DE/Home/home_node.html. Accessed 14 June 2018
8. Europeana Homepage. https://www.europeana.eu/portal/en. Accessed 14 June 2018
9. SHARE-VDE Homepae. http://www.share-vde.org/sharevde/clusters?l=en. Accessed 14 June 2018
10. VIAF Homepage. https://viaf.org/. Accessed 14 June 2018
11. LC NAF Homepage. http://id.loc.gov/authorities/names.html. Accessed 14 June 2018
12. LCSH Homepage. http://id.loc.gov/authorities/subjects.html. Accessed 14 June 2018
13. FAST Homepage. https://fast.oclc.org/searchfast/. Accessed 14 June 2018
14. GND Homepage. http://www.dnb.de/EN/Standardisierung/GND/gnd_node.html. Accessed 14 June 2018
15. ISNI Homepage. http://www.isni.org/. Accessed 14 June 2018

Assessing the Preservation of Derivative Relationships in Mappings from FRBR to BIBFRAME

Sofia Zapounidou[✉], Michalis Sfakakis[✉],
and Christos Papatheodorou[✉]

Department of Archives, Library Science and Museology, Ionian University,
Corfu, Greece
{l12zapo,sfakakis,papatheodor}@ionio.gr

Abstract. Support of the exploration user task demands the explicit representation of bibliographic families and of content relationships. Seamless navigation through differently modelled bibliographic datasets presumes the existence of mappings. Semantic interoperability through mappings will be evaluated using a testbed. This paper starts with the fine-tuning of a testbed for mappings from FRBR to BIBFRAME. Two *Gold Standards datasets* have been created along with a mechanism for the mapping of core entities and the derivation relationship from FRBR to BIBFRAME. This first attempt has revealed that derivations expressed at the FRBR *Expression* level are mapped to BIBFRAME more adequately than those expressed at the FRBR *Work* level.

Keywords: BIBRAME · Derivative bibliographic relationships · FRBR · Linked data · Interoperability · Mappings

1 Introduction

The *navigate and explore* user task [1, 2] will facilitate the exploration of bibliographic information. Recent studies have shown that organizing catalog records in bibliographic families enables exploration and, therefore, may be more conceivable to users [3–6]. Content relationships contribute to the formation of bibliographic families; their explicit representation will provide more navigation opportunities. The interpretation of bibliographic relationships has been clarified by several scholars [7–9]. Tillett in [7] identified seven types of content relationships: equivalence, derivation, descriptive, whole-part, accompanying, sequential, shared characteristic. Smiraglia explored the evolution of works [8] and coined the *bibliographic family* term [10] to express a group of related works that have common "ideational and semantic content" [8]. The original work carrying the common "ideational and semantic content" is considered the *progenitor* of the family, from which all the other works derive.

The bibliographic universe and library catalogs often include descriptions of works that are variations or mutations of another work. Examples include successive editions with revised content, translations, adaptations, abridgements, dramatizations, summarizations, etc. These cases may be described with derivative relationships that may

E. Garoufallou et al. (Eds.): MTSR 2018, CCIS 846, pp. 230–241, 2019.
https://doi.org/10.1007/978-3-030-14401-2_22

enable navigation between members of the same bibliographic family, or between different bibliographic families. Moreover, there are studies proving significant proportions of derivative works in catalogs. Tillett found that the 16.4% of the Library of Congress Catalog records she used as her sample, contained derivative works [7]. Smiraglia discovered that nearly half (49.9%) of the works in his Georgetown University sample were derivative works [8].

Bibliographic conceptual models, such as FRBR [11], the consolidated FRBR named IFLA-LRM [12], BIBFRAME [13], define constructs for the formal representation of bibliographic relationships. Seamless exploration of bibliographic data will demand navigation through different representations of bibliographic data, through different models' instances. However, the semantic and structural heterogeneities between the models may obstruct navigation and exploration of data as well as interoperable data interchange [14]. Some members of a bibliographic family may be represented in one model, while other members of the same bibliographic family may be represented using another model's semantics. Reliable and efficient mapping algorithms between models are needed to enable interoperability. One technique to evaluate mappings is to compare them against a *Gold Standard*.

Given that (a) future catalogs need to support the *explore* user task, (b) explicit representation of relationships provide navigation opportunities, (c) derivations are really common in the publishing world and library catalogs, (d) navigation through the bibliographic universe will demand the seamless exploration of bibliographic data represented in different models' semantics, and, therefore, mappings are needed, and (e) the existence of mappings between library data models [14, 15], we developed a testbed for the evaluation of mappings from FRBR to BIBFRAME. In this paper, the implemented mapping mechanism focuses on the preservation of derivative bibliographic relationships after mappings from FRBR to BIBFRAME 2.0. In the next section we present the steps and the main decisions taken for the creation of the two *Gold Standard datasets*. Section 3 presents the main issues tackled by the mapping mechanism, while Sect. 4 provides a qualitative discussion about the results of the mapping and its fine tuning.

2   Gold Standard Datasets

For the purpose of studying derivations, different kinds of publications, such as translations, adaptations, abridgements, dramatizations, were considered by a librarian. Popular works are expected to have more derivations and large bibliographic families. According to Smiraglia [8], the older the publication date of a progenitor work, the greater the possibilities of this progenitor work having derivative works. Thus, priority during the selection was given to classical and well-known works, namely *Cien años de soledad, Crime and Punishment, Don Quijote, Faust, Iliad, Karamazov Brothers, Madame Bovary, Odyssey, The Scarlet letter, Tom Sawyer, Wuthering Heights*. The publishing history of each family was studied to identify important and interesting instances of the variant derivation types, such as the Chapman translation and adaptations in the *Odyssey* family, or the Lombardo's *Odyssey* translation in multiple content types (original text, sound recording, braille). Close examination of all publications was not possible, and we had to (1) rely upon the information of MARC21 records including notes and (2) use other sources describing the publications, such as a Wikipedia page for the translations of Homer or online bookstores. Afterwards, 256 records have been collected in total. They were mostly downloaded from the Library of Congress. Different types of derivations reflecting the evolution of the content in the bibliographic families are included in the dataset; the most common derivation ones are translation and adaptation. The selected families and the number of records for each of them are: *Cien años de soledad* (15 records), *Crime and Punishment* (29 records*), Don Quijote* (11 records), *Faust* (28 records), *Iliad* (25 records), *Karamazov Brothers* (21 records), *Madame Bovary* (32 records), *Odyssey* (20 records), *The Scarlet letter* (24 records), *Tom Sawyer* (31 records), *Wuthering Heights* (20 records).

Two *Gold datasets* have been created, one for each model, FRBR and BIBFRAME respectively, by identifying the core entities/classes and their relationships incorporated into the 11 bibliographic families, out of the 256 records. Each dataset consists of the core entities'/classes' instances and of the relationships between them. It is worth noting that only core classes have been used so far, avoiding the representation of subjects and other entities. Representation of aggregates and other types of relationships, e.g. reproductions, whole-part relationships are out of the scope of this work and have not been systematically represented in the *Gold datasets*.

To represent the core entities and their relationships contained in the *Gold* FRBR *dataset*, the RDA vocabulary [16] has been used. The *Gold* FRBR *dataset* includes 72 *Work* entity instances, 229 *Expressions* having 257 *Manifestations*. The cataloguing approach implemented regarding the *Gold* FRBR *dataset* has been:

1. Derivation relationships have been used following the FRBR rules [11]. All FRBR relationships used in the dataset are presented in Table 1 along with their corresponding RDA properties. All occurrences are presented per family in Table 2.
2. All literal translations are represented at the *Expression* level; a *has a translation (rdae:P20171 is translated as)* relationship is represented only when the source text used for the translation is known or there is an explicit statement in the MARC record, e.g. in the Crime & Punishment family, some records include the phrase "translated from the Russian by…". Otherwise, *Expression* instances carrying literal translations are independent to one another being, though, realizations of the same *Work* instance. In this case, the translation could be implied indirectly by the use of different values for the *rdae:P20006 has language of expression* property.
3. Other derivation relationships are represented either at the *Work* or the *Expression* level, according to the model specification, using the corresponding RDA property. Abridgements and revisions are all represented at the *Expression* level, while adaptations, dramatizations, etc. are represented at either the *Work* or the *Expression* levels. When represented at the *Expression* level, the source text for the derivation is known. When represented between *Work* instances, the source text is not known.

Table 1. The FRBR derivation relationships used in the *Gold dataset* along with their corresponding RDA properties

Relationship	Name of relationship	Inverse relationship	Domain/Range	RDA property
Translation	Has a translation	Is a translation of	[E-E] (same work)	rdae:P20171 is translated as
Revision	Has a revision	Is a revision of		rdae:P20211 is revised as
Abridgement	Has an abridgement	Is an abridgement of		rdae:P20166 is abridged as (expression)
Adaptation	Has adaptation	Is an adaptation of	[E - E] (different works)	rdae:P20153 is adapted as (expression)
			[W-W]	rdaw:P10155 is adapted as (work)
				rdaw:P10236 is adapted as opera (work)
				rdaw:P10076 is adapted as radio program (work)
				rdaw:P10113 is adapted as libretto (work)
Transformation	Has a transformation	Is a transformation of	[W-W]	rdaw:P10016 is dramatized as (work)

4. In many cases illustrations were considered as integral to the intellectual realization of a *Work*, thus, triggering a new *Expression* instance.
5. *Person* agents were connected with *owl:sameAs* properties to their respective LCNAF [17] or VIAF ID [18]. There is a small number of *Person* instances that an ID has not been found neither in LCNAF, nor in VIAF.

The *Gold* BIBFRAME *dataset* has been created in a semi-automated way. The 256 MARC21 records were converted in BIBFRAME using the BIBFRAME MARC2BF2 [19] conversion software. To represent the core classes and the different types of derivative relationships between the members of the 11 bibliographic families described above, we edited the MARC2BF2 software's output performing the following tasks: (1) Create one instance of the BIBFRAME *Creative Work* class (*bf:Work*) for the representation of each family's progenitor in its representative language, e.g. *Iliad* in ancient Greek, *Don Quijote* in Spanish. These *bf:Work* instances were created only when there was a need to represent a specific relationship (e.g. translation) between them and other *bf:Work* instances already in the MARC2BF2 output (2) Use bibliographic relationships based on all record's information including human-readable information, e.g. notes in 5XX fields (3) Use id.loc.gov vocabularies, namely MARC Code List for Relators, LC Name Authority File, MARC Genre/Terms Scheme.

Table 2. Occurrences of derivation relationships in the *Gold* FRBR *dataset*

Family	Domain: Expr. - rdae:				Domain: Work – rdaw:					Total
	P20171	P20211	P20166	P20153	P10155	P10236	P10076	P10113	P10016	
Cien años	5									5
Crime&P	10	3		1	4				4	22
DonQuijote	2				1					3
Faust	2				3	1				6
Iliad	2	5	4	4	1					16
Karamazov	9	3		2	2				2	18
MmeBovary	2			1	3		1			7
Odyssey	5	3	1	4	1					14
ScarletLett	3				4	2			3	12
TSawyer		1		1	5				1	8
Wuthering	3				5		1			9
Total	**43**	**14**	**6**	**13**	**29**	**3**	**1**	**1**	**10**	**120**

The *Gold* BIBFRAME *dataset* includes 230 instances of the *Creative Work* class and 257 instances of the *bf:Instance* class. It is worth noting that the MARC2BF2 convertor creates a new *Creative Work* instance for illustrations, which is not always the case as referred in the fourth case of the cataloguing approaches applied to the *Gold* FRBR *dataset*. Considering that to each FRBR *Work* and *Expression* pair corresponds one *bf:Work* and to each FRBR Manifestation corresponds one *bf:Instance*, these numbers verified the application of the same rules for the representation of the core classes in both *Gold Standard datasets*.

BIBFRAME permits derivation relationships to be used with *Creative Work* or *bf: Instance* class instances [13]. BIBFRAME identifies also the generic *bf:hasDerivative* relationship, which has as subproperties the *bf:translation* and the *bf:originalVersionOf* ones. Both subproperties can be used with *Creative Work* or *bf:Instance* classes. The *bf:originalVersionOf*, as the MARC21 to BIBFRAME conversion specifications describe, shall be used mostly at the *bf:Instance* level accommodating information found in the MARC21 534 field. Therefore, all derivation relationships, except for translation, may be represented with the *bf:hasDerivative*. Even though BIBFRAME permits to represent derivations between both *bf:Works* and *bf:Instances*, in our dataset they were represented between *bf:Works*. In the case of translations, we added a translation relationship (*bf:translation*) between the *bf:Work* instance carrying the original text and all other *bf:Work* instances carrying the text in other languages without considering the source text used for the translated *bf:Work(s)*. Thus, the number of the represented translations is increased in the *Gold* BIBFRAME *dataset*. For the representation of the adaptations, abridgements, dramatizations, etc. the *bf: hasDerivative* and its inverse *bf:derivativeOf* have been used. All property occurrences per family are presented in Table 3.

Table 3. Occurrences of derivation relationships in the *Gold* BIBFRAME *dataset.*

Family	bf:translation	bf:hasDerivative	Total
Cien años	5	0	5
Crime&P	15	12	27
DonQuijote	5	1	6
Faust	17	4	21
Iliad	20	14	34
Karamazov	15	9	24
MmeBovary	13	4	17
Odyssey	12	9	21
ScarletLett	10	8	18
TSawyer	8	8	16
Wuthering	6	8	14
Total	**126**	**77**	**203**

3   Core Entities and Derivation Mappings

There is a semantic difference between the FRBR *Work* entity and the BIBFRAME *Creative Work* class. The former represents only the ideas of the intellectual creation, while the latter represents both the ideas and the signs realizing them. Therefore, the standard mapping is that a whole FRBR '*Work–is realized through-Expression*' path is mapped to a *bf:Work* instance. Consequently, explicit relationships between FRBR *Work* instances or between FRBR *Expression* instances can be mapped to relationships between instances of the *bf:Work* class. Merging two entities in one and creating instances of the *bf:Work* class for all pairs between a *Work* and its related *Expressions* may seem straightforward. Yet, as described later in the section, the mapping of *Work* relationships to all its mapped *bf:Work* instances, creates many useless and sometimes "noisy" relationships in BIBFRAME.

The mappings of FRBR core entities and of derivation relationships are presented in Table 4. Due to the mapping of a FRBR path (*Work–is realized through-Expression*) to a *bf:Work*, the mapped *bf:Work* carries all attributes and relationships of both FRBR entities in the path (*Work* and *Expression*). If an FRBR *Work* participates in more than one '*Work–is realized through-Expression*' paths, then all mapped *bf:Work* instances shall carry the *Work's* attributes and relationships. Consequently, the attributes and the relationships of an FRBR Expression will be mapped to and carried by the *bf:Work* created by the FRBR *Expression* and the *Work* it realizes.

Figure 1 presents the mapping of three derivation relationships: literal translation represented at the *Expression* level with the presence/absence of the '*has a translation*' relationship, and adaptation represented between *Works*. There are three *Expressions* of the Bronte's *Wuthering Heights Work* depicted in Fig. 1: the first one is the original English text and the other two are translations in Armenian and French. The source text used for the Armenian text is known, while the source text used for French translation is not known, thus lacking the existence of the translation relationship (*has translation* property). There is also an adaptation (dramatization) of the *Wuthering Heights* play

Table 4. Mapping FRBR core entities and derivation relationships to BIBFRAME

FRBR	RDA	BIBFRAME
Work-is realized through-Expression	rdac:C10001 - rdaw:P10078 - rdac: C10006	bf:Work
Manifestation	rdac:C10007	bf:Instance
Has a translation	rdae:P20171 is translated as	bf:translation
Has a revision	rdae:P20211 is revised as	bf: hasDerivative
Has an abridgement	rdae:P20166 is abridged as (expression)	
Has adaptation	rdae:P20153 is adapted as (expression)	
	rdaw:P10155 is adapted as (work)	
	rdaw:P10236 is adapted as opera (work)	
	rdaw:P10076 is adapted as radio program (work)	
	rdaw:P10113 is adapted as libretto (work)	
Has a transformation	rdaw:P10016 is dramatized as (work)	
Has an imitation	rdaw:P10117 is imitated as (work)	

Work by B. J. Taylor. This *Work* has two realizations, one in English and one in German. The mapping of the five FRBR '*Work–is realized through-Expression*' paths to five *bf:Work* instances is depicted using a differently-dashed shape surrounding each path. Mappings are depicted using bold arrows. In BIBFRAME five instances of the *bf: Work* are created, two of them (carrying the English text and the Armenian translation of *Wuthering Heights*) are related to one another with the *bf:translation* relationship. The third *bf:Work* instance representing the French translation is not related to the other two *bf:Work* instances that carry the same progenitor *Work's* ideas (*Wuthering Heights*) in different signs (English and Armenian texts). The other two *bf:Work*

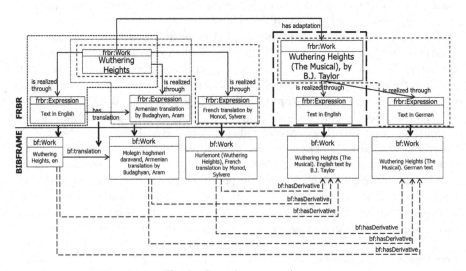

Fig. 1. Core classes mapping

instances represent the English and the German translation of the *Wuthering Heights* play. All three *bf:Work* instances carrying the ideas of the *Wuthering Heights Work,* also carry the adaptation relationship with all *bf:Works* carrying the ideas of the *Wuthering Heights* play *Work.* The *has adaptation* relationship is mapped to the *bf: hasDerivative* relationship. After the mapping, six *bf:hasDerivative* relationship instances are created. For readability reasons, they are all depicted with dashed lines.

4   Datasets and Mapping Assessments

The datasets were uploaded to a Virtuoso RDF store and the mapping has been implemented using the XSLT[1] language. This implementation transforms the FRBR *Gold dataset* to a new BIBFRAME dataset, named BIBF1. Comparing the two BIB-FRAME datasets (*Gold* and BIBF1) provides an insight for bibliographic relationships and ushers the fine-tuning of the FRBR to BIBFRAME mapping process.

A screenshot of the mappings implementation is displayed in Fig. 2. For each progenitor work of a family (Fig. 2a), the total number of *Expressions* is given (Fig. 2b). For each *Expression* the number of *Manifestations* embodying it, is also displayed (Fig. 2c). Then, the *bf:Work* created after the mapping of the '*Work–is realized through-Expression*' path is displayed (Fig. 2d) along with its attributes and relationships. In Fig. 2, a part of the *Wuthering Heights* family mappings is displayed. The progenitor *BronteWutheringHeights* has 10 *Expression* instances in our dataset. The first one displayed is the *WutheringHeightsArmenian*, an Armenian translation by Aram Budaghyaně. The *bf:Work* instance created after the mapping is the one with the URI   http://dlib.mappings.LRM2BF.org#WorkExpression_BronteWutheringHeights_ WutheringHeightsArmenian. On the right side of the screen, the *bf:Instances* of each mapped *bf:Work* are presented (Fig. 3).

Table 5 presents the classes of the three datasets per bibliographic family to measure the accuracy of the implemented mapping. The comparison between the *Gold* BIBFRAME and BIBF1 *datasets* showed that the 98% of *bf:Works* are identical. This difference is due to the existence of slightly different number of FRBR *Expressions* and *bf:Works* in the *Gold* FRBR and BIBFRAME *datasets* respectively, implied by each model's representation assumptions, as described in Sect. 2 for the *Gold* BIBFRAME development. Most of the differences are due to illustrations; if the illustrations were thought as integral to the text, a new *Expression* was created in the *Gold* FRBR *dataset.* When illustrations were thought as not integral to the intellectual realization of a *Work,* they were considered as *Expressions* of another separate *Work* embodied in the same *Manifestation* with the text (aggregate *Manifestation*). These separate illustration *Works* will be added in future updates of the dataset. There is no BIBFRAME guideline regarding the representation of aggregates. Therefore, all realizations with illustrations were considered as new *bf:Work* instances. There is a 100% match between the *bf: Instances* of the two BIBFRAME (*Gold* and BIBF1) datasets.

---

[1] http://83.212.114.162/bibdata_mappings/displayMappings.php.

http://dbis.ionio.gr/Datasets/gold-frbr_derivations_v0.1#BronteWutheringHeights **(a)**
Wuthering Heights
has 10 Expression(s)(b)

http://dbis.ionio.gr/Datasets/gold-frbr_derivations_v0.1#WutheringHeightsArmenian
has 1 Manifestation(s) (c)

txt (arm)

<bf:Work   **(d)**
rdf:about="http://dlib.mappings.LRM2BF.org#WorkExpression_BronteWutheringHeights_Wut
heringHeightsArmenian" > <rdf:type rdf:resource="http://id.loc.gov/ontologies/bibframe/Text"
/> <bf:language > <bf:Language rdf:about="http://id.loc.gov/vocabulary/languages/arm" />
</bf:language> <bf:title > <bf:Title > <bf:mainTitle >Wuthering Heights</bf:mainTitle>

Fig. 2. FRBR mappings to BIBFRAME for *Wuthering Heights*, *bf:Work* carrying the Armenian translation

http://dbis.ionio.gr/Datasets/gold-frbr_derivations_v0.1#man201
Molegin hoghmeri daravand

Nairi, Erevan, 1992.

<bf:Instance rdf:about="http://dlib.mappings.LRM2BF.org#Instance_man201" > <bf:title >
<bf:Title ><bf:mainTitle >Molegin hoghmeri daravand</bf:mainTitle></bf:Title></bf:title>
<bf:responsibilityStatement>vep Émili Bronte ; [anglerenits' t'argmanets', Aram Budaghyanĕ]
</bf:responsibilityStatement><bf:provisionActivity> <bf:ProvisionActivity> <rdf:type

Fig. 3. Mapping the FRBR *Manifestation* to *bf:Instance* for the Armenian translation of the *Wuthering Heights*

Table 6 presents all derivation relationship occurrences per bibliographic family. In the *Gold* FRBR *dataset* there are 43 occurrences of the translation relationship, first column of Table 6. All of them correspond to literal translations for which the source text is known and, therefore, they were expressed between FRBR *Expressions*. In total, there are 126 literal translations in the dataset. The absence of the translation property for the 83 literal translations for which the source text is not known, does not hinder exploration due to their membership in a family. In the *Gold* BIBFRAME *dataset*, there are 126 occurrences of the *bf:translation* relationship. When we created the *Gold* BIBFRAME *dataset* we purposely added *bf:translation* relationships to ground exploration between *bf:Works*. Therefore, the number of 126 *bf:translation* relationship occurrences is identical to the 126 literal translations in the FRBR dataset. All mappings from FRBR were successfully mapped in the BIBF1 dataset.

FRBR is more granular on derivation relationships by identifying more specific types of derivation than BIBFRAME does, such as adaptation, dramatization, abridgement, revision. In the *Gold FRBR dataset* there are 77 occurrences of the derivation relationship either between *Works* or between *Expressions* (Table 2). All derivation types presented in Table 1 have been used in our dataset. The instances of each relationship used in the *Gold* FRBR *dataset* per family appear in Table 2. In the *Gold* BIBFRAME *dataset* there exist 77 occurrences of the *bf:hasDerivative* relationship.

Table 5. Occurrences of core entities in the three datasets

Family	Gold FRBR			Gold BIBFRAME		BIBF 1	
	Works	Expres.	Manifest.	Works	Instances	Works	Instances
Cien años	3	9	15	9	15	9	15
Crime&P	9	25	29	25	29	25	29
DonQuijote	4	11	11	12	11	11	11
Faust	9	29	28	29	28	29	28
Iliad	3	24	25	26	25	24	25
Karamazov Brothers	5	20	21	20	21	20	21
Madame Bovary	8	27	32	27	32	27	32
Odyssey	3	17	20	17	20	17	20
ScarletLett	12	22	24	21	24	22	24
TSawyer	8	28	32	27	32	28	32
Wuthering	8	17	20	17	20	17	20
Total	**72**	**229**	**257**	**230**	**257**	**229**	**257**

Table 6. Occurrences of translation and other derivations in the three datasets

Family	Gold FRBR			Gold BIBFRAME		BIBF 1	
	Trl	LitTrl	Deriv	Trl	Deriv	Trl	Deriv
Cien años de soledad	5	5	0	5	0	5	0
Crime & Punishment	10	15	12	15	12	10	108
Don Quijote	2	5	1	5	1	2	4
Faust	2	17	4	17	4	2	42
Iliad	2	20	14	20	14	2	33
Karamazov brothers	9	15	9	15	9	9	53
Madame bovary	2	13	5	13	4	2	80
Odyssey	5	12	9	12	9	5	35
Scarlet letter	3	10	9	10	8	3	79
Tom sawyer	0	8	8	8	8	0	128
Wuthering heights	3	6	6	6	8	3	60
Total	**43**	**126**	**77**	**126**	**77**	**43**	**622**

Mapping the 77 occurrences of derivative relationship from FRBR to BIBFRAME, has created 622 occurrences of the *bf:hasDerivative* relationship in the BIBF1 dataset, while the respective occurrences in *Gold* BIBFRAME are 77. The mapping of the FRBR '*Work-is realized through-Expression*' path to a *bf:Work* instance is the contributing factor for the great number of *bf:hasDerivative* occurrences in BIBF1. As an example, the *Crime & Punishment progenitor Work* has 17 *Expressions* and 6 derivation relationships with other *Works*. Therefore, each one of the 17 *bf:Work* instances created after mappings, carries at least 6 *bf:hasDerivative* relationships with a total of 102 occurrences! Some of the 17 FRBR *Expressions* had their own derivation relationships; the *bf:Works* in this case carry the 6 *bf:hasDerivative* relationships mapped from the FRBR *Work's* relationships plus the *bf:hasDerivative* relationships mapped from the FRBR *Expression's* relationships. Thus, the total number of occurrences increases even more.

It is anticipated that this anomaly will be resolved by the extension of the mapping rule that maps FRBR to a more specific BIBFRAME representation. Moreover, alternative BIBFRAME representation with the proper rules may be considered, such as a) *Expression*-agnostic *bf:Work* instances serving as *progenitors* and b) *bf: hasExpression* property instances to relate *bf:Work* instances belonging in the same family. Both representations have been presented in [15].

5 Discussion

Exploration through the bibliographic universe may be supported by the explicit representation of bibliographic relationships among their members. Both FRBR and BIBFRAME facilitate the representation of bibliographic relationships. Successful mappings with a high accuracy may be implemented from FRBR to BIBFRAME. The mapping approach exhibited high levels of success in mapping core entities and the translation relationship. Even though the mapping of other derivative relationships has been successful, yet it produced too many occurrences of the *bf:hasDerivative* relationship after the mappings.

Effort has been given to consistently develop and accurately describe the *Gold Standard* FRBR and BIBFRAME *datasets* representing the core entities and their derivation relationships as they evolved in well-known publications. Our goal is to use *the Gold Standard datasets* for assessing the effectiveness of various processes, such as entity extraction from bibliographic sources, or mapping instances between FRBR and BIBFRAME. The *Gold Standard datasets* will be enriched with more entities, attributes and content relationships to achieve fine-tuning of the testbed.

Testing mappings from FRBR to BIBFRAME will be continued since RDA implements the FRBR [20] and due to the anticipation that great numbers of RDA aligned MARC21 records will be converted in BIBFRAME. Other mapping approaches will be tested using the testbed to check mappings from FRBR to alternative BIBFRAME representations, such as the ones presented in [15]. Even though these alternative BIBFRAME representations remain within the semantics of the BIBFRAME model, it is unknown if they too remain within the scope of the model. The publication of IFLA-LRM [12] and the revision of RDA vocabularies will be exploited in the future to test the mappings from the LRM to BIBFRAME.

References

1. IFLA: Statement of International Cataloguing Principles (2009). http://www.ifla.org/publications/statement-of-international-cataloguing-principles
2. IFLA: Statement of International Cataloguing Principles (ICP) (2016)

3. Hickey, T.B., O'Neill, E.T.: FRBRizing OCLC's WorldCat. Cat. Classif. Q. **39**, 239–251 (2009). https://doi.org/10.1300/J104v39n03_15
4. Zhang, Y., Salaba, A.: What do users tell us about FRBR-based catalogs? Cat. Classif. Q. **50**, 705–723 (2012). https://doi.org/10.1080/01639374.2012.682000
5. Merčun, T., Žumer, M., Aalberg, T.: Presenting bibliographic families: designing an FRBR-based prototype using information visualization. J. Doc. **72**, 490–526 (2016). https://doi.org/10.1108/JD-01-2015-0001
6. Merčun, T., Žumer, M., Aalberg, T.: Presenting bibliographic families using information visualization: evaluation of FRBR-based prototype and hierarchical visualizations. J. Assoc. Inf. Sci. Technol. **68**, 392–411 (2016). https://doi.org/10.1002/jasist.23659
7. Tillett, B.: Bibliographic relationships: toward a conceptual structure of bibliographic information used in cataloging. Thesis, University of California (1987)
8. Smiraglia, R.: Authority control and the extent of derivative bibliographic relationships. Thesis, University of Chicago (1992)
9. Vellucci, S.L.: Bibliographic relationships among musical bibliographic entities: a conceptual analysis of music represented in a library catalog with a taxonomy of the relationships discovered. Thesis, Comlumbia University (1995)
10. Smiraglia, R., Leazer, G.: Derivative bibliographic relationships: the work relationship in a global bibliographic database. J. Am. Soc. Inf. Sci. **50**, 493–504 (1999)
11. IFLA Study Group on the Functional Requirements for Bibliographic Records. Functional Requirements for Bibliographic Records Final Report. IFLA, The Hague (2009)
12. Riva, P., Le Boeuf, P., Žumer, M.: IFLA Library Reference Model: A Conceptual Model for Bibliographic Information. IFLA, Den Haag (2017)
13. BIBFRAME Model, Vocabulary, Guidelines, Examples, Analyses. https://www.loc.gov/bibframe/docs/index.html
14. Zapounidou, S., Sfakakis, M., Papatheodorou, C.: Representing and integrating bibliographic information into the semantic web: a comparison of four conceptual models. J. Inf. Sci. **43**, 525–553 (2017). https://doi.org/10.1177/0165551516650410
15. Zapounidou, S., Sfakakis, M., Papatheodorou, C.: Preserving bibliographic relationships in mappings from FRBR to BIBFRAME 2.0. In: Kamps, J., Tsakonas, G., Manolopoulos, Y., Iliadis, L., Karydis, I. (eds.) TPDL 2017. LNCS, vol. 10450, pp. 15–26. Springer, Cham (2017). https://doi.org/10.1007/978-3-319-67008-9_2
16. RDA Registry: Elements. http://www.rdaregistry.info/Elements/
17. Library of Congress Name Authority File (NAF). http://id.loc.gov/authorities/names.html
18. OCLC: VIAF The Virtual International Authority File. https://viaf.org/
19. Library of Congress: Marc2bibframe2. https://github.com/lcnetdev/marc2bibframe2
20. RDA technical guidelines. https://github.com/RDARegistry/RDA-Vocabularies/wiki/RDA-Technical-Guidelines

Metadata Standards for Palm Leaf Manuscripts in Asia

Nisachol Chamnongsri[(✉)]

School of Information Technology, Suranaree University of Technology,
Nakhon Ratchasima, Thailand
nisachol@sut.ac.th

Abstract. The goal of this research is to facilitate, as effectively as possible, user access to and use of the knowledge recorded on palm leaf manuscripts (PLMs). At the same time, the schema should serve as a standard information structure to be used in the management of PLMs and other digitized ancient documents. This will also make the linking of Asian cultural heritage and wisdom with those of countries in this region possible via the internet. Accordingly, this research aims to develop metadata schema for the management of PLMs collections to increase efficiency in the search, access, use, and management. There are four parts in this study: (1) the current state of PLMs management in Asia and the use of PLMs metadata schema in working projects were investigated, then (2) the elements were analyzed and grouped by functions, (3) the core elements were matched to KKUPLMMs 2012, 2015 and IFLA LRM User Tasks and (4) a Focus group was set up to evaluate the framework.

Keywords: Metadata · Palm leaf manuscripts · Ancient documents · Cultural heritage

1 Introduction: The PLMs Characteristics; Values; Problems of Management, Access and Use; Digitization and Metadata

Palm Leaf Manuscripts (PLMs) are the ancient documents form that comprises a significant documentary heritage of the people in South Asia and South East Asia. These manuscripts contain a vast amount of knowledge on Buddhism, tradition and beliefs, customary law, traditional medicine, astrology, history, folktales, etc. PLMs vary in size and styles, and each country has their unique characteristics. For example, PLMS in Thailand are generally 5–6 cm. in width and 50–60 cm. in length with 48 pages per fascicle (24 leaves written on both sides). PLMs can be as short as 15 cm. or as long as 80 cm. and can vary according to the number of pages. Ancient people used PLMs of different sizes for different purposes: for example, in Thailand the longer PLMs were used as a textbook to record Buddhist stories and doctrines, while the shorter ones were used as notebooks to record local wisdom related to daily life. The languages written in PLMs were both local and undergoing shift (such as Balinese, Thai, Lao, Khmer, Sanskrit), and the manuscripts were written in archaic orthographies, requiring expert

E. Garoufallou et al. (Eds.): MTSR 2018, CCIS 846, pp. 242–254, 2019.
https://doi.org/10.1007/978-3-030-14401-2_23

translation. Because the length of PLMs is determined by its physical dimensions rather than its content, a single manuscript may record many stories, or a single story may require more than one manuscript. PLMs in the past were recordings of stories and knowledge that had been passed on by local wise men.

Currently, many PLMs preservation projects in South Asia and South-East Asia have attempted to collect PLMs from various monasteries and digitize them to make it easier for users to access and use, and for project staff to translate and preserve them. India's Ministry of Tourism and Culture has established The National Mission for Manuscripts in 2003 to preserve the vast manuscript wealth of the country. India has an estimate of ten million manuscripts, probably the largest collection in the world. The Mission has the mandate of identifying, documenting, conserving and making accessible the manuscript heritage of the country. It has developed metadata and digitization standards for palm leaf manuscripts and made them available on their website for public access. The project has tried to collect the PLMs and conserve their physical condition before microfilming for conservation purpose [1]. To support user access, they digitize the PLMs and use open source software, DSpace, as an online database [2]. National library of Laos also has a huge PLMs collection. They microfilm PLMs in their collection and then digitize the microfilms and develop online database to allow easy 24-h access from anywhere [3]. In Indonesia, the National Library of Indonesia has assigned many places in Indonesia to hold the collection. Their PLMs collection is still quite small, so the PLMs metadata is put in the Library OPAC [2]. In Sri Lanka, the national library has a PLMs conservation and digitization project but the standards for the PLMs have not been set up yet [2]. In Thailand, two groups are working actively on PLMs preservation: universities and national libraries. PLMS are digitized and microfilmed. Nevertheless, only five projects have developed online databases and open to public access [4].

In order for the digitized document to be effectively accessed, retrieved, and used, a metadata record – structured data used to describe a set of data about the resource – needs to be created. For a digitized document made up of many elements and consisting of various types of files kept on different servers, metadata is the tool used to describe the features of these documents and facilitate the finding, access and retrieval of the digitized document. Metadata also supports the display of a document record in the correct structure and facilitates management of the resource by providing information about construction, facilitating interoperability and legacy resource integration, providing digital identification and supporting archiving and preservation and access rights [5, 6]. Thus, metadata is now playing an important role as the information representation in a digital library, digital museum, and digital archive environment, especially for cultural heritage collection.

However, the literature review revealed there is no metadata standard to describe palm leaf manuscripts. From the previous research [7], each PLMs preservation project has tried to develop their own description schema for the PLMs in their collection. The different projects created metadata in different ways and for different purposes. Some of them describe PLMs based on library catalog which does not match the requirements of museums and archives. On the other hand, describing it the way museums do would treat PLMs as antiques rather than information resources. This is about physical conservation rather than provision of access to their content. Besides, the number of metadata experts is limited while ancient manuscripts in each region have unique characteristics that require expertise in reading and specifying.

2 Metadata

Metadata schema is a set of metadata elements which includes the definition of elements representing the attributes of a resource, and each element can have one or more values. The design of a metadata schema requires a clear set of attributes and values to enable both human and computers to process and use the metadata. At the same time, a good metadata schema must be easy to learn and use. Metadata that is too specific or too detailed will result in the waste of time and money in its construction and maintenance [8, 9]. According to the IFLA guidance on the nature, implementation, and evaluation of metadata schemas in libraries, *"The choice of a metadata schema or schemas to be used in creating the surrogate records for uniquely identifying and linking to digital items or objects in a collection will depend on where and how the resources will be access and used...metadata schema may also depend on the desire degree of granularity, or the amount of detail to be captured and represented in the metadata record"* [10].

Thus, before designing metadata to describe a collection, the system designer should know the document they are going to describe as well as user's expectations on the new metadata since the purpose is to help users gain more efficiency in searching for the desired documents. Previous studies revealed that the main reason users did not use the metadata was because they find it useless, insufficient, difficult to understand, and difficult to use.

3 The Research Objectives

The goal of this research is to facilitate, as effectively as possible, user access and use of the knowledge recorded on PLMs. The schema should also serve as a standard information structure to be used in the management of PLMs and other digitized ancient documents. This will enable the linking of Asian cultural heritage and wisdom with those of countries in the region via the internet. Accordingly, this research aims to develop a framework of metadata for the management of PLMs collections in both digital and original PLMs to increase efficiency in the access, use, and management.

4 Research Methodology

This study consists of four parts: (1) the investigation of the current state of PLMs management in Asia, and the current use of PLMs metadata schema in working projects, (2) the analysis and grouping by functions of the elements, (3) the comparison to the previous KKUPLMMs 2012 and 2015 metadata schema based on IFFLA Functional Requirements for Bibliographic Records (FRBR), where the metadata development process is conducted on the integration of the concept of system development life cycle and metadata life cycle model which composes of three main steps: (1) metadata requirement analysis (2) design and development of metadata schema and (3) evaluation of metadata schema. Among the three steps, requirement analysis is very important since it investigates data to determine the requirement of the desired metadata and its function in PLMs management. The baseline data actually comes from series of studies including; users' behaviors and needs analysis, PLMs physical characteristics and the subject content structure, recording in their fascicles, examination, and the current stage of PLMs management and its problems in each context investigation. And (4) a group discussion at PLMs workshop to evaluate core metadata elements framework (Fig. 1).

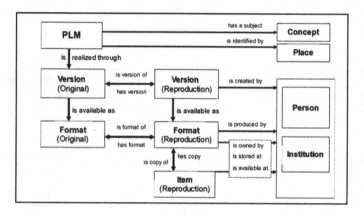

Fig. 1. KKUPLMs model applied from FRBR model [7]

5   Current Metadata Schemas Used to Describe PLMs

In April 2017, a survey was conducted to investigate the current metadata schemas or description schemas which PLMs preservation projects use to describe PLMs in their collections; Are there any standards readily and more frequently used than others? What is the important information present in PLMs bibliographic records? Sixteen projects found on the internet are included in this study; 10 projects from Thailand, 2 projects from a library in England, 2 projects from a university library in USA, 1 project from the National Library of Laos, and a project by National Mission for Manuscripts (NMM), India. Besides Thailand and Laos, this survey did not find PLMs databases from other countries in South-East Asia and South Asia available on the internet despite the knowledge that there is a vast amount of PLMs and many PLMs conservation projects in these regions. Among the 16 projects surveyed, no standard was found to be used more frequently than others.

Table 1. The information present in the bibliographic records of 16 projects

	Attributes/Projects	1	2	3	4	5	6	7	8	9	10	11	12	13	14	15	16	Total
	Bibliographic Information																	
1	1. Title	1	1	1	1	1	1	1	1	1	1	1	1	1	1	1	1	16
2	2. Other Title / original Title											1	1			1	1	4
3	3. Uniform Title			1	1							1						3
4	4. Series		1												1			2
5	5. Note/History/Remarks	1	1	1	1	1								1		1	1	8
6	6. Commentary															1		1
7	7. Date of Inscription	1	1	1		1	1			1	1	1		1			1	10
8	8. Era									1								1
9	9. Date of Found														1			1
10	10. Inscriber/ Author		1			1				1						1	1	5
11	11. Patron (who pays for the inscription)		1							1						1		3
12	12. Donor/Sponsor									1		1						2
13	13. Commentator															1		1
14	14. Investigator									1					1			2
15	15. Subject /Category		1	1		1			1	1	1	1		1	1	1	1	11
16	16. Place of Original	1	1	1	1	1	1			1	1			1	1			10
17	17. Description /Abstract							1	1			1	1	1		1		6
18	18. literary style								1									1
19	19. Related documents								1									1
	Physical Characteristics																	
20	1. Type / Material							1	1	1	1	1		1		1	1	8
21	2. Script		1	1	1	1		1	1	1	1	1	1	1	1	1	1	14
22	3. Language		1	1	1	1		1	1	1	1	1	1	1	1	1	1	14
23	4. Dimensions (W x L) cm.		1	1	1							1	1	1	1	1	1	9
24	5. Illustration															1		1
25	6. Inscription Method		1	1						1								3
26	7. Cover Board (Character)		1	1	1							1		1				5
27	8. Cover Board (Dimensions)		1	1														2
28	9. Edition (edge style)		1	1								1		1				4
29	10. Label		1	1														2
30	11. Wrapper		1	1														2
31	12. Type of PLM (short, long)		1															1
32	13. Lines per page		1										1	1	1	1		5
33	14. Number of Pages	1	1		1	1		1				1	1	1	1	1	1	11
34	15. Number of Stories		1												1			2
35	16. Number of Fascicles/Bundles	1	1	1	1		1	1	1	1	1	1		1	1		1	13
36	17. Fascicle Number	1	1											1			1	4
37	18. Completion		1				1			1	1					1	1	6
38	19. Physical Condition		1			1	1			1					1		1	6
39	20. Missing portions															1		
	Administrative Information																	
40	1. Storage Location	1	1	1	1	1	1					1	1	1	1	1	1	12
41	2. Catalog source															1		1
42	3. Date of Reproduction (digitization, mic	1	1	1			1								1		1	6
43	4. Image Specification	1		1			1								1		1	5
44	5. Digitigal image file						1				1						1	3
45	6. Registration Number		1	1	1		1	1	1	1	1	1	1	1		1	1	13
46	7. Number of shelf/cabinet		1	1	1													3
47	8. Preservation Method		1	1			1			1				1				5
48	9. Microfilm Number	1	1															2
49	10. Collection Number		1	1											1			3
50	11. Right/Owner Ship					1	1		1	1			1	1				6
51	12. Publisher/Digitization lab									1			1	1	1			4
52	13. Image Legibility											1						1
		11	17	30	17	15	16	7	14	17	13	18	12	16	18	19	25	

1. The National Library of Thailand schema, used only by staff.
2. The National Library of Laos schema; used by National Library of Laos; Lanna (Northern Thailand) PLMs preservation project, Chiang Mai University and Isan (Northeastern Thailand) PLMs preservation project, Mahasarakham University.
3. NMM metadata schema, used in their own projects.
4. KKUPLMMs was developed in 2009 based on the study of requirement from PLMs users, PLMs preservation projects in Thailand, and the characteristics of PLMs in Thailand. Three PLMs preservation projects in Thailand have applied KKUPLMMs with their schemas to develop PLMs databases.
5. MARC21, a library standard, used by one library in USA to describe PLMs.

Fifty five elements were found from these 16 projects. They can be separated into three groups; (1) physical characteristics (20 element), (2) bibliographic information (19 elements), and (3) administrative information (13 elements). The largest number of elements found in one project is 30, the second is 25, and the third is 19. The smallest number is 7. The biggest group is 16-19 elements (8 projects). All of them are active projects that have been working on PLMs conservation for 10 years. As shown in Table 1.

There are 13 elements in 50% (8 of 16 projects) of the studied projects, including; Title, Script, Language, Number of Fascicles, Registration Number, Storage Location, Subject/Category, Number of Pages, Place of Original, Date of Inscription, Dimensions, Type/Material, and Note/History/Remarks. However, only "Title" appears in all 16 projects, while "Script" and "Language" appear in 14 projects. Besides, these first three elements are assigned as the main access points for all projects. From Table 2, looking at the types of information reveals;

- The physical characteristics information appear most often. They included 11 from 23 elements; Script, Language, Number of fascicle/bundle, Number of Pages, Dimensions (W × L), Type of Material, Physical Condition, Completion, Cover Board (Character), Lines per page, and. Information in this group is useful in identifying and selecting the PLMs.
- The second group is bibliographic information indicating the content of the PLMs. They included 7 from 23 elements; Title, Subject/Category, Place of Original, Date of Inscription, Note/History, Description/Abstract, and Inscriber/Author. This group is used to identify the content of the PLMs, and to find and explore the content recorded in the PLMs.
- The third group is administrative information, including 6 from 23 elements; Registration Number, Storage Location, Right/Ownership, Date of Reproduction, Preservation Method, and Image specification. This group is helpful in obtaining, and using the PLMs

However, half of the elements in each group were found less than 5 times. They are 12:19 in bibliographic information, 7:13 in physical characteristics, and 10:13 in administrative information. This is because when metadata was developed, different projects created metadata in different ways for different purposes. They concern the physical conservation administration rather than provide the content access. The PLMs are also treated as antiques, not information resources.

Table 2. The frequency of appearance of information present in the bibliographic records of the 16 projects

Elements (N = 23)	Number of projects it's found (N = 16)	Type of information
1. Title	16	Bibliographic information
2. Script	14	Physical characteristics
Language		Physical characteristics
3. Number of fascicle/bundle	13	Physical characteristics
Registration number/Identifier		Administrative information
4. Storage location	12	Administrative information
5. Subject/Category	11	Bibliographic information
Number of pages		Physical characteristics
6. Place of original	10	Bibliographic information
Date of inscription		Bibliographic information
7. Dimensions (W × L) cm.	9	Physical characteristics
8. Note/History	8	Bibliographic information
Type of material		Physical characteristics
9. Description/Abstract	6	Bibliographic information
Right/Ownership		Administrative information
Date of reproduction		Administrative information
Physical condition		Physical characteristics
Completion		Physical characteristics
10. Cover board (Character)	5	Physical characteristics
Lines per page		Physical characteristics
Preservation method		Administrative information
Image specification		Administrative information
Inscriber/Author		Bibliographic information

6   KKUPLMMs

From our previous research [7] on the development of metadata for management of a digitized palm leaf manuscript, we created Khon Kaen University Palm Leaf Metadata Schema (KKUPLMMs) which was revised in 2012 and 2015 [7, 11]. We studied four projects working on PLMs conservation and providing PLMs service in Thailand. The research found that the main access point that users employed when searching PLMs is "Title" because it was the only access point that indicated the content in the PLMs. While the other two access points, Script and Language which were provided by all projects were often used to limit search, identify, and select the PLMs rather than to find them. Moreover, users mentioned Place of Original (the place or geographic location where the PLM was found) was useful in conducting limited search. For the selection of PLMs, users mentioned the main information including Content (indicated by Tile, Abstract or Content Summary, Place of Found), Script, Language, Storage Place and User Restriction, and Physical Condition or the Completeness of the PLMs (no missing fascicles, no missing pages, and the document is not too damaged to read, and the writing is readable). Some of them considered the age of the PLMs, the place where the PLM was found, and its literary style. Furthermore, users also needed to search for other versions or related works (translations, research reports etc.) of the required PLMs.

Regarding the important information present in the bibliographic records of PLMs created by the PLMs preservation projects in Thailand, it was found that four type of information out of 34 (Title, Note or History, Number of Fascicles, and Storage Location) were present in all projects. These information presents information relating to the content topic, the completion of the content, the place where the PLM was inscribed and the location where the PLM is stored, which are the most important details of information in the selection of PLMs. The finding suggests that the perception of the KKUPLMMs usefulness is more significant with users' that are more experienced with the PLMs. Finally, the PLMs metadata schema developed for palm leaf manuscripts consists of 76 properties (34 core elements and 42 element refinements) to describe all versions and formats of PLMs. It can support users in searching for the PLMs as well as staff in managing collections of PLMs.

7 Matching with IFLA User Tasks

The five generic user tasks (find, identify, select, obtain, explore) employed while users search for bibliographic records serve as a statement of the IFLA LRM model's functional scope and confirm its outward orientation to the end-user's needs. The five user tasks phrased from the point of view of supporting the user's ability to carry them out include; [12].

- Find, to bring together information about one or more resources of interest by searching on any relevant criteria.
- Identify, to clearly understand the nature of the resources found and to distinguish between similar resources.
- Select, to determine the suitability of the resources found, and to be enabled to either accept or reject specific resources.
- Obtain, to access the content of the resource.
- Explore, to discover resources using the relationships between them and thus place the resources in a context.

To meet users' information needs, the five user tasks and KKUPLMMs 2015 which was based on FRBR model and user study were used to match with the elements. When matching 23 elements presented in the bibliographic records of the 16 projects to the five tasks of Functional Requirement of Bibliographic Records; find, identify, select and obtain (shown as Table 3) we found that all five tasks have elements responding to:

Table 3. The comparison of main elements of KKUPLMMs 2012, 2015, and 2017 survey and matching with IFLA LRM 5 Tasks

PLMM in 2012	PLMM in 2015	2017 (survey ranking)	IFLA LRM 5 Tasks
Content information			
1. PLMs' title/Stories' title	1. Title	1. Title (1)	Find, Identify, Select, Explore
2. Uniform title	2. Uniform title	-	Find, Explore
3. Keyword	3. Keyword	-	Find, Explore
4. Subject/Subject heading	4. Subject	2. Subject/Category (5)	Find, Explore
-	5. Summary	3. Description/Abstract (9)	Find
5. Literary style	6. Literary style	-	Find, Identify, Select
6. Where the PLM was found	7. Place found	4. Place of original (5)	Find, Identify, Select, Explore
7. Time period/Date of inscription	8. Date of inscription	5. Date of inscription (6)	Find, Identify, Select, Explore
		6. Note/History (8)	Identify, Select
Physical characteristic information			
8. Script	9. Script	7. Script (2)	Find, Identify, Select, Explore
9. Language	10. Language	8. Language (2)	Find, Identify, Select, Explore
10. Physical characteristics	11. Physical characteristics	9. Completion of volume (if it includes many fascicles) (10)	Identify, Select
-	11.1 Dimension	10. Dimensions (W x L) (7)	Identify
-	11.2 Number of pages	11. Number of pages (5)	Identify
-	11.3 Number of fascicles	12. Number of fascicle/Bundle (3)	Identify
-	11.3 Physical condition	13. Physical condition (10)	Identify, Select
-	-	14. Lines per page (10)	Identify
-	-	15. Cover board (Character) (10)	Identify
11. Form of PLM	12. Form of PLM	16. Type of material (8)	Identify, Select
Administrative information			
12. Storage place	13. Storage place	17. Storage location (4)	Select, Obtain, Explore
13. Holding location	14. Holding location	-	Obtain, Explore
14. Owner	15. Owner	18. Right/Ownership (9)	Select, Obtain, Explore
15. Copyright statement			Select, Obtain

(*continued*)

Table 3. (*continued*)

PLMM in 2012	PLMM in 2015	2017 (survey ranking)	IFLA LRM 5 Tasks
	16. Copyright statement		
16. Use restriction	17. Use restriction	-	Select
17. Access methods	18. Access methods	-	Obtain
18. Date of preservation	19. Date of preservation	-	
19. Preservation methods/Preservation actions taken	20. Preservation methods	19. Preservation method (10)	
20. Technical information	21. Technical information	-	Obtain
21. Producer	22. Producer	-	
22. Date of registration	23. Date of registration	-	
23. Negotiation terms	-	-	Select
-	-	20. Registration number (3)	Obtain

- To identify PLMs or distinguish between several PLMs with the same title and/or characteristics. There are 15 elements supporting this task; including all physical characteristic information such as Script, Language, Number of Fascicle, Physical Condition and etc. and some elements from content information: Title, Place of Original, Date of Inscription, and Note/History.
- To find PLMs that correspond to the user's stated search. Six elements support this task: Title, Subject/Category, Script, Language, Place of Original, and Date of Inscription.
- To select the PLMs that are appropriate to the user's needs. There are 10 elements in this group; Title, Place of Original, Date of Inscription, and Note/History, Script, Language, Completion of Volume, Physical Condition, Type of Material, Storage Location, and Right/Ownership.
- To acquire or obtain access to the PLMs described. The user has the ability to download or loan an entity. There are four elements supporting this task; Registration Number, Storage Location, and Right/Ownership.
- To explore the related PLMs, there 9 elements in this group; including Title, Subject, Original Location, Date of Inscription, Script, Language, Storage Location, and Owner.

Then, the result of this research was prepared as background information for the participants to join a discussion in the PLMs workshop which was arranged one month later. The background information was sent to the participants three weeks before the workshop.

8 The Group Discussion at the PLMs Workshop

The two-day workshop at the National Library of Sri Lanka held by IFLA was arranged on September 6–7, 2017. Twelve experts in metadata and manuscripts from PLMs preservation projects in various organizations, from seven countries participated in this workshop. The organizations represented were IFLA; SEAMEO SPAFA; Technical University of Cologne, Germany; Khon Kaen University, Thailand, Suranaree University of Technology, Thailand; Jawaharlal Nehru University, India; National Library of Laos; National Library of Indonesia; University Kelaniya, Sri Lanka; National Library of Sri Lanka; and IPSIFCA/AO, Sri Lan Ka.

The first day started with the researcher, as the facilitator, presenting the background paper to outline the variety of current standards in use, the diversity of using metadata for PLMs descriptions, the problems caused by the lack of a unified metadata set of standards for the materials, then posing questions to invite the participants to tackle the problems and find constructive solutions.

The second day started with the researcher presenting the methodology of PLMs metadata development: a case study of Thailand (KKUPLMMs). The research framework was based on the System Development Lifecycle and Metadata Life Cycle Model which is composed of three main steps: (1) metadata requirement analysis (2) design and development of metadata schema and (3) evaluation of metadata schema; and using FRBR model proposed by IFLA in 1998 [13] to define a structured framework of metadata schema and relationships between metadata records by focusing on the kinds of resources that a data record describes. Among the three steps, requirement analysis was highlighted. After that, the workshop participants were invited to find constructive solutions. The three mains questions; Do you agree to create and develop metadata standards for palm leaf manuscript in the region? If then, what are the restrictions in your region to create a joint metadata framework for palm leaf manuscripts to ensure access? How to be successful in metadata standard creation in the region? Then Tables 1, 2 and 3 were presented for further discussions.

All participants strongly agreed to jointly develop metadata standard for PLMs management. At the beginning, the participants suggested creating core metadata elements framework which can support two main functions of PLMs management: preservation and access. However, the important data for setting metadata requirement should be derived from the involved parties which include PLMs users such as historians, researchers in various fields, academics, graduate students and those who work with PLMs collection such as librarians, information scientists, curators and experts in ancient languages, etc.

In order to initiate metadata standard by creating the metadata information framework, the participants decided to use metadata elements which were analyzed from the elements shown in metadata schemes used in the 16 projects (Table 1), as a guideline for selecting the core elements of metadata for PLMs management. The principles of selecting metadata elements based on PLMs management functions are: preservation and access. After discussion and consideration, the group created the first draft of metadata core elements containing 39 elements which can be divided into 3 groups by functions; access (15 elements), management (15 elements), and administration (9 elements) [2].

9 Conclusion and Future Works

Since 2012 when the KKUPLMMs was announced, many PLMs preservation projects in Thailand have applied KKUPLMMs with their schemas to develop PLMs databases. On the other hand, the PLMs databases we found in western countries belong to academic library and national library. This group describes the PLMs as library resources. They do not specifically give physical description or physical condition. PLMs are ancient documents with unique characters and usage, thus they need a specific framework to describe. The core PLMs description framework from the workshop has shown that the participants have more concern about user access. However, PLMs being ancient documents also require management and administration.

When the core elements from the workshop were compared to KKUPLMMs, it was found that they were the same as twenty eight elements from KKUPLMMs 2012 and fourteen elements from KKUPLMMs 2015 (the brief version). It can be said that the metadata development framework presented at the workshop has the potential to be used in a metadata research. The behaviors of PLMs users in each country should also be investigated to obtain the data for setting basic requirements of PLMs metadata. The experts from each country should reconsider and try to implement the metadata core elements in their own PLM management context, and consequently, give feedback on the problems and provide suggestions to the group. This information will be very useful in developing the metadata standards for PLMs management that can be applied in each country. This is to ensure that researchers, students and people who are interested in PLMs in the region and other parts of the world can access, use, and share their memories, knowledge, and cultures while the PLMs are well preserved for the future.

Acknowledgments. I would like to thank the International Federation of Library Association and Institutions (IFLA) and National Library and Documentation Services Board (NLDSB), Sri Lanka for the workshop grant support.

References

1. National Mission for Manuscripts. https://www.namami.gov.in/history. Accessed 12 Aug 2018
2. The Scoping IFLA Workshop on Palm Leaf Manuscripts: Preserving Cultural heritage, 22 November 2017. https://www.ifla.org/files/assets/hq/plm2017_scopingworkshopreport.pdf. Accessed 12 Aug 2018
3. Digital Library of Lao Manuscripts. http://www.laomanuscripts.net/en/index. Accessed 12 Aug 2018
4. Chamnongsri, N., Manmart, L.: Metadata Standards for Palm Leaf Manuscripts: A Background Paper for IFLA Palm Leaf Manuscripts Workshop, 6–7 July 2017, Colombo, Sri Lanka, May 2017
5. Hughes, L.M.: Digitizing Collections Strategic Issues for the Information Manager. Facet, London (2004)
6. NISO: Understanding metadata. NISO Press, Bethesda (2004)

7. Chamnongsri, N.: Metadata development for management of a digitized palm leaf manuscript. Thesis [Ph.D.], Khon Kaen University, Khon Kaen (2009)
8. Long, X., Ling, C.: Design and implementation of Chinese university rare book digital library (2001). http://www.idl.pku.edu.cn/pdf/NIT-metadata%20paper.pdf. Accessed 21 May 2009
9. Haynes, D.: Metadata for Information Management and Retrieval. Facet, London (2004)
10. IFLA Section on Cataloguing. Guidance on the Nature, Implementation, and Evaluation of Metadata Schemas in Libraries (2005). http://www.ifla.org/files/catalogung/pubs/metadata_schemas-20050731.pdf. Accessed 12 Aug 2018
11. Manmart, L., Chamnongsri, N., Wuwonge, W., Sugimoto, S.: Metadata development for palm leaf manuscripts in Thailand. In: DCMI International Conference on Dublin Core and Metadata Applications, [S.l.], pp. 95–105 (2012). ISSN 1939-1366
12. Riva, P., Bœuf, P.L., Žumer, M.: IFLA Library Reference Model: A Conceptual Model for Bibliographic Information. CH Den Haag Netherlands: IFLA (2017)
13. IFLA Section on Cataloguing. Functional Requirements for Bibliographic Records: final report. K.G. Saur München: IFLA (1998)

Knowledge IT Artifacts (KITA) in Professional Communities and Aggregations

Knowledge Artifacts for the Health: The PERCIVAL Project

Fabio Sartori[✉], Riccardo Melen, Matteo Lombardi, and Davide Maggiotto

REDS Lab - Department of Computer Science, Systems and Communication,
University of Milan - Bicocca, viale Sarca, 336, 20126 Milan, Italy
sartori@disco.unimib.it

Abstract. Quality of life (QoL) of patients affected by chronic diseases
and their caregivers is a very important and inter-disciplinar research
topic. From recent literature, it emerges the need for new methodologies
capable to reduce the impact of a chronic disorders on everyday life of
affected people and their relatives, especially when they are geographi-
cally far from care centers: the *PERsonal Care Instructor and VALuator*
(PERCIVAL) project, collaboration between the REDS Lab and Educational Factory srl, is a first attempt to build up an integrated environment
to promote the sharing, deliberation and monitoring of decisions about
different aspects of chronic diseases among all the actors involved.

Keywords: Wearable devices · Knowledge artifacts · e-Health ·
Quality of life

1 Introduction

Quality of life (QoL) of patients affected by chronic diseases and caregivers is
a very important and interdisciplinary research topic. For example, it emerges
[1,2] the need for new methodologies capable to reduce the impact of neuro-
degenerative disorders on everyday life of affected people and their relatives.

In particular, it is often highlighted how the evolution of chronic diseases
over the time brings to a substantial stability of QoL and depression in patients;
on the contrary, the burden and depression of caregivers significantly increase.

It is clearly pointed out how interventions to improve the communication
effectiveness between patients and caregivers might increase the psychological
well-being of both parties, helping patients to be more aware of their caregivers'
needs, and caregivers to get more apt to accept their difficult but important
role. Thanks to the available wearable technologies, our goal is creating new
ways to mean the communication among patients, caregivers and professionals,
in order to improve the psychological well-being and QoL of them all. Such
technologies are not invasive and allow to check a huge number of parameters
continuously, with benefits from the control of physical and psychological status
of patient-caregiver pairs' point of view, providing the professionals with effective
and efficient interventions' tool. The main objective of the PERCIVAL project is

© Springer Nature Switzerland AG 2019
E. Garoufallou et al. (Eds.): MTSR 2018, CCIS 846, pp. 257–267, 2019.
https://doi.org/10.1007/978-3-030-14401-2_24

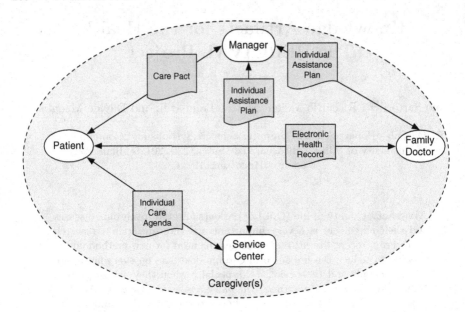

Fig. 1. The actors and information flow introduced by the reformed Healthcare System of Lombardy.

to design and implement a complete conceptual and computational framework to share information and knowledge among all the people involved in the treatment of chronic diseases, taking care of the heterogeneous nature of related information and knowledge by means of *knowledge aritfact* notion. The PERCIVAL project is intrinsically correlated to important organizational change that are occurring in north of Italy, and in particular within the Lombardy region.

The Lombardy region has recently developed an innovative reform[1] of regional Healthcare System. One of the main important points is the formalization of an integrated management of chronic patients, making the public administration responsible for the correct and complete prescription of diagnostic exams, drugs, professional visits and so on. Figure 1 shows the main *actors* and *artifacts* involved as well as a sketch of the information flows among them.

– *Patient*: he/she chooses the Manager, together with he/she defines the *Care Pact* (CP);
– *Manager*: the Manager is the most important innovation of the reform; it could be the *family doctor* or not; it defines the care-pact with the patient as well as the *Individual Assistance Plan* (IAP) according to the Region guidelines; it collaborates with the family-doctor (if different from the Manager), sharing the IAP with him/her;

---

[1] See http://www.lombardiasociale.it/wp-content/uploads/2015/10/LR-23_2015.pdf.

- *Family Doctor*: he/she is the main reference of the patient, collaborating with the Manager in the redaction of IAP or suggesting further information to modify it; the family doctor shares the *Electronic Health Record* (EHR) with the patient;
- *Service Center*: it supports the Manager, checking for the correspondence between IAP and regional guidelines; it supports the patient in the management of his/her *individual-care agenda* (ICA).

Caregivers are not directly involved by the reform, but, indeed, indirectly. Patients are classified on three distinct levels of chronicity:

- *Level 1*: characterized by very high clinical fragility, where the main pathology is associated to three others at least, for a total of four or more contemporary diseases;
- *Level 2*: characterized by medium-high clinical fragility, where the main pathology is associated to two others at most, for a total of two or three contemporary diseases;
- *Level 3*: characterized by initial stages of clinical fragility, where the main pathology is not associated to others.

While patients at Level 3 can be followed by the family-doctor, who merges its usual role with the Manager one, the choice of a Manager for patients at Levels 2 and 3 should be mandatory. Entering the new healthcare system is not easy for these kinds of people, who must be supported by their caregiver(s), usually a member of their family or a collaborator.

For this reason, the role of caregivers is crucial, although it has not been formally recognized by the reform: caregivers support the patient to understand the chronic state of his/her disease(s), check he/she follows the medical prescriptions, accompany him/her on therapies, analysis and examinations.

Caregivers are fully involved in the case management plan, and their QoL is often more affected by it than the patient's one: the main goal of the PERCIVAL project is to develop an integrated environment that allow to increase their QoL level through the sharing of important information and deliberations about the patient with all the "institutional partners" described above.

The PERCIVAL project is recently started and will finish at the end of the year. In this paper, we propose an overview of it from the practical point of view, specifying its main important issues in a very specific case study: the support of patients affected by diabetes. Section 2 briefly introduces the notion of *higher level knowledge artifact* and its relationship with the problem tackled in PERCIVAL. Section 3 will describe the current state of implementation of the PERCIVAL system in the project case study. Finally, Sect. 4 will end the paper with some considerations about the rest of the project.

2   PERCIVAL Development

The PERCIVAL project aims at the adoption of wearable expert systems paradigm [3] to develop a virtual community [4] of people involved in chronic patients support. Figure 2 shows a sketch of the system architecture: wearable

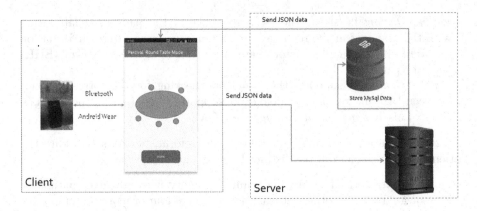

Fig. 2. The draft client-server architecture of PERCIVAL.

devices are used to detect physiological data from off-the shelf sensors [5]; these data are collected by the PERCIVAL app and sent to the server, where they are stored and used for deliberations about actions to be performed.

These actions depend on both the considered knowledge model and the kind of users they interest to: given that the wearable expert system is based on KAFKA [6], different kinds of knowledge can be represented and correlated; in particular, KAFKA is focused on the acquisition and representation of functional, procedural and experiential knowledge.

By definition [7], functional knowledge is related to the *functional representation* of a product, that *consists of descriptions of the functionality of components (or (sub-) systems) and the relationship between them*. To properly capture such relationships, the authors suggest the adoption of ontologies (being able to deal with the semantics of relations); in PERCIVAL, functional knowledge is related to the identification of users and artifacts they can access to, together with the operations they can perform on them. To this scope, the PERCIVAL system introduces the *round table* abstraction to describe the virtual community involved in the chronic disorder management: a user can participate with a specific role (i.e. the ones specified by the Reform plus the caregiver), sharing information and knowledge with others according to it.

Basically, the round table provides the members of the community with an immediate feedback about the virtual presence of others within the system. When a member is present, he/she can access all the knowledge and information stored in or accessible via the PERCIVAL system; such resources are archived in specific *artifacts*, that are CP, EHR, IAP and ICA, as well as in *instructor and evaluation modules*, that are software components devoted to perform artifacts modifications; the way artifacts can be managed by the user (through a specific module) depends on the privileges he/she has, as summarized in Table 1, where artifacts are listed in the rows, users and their privileges in the columns.

Table 1. Summarization of round table participants on PERCIVAL resources

User type	P			M			FD			SC			C		
Privilege	R	W	A	R	W	A	R	W	A	R	W	A	R	W	A
Care pact	X	X	X	X	X	X	X	-	-	X	-	-	X	-	-
Electronic health record	X	-	-	X	-	-	X	X	X	X	-	-	X	-	-
Individual assistance plan	X	-	-	X	X	X	X	-	X	X	-	-	X	-	-
Individual care agenda	X	-	X	X	-	-	X	-	-	X	X	X	X	-	-

Procedural knowledge is defined in [8] as the *understanding of how to apply the concepts learned in any problem solving situations*. This means that procedural knowledge concerns how to combine concepts to solve a problem. In other words, procedural knowledge is devoted to explain the different steps through which a result is obtained, but it doesn't specify anything on how those steps are implemented. In PERCIVAL, procedural knowledge can be meant as a sequence of steps to perform for the implementation of a specific action prescribed by functional knowledge. For example, the patient should accomplish a sequence of activities defined by the manager in the IAP artifact: this activities, from the patient point of view, are a representation of the procedural knowledge modeled by the manager to support him/her in tackling the chronic disease. According to the chronic level of the disorder, the procedural knowledge will define one or more sequences of activities: these sequences could be correlated or not, depending on the nature of the disease.

Finally, some authors defined [9] experiential knowledge as *knowledge derived from experience*. It is important because *it can provide data, and verify theoretical conjectures or observations*. Experiential knowledge, that can remain (partly) tacit, allows to describe aspects that procedural knowledge is not able to represent, and opportune tools are needed to capture it; in PERCIVAL, experiential knowledge could be devoted to avoid negative side-effects due to the correlation between the flows of procedural knowledge, or the implementation of reasoning processes made by domain experts, in particular the manager and the family-doctor, to perform opportune actions on artifacts. For example, the detection of physiological parameters, like e.g. heart beat rate or body temperature and their usage to prescribe new therapies or analysis.

3 Case Study: PERCIVAL for Diabetes Treatment

Chronic diseases are often characterized by the emerging of multiple disorders. Thus, chronic patients are subject to different, contemporary and heterogeneous therapies. The main problem from the medical point of view is to find a correct trade-off among them: drugs must be taken at different or the same time according to possible side-effects, possible psychological support could be necessary as well as adequate physical training and diet programs. In the PERCIVAL project, we are focusing on diabetes, that is one of the most important chronic disorder to face with according to regional reform guidelines.

The American Diabetes Association defines diabetes [10] as *a group of metabolic diseases characterized by hyperglycemia resulting from defects in insulin secretion, insulin action or both. The chronic hyperglycemia of diabetes is associated with long-term damage, dysfunction, and failure of different organs, especially the eyes, kidneys, nerves, heart and blood vessels.* The number of people affected by this disturb is continuously increasing: in Italy, 12% of population in the 50–69 years old interval is affected by diabetes, and the World Health Organization estimates the number of patients in the world will duplicate within 2025. Due to the heterogeneous nature of complications, diabetes is one of the most important cost item in the Public Health balance of Italy as well as many other countries. It has been calculated that Italian National Health Service spends about 2600 euro per year for each person affected by diabetes.

Moreover, a diabetes diagnosis is often correlated to the emerging of important psychological side-effects, both in the patient and his/her relatives. Psychological support is really important in the treatment of patients [11], that must be continuously monitored and stimulated toward a full self-management of their motivation to follow therapies and good lifestyles [12]. The proper support of caregivers is even more crucial: many studies, like e.g. [13] point out the extremely heavy burden suffered by relatives of the patient, especially in the early stages of a chronic disease. To fall in depression is highly probable, due to many factors, and the overall QoL of caregiver is generally worse than the sick person.

The main aim of the PERCIVAL project is increasing the QoL of patients and caregivers through the development of an integrated framework that supports them at different levels of granularity. In the next sections the first part of the project will be presented, devoted to developing a module to check and support the physical and psychological well-being state of the patient.

Figure 3 shows a sketch of the main elements of the PERCIVAL project. From the conceptual point of view, PERCIVAL is composed by three main parts: the *Round Table Mode*, the *Artifacts* and the *Instructors and Evaluation Modules*. The first one is devoted to the design of the community of users involved in the system. Each of them has a specific interface to register in the system, specifying its role and permissions, as well as the values for the main attributes. The role defines the set of operations a specific user can perform on artifacts, that are passive entities representing the documents necessary to register all the information about the chronic disorder of the patient. Operations are accomplished by means of opportune modules. In the figure, the flow from *Patient* role to *Individual Care Agenda* by means of the *MoveUp* module is shown. The MoveUp module is the first prototype of the *Instructor and Evaluation Modules* component of PERCIVAL: it aims to give a qualitative and quantitative evaluation of the psychological and physical well-being of a patient through the determination of self-efficacy and METs produced by the user during suggested training sessions. Indeed, physical activity is crucial for keeping under control the evolution of diabetes; thus, the PERCIVAL system aims at providing the patient with a training plan tailored on his/her physical and mental state. The details about the computational model behind the MoveUp module are out of the paper scope: they can be found in [14].

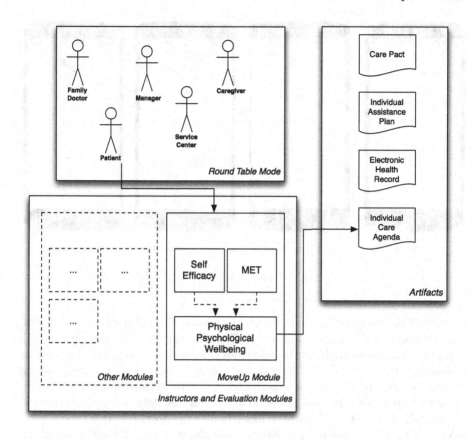

Fig. 3. The main elements of the PERCIVAL project.

Figure 4 illustrates the main components of the graphical user interface for the patient characterization in PERCIVAL. The user is asked to specify his/her age (step 2. in the figure), that is necessary to the MET sub-module of MoveUp, and other parameters (step 3. in the figure) like *weight* and *waistline*, that are useful to evaluate possible benefits or drawbacks emerging from suggested physical activities. Finally, the figure shows (step 4.) the interface for the collection of values to evaluate self-efficacy of the user after a physical activity.

Figure 5 presents a sketch of the recommendations made by MoveUp to evaluate the subject well-being. First of all, the *individual care agenda* is automatically updated on the basis of previous training sessions results, considering both MET calculus and self-efficacy statement (step 1. in the figure). This artifact has been thought as a *calendar*, where all the actions related to the diabetes treatment will be annotated day by day. In this way, the individual care agenda will be shared among the different actors involved in the round table, that will be notified when changes occur. Currently, only the MoveUp module has been developed that automatically modifies the artifact; the user can manually place

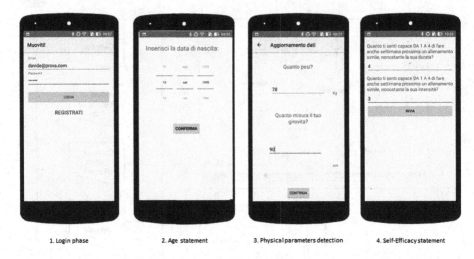

Fig. 4. The round table GUI.

the activities suggested by the system to fit better with other duties (e.g. therapies, examinations, analysis, and so on). The calendar provides the patient with
important information about the event (step 2. in the figure), like the weather
forecasting, the duration and intensity of the activity to do, with the possibility for the user to change the position of the activity in the agenda. Finally,
the system supports the user in collecting significant data when the activity is
accomplished (step 3. in the figure), in particular the *heart-beat rate* necessary to
calculate the MET amount, a visual warning about the correct execution of the
activity, and the shortcuts to statistics and graphs about the results obtained.

Finally, Fig. 6 illustrates how the patient performance has varied over the
time, to provide each member of the round table with an immediate feedback
about the results obtained day by day and week by week. In particular, MoveUp
currently allows to visualize the heart-beat rate graph of the last training session
(step 1. in the figure), the curves of weight (step 2. in the figure) and waistline
(step 3. in the figure) variations week by week, the burned calories graph, session by session (step 4. in the figure) and the percentage of *intense* activity with
respect to *moderate* activity (step 5. in the figure). All these information are
stored to be used for next recommendations (e.g. increase the MET amount for
the next week, decrease it or leave it unchanged) and crossed with psychological determinant stated in a qualitative way (e.g. the self-efficacy as introduced
above) and/or shared with other members of the round table for their actions
on the artifacts.

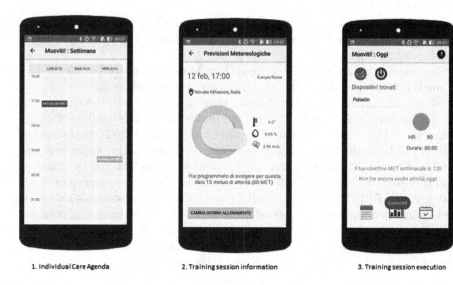

Fig. 5. The MET calculus GUI.

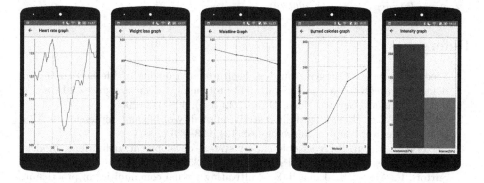

Fig. 6. The monitoring of physiological parameters in PERCIVAL

4   Conclusion

This paper has presented an innovative project in the Healthcare domain, namely PERCIVAL. The project aims to develop a framework to share information, knowledge and documents among all the subjects involved in the recent reform of Lombardy Healthcare System. The reform focused on the identification of Managers to support properly chronic patients affected by multiple disorders.

In particular, the PERCIVAL project is centered on people affected by diabetes, one of the most invasive diseases, causing many problems to the human body. The project is oriented to improve the QoL of patients and their caregivers, through the monitoring of physiological and psychological parameters, exploiting them to help users following prescriptions, therapies and suggestions for optimal life-styles.

The round table abstraction has been thought as a mean to allow all the professionals indicated by the reform to participate to a virtual community, sharing the main artifacts concerning the disorder treatment. Currently, the patient role is under investigation, with the design and implementation of modules for supporting its inclusion. In particular, this paper has presented the MoveUp module of PERCIVAL, devoted to suggest a personalized plan of training to prevent possible heart complications, that are very frequent in people affected by diabetes.

Future work will consider other aspects of the diabetes treatment cycle: in particular, the PERCIVAL project will focus on diet and pharmacological therapies to build up a complete, integrated framework to improve the QoL of patients. Then, the developed prototype will be extended to characteristics of other roles involved, in order to deliver a configurable environment for the sharing of knowledge and information among all the round table participants.

Aknowledgements. The PERCIVAL project is a collaboration between the REDS Laboratory of the University of Milano-Bicocca and Educational Factory srl. The project is partially funded by Lombardy Region in the frame of *Innodriver* programme (grant nr. *Innodriver-S3-2018-709672*).

References

1. Riedijk, S., et al.: Caregiver burden, health-related quality of life and coping in dementia caregivers: a comparison of frontotemporal dementia and Alzheimer's disease. Dement. Geriatr. Cogn. Disord. **22**(5–6), 405–412 (2006)
2. Gauthier, A., et al.: A longitudinal study on quality of life and depression in ALS patient-caregiver couples. Neurology **68**(12), 923–926 (2007)
3. Sartori, F., Melen, R.: Wearable expert system development: definitions, models and challenges for the future. Program **51**(3), 235–258 (2017)
4. Sartori, F., Melen, R., Pinardi, S.: Cultivating virtual communities of practice in KAFKA. Data Technol. Appl. **52**(1), 34–57 (2018)
5. Pinardi, S., Sartori, F., Melen, R.: Integrating knowledge artifacts and inertial measurement unit sensors for decision support. In: KMIS, pp. 307–313 (2016)
6. Sartori, F., Melen, R.: Time evolving expert systems design and implementation: the KAFKA approach. In: International Joint Conference on Knowledge Discovery, Knowledge Engineering and Knowledge Management-12/14 Novembre, vol. 2, pp. 84–95 (2015)
7. Kitamura, Y., Kashiwase, M., Fuse, M., Mizoguchi, R.: Deployment of an ontological framework of functional design knowledge. Adv. Eng. Inf. **18**(2), 115–127 (2004)
8. Surif, J., Ibrahim, N.H., Mokhtar, M.: Conceptual and procedural knowledge in problem solving. Procedia - Soc. Behav. Sci. **56**, 416–425 (2012)
9. Niedderer, K., Reilly, L.: Research practice in art and design: experiential knowledge and organised inquiry. J. Res. Pract. **6**(2), 2 (2010)
10. Association, A.D., et al.: Diagnosis and classification of diabetes mellitus. Diab. Care **37**(Suppl. 1), S81–S90 (2014)

11. Shigaki, C., et al.: Motivation and diabetes self-management. Chronic Illn. **6**(3), 202–214 (2010)
12. Ockleford, E., Shaw, R.L., Willars, J., Dixon-Woods, M.: Education and self-management for people newly diagnosed with type 2 diabetes: a qualitative study of patients' views. Chronic Illn. **4**(1), 28–37 (2008)
13. Adelman, R.D., Tmanova, L.L., Delgado, D., Dion, S., Lachs, M.S.: Caregiver burden: a clinical review. JAMA **311**(10), 1052–1060 (2014)
14. Baretta, D., et al.: Wearable devices and AI techniques integration to promote physical activity. In: Proceedings of the 18th International Conference on Human-Computer Interaction with Mobile Devices and Services Adjunct, pp. 1105–1108. ACM (2016)

Artfacts - A Platform for Making Sense of and Telling Stories with Cultural Objects

Leonardo de Araújo[✉]

Universität Bremen, Bibliothekstraße 1, 28359 Bremen, Germany
araujo@informatik.uni-bremen.de

Abstract. This paper presents the conceptualization, implementation, and evaluation of a Fast-speed IT Platform called *Artfacts*, which was designed within the context of the Two-speed IT Infrastructure, where a foundational, stable, and slow infrastructure is complemented by a creative, experimental, and agile additional infrastructure capable of promptly responding to the needs of communities. The platform is an attempt to digitally incorporate strategies for making sense and reusing digital collections and mitigate problems concerning specialized knowledge required for profiting from the affordances of data repositories as a creative material. In this sense, through the cartography of information, the platform aims at widening the participation of individuals with no technical background in the development and maintenance process of interpretive applications, no matter whether within cultural institutions or events such as hackathons for cultural heritage. Artfacts intermediates the reinterpretation of cultural datasets and the fabrication of interpretive applications by means of a flexible, general, and interoperable data model that is able to adapt to the demands of storytellers, and an open-ended Object-Oriented UI that enables analysis and experimentation by arranging and rearranging data elements into digital narratives.

Keywords: Digital storytelling · Data model · Digital collections · Heritage interpretation · Hackathons · Knowledge map · GLAMs

1 Introduction

There is an increasing awareness of the potentialities of digital collections serving as a powerful creative material for the production of engaging stories about heritage. In this sense, the number of memory institutions that try to find new meanings and applications to their data assets is increasing. One must only look at the participation of GLAMs in events such as hackathons for cultural heritage, where digital collections provide the foundation for the conceptualization and development of a range of interpretive applications. The creative potentialities of participatory initiatives are however constrained by traditional infrastructures that do not provide flexibility for algorithmically representing and interpreting

© Springer Nature Switzerland AG 2019
E. Garoufallou et al. (Eds.): MTSR 2018, CCIS 846, pp. 268–279, 2019.
https://doi.org/10.1007/978-3-030-14401-2_25

heritage. Although inflexible infrastructures do present benefits for institutions, since they enforce straightforward workflows and solid administrative practices, the open-endedness necessary to support creativity is lacking. Flexibility and inflexibility, open and closed-endedness, novelty and tradition however do not need to be dealt in binary terms, but they can instead co-exist. Oomen et al. [9] build on the ideas of Bossert et al. [2] to propose a *Two-speed IT architecture* that is adapted to the Cultural Sector. This Two-speed IT Approach consists of adopting two different digital strategies - slow and fast - in order to pre- serve the stability of core institutional practices, but at the same time innovate by adapting and responding faster to the needs of communities. Oomen et al. [9, p. 51] define Slow- and Fast-speed IT Strategies as:

- `Slow-speed IT Strategy`: *"standardized and off-the-shelf solutions that are used to secure 24/7 service. The solutions are updated following service-level agreements with suppliers. In the heritage domain, good examples are systems for managing storage, cataloguing, play-out and ordering. Given the impact, the frequency of updating applications in the 'slow' ecosystem is measured in months or years rather than weeks."*
- `Fast-speed IT Strategy`: *"tailor-made solutions that cater to very specific user requirements and are used to experiment with new technologies. Opposed to systems that are 'core' (for instance the storage systems), applications developed in the 'fast' speed do not have very stringent requirements regard- ing stability and minimum 'uptime'(i.e. they are in some cases maintained by developers themselves). For instance: experimental visualizations of datasets, automatic metadata extraction services and online magazines linked to cur- rent exhibits."*

In technical terms, Oomen et al. [9] include under the definition of a *Slow-speed IT Strategy* Information Systems (ISs) responsible for storage and cataloguing, which, in the case of cultural institutions, are responsibilities delegated to Col- lection Management Systems (CMSs). On the other hand, the *fast-speed digital strategy* enables experimentation through the development of tailor-made solu- tions that are built upon e.g. online data repositories and APIs (see [9, p. 50]). It is indeed possible to see examples of this Two-speed IT Architecture Approach in the cultural heritage sector by institutions that e.g. adopt the guidelines pro- posed by the OpenGLAM initiative[1] and take part in hackathons.

2 Conceptualization

2.1 Problems and Requirements

Belonging to a traditional Slow-speed IT Infrastructure, CMSs are designed for the administration of institutional workflows and core cultural assets, which are rendered as digital collections. CMSs focus on tasks, such as the digital description of artifacts, their indexation, their search and retrieval, among others

---

[1] https://openglam.org/.

(see [1,10]). As core administrative and organizational tools, CMSs restrict themselves to a pre- and well-defined set of description fields arranged in forms. Therefore, they enforce workflows and the fulfillment of pre-defined goals. In addition, because they are simple to use, individuals from curatorial, educational, and research departments do not need technical training in order to work with these systems. CMSs are however not suitable for the interpretation of heritage. Apart from being user-friendly, the requirements of ISs to satisfy the principles of Heritage Interpretation[2] (HI) must afford the full range of combinatorial possibilities necessary for telling stories with data objects. This combinatorial approach is incompatible with pre-defined outcomes. In this sense, ISs that aim at serving as a tool for HI need to go beyond over focusing on the administrative description of cultural objects, the enforcement of workflows[3], and the interoperability of the data model. As storytelling depends largely on the storyteller, no pre-defined data model is capable of predicting all elements of a story. The system must then present the storyteller with user-friendly data-driven tools that are able to express his or her personal perspectives. Enriching digital collections so that visibility to certain topics is enabled, is key for producing compelling interpretations. Thus, it is proposed that the means for affording HI is via the maximization of usability, speed, and flexibility in which cultural data can be reused, recontextualized, and enriched by storytellers. That can be achieved by:

- **General and Extensible Data Model**: general data models, such as Dublin Core, present both advantages and disadvantages. They are designed to be simple and generic, and therefore of easier usage and adoption. However, they lack granularity for a more detailed representation of objects. On the one hand, a data model that aims at storytelling should be generic in order to be user-friendly, so that individuals from curatorial and educational departments can adopt the system. On the other hand, it should also be easily expandable, so that it can be adapted to the needs of the storyteller.
- **Data-driven and Object-Oriented UI (OOUI)**: the data model described above must be accompanied by an interface that is able to provide storytellers with the necessary means for not only the arrangements of cultural objects, but also the extension of the data model. The main goal of such a data-driven and object-oriented approach is not to enforce workflows, but to afford a possibility space where narratives are generated from the open-ended combination of objects and their behaviors. Usability should also be a concern of the OOUI so that high accessibility can be provided.

---

[2] This term is vastly discussed within the cultural heritage sector and has as one of its basis the principles proposed by Freeman Tilden [3].

[3] Form-Based User Interfaces, predominately employed by CMSs, are used to model simple and well-defined use cases/workflows and enforce them by guiding and restricting the interactions of the user through limited input elements (see [11]).

2.2 Solution

The Artfacts Platform does not aim at replacing existing CMSs (see *Collection Management System* on Fig. 1), but instead at providing an extra semantic layer on top of the existing infrastructures for enabling institutions to create new or (re-)interpret, reuse, and deploy enriched data repositories (see *External Data Sources* on Fig. 1). The Artfacts Platform was conceptualized to fulfill the requirements necessary for expressing compelling stories that can be rendered as interpretive applications, named here as *Digital Interpretive Artifacts* (DIAs)[4].

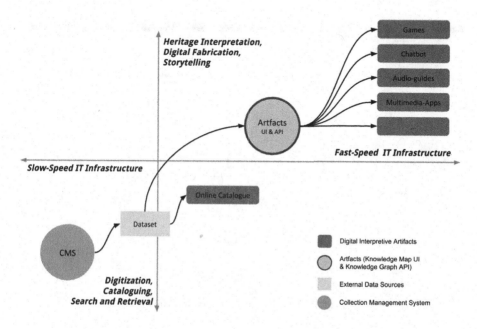

Fig. 1. Artfacts in the context of a Two-speed IT infrastructure

The platform can be characterized as a Fast-speed IT Infrastructure, not being therefore a *core* institutional system, but an add-on that offers a pragmatic approach to the way digital collections are reutilized. The main goal of the platform is to afford the production of digital storytelling through DIAs. Therefore, the Artfacts Platform is not a system to be used to look up information. The analysis and (re-)interpretation of digital collections is done through the cartography of information as object-oriented data structures called

---

[4] Commonly used in exhibitions, DIAs support audiences in interpreting collections. They can be e.g. audio-guides, chatbots, interactive multimedia exhibits, augmented reality apps, and so on (see Fig. 1).

Knowledge Maps (KMs - see Fig. 2). At the heart of the Artfacts Platform, KMs[5] are semantic-rich network diagrams based on the Schema.org's Vocabulary[6] and the Simple Knowledge Organization System (SKOS)[7]. KMs do not enforce workflows, but instead present the user with a possibility space, in which scenarios are composed by combining different objects among themselves. In this sense, creativity is enabled by the KMs' combinatorial capabilities. Besides serving as tools for the (re-)interpretation of digital collections, KMs can also be directly used as interfaces to organize and control the flow of system events and user actions of third-party applications.

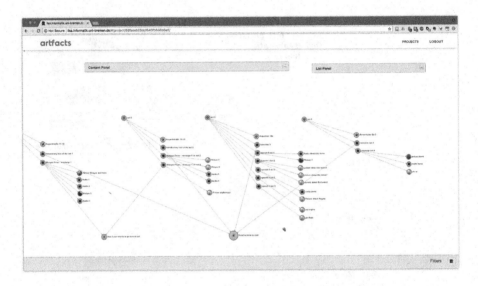

Fig. 2. Overview of the User Interface

Although highly malleable and open-ended, KMs require no special training for their manipulation [12]. In addition, the platform also presents accessible strategies for quickly converting unstructured narratives (statements) into structured representations through its Tagging System (see item Sect. 4).

---

[5] KMs are visual graph organizer that serve as a method for supporting the human cognitive handling of concepts. [4] defines KMs as *"a graphical display of information in which the importance and relationships between the various elements of knowledge are portrayed in the form of a map"* [4]. As Concept Maps, KMs obey a rhizomatic model where their links are directional and labeled. Most importantly, their unique characteristic is that they require a standardized vocabulary, and do not have predefined starting and ending nodes [5].

[6] https://schema.org/.

[7] https://www.w3.org/TR/skos-reference/.

3 Artfacts' Data Model

Artfacts' Data Model (ADM) was designed with the following considerations. Firstly, the ADM needed implement digital versions of KMs preserving their capacity of providing a framework for action-based understanding. Secondly, the ADM needed to be machine-readable and allow some degree of interoperability so that mapping between other Data Standards is possible. Thirdly, the ADM needed to be adaptable to the specificities of storytellers. And finally, the ADM should support production and management of DIAs. The model can be described as such:

- skos:Collection
  - E1 artfacts:CollectionNode: *A collection of collections representing a statement.*
    - E2 artfacts:MainCollectionNode: *A collection of collections representing the entities of a statement.*
    - E3 artfacts:EntityCollectionNode: *A collection of concepts representing the subject or object of a statement.*
- skos:Concept
  - E4 artfacts:Node: *The most generic entity type.*
    - E5 artfacts:Action: *Based on* schema:Action. *An action performed by an agent. The execution of the action may produce a result.*
    - E6 artfacts:Artifact: *Based on* schema:CreativeWork. *The most generic kind of creative work, including artworks, books, movies, photographs, software programs, etc.*
    - E7 artfacts:Concept: *Based on* schema:Intangible. *A utility class that serves as the umbrella for a number of 'intangible' things, such as an abstract idea or notion; a unit of thought.*
    - E8 artfacts:Event: *Based on* schema:Event. *An event happening at a certain time and location, such as a concert, lecture, or festival. Repeated events may be structured as separate Event objects.*
    - E9 artfacts:Institution: *Based on* schema:Organization. *An institution such as a museum, library, archive, school, NGO, etc.*
    - E10 artfacts:Location:*Based on* schema:Place. *Entities that have a somewhat fixed, physical extension.*
    - E11 artfacts:Person: *Based on schema:Person. A person (alive, dead, undead, or fictional).*
    - E12 artfacts:Quality: *Based on* schema:QualitativeValue. *A characteristic of an entity, e.g. large, medium, small-sized institution.*
    - E13 artfacts:Quantity: *Based on* schema:Quantity. *Quantities such as distance, time, mass, weight, etc.*
    - E14 artfacts:PropertyNode: *Assigns an additional property that offers structured values to an entity.*
      - E15 artfacts:RelationshipValue: *Assigns a string to an entity property.*
      - E16 artfacts:NodeClass: *The classification of an entity.*
      - E17 artfacts:ExtraValue: *Assigns a string to an entity property.*
      - E18 artfacts:Boolean: *Assigns a boolean value to an entity.*

· **E19** `artfacts:Unit`: *Assigns to an entity a structured value indicating the quantity, and unit of measurement.*

· **E20** `artfacts:URI`: *Assigns a Data type:URI to an entity.*

· **E21** `artfacts:GPS`: *Assigns geographic coordinates to an entity.*

· **E22** `artfacts:Date`: *Assigns to an entity a date value in ISO 8601.*

· **E23** `artfacts:Medium`: *Assigns to an entity a downloadable media object (image, video, audio).*

· **E24** `artfacts:Hook`: *Assigns to an entity an agent for controlling a device or application.*

· **E25** `artfacts:WebAddress`: *Assigns a data type:URL to an entity.*

4   The Tagging System

Artfacts provides the user with the option to construct KMs semi-automatically by tagging entities from statements using its *Core Tagging Vocabulary* (see Sect. 3 from E5 to E14). The conceptualization of this feature drew inspiration from *Qualitative Data Analysis Systems* (QDAS) that use Grounded Theory[8] as method for the analysis of collected media resources, such as text, audio, and video. As in Grounded Theory, these systems employ *coding* as a fundamental analytic process, and the *code* as its core unit. According to Johnny Saldaña, *"a code in qualitative inquiry is most often a word or short phrase that symbolically assigns a summative, salient, essence-capturing, and/or evocative attribute for a portion of language-based or visual data"* [8]. In QDAS, a portion of these *language-based or visual data* is defined as *indicators* [7].

The Coding System employed by QDAS is however different from the Tagging System employed by Artfacts. That is because, Artfacts' Tagging System is more granular and aims ideally at the extraction of triples from statements. In order to be successful, the tagging process must necessarily extract at least one entity that is assigned as subject (`artfacts:hasCollectionWithSubject (x, y)`) of the statement. In addition, a statement may also contain several objects (`artfacts:hasCollectionWithObject(x, y)`). The system converts all the entities into nodes. Finally, relationships are also established between the subject and object(s). Relationship labels can be also assigned by adding an extra property to them (`artfacts:RelationshipValue`).

For example, the KM shown on the Fig. 2 partially depicts how the guided tours for the chatbot *Marbles of Remembrance* (see item Sect. 5) was modeled. A tour was defined as having several parts (or *acts*), which were associated to a particular address in Berlin, Germany. Each *act* should start with an introduction, and be accompanied by messages associated to an avatar, in this case *Maayan Freier*, who would be the digital surrogate for interacting with the user.

---

[8] Grounded Theory is a research method that is used to develop a theory by detecting patterns in data. In other words, *"Grounded Theory is the generation of theories from data."* [6].

A part of this KM was extracted from the following statement: *"**Act 1** starts at **Auguststraße 11–13** and it contains **Introduction, MSG1 - Follow the Map, MSG2 - Present Mom's Picture, MSG3 - About 2. jüdische Volksschule**"*. On the figure above (see Fig. 3), it is possible to see the tagged statement on the component *Content Panel* of the Artfacts' User Interface.

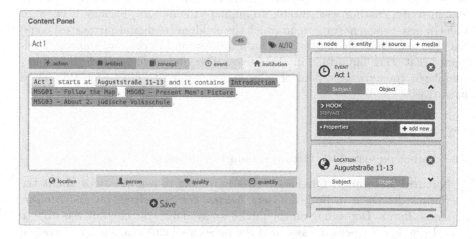

Fig. 3. Content Panel and the Tagging System

5 Evaluation

In addition to a usability test that was applied in order to evaluate Artfacts' vocabulary and the Tagging System[9] (see [12]), a case study was organized in order to gather insights on the limitations and effectiveness of the Artfacts Platform as a tool for telling stories with digital collections. The study was carried out during the 2017 edition of the hackathon Coding da Vinci (CdV), which offered a good setting for assessing the platform. The CdV is an event joint by several cultural institutions and participants from a variety of technical, artistic, and cultural backgrounds. Concerning the research goals, the case study focused on analyzing how well Artfacts was able to both support the manipulation of data objects by individuals with no technical background, and cope with the demands of an interdisciplinary team within a demanding and creative working environment. The platform needed to accommodate fast-changing requirements during intensive iterative development cycles, which are typical in a Fast-speed setting. As part of the study, the chatbot *Marbles of Remembrance* was conceptualized and implemented.

---

[9] The usability test was applied in the first version of the platform.

5.1 Concept

The team members worked with a subset (*Karten der Schuelerkartei*) comprised of almost 11 thousand registration cards of Jewish children that suffered persecution during the Nazi Regime. The dataset was provided by the International Tracing Service[10], which is an archive and bureau for documenting and tracing persecuted individuals and liberated survivors from German National Socialism. The idea of a chatbot was suitable to animate the dataset, because it engaged users in first-person narratives, in which the children (as digital surrogates) could tell their stories by taking the user on a tour around Berlin and showing landmarks that were important in their lives. The *Stolpersteine Berlin*[11] dataset completed the necessary pool of information needed to create location-based narratives.

5.2 Implementation

The chatbot presented the three main functionalities:

- **Natural Language Queries:** Users were able to ask questions about the victims described in both datasets *Karten der Schuelerkartei* and *Stolpersteine Berlin*. Depending on the metadata available, the chatbot was able to tell whether the person was one of the persecuted children, show registration cards, birth and death dates, and whether the person was able to survive and emigrate. Furthermore, since the records of both datasets were crossed, the chatbot could show the person's address on a map.
- **Guided Tours:** The chatbot provided guided-tours following the narratives of particular children. These stories are the most compelling part of the concept, because the user has the chance to get a deeper impression on how the Jewish children lived, how they saw the world, and visit the places that were part of their routine during the WWII. The guided-tours are location-based, meaning that the stories were connected to landmarks in the city.
- **Notifications:** Because the Charbot used the Telegram web services[12], the user was able to share its live location with the chatbot. Depending on the current GPS coordinates of the user, the chatbot app would notify him or her about *Stolpersteine* within a certain radius.

The chatbot[13] used Telegram (Server API and the Telegraf Client API[14]) for handling the communication with the user. The app identified the type of message and redirected it to the proper component. Natural language queries were sent to an external webservice called DialogFlow[15] so that entities and

---

[10] https://www.its-arolsen.org/.

[11] https://www.stolpersteine-berlin.de/.

[12] https://core.telegram.org/.

[13] The chatbot is available as open source on: https://github.com/leonardomra/berlinbot-codingdavinci.

[14] https://github.com/telegraf/telegraf.

[15] https://dialogflow.com/.

intents could be extracted from the text messages. The system compared then the intent received from DialogFlow with a dictionary of methods implemented in the chatbot app. If the chatbot component *Message Analyzer* identified the input from Telegram as a guided-tour request, the chatbot app would redirect the message to the component *Story Module*, which was in charge of accessing and translating KMs contained in Artfacts' projects into the guided-tour narratives.

In Artfacts, the KMs were used to model the stories that were told as location-based tours. The tours were composed by different types of nodes that were defined by adding extra metadata to the subject of the statements using the property `artfacts:Hook`. On the Fig. 3, it is possible to see the property `artfacts:Hook("StoryAct")` being assigned to the subject represented by the entity `"Act 1"`. A schema was then defined obeying the following structure:

- A node representing a tour of assigned property `artfacts:Hook("Story")` pointed to another node of type `artfacts:Person` with an assigned property `artfacts:Hook("Actor")` and that was connected to a data point in the dataset that represented one of the victims.
- The node representing the tour could point to one or many other nodes designated to represent the act(s) or parts of a tour. These nodes were assigned the property `artfacts:Hook("StoryAct")`.
- Each node of assigned property `artfacts:Hook("StoryAct")` was pointed to a node of assined property `artfacts:Hook("Location")` that contained, among others, GPS metadata defined by `artfacts:GPS`.
- Moreover, nodes of assigned property `artfacts:Hook("StoryAct")` could also point to one or many nodes of assigned property `artfacts:Hook` `("Narrative")` and `artfacts:Hook("Speech")`, which were responsible for storing information relative to the messages used for the conversation with the user.
- Nodes of assigned property `artfacts:Hook("Speech")` could also be connected to nodes of assigned type `artfacts:Hook("Medium")`, used to reference and deliver audio, video, and picture files during the conversations.
- Finally, nodes of assigned property `artfacts:Hook("Narrative")` and `artfacts:Hook("Speech")` could be connected to nodes of assigned property `artfacts:Hook("UserAction")`, which had as functions either pausing the story and waiting for the user to press a button, or watching for a confirmation that the user has reached a certain landmark.

5.3   Observations and Conclusions

The case study suggests that the Artfacts Platform is particularly beneficial for rapid prototyping. Its OOUI is of flexible adaptability and easy to understand and use. The team was composed by a programmer and three other members with either little or no experience in programming (content producers). While the programmer was in charge of coding the chatbot, the other team members were responsible for cleaning and refining the datasets, and producing extra content by researching about specific children who were to be the subjects of the guided-tours. Artfacts provided autonomy to non-programmers, since they could produce and concurrently improve the guided-tours with the Artfacts Platform (Fig. 4). They were able to immediately modify the tours on a no-code basis and on-site if they realized that e.g. a land-mark should be presented before, or a message was too long to be read while on a busy street. In addition, the Artfacts Platform contributed to the visibility of particular topics that otherwise would be invisible if content producers were not given the autonomy to research and digitally represent their findings as structured narratives. The dataset *Karten der Schülerkartei* represented only the information contained on the registration cards. Particular events on the lives of the children were therefore invisible, because they were not registered. By enriching the information contained in the dataset *Karten der Schülerkartei*, content producers were able to create stories that appealed emotionally to the audience. Based on these observations, the study suggests that Artfacts raised the overall quality and speed of the development process, and contributed to the visibility of important topics. These factors highly likely helped the project to be honored with a prize at the hackathon finals [13].

Fig. 4. CdV participants using the Artfacts Platform

It is also important to point out some limitations of the Artfacts Platform. The platform does not provide a solution that completely eliminates the need for programming. Although this is in fact not the objective of the platform, to provide greater leverage to non-programmers would be beneficial to widening the participation in regard to the way heritage is represented and digitally interpreted. Because of the flexible data model and OOUI, the platform is already able to adapt to different concepts and implementations of interpretive applications, and offer indeed some leverage to non-programmers. However, further development is necessary to augment these capabilities. Finally, KMs are proposed here as accessible scaffoldings to deal with information and institutional work. However, a long term study is required to verify how KMs would suit personal working styles as part of the institutional work carried out within GLAMs by e.g. curators, researchers, and educators.

References

1. Stiller, J.: From curation to collaboration, April 2014. https://doi.org/10.18452/16944, https://edoc.hu-berlin.de/handle/18452/17596. Accessed 26 Feb 2018
2. Bossert, O., Harrysson, M., Roberts, R.: Organizing for digital acceleration: making a two-speed IT operating model work - McKinsey & Company. https://www.mckinsey.com/industries/high-tech/our-insights/organizing-for-digital-acceleration-making-a-two-speed-it-operating-model-work. Accessed 24 Apr 2018
3. Tilden, F.: Interpreting Our Heritage, 3d edn. Chapel Hill Books. University of North Carolina Press, Chapel Hill (1977). ISBN 978-0-8078-4016-0
4. Hanewald, R., Ifenthaler, D.: Digital knowledge mapping in educational contexts. In: Ifenthaler, D., Hanewald, R. (eds.) Digital Knowledge Maps in Education, pp. 3–15. Springer, New York (2014). https://doi.org/10.1007/978-1-4614-3178-7_1
5. O'donnell, A., Dansereau, D., Hall, R.: Knowledge maps as scaffolds for cognitive processing. Educ. Psychol. Rev. **14**(1), 71–86 (2002)
6. Walsh, I., Holton, J.A., Bailyn, L., Fernandez, W., Levina, N., Glaser, B.: What grounded theory is... a critically reflective conversation among scholars. Organ. Res. Methods **18**(4), 581–599 (2015)
7. Holton, J.: The coding process and its challenges. Grounded Theory Rev. **9**(1), 21–40 (2010)
8. Saldana, J.: The Coding Manual for Qualitative Researchers, 3rd edn. SAGE, Los Angeles, London (2016)
9. Oomen, J., Brinkerink, M., Huurnink, B., Schuurman, J.: Changing gears: fast-lane design for accelerated innovation in memory organisations. In: Sustainable Audiovisual Collections Through Collaboration: Proceedings (2017)
10. Carpinone, E.: Museum collections management systems: one size does not fit all. Seton Hall University Dissertations and theses (ETDs), May 2010
11. Wroblewski, L.: Web Form Design: Filling in the Blanks. Rosenfeld Media, Brooklyn (2008)
12. de Araújo, L., Ramos, D.C.: Automatic tagging as a support strategy for creating knowledge maps. J. Syst. Cybern. Inf. **15**(3), 32–40 (2017)
13. Ergebnisse Coding da Vinci Preisverleihung. https://codingdavinci.de/news/2017/12/03/ergebnisse.html. Accessed 9 July 2018

A Semantic-Based Metadata Schema to Handle System and Software Configuration

Ricardo Eito-Brun[(✉)]

Universidad Carlos III de Madrid, c/Madrid, Getafe (Madrid), Spain
reito@bib.uc3m.es

Abstract. Configuration management is a key process in the system and software engineering. Product integrity is a key requirement in the development of software-based solutions, and Configuration Management defines the set of practices aimed to ensure the consistency and coherence of the product during its full life cycle. Although there are different standards that establish the principles of Configuration Management, in complex projects that require the interaction of several entities and companies, a more precise, detailed specification about how to report, compare and handle configuration data is needed. This constitutes an interesting opportunity for metadata management professionals.

This contribution presents the development of a tool for managing configuration management data. The case study - developed in the context of a system engineering company – makes use of semantic web languages (RDF, OWL) and technologies to support engineers in the registration, analysis, reporting and auditing of products' configuration. The solution defines different metadata used to handle configuration status, and a technical solution to handle them.

Keywords: Configuration management · RDF · Ontologies ·
Information management

1 Introduction

System and software process reference models and methodologies include Configuration management (CM) as part of the support processes that companies must put in place as part of a complex system engineering program. According to the ISO/IEC 12207:2008 standard, the aim of Configuration management is "to establish and maintain the integrity of all identified outputs of a project or process and make them available to concerned parties" [1].

Literature and standards offer additional definitions of this process. The Systems Engineering Handbook developed by INCOSE refers to "the discipline of identifying and formalizing the functional and physical characteristics of a configuration item at discrete points in the product evolution for the purpose of maintaining the integrity of the product system and controlling changes to the baseline." [2]. Sector specific

© Springer Nature Switzerland AG 2019
E. Garoufallou et al. (Eds.): MTSR 2018, CCIS 846, pp. 280–287, 2019.
https://doi.org/10.1007/978-3-030-14401-2_26

standards like Automotive SPICE [3] maintain the purpose of the process as defined in ISO/IEC 12207 and defines the process outcomes or results of the process:

- "a configuration management strategy is developed;
- all configuration items generated by a process or project are identified, defined and baselined according to the configuration management strategy;
- modifications and releases of the configuration items are controlled;
- modifications and releases are made available to affected parties;
- the status of the configuration items and modifications is recorded and reported;
- the completeness and consistency of the baselines is ensured; and
- storage of the configuration items is controlled."

CM process involves different activities, starting with the identification and naming of the items that will be part of the system/software products, the formal tracking and control of changes made in the product during its development and evolution, the reporting the configuration status, and the audits on the product configuration.

As part of the planning of the process, companies must start with the identification of the different configuration items (CIs) that shall be part of the final product, with a clear definition of the guidelines used to name them and to handle their evolution during the project.

Formal change management is also part of configuration management, although in some reference process models like Automotive SPICE maintain a specific process for Change request management, which is clearly linked to Configuration management practices.

Finally, the concept of audits in configuration management implies the objective, independent verification of the final product configuration, checking that it is composed by the different components that were agreed and reported in the design baseline.

All these activities require, and are based on, the accurate recording of metadata about:

- the envisioned structure of the final product (called the as-design baseline),
- the characteristics of the items and components that will be purchased, developed and later integrated in the final product, and
- the final configuration of the product (called the as-built baseline).

Metadata plays a key role in the reconciliation of the as-design and as-built baselines, which is one of the objectives of the product configuration audits. This reconciliation shall compare the structure and components of the planned vs the final product, and identify any difference. These differences must be analysed and properly justified.

The configuration management process must handle a complex network of related data. It is in fact a process that is tightly coupled with logistic and procurement activities, as configuration management consumes and reuse the data generated by the design and acquisition process. Configuration management also interfaces with other engineering and support processes, like support and operations activities: once the product has been built and released, operators and staff in charge of maintenance activities must still maintain the product configuration data, and record any imple-mented change. Configuration management data must also be linked to operation manuals and user guides that explain operators how to handle component replacements and how to respond to obsolescence issues.

As a conclusion, it can be stated that the management of configuration data is a continuous, regular activity that starts with the first steps of the product design and lasts during the whole product life cycle. Metadata accuracy is a critical requirement to ensure the integrity of the product and avoid errors during the different phases.

2 Configuration Management Life Cycle

Configuration Management activities start at the beginning of the engineering process, with the identification of the components – software and hardware – that will be part of the final product.

Different standards use different terms to refer to the documents and work products where configuration management data is recorded. In this study, we use as a reference the ECSS standard ECSS-M-ST-40C (2009) [4], which defines different work products related to configuration management. Typical products aimed to keep the information and data recorded in the initial steps of the design activities are the product tree and the list of configuration items. Both documents have a different purpose: the product tree is a direct output of the engineering design process; the list of configuration items – traced to the items identified in the product tree - provides the enumeration and listing of all the planned configuration items. These documents require the maintenance of the data concerning the relationships between the different configuration items, being typical relationships the meronymy (is part of) and dependencies (e.g., technical compatibility between different versions of software or hardware components).

The relationship between the design activities and the configuration management process must also be reflected and recorded in subsequent documents. The cited standard defines a separate document – the Configuration Item Data List or CIDL, aimed to keep the relationship between the configuration items and the documents that specify its design. CIDL is an interesting work product from a metadata management perspective, as it requires the establishment of links between software and/or hardware components and documents. Once this relation is established, any evolution of the design documentation must be tracked and checked to ensure that it is propagated to the specifications that shall guide the manufacturing and production of the related configuration item.

Once the design is baselined, manufacturing and component integration activities can start. As a result, the acquired or manufactured components shall be integrated until the final product is built. A separate document is defined in the referred standard to reflect the as-built configuration of the final product: the As-Built Configuration List or ABCL. ABCL data are traced to the CIDL, as the as-built configuration should be fully compatible with the as-designed, with minor or no differences at all. Of course, in the development of a large, complex project, this consistency or equivalence is hard to guarantee, as different issues may happen during the process, e.g., the need of replacing one planned component or version by a new one or by a suitable alternative due to manufacturing constraints or failure of suppliers to provide it on time.

Regardless the causes of these potential issues, deviations between the as-designed and the as-built configuration may happen, and they must be identified and formally justified by means of a new document, the request for waiver, which must be submitted to the customers' approval.

As stated in the introductory section, configuration data life cycle extends beyond the final release of the product (whose configuration is reported in the ABCL document). During operations, the changes in the product shall be recorded, and the compatibility between the replacements of components must be ensured to keep the system integrity. Typically, the evolution of the product configuration after its release, and once its operational usage starts, are kept in a separate document: the logbook, where the interventions and replacements completed by operators are recorded.

3 Configuration Management Metadata

The standard used as a reference in this work, ECSS-M-ST-40C, establishes a set of documents used to report the status of the product configuration at different stages. To the documents mentioned in the previous section we should add additional reports like the software configuration file and the configuration status accounting report. The first one, which applies to software products, contains the list of source code and configuration files that are needed to build a software product; the second one has the purpose of listing all the documents related to the product and its development, making a distinction between the applicable and obsolete versions.

The standard just defines the purpose of the document and provides a Document Requirements Definition (DRD) with the table of contents and sections each document must contain. The main limitation of this standard is that it does provide neither a detailed description of the data that must be provided for each configuration item, nor the relationships that could be established between them.

As an example, the description of the ABCL DRD is summarized below:

D.1.2 Purpose and objective

The objective of the as built configuration list (ABCL) is to provide a reporting instrument defining the as built status per each serial number of configuration item subject to formal acceptance.

D.2 Expected response

D.2.1 Scope and content

<1> Introduction

a. The introduction shall describe the purpose and objective of the as built configuration list.

<2> Applicable and reference documents

a. The as built configuration list shall list the applicable and reference documents in support to the generation of the document.

<3> List

a. The as-built configuration list shall list all discrepancies between the as-designed configuration documented in the configuration item data list and the as-built configuration documented by nonconformance reports or waivers.

b. The ABCL configuration item breakdown section, obtained from the equivalent configuration item data list section, shall be completed by adding the following information:

1. *serial number identification;*
2. *lot or batch number identification;*
3. *reference(s) of applicable nonconformance report(s) or request for waiver(s)."*

From the joint analysis of these DRDs it is feasible to identify the different data that are needed to support an effective configuration management process and report the configuration status at the different stages of the product ensuring the compliance with these standards.

The availability of a shared metadata schema with the capability of accommodating the different data needed by the Configuration management – as well as related process like logistics management or procurement, helps ensure the compatibility between the tools used by different companies and constitutes the basis for the creation of an automated document exchange process between all the involved parties.

With this purpose, a metadata schema was developed with the help of semantic languages (RDF/OWL) with the help of the TopBraid Composer tool. The selection of the Semantic Web standards is considered a relevant step to ensure data exchange capabilities, data aggregation for configuration data of complex products, and to support the implementation of automated checks and verification tasks (e.g., the reconciliation of the as-designed and as-built configurations). Other verification tasks typically conducted during configuration audits, which could benefit from a semantic organization of the data include:

- Avoiding errors like duplicated references to the same configuration items at different parts of the assembled product(s).
- Identification of errors in product references (part numbers or serial numbers) between the product tree, as-designed or as-built configuration reports.
- Identification of differences between the as-built and the as-designed configuration.
- Ensuring that any difference between the as-built and the as-designed configuration is related to a formal deviation or request for waiver.
- Identify formal deviations or waivers that are not traced to a problem identified during the configuration audit.
- Identify configuration items with missing design documentation or specifications. Identify products with references to obsolete components.

The identification of the entities and data to be handle by the proposed schema was made through the analysis of the DRD provided in the reference standard, and the analysis of a set of configuration management reports, logistic data and operation manuals. Interviews with staff involved in configuration management activities were also conducted to obtain their feedback and additional data. The expected content of the DRD acts as the typical competence questions that are described as the starting point for building ontologies in different methodologies [5, 6].

The schema identifies the following classes:

- Configuration Item, as a general concept that can be assembled in an upper level configuration item. Configuration items are characterized by different properties, and a distinction can be made between software and hardware configuration items, and between procured and developed configuration items. This distinction is made as part of the class hierarchy. Configuration items are also divided into:
  - Component, which refers to a configuration items used as part of the as-design configuration. They are specific product that can be chosen as a design option.
  - Recurrent unit, as a specific manufactured unit of one component. These are the types of configuration items used as part of the as-built configuration.
- Final product, as an item that is the result of assembling different, lower-level configuration items, and that is not assembled in an upper-level product.
- Documents, a general concept that refers to the documents that specify the technical characteristics of the configuration items, and provide guidelines and recommendations on their use and operation.
- Configuration reports, to refer to the different reports used to report the configuration data. This class is relevant as – to ensure the homogeneous reporting of configuration data, a separate entity is needed with clear links (i.e. properties) between the report and the configuration (for the final product or for an intermediate version of a configuration item) that is being reported.

The metadata schema becomes more complex when dealing with the properties. Ontology development makes a distinction between data and object properties. Data properties identified during the analysis of the DRD and configuration reports were used to record data about different aspects of the configuration items: identifiers and description, part and serial numbers for hardware items, manufacturer type code, acquisition and replacement values, date of entry into the inventory, date of purchase or production, estimated cost of dismantling the asset, status (in progress, accepted by the Contracting Authority, rejected, …), life duration in months, custodian, contract number, related WBS Code, current and planned physical location, method of disposal clearances with regard to international security regulations, etc. Data properties are also used to make a distinction between components and their recurrent units: besides the typical distinction made with the serial number and the part numbers (part numbers assigned to the component and the serial number to each recurrent unit), although the schema makes a distinction at the class level between component and recurrent unit.

In the case of procured software configuration items, other properties like version number, types of licenses, licence expiry dates, physical file names and location in repositories, etc., were identified. Domain and range restrictions were used to establish the relationships between properties and classes when necessary.

Additional properties were defined to record the different types of relationships that can be established between the configuration items as they are assembled in a higher-level configuration item or in the final product. These relationships include:

- Meronymy (is part of and the opposite one, composed by). This is the basic relation that reflects the assembly and aggregation of one or several units of a configuration item.

- Dependency. This relation is used to reflect a dependency between a specific component (or component and version) of a configuration item with other configuration item it must interface or interact.
- Equivalence. This relation is used to identify items that can be used as alternatives to another configuration item.
- Compatibility. This relation – to be recorded and identified as part of the as-design configuration – registers the compatibility between configuration items and versions of the configuration items.
- Deployment. To indicate the relationship between software and hardware configuration items, and indicate in which hardware is running a specific software program.

The last three relations and their related properties shall be used in the definition of the as-designed configuration. The as-built configuration shall not include any of these properties, although they are quite relevant to support checks and to identify potential errors when updating components of the as-built configuration (e.g., trying to replace an existing item with another one that is not compatible with the existing configuration).

4   Conclusions

The developed schema has been validated against the configuration management data collected in two real projects, and it has shown its capability to record and accommodate the configuration management data requested in the standard used as a reference. The project's existing documents (CIDL, ABCL, inventory list, etc.) were processed to generate a set of triples that were later loaded into the semantic repository. The incorporation of these data led to some minor adjustment in the proposed schema of properties and classes. The possibility of generating the different documents – aligned with the DRD – was also validated by means of a different SPARQL queries built on top of a semantic repository based on Ontotext GraphDB.

One of the potential constraints that was identified during the initial steps of the project was the maintainability of the configuration management data. Regarding this point, it can be stated that there are no constraints due to the flexibility of the proposed data model and the fact that data can be added at the different steps just by adding new triples to the data set that represents the product configuration. The evolution of the configuration data sometimes require the addition of validity periods, for example, to record that one component has been replaced by another one within an assembly, and that the replaced component was in operation during a specific time period. In these cases, different classes are needed and were incorporated to the ontology schema, like Intervention and InOperationPeriod, both having an start and ending time tags.

As a summary, it can be concluded that:

- Semantic data modelling standards offers more flexibility both for data maintenance and for data querying, compared with the more restricted models that are characteristic of relational databases.

- SPARQL language and end-points offer a kind of universal API (Application Programming Interface) that can be used as a general-purpose access method to any configuration data, avoiding the need of working with predefined, custom-developed APIs to support queries and the exchange of information between parties.
- The model works as an intermediate schema to which other existing, proprietary based applications and data models can be mapped to ensure the exchange of data between heterogeneous applications.

References

1. ISO/IEC 12207:2008. System and Software Engineering - Software Life Cycle Processes, 2nd edn. (2008)
2. INCOSE. Systems Engineering Handbook: A Guide for System Life Cycle Processes and Activities, 4th edn. 304 p. (2015). ISBN 978-1-118-99940-0
3. VDA QMS. Automotive SPICE Process Assessment/Reference Model, v3.1 (2017)
4. ESA. ECSS-M-ST-40C Rev. 1. Space Project Management. Configuration and Information Management. ESA-ESTEC. ECSS Secretariat (2009)
5. Park, J., Sung, K., Moon, S.: Developing Graduation Screen Ontology Based on the METHONTOLOGY Approach. In: Networked Computing and Advanced Information Management NCM 2008. Fourth International (2008)
6. Corcho, O., Fernández-López, M., Gómez-Pérez, A., López-Cima, A.: Building legal ontologies with METHONTOLOGY and WebODE. In: Benjamins, V.R., Casanovas, P., Breuker, J., Gangemi, A. (eds.) Law and the Semantic Web. LNCS (LNAI), vol. 3369, pp. 142–157. Springer, Heidelberg (2005). https://doi.org/10.1007/978-3-540-32253-5_9

Digital Humanities and Digital Curation (DHC)

Connecting and Mapping LOD and CMDI Through Knowledge Organization

Francesca Fallucchi[1,2(✉)] and Ernesto William De Luca[1,2]

[1] DIII, Guglielmo Marconi University, Rome, Italy
{f.fallucchi,ew.deluca}@unimarconi.it
[2] DIFI, Georg Eckert Institute, Braunschweig, Germany
{fallucchi,deluca}@gei.de

Abstract. This paper explains the connection and mapping of knowledge representations between RDF and CMDI. Therefore, the challenge is to create a bridge between Linked Open Data (LOD) and the Component MetaData Infrastructure (CMDI) to ensure that the limits of the two paradigms are compensated and strengthened to create a new hybrid approach. While on the one hand, CMDI is easier to use for modelling purposes, the Metadata is not descriptive enough for a document to be easily discoverable using Linked Data (LD) technologies to publish and to enrich the document's content. Yet on the other hand, the explicit semantics and high interoperability of LOD have many advantages, but its modelling process is too complex for non-expert users. Here we show how knowledge organization plays a crucial role in this issue.

Keywords: Component MetaData Infrastructure (CMDI) ·
Linked Open Data (LOD) · Metadata for language resources ·
Digital humanities · Knowledge Organization (KO)

1 Introduction

Knowledge Organization (KO) is a branch of Library and Information Science (LIS) that includes activities such as classification, indexing and creating document descriptions, performed mostly by librarians, archivists, and information specialists as well as by computer algorithms. This field of study deals with the nature and quality of knowledge organising processes (such as taxonomies and ontologies) as well as the knowledge organising systems used to organise documents, document representations and concepts [1, 2].

The relevance of this research area has changed considerably with the emergence of the digital era and the World Wide Web. Due to the increasing amount of available data, adequate structuring systems are needed to help researchers find relevant information. In addition, standardised and faceted access to knowledge is required for the provision of a data model capable of dealing with large amounts of data from various domains in the digital world. Such a standardised and faceted way of accessing knowledge has been analysed and is increasingly being used in the design of webpages [3] and for personalised information through the use of User Profiles [4].

In this paper, we discuss the current state of KO-based research and systems, focusing especially on library systems and acknowledging the new challenges emerging within the

© Springer Nature Switzerland AG 2019
E. Garoufallou et al. (Eds.): MTSR 2018, CCIS 846, pp. 291–301, 2019.
https://doi.org/10.1007/978-3-030-14401-2_27

different LIS disciplines. In particular, we analyse two paradigms (LOD and CMDI) which are normally used independently, then connect them to ascertain the respective advantages of such a system and attempt to solve any subsequent weaknesses.

We then analyse the current state of classification: from conventional classification schemes (see Sect. 2) used for organising knowledge to new developments in library classification that provide for modern knowledge representation and consider semantic information. This information can be extracted and linked, such as in the LOD structures (see Sect. 2.1) and linguistically, such as in WordNet domains and similar structures (see Sect. 2.2).

In Sect. 3, we describe the standard for making linguistic resources accessible to researchers through metadata description. We analyse the structural standards for metadata from a bibliographic point of view, using metadata standards such as MARC (see Sect. 3.1), and the new developments in metadata infrastructures from an infrastructure point of view, such as CMDI (See Sect. 3.2).

In Sect. 4, we analyse the similarities and differences between the modern representation of knowledge and the new developments in metadata infrastructures.

The paper then describes a new hybrid approach to create a bridge between LOD and CMDI (see Sect. 5), we conclude by describing a selection of emerging strategies (see Sect. 6).

2   Classification Schemes

Classification schemes are defined as a list of classes arranged according to a set of predefined principles for the purpose of organising items in a collection or entries in an index, bibliography or catalogue into groups based on their similarities and differences in order to facilitate access and retrieval.

Library classification schemes are tools that allow us to allocate a class mark, an artificial notation comprising alphanumeric characters and punctuation marks, to every item based on its subject content so that library staff can preserve all the related items together on the library's shelves. Since the nineteenth century many library classification schemes have been developed [5].

The most important international classifications schemes are the classification used by the Library of Congress (LCC) [6], the Dewey Decimal Classification (DDC) [7], the Universal Decimal Classification (UDC) [8] and the Information Coding Classification (ICC) [9]. Nowadays, in order to organise digital content in a standardised classified structure, we need to remain close to the ideas of Melvil Dewey and his decimal system, which is indeed the simplest and most adequate approach for this purpose; for humans as well as for computers.

A variety of other classification schemes have also been generated in public and university libraries. Taking all of the conventional classification schemes into consideration, we can say that these are inadequate because of their intrinsic structures and characteristics and the fact that they are most often bound to their respective domains. A further problem with conventional classification systems is their construction, which is oriented according to each discipline. This implies finite extendability and eventually obsolescence.

We believe that we need to examine more accurately the possibility of implementing a more general data structuring approach in order to gain more flexibility with regard to semantic information.

2.1 Classification Schemes and Linked Open Data

In a recent survey, current library systems were analysed for their implementation of and experimentation with LOD and a roadmap showed a possible modernisation solution using these new technologies [10].

This survey aims to outline the variety of stages of adoption and readiness regarding the implementation of and experimentation with LOD.

Different other work has been done in publishing the DDC, the Virtual International Authorities File (VIAF) [11] and the Faceted Application of Subject Terminology (FAST) [12] as LD by the Online Computer Library Center (OCLC).

2.2 WordNet and Linked Open Data

WordNet [13] is one of the largest and most important lexical databases in English. There has been much research on ontology-lexicon interfaces and the question of how semantic web ontologies and lexical databases such as WordNet relate to each other [14] and could be integrated [15–17]. Several versions of the Princeton WordNet (PWN) [18] have become an integral part of the LLOD cloud [19].

In contrast to most similar projects, they have been focusing on providing the means for universal identifiers for words, in common with the Global WordNet Grid initiative [20]. This would facilitate linking to other relevant lexical resources. In this context, a list of guidelines for creating LD versions of WordNet has been published [21]. These guidelines advise on the selection of appropriate vocabularies (such as lemon and RDF/SKOS), on the RDF generation process, and on URIs published in RDF during the last decade.

For example, Van Assem et al. [22] have created an version of an RDFS/OWL representation of PWN, while Graves and Gutierrez [23] have also discussed and presented a PWN-RDF version. De Luca et al. [24] converted the EuroWordNet representation into RDF/OWL format and extended it using lexical resources [25]. The LLOD cloud has also been advocated by [24, 26].

3 Metadata Standards

Descriptive metadata characterises a resource with keyword-value pairs. It has become increasingly important to manage and find electronic resources in a time where the sheer amount of resources and the complexity of the relations between them are expanding rapidly and unpredictably.

The use of such descriptions allows researchers clearer and easier access to available resources. In this ways, users can manage and find research data beyond traditional publications.

Metadata has always been a key issue for libraries and archives and thus has a long and complex history [27]. Metadata for language resources and tools exists in a multitude of formats. Often these descriptions contain specialised information for a specific research community [28]; knowledge organization systems are used in almost activity such as cultural heritage [29–33], the public administration domain [34–36], humanitarian assistance and disaster relief [37–39], while health [40–42] and Industry 4.0 [43, 44] present many new challenges.

The systematic description of books, sound and video recordings, and other artefacts, has a long tradition in the field of LIS [45]. Such descriptions were traditionally used in library catalogues until the 1980 s, when libraries converted their catalogue data to digital databases.

For correct cataloguing of such resources, information about their creators, titles, formats, dimensions, subject terms etc. are aggregated in bibliographic records. In addition, the use of metadata schemas for the digital storage of information became important in the 2000 s, where the existing metadata were then used to describe digital data using metadata standards.

A number of dominant metadata standards exist to record resource information, such as MARC, Dublin Core (DC), MODS, etc. [46, 47]. Metadata management remains a crucial aspect in the life cycle of language resources, especially, if we analyse the schemas, structural standards for metadata within the fields or elements where the data resides and new developments in metadata infrastructures, such as CMDI provided by CLARIN.

3.1   Bibliographic Metadata Standards

Structural standards define the fields and the information types to be recorded. The first step for a good metadata structure is to start with a high level of granularity. It is almost always easier to migrate data from a highly granular structure to a more simple structure than to parse single elements into multiple elements.

The structural standards often determine the syntactical standards. Sharing information about resources between institutions that adopt different metadata standards requires a crosswalk.

A crosswalk attempts to map the elements in one metadata format or schema to the semantically equivalent elements in another schema. In the Library Sciences, there are a number of established metadata crosswalks, for instance, from DC to MARC 21 [48] and from MARC 21 to DC [49]. Mapping one metadata standard to another is not an easy task [50–52]. Frequently no one-to-one mapping exists from a given data descriptor of the source metadata format to another descriptor in the target format. Either no such mapping can be found, or many-to-one or one-to-many mappings need to be constructed.

A team working for CLARIN analysed available metadata sets and concluded that they are insufficient to cover the whole domain of LR because the sets have either too much or too little specificity but also because the terminology used in the different metadata sets does not always fit with the terminology of a specific sub-domain or community. The variety of subdomains in linguistic research has helped to demonstrate that a single metadata schema cannot succeed in conquering all sub-fields in linguistics.

The differences in needs, terminology and traditions will prevent uptake and acceptance of such a schema. Therefore the CLARIN team decided to create a metadata infrastructure based on components that would be flexible enough to allow users to create their own metadata sets by aggregating different metadata components.

3.2 Metadata Infrastructures

CMDI incorporates a flexible method for creating metadata descriptions and maintaining semantic interoperability [53]. CMDI benefits from the consolidate structure of the model and the schema. The last version of CMDI also offers a new means of lifecycle management, introduced to avoid the proliferation of components, a new mechanism for external vocabularies that will contribute to more consistent use of controlled values and cues for tools that will allow improved presentation of the metadata records to the end users.

Making linguistic resources accessible via standard library catalogues is significant, because their CMDI-based metadata records cannot simply be ingested into existing library catalogues. In the library world, only a few established metadata standards are used within library catalogues and CMDI is practically unknown. For librarians, CMDI is not an acceptable format, as it does not fit their cataloguing infrastructure.

To better connect to the library world, and to allow librarians to enter metadata for linguistic resources into their catalogues, we need to convert CMDI-based metadata to a bibliographic metadata standard. For this reason, a crosswalk is required, which allows mapping between these two standard processes, starting with the mapping of the relationships and equivalences between the different metadata fields. It is therefore necessary to convert rich and discipline-specific metadata such as CMDI-based formats to library-specific formats such as MARC.

The general and rather fluid nature of CMDI, however, makes it hard to map arbitrary CMDI schemas to metadata standards such as DC or MARC, which have a mature, well-defined and fixed set of field descriptors. There is no universal crosswalk available that enables map from CMDI to bibliographic standards and back. In the CLARIN context, there are a number of crosswalks in use. Zhang et al. [54] describe the use of CMDI at the Meertens institute to convert metadata from various formats into CMDI.

A general mapping of CMDI-based metadata to bibliographic standards such as DC and MARC 21 is presented in NaLiDa [45]. They attempted to minimise the information loss when mapping to DC and MARC 21. An environment is described in [55], which converts existing resources from the TEI- to the CMDI-format to make resources available for harvesters included in the CLARIN metadata aggregators, such as the CLARIN VLO.

A plethora of resource inventories and catalogues has been proposed to address this need. However, almost all of them are based on a single metadata scheme, forcing the resource providers to trade accuracy in favour of compatibility. CLARIN established the possibility for institutions to become CLARIN centres if they offer the CMDI records they create for harvesting via the Open Archives Initiative's Protocol for Metadata Harvesting (OAI-PMH) [56].

4   Bridge Between Metadata and LOD

The wider Linked Open Data ecosystem and the Semantic Web in general are built on the bedrock of shared, unique identifiers. Libraries have a long history of shared data governance and standards, and as such, library culture is well suited to transitioning to LD. Some institutions have already carried out research and worked on approaches for the extraction and publication of library digital collections as LD.

Lampert et al., in [57] and [58], demonstrate that the transformation of digital collection's metadata into LD is feasible and a very promising investment that can increase the discoverability of materials in current systems that provide limited metadata schema choices and where it is not possible to create explicit connections between related contents from different digital collections. For instance, tools such as Open-Refine [56] help guide digital collection managers through the processes of data transforming, reconciliation, and LD generation.

Other tools help knowledge visualisation in many ways, for example semi-automatically creating GUIs, as SAGG does [59], or creating dashboards which are realised through the business intelligence tools integrated in DAF [60], as described in [36]. An open access repository is extracted and published as LD by directly mapping metadata from the database schema into RDF format. OAI2LOD [61] is a tool based on the D2RQ [62] architecture and the OAI-PMH protocol and is used for republishing the University of Vienna DSpace repository according to the LD 5 stars deployment scheme [63].

Results like those in [57, 58, 61, 64, 65] show that, in the digital repositories, the LOD paradigm facilitates: *integration*, typically materialised using OAI-PMH harvesting interfaces, *expressiveness* in describing the information, and *query answering*.

4.1   MARC to LOD

In describing the information, LOD differs from MARC. A key differentiator is that MARC is based on records whereas LOD is based on graphs. Unlike knowledge graphs, which are theoretically infinite, records have a fixed number of fields and subfields.

Graph-based knowledge systems simultaneously strengthen the ability to describe objects using reputable controlled vocabularies while at the same time providing an extendibility that allows users to add new knowledge nodes (fields) to their descriptive graphs. MARiMbA is a tool for automating the transformation and linkage of the library dataset to RDF [66] and which also allows domain experts to map library metadata into highly specialised IFLA [67] library models using spreadsheets.

4.2   CMDI and LOD

In the CMD2RDF project, CLARIN-NL supported the implementation of mapping from Component Metadata (CMD) to RDF [68]. For this the XML-based records have to be transformed into RDF without any loss of information. This is difficult to achieve because usually, such as in [21], the set already mapped to DC by the OAI-PMH provider is converted to RDF but a subset of the information is lost.

The flexibility of CMDI also means that in such a generic transformation a fixed metadata RDF schema, like the Data Catalog Vocabulary (DCAT), is not directly applicable as it would require mapping to the fixed schema to be individually designed and maintained for every CMD profile encountered. But as shown below, more generic RDF vocabularies do play a role in transformation. These graphs should be made accessible to end-users, either as a downloadable file or via a SPARQL endpoint. In [69] the execution of mapping for records in CMDI from XML to RDF is described.

We will then explain the connection and mapping of knowledge representations between RDF and CMDI in order to offer a sense of its potential and opportunities for cross-fertilisation with other LD resources.

5 Our Hybrid Approach

The challenge is to create a bridge between LOD and CMDI to ensure that the limitations of the two paradigms are compensated for and that they are subsequently strengthened in order to create a new hybrid approach.

We try to overcome the most significant limitation of metadata, which is that is not descriptive enough for a document to be easily discoverable using LD technologies to publish and to enrich the document's content. In this case a document would be easily discoverable. Furthermore, we try to overcome the principal limit of LOD, which is problematic modelling by non-expert users, by using CMDI metadata modelling systems.

1. The need of actual classification schemes in an LOD representation, which will also result in the finalisation of the Lexicon of Knowledge Fields.
2. The development of facets classification into an interoperable instrument.
3. The need to connect facets classification with other existing classifications, thesauri, ontologies, etc., to provide general or specific information for an area.
4. The need to link the facets with existing standard data, also internationally and therefore multilingually.
5. The need for conceptual modeling resources in a digital repository.
6. The need for design CMDI components/profiles to encode specific descriptive features of the resources.
7. The need to reuse appropriate CMDI metadata schemas to describe metadata components that bundle descriptions for certain resource characteristics.
8. The need to create a suitable metadata profile to describe resources.
9. The need to extract the metadata content from a digital repository and generate a semantically enriched LD dataset
10. The need to use a built-in OAI-PMH access point that allows CMDI records to be made available in VLO.

Fig. 1. Tasks for connecting and mapping LOD and CMDI

Our aim is to define an interoperable, standardised, multilingual point of entry to all available data on textbook research across a range of formats. We want to define a CMDI semantic representation, which allows us to model all the knowledge fields in the world and integrate them into the available LOD Cloud. We summarise the desiderata related to LOD and CMDI tasks in Fig. 1. The largest spectrum of disciplines can be used to provide a variety of use cases needed to test the system's results.

6 Conclusion

The need for homogeneous access to archives and research infrastructures shows the need to establish a common standard, covering metadata, content, and inferred knowledge.

Unfortunately, with emerging data formats, no suitable standard yet exists. There is a wide variety of data, metadata formats and schemas that cover more information than just bibliographic catalogue records. While bibliographic catalogue records describe a resource, metadata encourages interoperability thus facilitating resource discovery by expanding the amount of searchable information. Here the two key aspects are: the guarantee of interoperable implementation and the sharing process of standardisation. Seeing as how metadata is not descriptive enough for a document to be easily discoverable, we propose to publish and enrich its content using LD technology.

The advantages of such technology, when well used, are the explicit semantics and high interoperability. Nevertheless, LD technology is difficult for non-expert users to model. For this reason, we propose to investigate the possibility of using CMDI to overcome these modelling problems. Our paper contributes to research in the field of knowledge organization within information science by providing a modern knowledge representation that considers semantic information. This information can be extracted and linked with LD paradigms and demonstrated by developing records using CMDI. In the future we want to develop a system for this purpose using as large a spectrum of disciplines and use cases as necessary to test the system's results.

References

1. Hjørland, B.: What is knowledge organization (KO)? Knowl. Organ. **35**, 86–101 (2008)
2. Luca, D., et al.: Using clustering methods to improve ontology-based query term disambiguation. Int. J. Intell. Syst. **21**(7), 693–709 (2006)
3. La Barre, K.: The use of faceted analytico-synthetic theory as revealed in the practice of website construction and design. Ph.D. dissertation, Indiana University (2006)
4. Plumbaum, T., et al.: User modeling for the social semantic web. In: Proceedings of the Second International Conference on Semantic Personalized Information Management: Retrieval and Recommendation - Volume 781, pp. 78–89. CEUR-WS.org (2011)
5. Lorenz, B.: Systematische Aufstellung in Vergangenheit und Gegenwart 2003 (2003)
6. Library of Congress Classification. https://www.loc.gov/catdir/cpso/lcco/
7. Dewey Decimal Classification. https://www.oclc.org/dewey/features/summaries.en.html
8. Universal Decimal Classification. http://www.udcc.org/index.php/site/page?view=about

9. Dahlberg, I.: The information coding classification (ICC): a modern, theory-based fully-faceted, universal system of knowledge fields. Axiomathes **18**(2), 161–176 (2008)
10. Smith, M., et al.: Survey of Current Library Linked Data Implementation (2017). https://bibflow.library.ucdavis.edu/xi-survey-of-current-library-linked-data-implementation/
11. VIAF Homepage. https://viaf.org/
12. FAST Homepage. http://fast.oclc.org/
13. Fellbaum, C.: WordNet: An Electronic Lexical Database. MIT Press, Cambridge (1998)
14. Hirst, G.: Ontology and the Lexicon. In: Staab, S., Studer, R. (eds.) Handbook on Ontologies, pp. 269–292. Springer, Heidelberg (2009). https://doi.org/10.1007/978-3-540-24750-0_11
15. Buitelaar, P.: Ontology-based semantic lexicons: mapping between terms and object descriptions. In: Ontology and the Lexicon, pp. 212–223. Cambridge University Press (2010)
16. Kunze, C., et al.: Repräsentation und Verknüpfung allgemeinsprachlicher und terminologischer Wortnetze in OWL. Zeitschrift für Sprachwiss. **26**(2), 267–290 (2007)
17. Lüngen, H., et al.: Modelling and processing WordNets in OWL. In: Mehler, A., Kühnberger, K.U., Lobin, H., Lüngen, H., Storrer, A., Witt, A. (eds.) Modeling, Learning, and Processing of Text Technological Data Structures, pp. 347–376. Springer, Heidelberg (2011). https://doi.org/10.1007/978-3-642-22613-7_17
18. WordNet, A Lexical Database for English (2015). https://wordnet.princeton.edu/
19. Chiarcos, C., et al.: Towards a linguistic linked open data cloud: the open linguistics working group. Trait. Autom. des Langues **52**(3), 245–275 (2011)
20. Pease, A., Fellbaum, C., Vossen, P.: Building the Global WordNet Grid (2008)
21. McCrae, P., et al.: Guidelines for Linguistic Linked Data Generation: WordNets (2015)
22. Van Assem, M., Gangemi, A., Schreiber, G.: Conversion of WordNet to a standard RDF/OWL representation. In: International Conference on Language Resources and Evaluation, pp. 237–242 (2006)
23. Raves, A., Gutierrez, C.: Data representations for WordNet: a case for RDF. In: Sojka, P., Choi, K.-S., Fellbaum, C., Vossen, P. (eds.) Proceedings of the 3rd International WORDNET Conference, pp. 165–169 (2006)
24. De Luca et al., Converting EuroWordNet in OWL and Extending It with Domain Ontologies (2007)
25. De Luca, E.W.: Aggregation and Maintenance of Multilingual Linked Data. Semi-Automatic Ontology Development: Processes and Resources Book. IGI Global, Pennsylvani (2012)
26. De Luca, E.W., Dahlberg, I.: Including knowledge domains from the ICC into the multilingual lexical linked data cloud, vol. 14 (2014)
27. Infographic-The History of Metadata. https://www.m-files.com/en/infographic-the-history-of-metadata
28. CMDI Metadata - The Language Archive. https://tla.mpi.nl/cmdi-metadata/
29. Beccaceci, R., et al.: Education with 'living artworks' in museums. In: CSEDU 2009 - Proceedings of the 1st International Conference on Computer Supported Education, vol. 1 (2009)
30. Arcidiacono, G., et al.: The use of lean six sigma methodology in digital curation. In: CEUR Workshop Proceedings, no. 2014 (2016)
31. Hernández, F., et al.: Building a cultural heritage ontology for Cantabria. In: Annual Conference of CIDOC Athens, pp. 1–14 (2008)
32. Hyvönen, E.: Publishing and using cultural heritage linked data on the semantic web. Synth. Lect. Semant. Web Theory Technol. **2**(1), 1–159 (2012)
33. Accardi, A.R.D., et al.: Digital museums of the imagined architecture: an integrated approach. DISEGNARECON **9**, 15.1–15.11 (2016)

34. Fallucchi, F., et al.: Ontology-driven PA web hosting monitoring system, vol. 8842 (2014)
35. Bianchi,M., et al.: Service level agreement constraints into processes for document classification. In: ICEIS 2014-Proceedings of 16th International Conference on Enterprise Inform. Systems, vol. 1 (2014)
36. Fallucchi, F., et al.: Analysing and visualizing open data within the data & analytics framework. In: Digital Library Track 12th Metadata and Semantics Research Conference (2018)
37. Zhang, D., et al.: A knowledge management framework for the support of decision making in humanitarian assistance/disaster relief. Knowl. Inf. Syst. 4(3), 370–385 (2002)
38. Fallucchi, F., et al.: Supporting humanitarian logistics with intelligent applications for disaster management. INTELLI 2016, 64 (2016)
39. Fallucchi, F., Tarquini, M., De Luca, E.W.: Knowledge management for the support of logistics during humanitarian assistance and disaster relief (HADR). In: Díaz, P., Bellamine Ben Saoud, N., Dugdale, J., Hanachi, C. (eds.) ISCRAM-med 2016. LNBIP, vol. 265, pp. 226–233. Springer, Cham (2016). https://doi.org/10.1007/978-3-319-47093-1_19
40. Ferroni, P., et al.: Risk assessment for venous thromboembolism in chemotherapy-treated ambulatory cancer patients. Med. Decis. Mak. 37(2), 234–242 (2017)
41. Ferroni, P., et al.: Validation of a machine learning approach for venous thromboembolism risk prediction in oncology. Dis. Markers 2017, 1–7 (2017)
42. Scarpato, N., et al.: E-health-IoT universe: a review. Int. J. Adv. Sci. Eng. Inf. Technol. 7(6), 2328–2336 (2017)
43. Pieroni, A., et al.: Industry 4.0 revolution in autonomous and connected vehicle a non-conventional approach to manage big data. J. Theor. Appl. Inf. 96(1) (2018)
44. Pieroni, A., et al.: Smarter city: smart energy grid based on Blockchain technology. Int. J. Adv. Sci. Eng. Inf. Technol. 8(1), 298–306 (2018)
45. Zinn, C., Trippel, T., Kaminski, S., Dima, E.: Crosswalking from CMDI to dublin core and MARC 21. In: International Conference on Language Resources and Evaluation, no. i, pp. 2489–2495 (2016)
46. Hillmann, D.I., et al.: Metadata standards and applications. Ser. Libr. 54(1–2), 7–21 (2008)
47. DCMI: DCMI Metadata Terms. http://www.dublincore.org/documents/dcmi-terms/
48. The Dublin Core to MARC crosswalk. http://www.loc.gov/marc/dccross.html
49. The MARC to Dublin Core crosswalk. http://www.loc.gov/marc/marc2dc.html
50. Woodley, M.S.: Crosswalks, metadata harvesting, federated searching, metasearching: using metadata to connect users and information. In: Introduction to Metadata, pp. 1–25 (2008)
51. Godby, C.J., et al.: A Repository of Metadata Crosswalks. D-Lib Mag. vol. 10, no. 12 (2004)
52. Pierre, M.S., LaPlant, W.P.: Issues in crosswalking content metadata standards. Bethesda MD Natl. Inf. Stand. Organ. 7, 01–16 (1998)
53. Broeder, D., Windhouwer, M., Van Uytvanck, D., Goosen, T., Trippel, T.: CMDI: a component metadata infrastructure. In: Describing LRs with Metadata: Towards Flexibility and Interoperability in the Documentation of LR Workshop Programme (2012)
54. Zhang, J., Kemps-Snijders, M., Bennis, H.: The CMDI MI search engine: access to language resources and tools using heterogeneous metadata schemas. In: Zaphiris, P., Buchanan, G., Rasmussen, E., Loizides, F. (eds.) TPDL 2012. LNCS, vol. 7489, pp. 492–495. Springer, Heidelberg (2012). https://doi.org/10.1007/978-3-642-33290-6_57
55. Fallucchi, F., et al.: Creating CMDI-profiles for textbook resources. In: Digital Library Track 12th Metadata and Semantics Research Conference 23–26 October 2018, Limassol, Cyprus (2018)
56. OAI-PMH. http://www.openarchives.org/OAI/openarchivesprotocol.html
57. Lampert, C.K., Southwick, S.B.: Leading to linking: introducing linked data to academic library digital collections. J. Libr. Metadata 13(2–3), 230–253 (2013)

58. Southwick, S.B.: A guide for transforming digital collections metadata into linked data using open source technologies. J. Libr. Metadata **15**(1), 1–35 (2015)
59. Scarpato, N., Alessio, G.: SAGG: a novel linked data visualization approach. J. Theor. Appl. Inf. **95**(22), 6192–6203 (2017)
60. Lillo, R.: Data and analytics framework. how public sector can profit from its immense asset, data. In: Leuzzi, F., Ferilli, S. (eds.) TRAP 2017. AISC, vol. 728, pp. 3–9. Springer, Cham (2018). https://doi.org/10.1007/978-3-319-75608-0_1
61. Haslhofer, B., et al.: The OAI2LOD Server:Exposing OAI-PMH Metadata as LD (2008)
62. D2RQ. http://d2rq.org/
63. Linked Data 5. http://www.w3.org/DesignIssues/LinkedData.html
64. Konstantinou, N., Spanos, D.-E.: Creating linked data from relational databases. Materializing the Web of Linked Data, pp. 73–102. Springer, Cham (2015). https://doi.org/10.1007/978-3-319-16074-0_4
65. Koutsomitropoulos, D.A., et al.: Herding linked data: semantic search and navigation among scholarly datasets. Int. J. Semant. Comput. **09**(04), 459–482 (2015)
66. Vila-Suero, D., et al.: A library linked dataset. Semant. Web **4**(3), 307–313 (2013)
67. IFLA. https://www.ifla.org/
68. Durco, M., et al.: From CLARIN component metadata to linked open data. In: Proceedings of the 3° Workshop on LD in Linguistics (LDL 2014).LREC 2014. Reykjavik, Icel (2014)
69. Windhouwer, M., et al.: CMD2RDF: building a bridge from CLARIN to linked open data. In: Data Archiving and Networked Services (DANS), pp. 95–103. Ubiquity Press (2017)

Creating CMDI-Profiles for Textbook Resources

Francesca Fallucchi[1,2(✉)] ⓘ, Hennicke Steffen[2] ⓘ,
and Ernesto William De Luca[1,2] ⓘ

[1] DIII, Guglielmo Marconi University, Rome, Italy
{f.fallucchi, ew.deluca}@unimarconi.it
[2] DIFI, Georg Eckert Institute, Braunschweig, Germany
{fallucchi, hennicke, deluca}@gei.de

Abstract. This paper analyses the establishment of a common infrastructure standard covering metadata, content, and inferred knowledge to allow collaborative work between researchers in the humanities. Interoperability between heterogeneous resources and services is the key for a properly functioning infrastructure. In this paper, we present a digital infrastructure of our textbook-related services and data, which are available and open for researchers worldwide. In this process we adhere to established standards and provide APIs for other services. In order to integrate our resources and tools into the CLARIN infrastructure and make them discoverable in the VLO (Virtual Language Observatory), we decided to use CMDI (Component MetaData Infrastructure). We focus in this paper on the creation process for a CMDI metadata profile which fulfils the needs of our projects.

Keywords: Component MetaData Infrastructure (CMDI) ·
VLO (Virtual Language Observatory) · CLARIN · Textbook ·
Metadata for language resources · Digital humanities

1 Introduction

The traditional organisation and retrieval of information in libraries is well established, has well-defined standards and allows documentation, collaboration and sharing of data and agreement on quality expectations. On the other side, digital libraries present new possibilities for accessing information. The traditional metadata-driven methods of library cataloguing are inadequate to fully describe digital objects in a new dynamic and content-driven environment [1]. Additionally, libraries from different countries may not share the same standards, so that interoperability is almost impossible. Tools and workflows are also often created for very specific purposes and areas, and therefore are difficult to share without a huge adaptation effort. Therefore, the use of standards for resource formats and metadata becomes crucial to enable resources to be easily discovered. The need of homogeneous access to libraries, archives and research infrastructures translates into the need to establish a common standard, covering metadata, content, and inferred knowledge. Unfortunately, there is not yet a suitable standard for emerging data formats [1]. There is a wide variety of metadata formats and

E. Garoufallou et al. (Eds.): MTSR 2018, CCIS 846, pp. 302–314, 2019.
https://doi.org/10.1007/978-3-030-14401-2_28

schemas, which cover more information than bibliographic catalogue records. While traditional bibliographic catalogue records are typically limited to descriptions of a bibliographic information resource, emerging metadata formats encourage interoperability and facilitate resource discovery by expanding the amount of searchable information. The two key aspects here are (1) the guarantee of the interoperability implementation and (2) the sharing process of standardisation.

CLARIN [2] has provided *Component MetaData Infrastructure* (CMDI) to overcome the dispersion of data formats. CMDI provides a framework to describe and reuse metadata blueprints. Description building blocks ("components", which include field definitions) can be grouped into a ready-made description format (a "profile"). Both are stored and shared with other users in the CLARIN Component Registry (CCR) [3] to promote reuse. Each metadata record is then expressed as an XML file, including a link to the profile on which it is based. The CMDI approach combines architectural freedom when modelling the metadata with powerful exploration and search possibilities over a broad range of language resources [4, 5].

In this paper, we present a metadata infrastructure, which allows the co-existence of many different schemas and supports semantic interoperability by using a separate 'pragmatic reference system' for the semantics being implied. To support users with limited experience of creating new schemas and reusing existing work at a conceptual level, we chose to build upon an existing infrastructure, where small reusable sections of metadata schemas can be created and recombined to form completely new schemas. We describe a process to build resources using CMDI description and we test it on the textbook resources of the *Georg Eckert Institute* (GEI). The rest of the paper is organised as follows: after presenting the current state of the field of descriptive metadata (see Sect. 2) we focus on bibliographic metadata standards and their related infrastructures. We then discuss and define the idea of a 'textbook resource', a concept which is at the heart of our mapping process to CMDI (see Sect. 3). After a precise analysis of the existing resources (see Sect. 3.1), we define a conceptual model in particular (see Sect. 3.2) as a flexible interoperable metadata schema (components and profile) suitable for, but not limited to, describing resources. Furthermore, we explain the full CMDI metadata life cycle process which allows us to convert our resources to CMDI records (see Sect. 4). We conclude the paper by describing future work (see Sect. 5).

2   Related Work

Descriptive metadata characterises a resource with keyword-value pairs. It has become increasingly important to manage and find electronic resources in a time where the sheer amount of resources and the complexity of the relations between them are increasing exponentially and unpredictably. The use of such descriptions allows researchers clearer and easier access to available resources. In this way, users can manage and find research data which goes beyond traditional publications. Metadata has always been a key issue for libraries and archives [6]. Today, many tools exist, as well as a multitude of metadata formats for language resources. Often these descriptions contain specialised information for a specific research community [7] or are included in knowledge organisation systems used for cultural heritage [8, 9], in the Public Administration domain [10–12] or for humanitarian assistance and disaster relief [13–15] as well as for new challenges in Health [16–18] and Industry 4.0 [19, 20].

The CLARIN team analysed the available metadata sets and concluded that they are insufficient to cover the whole domain of language resources (LR) because the sets either lacked specificity or were too specific and also because the terminology used in the different metadata sets does not always fit with the terminology of a specific sub-domain or community. The variety of subdomains in linguistic research means that a single metadata schema cannot successfully cater to all sub fields of linguistics. The differences in needs, terminology and traditions will prevent uptake and acceptance of such a schema. Therefore, the CLARIN team decided to create a metadata infrastructure based on components that would be flexible enough to allow users to create their own metadata sets by aggregating different metadata components. CMDI has been one of the core pillars of CLARIN since the beginning of this initiative [21]. One of the key properties of CMDI is its flexibility, which makes it possible to create metadata records closely tailored to the requirements of resources, tools and services. CMDI also provides new means for lifecycle management, introduced to avoid the proliferation of components. Furthermore, new mechanisms for using external vocabularies will contribute to more consistent use of controlled values, and cues for tools will allow improved presentation of the metadata records to the end users.

Making linguistic resources accessible via standard library catalogues is significant, because their CMDI-based metadata records cannot be simply ingested into existing library catalogues. In the library world, only a few established metadata standards are used within library catalogues (e.g. MARC or DC). To better connect to the library world, and to allow librarians to enter metadata for linguistic resources into their catalogues, we need to convert CMDI-based metadata to a bibliographic metadata standard. CLARIN established the possibility for institutions to become a CLARIN centre if they offer the CMDI records they create for harvesting via the Open Archives Initiative's Protocol for Metadata Harvesting (OAI-PMH). One of CLARIN's central services, the Virtual Language Observatory (VLO) [22], is the metadata-based portal for language resources. The VLO provides access to the full set of harvested CMDI records and is completely based on the CMDI and ISOcat standards.

3   What Are Our Textbook Resources?

In order to extend the digital infrastructure within the CMDI profiles, we had to formalise our understanding of textbooks and develop a dedicated conceptual model. This work has been conducted within the *WorldViews* project which aimed to develop the digital research infrastructure at the GEI.

3.1   Available Infrastructure

The *Digital Information and Research Infrastructures* department (DIRI) [23] at the GEI conducts autonomous research within the digital humanities. The department analyses different resources and publications to discover how historians can be supported while working with digital resources [24]. One of the main goals of the DIRI department is to make our findings permanently available in digital form. Much of the GEI's research infrastructure and many transfer projects are currently focussed on being standardised and integrated [25]. For example, a middleware solution has been implemented in the WorldViews project [26–28] to facilitate data storage and reuse within the GEI context and beyond. The WorldViews project team has also built a multilingual digital resource for primary source material, containing digitised excerpts from textbooks from around the world on topics that are of global, transnational and interregional relevance. Furthermore, the project enhances discoverability, reusability, and sustainability of digital resources in cultural and historical research and in the digital humanities by applying tools and standards for creating a digital online platform for textbook sources. In this case, the conceptualisation and creation of CMDI, as well as TEI representation of the data output in WorldViews, have been the main means of accomplishing this goal. The WorldViews data is accessible through standard interfaces and exchange protocols, which serve as a use case to test improvements in the data infrastructure's ability to facilitate the data's long-term sustainability and reuse. We are currently intensifying the connection to global cultural heritage organisations such as the Deutsche Digitale Bibliothek [29] and Europeana [30] and we have presented a study where we show the connection and the mapping in the knowledge representations between RDF and CMDI [31].

The available infrastructure at the GEI provides the basis for using CMDI as a new standard of metadata to provide access to objects in digital libraries. CMDI has been used in WorldViews to create and implement appropriate metadata schemas for describing resources. The CMDI metadata modelling process allows the reuse of different sections of metadata schemas or metadata components, which bundle descriptions for certain resource characteristics. These components can be recombined to create a suitable metadata profile for describing a specific resource type. Thus, components contain metadata elements or other components, forming profiles used to describe either singular resources or sets of related resources such as collections, especially textbook resources.

3.2   Conceptual Modelling of Textbook Resources

The first important step in the creation of CMDI records was to establish a conceptual modelling view of the textbook sources. The most relevant metadata and textual features were developed from scratch after consulting historians at the GEI who identified three distinct types of resources:

- A **textbook** is the whole (view of a) textbook;
- A **source** is a particular and selective view of a textbook such as a specific chapter or an excerpt consisting of one or more pages taken from a textbook;
- A **contribution** is a scientific text such as a commentary or essay typically discussing a source as its topic.

One of the most important processes related to the planned formalisation was the digitisation and metadata editing process for these three resource types. For this purpose, the WorldViews team adapted and customised the open source software Goobi

[32], a collaborative digitisation workflow tool providing an adequate environment for workflow handling and metadata editing. The software organises the workflow into separate and clearly distinguishable steps such as scanning, OCR, metadata enrichment or quality assurance. These steps are organised into three different templates, one for textbooks, one for sources and one for contributions. Each template combines all necessary steps into a structured workflow that allows all relevant data to be created, input and exported for the presentation of each resource type in the WorldViews digital platform: primarily digitised images, TEI and CMDI files for full-texts and descriptive metadata, and METS-MODS for structural metadata.

Regarding metadata editing in Goobi, the metadata profile is generic, and most metadata is filled in manually, yet, where possible, based on controlled vocabularies. Only bibliographic data is harvested through the OPAC interface, thus also using the *Gemeinsame Normdatei* (GND) [33] data and the handle service provided by GBV Common Library Network [34]. The last step in each template is the mapping and exporting of the previously recorded data from Goobi to TEI, CMDI and METS-MODS documents, each based on specific schemas.

The TEI schema created for textbook sources focuses on basic elements for the selective and formal description of those structural and semantic features that are immediately relevant for WorldViews. For example, headings of sections or the semantics of particular paragraphs should provide the necessary semantic information to contextualise search results and to formulate more precise queries that target particular segments of the text. This schema is designed to provide the nucleus for more comprehensive descriptions of entire textbooks, such as those found in the GEI-Digital platform [1]. Goobi exports two kinds of TEI documents: TEI Sources (containing the metadata for source, textbook and the annotated full-text of the source) and TEI Contributions (containing the metadata and the full-text for the commentaries on the sources). By analysing the Goobi output and participating in a number of discussions between historians, domain experts, information scientist experts and computer science technicians we have been able to define the conceptual model necessary to model the existing resources in the CMDI world.

4   CMDI Metadata Records for Textbook Sources

With the CMDI framework, the CLARIN team has developed a standard for flexible structuring of metadata for language resources. By using CMDI, full-text resources can immediately be indexed by CLARIN's Virtual Language Observatory and analysed using its various tools and services such as Weblicht [35].

The use of CMDI descriptions for textbook resources allows internally standardised search and retrieval operations in federated search scenarios. The CMDI approach combines architectural freedom when modelling the metadata with powerful exploration and search possibilities over a broad range of language resources. In order to model textbook sources with CMDI different components are needed (see Fig. 1).

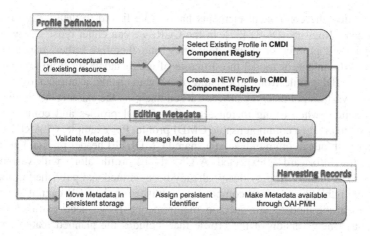

Fig. 1. Process of building GEI resources using CMDI description

The process of building the GEI resources using CMDI description includes three main steps:

- *Profile Definition*
  - define conceptual model of existing resources (see Sect. 3.2)
  - define CMDI profile: select existing profile in CCR or create a new profile in CCR.
- *Editing Metadata*: editing initially empty metadata record by choosing a profile in CCR
  - manage: edit the contents of the components and their elements.
  - validate: consistency checking and validation of value entered for the components and their elements.
  - CMDI XML is the format of the returned metadata.
- *Harvesting Metadata*: the metadata is available to host in VLO through OAI-PMH:
  - move metadata to persistent storage
  - assign persistent identifier
  - make metadata available through OAI-PMH

In the following subsections we explain the components of the system. In Sect. 4.1 we discuss the existing profile selected in CCR according to the Best Practice Guide for using CLARIN metadata components [36], and then in Sect. 4.2 the editing process of the metadata is described, including details on the editor employed. In Sect. 4.3 we report on some *general problems* and *mapping issues* resulting from the reuse of an existing profile. Finally, in Sect. 4.4 we describe the records which have been harvested via OAI-PMH.

4.1 Selecting an Existing Profile

In CMDI the syntax of a metadata set for a given resource type can be defined with reference to the semantics of each element in the CCR. To ensure semantic interoperability, the component elements have to be linked to data categories in the Data Category Registry (DCR) [37]. In the CCR, we can either reuse existing CMDI components and profiles or define new ones, and therefore either map to existing structures and content, or model the structure of the metadata set from scratch. When creating a CMDI profile from an existing metadata scheme, a number of challenges may arise at various points in the process: when mapping the existing structure onto the CMDI structure, when trying to reuse existing CMDI profiles and components and when trying to create a common usable CMDI profile. For example, CLARIN-DK [38] cooperates with other communities on a shared CMDI-TEI header profile, but its reuse is not as straightforward as expected. A CMDI-TEI profile along with various components has, as mentioned previously, already been defined and published in the CCR. The existing public profiles and components published in the CCR cannot be modified in order to accommodate our specific requirements. If we need extra elements or components a new version of the profile that includes the planned features must be created. However, if a slightly different structure is needed, the profile is no longer backwards compatible and will be treated as an entirely new profile (and not as a new version of the existing profile). However, the use of existing profiles and components is a very effective way to make repositories and infrastructures interoperable and is encouraged by CLARIN.

In our work, we decided to reuse existing profiles and components. This makes it easier for the users to understand and exchange metadata from different metadata providers avoiding fragmentation/inflation of profiles. We use the general workflow steps for the conversion of existing CMDI metadata to find an existing profile that can accommodate all needs of GEI resources. We started by analysing the TEI documents, extracted from Goobi, and their metadata specification in order to structure the metadata into attributes, elements and components in accordance with CMDI. We then scrutinised existing public CMDI profiles and components in the CCR. These must of course cover the same type of resources as the ones in focus, in this case the metadata fields from the TEI header. In the CCR there are three existing CMDI-TEI header profiles that cover the same type of GEI resources:

1. Creator: DK-CLARIN User
2. Creator: Axel Herold (DTA-Basisformat)
3. Creator: Matej Durco

No existing components completely fitted the structure in our TEI header specification but we selected CMDI-TEI header profile (GroupName: TEI CLARIN-DK, v1.0) [39] because it is the one that best covers the structure of our own TEI documents. The selected CMDI-TEI header profile allows the best reuse of existing components and elements for mapping with our resources metadata. This profile allows the conversion of all three distinct resource types as identified by the GEI historians and outlined above: textbooks, sources and contributions. By utilising an existing CMDI profile and applying our metadata representation requirements to that profile, we have committed to the idea of reuse as propagated by the CMDI community.

4.2 Creating and Managing Metadata

In order to check how the selected CMDI-TEI header profile allows the conversion of existing metadata for GEI TEI resources to CMDI, we created the CMDI instances using an existing editor. There are several existing editors that allow the creation and management of metadata with a given metadata schema that conforms to CMDI. For example, ProFormA2 is a web-based CMDI editor [40] and META-SHARE [41] offers metadata schemas for four resource types: corpus, lexical/conceptual resource, tool/services, and language description. Both currently appear to be of limited use for the full choice of CMDI profiles in the CCR. Arbil [42] is a general metadata editor, browser, and organiser tool for CMDI, IMDI and similar metadata formats [42]. There are other general purpose XML editors such as Oxygen [43] that are challenging to use for non-experts, since their use requires some insight in the XML technology. The IMDI-editor [39] and HTML5 web app CMDI Maker [44] allow users to load files that are part of a resource, to which the researcher can add metadata.

After an initial analysis of the advantages and disadvantages of the existing editors, we decided to use the COMEDI editor [45] to recreate and enrich GEI resources. COMEDI is a new CMDI-compatible editor, motivated by the wish to offer even more efficiency and user-friendliness and to overcome the disadvantages of other existing editors. We can create other sources by typing the selected CMDI-TEI header profile ID (ID: clarin.eu:cr1:p_1380106710826) for each GEI resource. New empty files based on the selected CMDI profile are created. In 'edit mode' we enter metadata extracted from the TEI files of the GEI resources. When we have entered a value for an element, the value is validated on the fly against the element description. Validation, controlled vocabulary, and autocompleting are indispensable tools to reduce the amount of inconsistencies and errors in the metadata, while also saving time for the metadata creator. The COMEDI editor validates input according to the ValueScheme specification in the element definition and displays the error message 'invalid input'. When we have finished editing all the metadata for the GEI resources, the validity of our metadata is indicated in the status row below the metadata record with the message: *The metadata record is valid.* When the metadata is complete and valid, we change the status to "published". Figure 2 shows some examples of new metadata records created for existing GEI resources. It is possible to download the CMDI records as XML files or as an HTML page and the metadata is available for hosting via an OAI-PMH endpoint.

Record name	Profile	CMDI Record XML	Owner	Status	
Click to view or edit the metadata record		Click to download			Delete
Deutsche Lieder Deutsche Lieder	teiHeader	[Download]	////////////////	published	·
Peace Conference in Munster1648 Peace Conference in Munster1648	teiHeader	[Download]	////////////////	published	·
People of Malaysia People of Malaysia	teiHeader	[Download]	////////////////	published	·
The Peoples of Sout-East Asia The Peoples of Sout-East Asia	teiHeader	[Download]	////////////////	published	·
What is a race - eng - What is a race - eng -	teiHeader	[Download]	////////////////	published	·
What is a race - ger - What is a race - ger -	teiHeader	[Download]	////////////////	published	·

Fig. 2. Examples of CMDI records created

4.3 Modelling Issues

We used existing profiles and components to allow interoperability between repositories and infrastructures. We were confronted with many difficulties and had to make
many compromises. Even though the syntax of the selected profile, TEI header, was
agreed upon by several scholars and metadata curators, as for all profiles and components in CCR, and the definitions of the metadata elements were given by TEI and
documented in the CCR with links to relevant definitions in CCR, the semantics of the
elements are not always clear and unambiguous since the syntax plays an important
role in the semantics. In addition, different operators from the same or from different
research communities edit and fill in the metadata in different ways, which in some
cases does not conform to the expected standard. We are aware of these issues and are
working to prevent problems in the metadata harvesting process for different environments. Other problems are present within the reuse of existing profiles because of
limitations or mapping issues. At the end of the metadata editing procedure, we
achieved an acceptable trade-off between interoperability and the loss of information
using existing profiles and components. In Table 1. General problems and mapping
issues. We describe the general mapping problems we encountered in the process of
converting our existing resources into the new CMDI world.

Table 1. General problems and mapping issues.

TEI	CMDI	Problems
\<author\> \<persName\> ...	*Component:titleStmt* *Element:author*	There is no *Component:Person*, to enter the author you must write the entire string with first and last name
\<publicationStmt\> \<publisher\> \<orgName role="project"\> ...	*Component:* *publicationStmt* *Element:publisher*	There is no attribute for the '@role = project' - important for facet searches in VLO
\<sourceDesc\> \<biblFull\>...	*Component:sourceDesc* *Component: biblStruct* *Component: monogr*	The mandatory biblStruct and monogr components are a problem in particular for contribution resources. We omit contributions altogether from the VLO in this case
\<sourceDesc\> \<biblFull\> \<titleStmt\> \<title level="m" type="main"\>.... \> ...	Component:sourceDesc Component: biblStruct Component: monogr Element: title	Element: title does not have type. Problems distinguishing between kinds of title (e.g. main, sub, ...) We do not distinguish between kinds of titles but concatenate everything into one \<title\> element
\<profileDesc\> \<textClass\> \<abstract...\> ...	Component:profileDesc Component:textDesc Element: purpose	We cannot convert sub-elements \<p\> and \<note\> into \<ab\> and we skip \<abstract\> altogether

4.4   Harvesting and Search Facets

The CMDI representation for full-text resources can immediately be indexed by CLARIN's Virtual Language Observatory and can be analysed using its various tools and services such as Weblicht. The CMDI description of GEI resources also allows for internally standardised search and retrieval operations in federated search scenarios. Furthermore, the COMEDI editor is a powerful tool that has a built-in OAI-PMH access point, which allows the immediate exportation of the records. A metadata file in COMEDI can be exported as a CMDI record, or embedded in an OAI-PMH wrapper.

As already mentioned, when the metadata is complete and valid, we change the status to 'published' as shown in Fig. 2. The new CMDI resources are then available for hosting via the OAI-PMH endpoint. After harvesting, the VLO fills a SOLR database. Since CMDI is a fairly flexible XML format, the information required for search facets can be encoded in different parts of the XML, depending on the repository or even depending on the resource. In order to alleviate this problem of flexible input formats the VLO relies on ISOcat data categories. These ISOcat data categories are mapped to the matching XPath for the specific CMDI file, based on the XSD of the CMDI profile. Each metadata record is then expressed as an XML file, including a link to the profile on which it is based. In Fig. 3. Conceptual model of the aggregation of values we show the conceptual links aggregating the values from those elements into the mapped facets in the VLO search index. We use the CLARIN Concept Registry (CCR) to create concept links in CMDI. This registry has relevant concepts based on the corresponding ISOcat data categories, which map all search facets available in the VLO to concept links and 'fallback' elements in CMDI. Thus, for each search facet, VLO checks a CMDI record for elements with certain concept links and then aggregates the values from those elements into the mapped facets in the VLO search index. This aggregation of values makes GEI resources available in CMDI-format and available for harvesting by CLARIN metadata aggregators such as the CLARIN VLO.

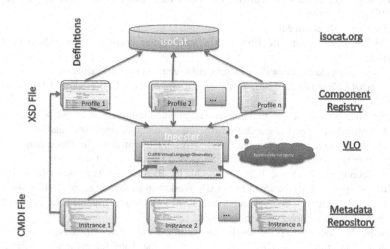

Fig. 3. Conceptual model of the aggregation of values

5   Conclusion

The use of standard formats and metadata for descriptions is crucial to enable the discovery of resources. This is necessary in libraries, archives and research infrastructures because of the heterogeneous data and metadata. We analysed CMDI, an infrastructure which permits many different schemas to co-exist and supports semantic interoperability by using a separate 'pragmatic reference system' for the semantics being implied. CMDI supports users with limited experience of the concept of creating new schemas and reusing existing work. We implemented an approach where small reusable sections of metadata schemas can be created and recombined to form complete new schemas. In this paper we presented our approach to building a CMDI profile for WorldViews, the digital humanities project conducted by the GEI. This project is an important step to getting our data into the CLARIN-infrastructure and is a blueprint for the CMDI usage for all areas of textbook research. We built an environment to convert our existing resources from the TEI- to the CMDI-format to make GEI resources available for harvesters included in the CLARIN metadata aggregators such as the CLARIN VLO. An existing profile was selected from CCR and details replaced with existing GEI resources. Thus, we created metadata records included in an OAI-PMH access point being available in the VLO. The environment has been built to make our digital services and our data available and openly accessible. We will address the problems that emerged during the conversion process by defining a new profile. We will also replicate the whole process to convert other types of resources. Our ultimate objective is to create a framework for converting and making all our resources available automatically.

References

1. Hillmann, D.I., Marker, R., Brady, C.: Metadata standards and applications. Ser. Libr. **54**(1–2), 7–21 (2008)
2. VLO. https://vlo.clarin.eu/
3. CLARIN Component Registry. https://catalog.clarin.eu/ds/ComponentRegistry/#/?_k= mxdsdz
4. Component-metadata. https://www.clarin.eu/content/component-metadata
5. CLARIN-D User Guide, Clarin-D Ap 5, vol. 1.0.1, no. CC BY-ND 3.0 DE, pp. 19–29 (2012)
6. Infographic. https://www.m-files.com/en/infographic-the-history-of-metadata
7. CMDI Metadata - The Language Archive. https://tla.mpi.nl/cmdi-metadata/
8. Beccaceci, R., et al.: Education with 'living artworks' in museums. In: Proceedings of the 1st International Conference on Computer Supported Education, vol. 1 (2009)
9. Arcidiacono, G., De Luca, E.W., Fallucchi, F., Pieroni, A.: The use of lean six sigma methodology in digital curation. In: CEUR Workshop Proceedings, no. 2014 (2016)
10. Fallucchi, F., Alfonsi, E., Ligi, A., Tarquini, M.: Ontology-Driven Public Administration Web Hosting Monitoring System, vol. 8842 (2014)
11. Bianchi, M., et al.: Service level agreement constraints into processes for document classification. In: ICEIS 2014 - Proceedings of the 16th International Conference on Enterprise Information Systems, vol. 1 (2014)

12. Fallucchi, F., Petito, M., De Luca, E.W.: Analysing and visualizing open data within the data & analytics framework. In: Digital Library Track of the 12th Metadata and Semantics Research Conference, 23–26 October 2018, Limassol, Cyprus., 2018

13. Zhang, D., et al.: A knowledge management framework for the support of decision making in humanitarian assistance/disaster relief. Knowl. Inf. Syst. **4**(3), 370–385 (2002)

14. Fallucchi, F., Tarquini, M., De Luca, E.W.: Supporting humanitarian logistics with intelligent applications for disaster management. INTELLI **2016**, 64 (2016)

15. Fallucchi, F., Tarquini, M., De Luca, E.W.: Knowledge management for the support of logistics during Humanitarian Assistance and Disaster Relief (HADR), vol. 265 (2016)

16. Ferroni, P., et al.: Risk assessment for venous thromboembolism in chemotherapy-treated ambulatory cancer patients. Med. Decis. Mak. **37**(2), 234–242 (2017)

17. Ferroni, P., et al.: Validation of a machine learning approach for venous thromboembolism risk prediction in oncology. Dis. Markers **2017**, 1–7 (2017)

18. Scarpato, N., Pieroni, A., Di Nunzio, L., Fallucchi, F.: E-health-IoT universe: a review. Int. J. Adv. Sci. Eng. Inf. Technol. **7**(6), 2328–2336 (2017)

19. Pieroni, A., Scarpato, N., Brilli, M.: Industry 4.0 revolution in autonomous and connected vehicle a non-conventional approach to manage big data. J. Theor. Appl. Inf. Technol. **96**(1), 10–18 (2018)

20. Pieroni, A., et al.: Smarter city: smart energy grid based on blockchain technology. Int. J. Adv. Sci. Eng. Inf. Technol. **8**(1), 298–306 (2018)

21. Broeder, D., Windhouwer, M., Van Uytvanck, D., Goosen, T., Trippel, T.: CMDI: a component metadata infrastructure. In: Describing LRs with Metadata: Towards Flexibility and Interoperability in the Documentation of LR Workshop Programme (2012)

22. CLARIN, Virtual Language Observatory (2016). http://vlo.clarin.eu

23. GEI: Digital Information and Research Infrastructures. http://www.gei.de/en/departments/digital-information-and-research-infrastructures.html

24. De Luca, E.W.: Digital infrastructures for digital humanities in international textbook research. In: Interdisciplinary Conference on Digital Cultural Heritage (DCH 2017) (2017)

25. De Luca, E.W., et al.: The repository of textbook research – integrating all open data on textbooks into a middleware with multilingual accessibility. In: Open Repositories Conference 2017 (2017)

26. Worldviews—A Digital Edition of International Textbook Sources. http://worldviews.gei.de/en/

27. Stahn, L., et al.: World views - a digital archive infrastructure for the GEI for international textbook research 1 introduction 2 GEI data, no. SDA, pp. 42–48 (2015)

28. Hennicke, S., De Luca, E.W., Schwedes, K., Witt, A.: WorldViews: Access to International Textbooks for Digital Humanities Researchers, pp. 254–256 (2012)

29. Deut. Digit. Bibliothek - Kultur und Wissen. https://www.deutsche-digitale-bibliothek.de/

30. Europeana Collections. https://www.europeana.eu/portal/de/

31. Fallucchi, F., De Luca, E.W.: Connecting and mapping LOD and CMDI through knowledge organization In: Track Digital Humanities and Digital Curation of the 12th Metadata and Semantics Research Conference, 23–26 October 2018, Limassol, Cyprus (2018)

32. Goobi: Over. of the funct.. https://www.intranda.com/en/digiverso/goobi/goobi-overview/

33. GND. http://www.dnb.de/DE/Standardisierung/GND/gnd_node.html

34. GBV. https://gso.gbv.de/

35. Weblicht Wiki. https://weblicht.sfs.uni-tuebingen.de/weblichtwiki/index.php/Main_Page

36. Clarin, T., et al.: Best practice guide for using CLARIN metadata components. https://www.clarin.eu/content/cmdi-best-practices-guide

37. The Data Category Repository. https://www.iso.org/sites/dcr-redirect/dcr.html

38. CLARIN-DK. https://clarin.dk/

39. IMDI-Editor The Lang. Archive. https://tla.mpi.nl/tools/tla-tools/older-tools/imdi-editor/
40. Dima, E., et al.: A metadata editor to support the description of linguistic resources. Proceedings of Eight International Conference on Language Resources and Evaluation, pp. 1061–1066 (2012)
41. Piperidis, S., et al.: META-SHARE: one year after META-SHARE, pp. 1532–1538 (2012)
42. Withers, P.: Metadata management with Arbil, pp. 72–75 (2008)
43. Weblet Importer. https://www.oxygenxml.com/
44. CMDI maker. http://class.uni-koeln.de/cmdi_maker/
45. Lyse, G.I., Meurer, P., De Smedt, K.: COMEDI: A component metadata editor. Sel. Pap. Clar. Annu. Conf. **2014**, 82–98 (2015)

European and National Projects

Towards a Knowledge Graph Based Platform for Public Procurement

Elena Simperl[1], Oscar Corcho[2], Marko Grobelnik[3], Dumitru Roman[4],
Ahmet Soylu[4(✉)], María Jesús Fernández Ruíz[5], Stefano Gatti[6],
Chris Taggart[7], Urška Skok Klima[8], Annie Ferrari Uliana[9], Ian Makgill[10],
and Till Christopher Lech[4]

[1] University of Southampton, Southampton, UK
[2] Universidad Politécnica de Madrid, Madrid, Spain
[3] Jožef Stefan Institute, Ljubljana, Slovenia
[4] SINTEF Digital, Oslo, Norway
ahmet.soylu@sintef.no
[5] Ayuntamiento de Zaragoza, Zaragoza, Spain
[6] Cerved Group Spa US, Milano, Italy
[7] OpenCorporates Ltd, London, UK
[8] Ministrstvo za javno upravo, Ljubljana, Slovenia
[9] OESIA Networks SL, Madrid, Spain
[10] OpenOpps Ltd, London, UK

Abstract. Procurement affects virtually all sectors and organizations particularly in times of slow economic recovery and enhanced transparency. Public spending alone will soon exceed EUR 2 trillion per annum in the EU. Therefore, there is a pressing need for better insight into, and management of government spending. In the absence of data and tools to analyse and oversee this complex process, too little consideration is given to the development of vibrant, competitive economies when buying decisions are made. To this end, in this short paper, we report our ongoing work for enabling procurement data value chains through a knowledge graph based platform with data management, analytics, and interaction.

Keywords: Procurement · Knowledge graphs · Analytics · Interaction

1 Introduction

Procurement affects virtually all sectors and organisations. In the public sector alone, spending on goods and services across the EU is estimated to exceed €2 trillion per annum[1]. Governments and state-owned enterprises are confronted with massive challenges: they must deliver services with greatly reduced budgets; prevent losses through fraud and corruption; and build healthy, sustainable

This work is funded by EU H2020 TheyBuyForYou project (780247).

[1] http://ec.europa.eu/DocsRoom/documents/20679.

E. Garoufallou et al. (Eds.): MTSR 2018, CCIS 846, pp. 317–323, 2019.
https://doi.org/10.1007/978-3-030-14401-2_29

economies. Managing these competing priorities is notoriously difficult. In times of slow economic recovery and enhanced transparency and accountability, there is a pressing need for better insight into, and management of government spending (cf. [1]). In the absence of data and tools to analyse and oversee this complex process, too little consideration is given to the development of vibrant, competitive economies when buying decisions are made.

To this end, within an EU project called TheyBuyForYou[2], we work towards enabling the procurement data value chains through a knowledge graph based platform paired with data management, analytics, and interaction. Our objective, from a technical point of view, is to build a technology platform, consisting of a set of modular, web-based services and APIs to publish, curate, integrate, analyse, and visualize a comprehensive, cross-border and cross-lingual procurement knowledge graph, including public spending and corporate data from multiple sources across the EU. In this context, the first challenge is the heterogeneity of the underlying data (cf. [5,10]), which covers structured (e.g., statistics, financial news) as well as unstructured (e.g., text, social media) sources in different languages and using their own terminology and formats (CSV, PDF, databases, websites, APIs etc.). A second challenge will be turning this vast array of information into a semantic knowledge graph [17,18], an interconnected semantic knowledge organization structure using Web URIs and linked data vocabularies, which can be analysed in depth to identify patterns and anomalies in procurement processes and networks. Finally, the last challenge is to support analytics and interaction with the knowledge graph by different groups of stakeholders.

In this short paper, we report our ongoing work. The rest of the paper is structured as follows. In Sect. 2, we present an overview of the related work. We present key challenges and our solution approach in Sect. 3 and Sect. 4 respectively, and finally we conclude the paper in Sect. 5.

2   Related Work

Although there is no single definition of a knowledge graph, from a broader perspective, we consider it as a graph describing real world entities and their interrelations (cf. [12,18]). They have become powerful assets for representing, storing, sharing, and accessing information both in academia, such as Yago [3] and DBpedia [9], and in industry such as Google's Knowledge Graph, Facebook's Graph Search, and Microsoft's Satori [17]. Different approaches and technologies could be used to construct knowledge graphs, such as ad-hoc approaches focusing on graph-oriented data storage and management built on relational and NoSQL databases and semantic approaches built on the Semantic Web technologies [8,18]. The Semantic Web offers relevant standards and technologies for representing, exchanging, and querying knowledge graphs. Typically, semantic knowledge graphs are stored or exported as RDF datasets and queried with

---

[2] https://theybuyforyou.eu.

SPARQL query language, while the semantics of such datasets are encoded in OWL 2 ontologies allowing logic-based reasoning[3].

There are various initiatives whose purpose is to create de-jure and de-facto standards for electronic procurement, including such as Open Contracting Data Standard (OCDS)[4] and TED eSenders[5]. However, these are mostly oriented to achieve interoperability (i.e., addressing communication between systems), document oriented (i.e., the structure of the information is commonly provided by the content of the documents that are exchanged), and provide no standardised practices to refer to third parties, companies participating in the process, or even the main object of contracts. This at the end generates a lot of heterogeneity. Procurement domain can take advantage of applying the Semantic Web approach by reusing existing vocabularies, ontologies, and standards [1]. Specifically in the procurement domain, these include among others PPROC ontology [10] for describing public processes and contracts, LOTED2 ontology [5] for public procurement notices, PCO ontology [11] for contracts in public domain, and MOLDEAS ontology [14] for announcements about public tenders. LOTED2 is considered as a legal ontology and is comparatively more complex and detailed with respect to MOLDEAS, PCO, and PPROC. The latter is concerned on reaching a balance between usability and expressiveness.

3 Challenges

The technical landscape for managing contracts is very complex, for example, contracts are handled using different tools and formats across departments. Procurement data has a large scale and covers structured as well as unstructured data sources in different languages, terminology, and formats. By delivering a knowledge graph integrating a variety of procurement related datasets and an open-source platform and APIs for decision support and analytics, a wide range of procurement business cases could be supported. However, there are challenges to be addressed.

3.1 Data Integration

Apart from lack of a common schema, there are several other problems due to ingestion of heterogeneous and often noisy data sources. Firstly, there could be duplicates (e.g., seemingly two different tenders actually refer to the same tender) and missing information. Secondly, mapping entities referred to in data sets is also considerable challenge. For example, linking company data across data sets needs to take into account that not only companies change names frequently, but names are reused; addresses are in multiple forms and often refer to trading or administrative addresses rather than registered addresses; and legal names are represented in multiple forms or languages.

---

[3] https://www.w3.org/standards/semanticweb/.
[4] http://standard.open-contracting.org/latest/en/.
[5] http://simap.ted.europa.eu/.

3.2 Data Analysis

Firstly, procurement documentation is typically available in the native language of the issuing organisation. Even in multi-lingual sources such as the Tenders Electronic Daily (TED), the documents in the language of the issuing country are a lot more detailed than their translations. Therefore, comparing and linking documents across languages for various analysis purposes, such as cross-lingual document clustering by topic, is challenging. Secondly, the stream of public spending documentation from governments is a large data source and requires real-time automatic analysis approaches. For example, TED alone is updated with roughly 1500 public procurement notices five times a week.

3.3 Human-Data Interaction

Buyers, suppliers, journalists, and citizens need tools to understand the complex space of procurement data. Potential solutions should go beyond the interactive visualizations offered by the most existing analytics software, better match individual information needs, be integrated with real-time automated analytics, and master the inherent properties of the underlying data, which is very diverse in terms of structure, vocabularies, language, and modality. Finally, there is also a need for improved methods to create interactive visualizations that communicate findings intelligibly. Existing tools often tell an implicit story and are difficult to replicate or integrate with other analytics sources.

4 TheyBuyForYou Approach

We are building an integrated information hub with a semantic knowledge graph for public procurement and company data in order to support: (i) economic development by facilitating better outcomes from public spending for SMEs; (ii) demand management by spotting trends in public spending to achieve long-term goals such as savings; (iii) competitive markets by promoting healthier competition and identifying collusions and other irregularities; (iv) and supplier intelligence by advanced analytics. We will address the aforementioned challenges as described in the followings.

4.1 Knowledge Graphs

We are creating a knowledge graph primarily integrating and linking two large open databases: core company data provided by OpenCorporates[6] and tenders and contracts data provided by OpenOpps[7] in the OCDS format. Once the data is extracted from the aforementioned databases through an extract-transform-load (ETL) process, it needs to be integrated into a common ontology built on existing ontologies and vocabularies, possibly with extensions, and entities

---

[6] https://opencorporates.com.
[7] https://openopps.com.

need to be linked across data sets. The resulting knowledge graph will be published through open APIs and a SPARQL endpoint. A range of data curation mechanisms need to be applied, including the identification and resolution of duplicates, and the completion of missing information by using heuristic and machine learning (ML) approaches as well as manual input from citizens. Additional links between the data sources, for instance between entities in procurement documents and data and the entities coming from business registries, could be discovered through using data reconciliation algorithms, a combination of heuristics, explicit sets of rules, and clustering algorithms (cf. [2,6]).

4.2 Cross-Lingual and Real-Time Analytics

Cross-lingual document comparison and linking approaches could be adapted to public spending documentation (cf. [7]). In natural language processing, a typical approach to document analysis is to represent each document as a vector of semantic concepts and terms from the document resulting in different vector space for each language. In order to compare vectors from different spaces, we use an approach based on canonical correlation analysis to find a mapping to a common semantic vector space, which preserves document similarities within individual languages while enabling their comparison across languages. As a first application, we are implementing anomaly detection, also known as outlier detection. It is the task of identifying data points or groups of data points that in some sense diverge from normal behaviour (cf. [4]). This is highly relevant in the domain of public spending, where we are interested in both individual exceptional cases as well as large and systematic patterns standing out from the norm, whether they represent examples of good public procurement practice or possible cases of corruption.

4.3 Data Visualisation, Storytelling and Narratives

A visual solution should allow for exploratory navigation of the content space (in reflection to and exploring temporal developments); following links to the used content and their provenance; and providing links to alternative visualizations. Especially, approaches targeting the visualization and understanding of temporal aspects [15] and dynamics, and the visualization of highly networked content [16] drive our work. We employ storytelling methods to create visualizations by using narratives, which are compact, yet coherent natural language summaries of data [13]. A tool is being developed to create machine-readable specification of infographics, deployed using open standards, e.g., JSON and linked data, and that can be easily shared and linked to other media, maintains links to the identifiers of the data and ontologies they refer to, and integrates cross-lingual real-time analytics capabilities. To enhance the natural language generation methods in use, we will compile a collection of data design patterns from the procurement knowledge graph to generate end-user configurable storification templates.

5   Conclusions

We presented key challenges and a solution approach, using knowledge graphs, data analysis and interaction, for enabling procurement data value chains. We will also build a series of toolkits and portals on top of our solution to allow various stakeholders to explore and understand how public procurement decisions affect economic development, efficiencies, competitiveness and supply chains.

References

1. Alvarez-Rodríguez, J.M., et al.: New trends on e-procurement applying semantic technologies: current status and future challenges. Comput. Ind. **65**(5), 800–820 (2014)
2. Araújo, S., et al.: SERIMI: class-based matching for instance matching across heterogeneous datasets. IEEE Trans. Knowl. Data Eng. **27**(5), 1397–1410 (2015)
3. Biega, J., et al.: Inside YAGO2s: a transparent information extraction architecture. In: Proceedings of the 22nd International Conference on World Wide Web (WWW 2013), pp. 325–328. ACM, New York (2013)
4. Chandola, V., et al.: Anomaly detection: a survey. ACM Comput. Surv. **41**(3), 15:1–15:58 (2009)
5. Distinto, I., et al.: LOTED2: an ontology of European public procurement notices. Semant. Web **7**(3), 267–293 (2016)
6. Dorneles, C.F., et al.: Approximate data instance matching: a survey. Knowl. Inf. Syst. **27**(1), 1–21 (2011)
7. Fortuna, B., et al.: A kernel canonical correlation analysis for learning the semantics of text. In: Kernel Methods in Bioengineering, Communications and Image Processing (2006)
8. Kharlamov, E., et al.: Ontology based data access in statoil. Web Semant.: Sci. Serv. Agents World Wide Web **44**, 3–36 (2017)
9. Lehmann, J., et al.: DBpedia - a large-scale, multilingual knowledge base extracted from Wikipedia. Semant. Web **6**(2), 167–195 (2015)
10. Muñoz-Soro, J.F., et al.: PPROC, an ontology for transparency in public procurement. Semant. Web **7**(3), 295–309 (2016)
11. Necaský, M., et al.: Linked data support for filing public contracts. Comput. Ind. **65**(5), 862–877 (2014)
12. Paulheim, H.: Knowledge graph refinement: a survey of approaches and evaluation methods. Semant. Web **8**(3), 489–508 (2017)
13. Portet, F., et al.: Automatic generation of textual summaries from neonatal intensive care data. Artif. Intell. **173**(7), 789–816 (2009)
14. Rodríguez, J.M.Á., et al.: Towards a Pan-European e-procurement platform to aggregate, publish and search public procurement notices powered by linked open data: the moldeas approach. Int. J. Softw. Eng. Knowl. Eng. **22**(3), 365–384 (2012)
15. Shanbhag, P., et al.: Temporal visualization of planning polygons for efficient partitioning of geo-spatial data. In: Proceedings of the IEEE Symposium on Information Visualization (InfoVis 2005). IEEE Computer Society, Washington, DC (2005)
16. Smith, M.A., et al.: Analyzing (social media) networks with NodeXL. In: Proceedings of the 4th International Conference on Communities and Technologies, pp. 255–264. ACM, New York (2009)

17. Suchanek, F.M., et al.: Knowledge bases in the age of big data analytics. Proc. VLDB Endowment **7**(13), 1713–1714 (2014)
18. Yan, J., et al.: A retrospective of knowledge graphs. Front. Comput. Sci. **12**(1), 55–74 (2018)

Metadata for Large-Scale Research Instruments

Vasily Bunakov[✉]

Science and Technology Facilities Council, Harwell OX11 0QX, UK
vasily.bunakov@stfc.ac.uk

Abstract. The work outlines diverse effort of a few initiatives for metadata and attribution mechanisms that can be used for large-scale instruments hosted by shared research facilities. Specifically, the role of persistent identifiers and associated metadata is considered, in relation to cases where the use of references to large-scale instruments can support research impact studies and Open Science agenda. A few routes for the adoption of large-scale instruments metadata are outlined, with indication of their advantages and limitations.

Keywords: Large-scale instruments · Research facilities ·
Research attribution · Persistent identifiers ·
Research information management · Impact studies · Open science

1 Introduction

Large-scale research facilities such as synchrotron radiation sources, neutron sources or powerful lasers offer shared access to a variety of scientific instruments and are a prominent part of the research landscape for the last few decades. The notion of "instrument" in such facilities differs from that in other research contexts, as a facility instrument is often a complex set of equipment that evolves through time, may support multiple experimental techniques and requires specific research and technology expertise for its development and practical use. A facility instrument involves an organizational aspect and may be operated by a dedicated administrative unit; the instrument may have specific sources of funding and specific collaborations that perform the instrument support and upgrades.

Visitor scientists apply for a share of time on large-scale instruments in order to conduct their own research driven by their own research agenda. Depending on the nature of a particular research, the involvement of the host instrument specialists (instrument scientists) may be more of a supporting nature, or can make crucial contribution to research results. This leads to various practices of research attribution across different disciplines and research contexts, with the perceived tendency to the less frequent attribution given to instrument scientists [3].

There is a growing understanding that not only instrument scientists, but the instruments themselves deserve proper attribution in research outputs such as research papers, as this can contribute to impact studies that influence next rounds of investment in the large-scale instruments and in facilities as a whole. The problem of instruments attribution can be addressed using different information management techniques; as an example, larger facilities can afford hiring a dedicated bibliographer who traces research papers down to particular instrument-specific awards that allowed raw data collection in the first place. Another approach is implementing certain policies that require visitor scientists to attribute their research outputs with clear references to instruments. In addition or alternatively, a certain level of information management automation can be introduced, so that when visitor scientists are granted with their timeshare of a large-scale instrument, their personal records in a publically available (harvestable) registry are automatically updated with proper references. Irrespective of the approach to attribution, the large-scale instruments require clear and persistent identity as a part of quality instrument metadata.

This work first introduces a few Open Science cases beyond impact studies that can be supported by quality metadata for large-scale instruments. It then outlines a few approaches to the instruments attribution that imply a few routes for the instruments metadata adoption by research facilities. It further suggests reasonable priorities for different adoption routes.

2 Open Science Cases for Large-Scale Instruments

Clear research attribution aimed at impact studies can be an immediate driver why research facilities should consider better metadata for their instruments, but this is not the only case where quality instrument metadata is required. FAIR principles [14] that initially promoted research data Findability, Accessibility, Interoperability and Reuse are now advised for their application to related algorithms, tools, workflows, protocols and services [1]. Instruments are now considered an essential part of research workflows that should support Open Science [2].

There are a few aspects of Open Science that facilities may want to explore through better metadata for instruments:

- Research trends and research frontiers studies; this may contribute to evidence-based planning for instruments and facilities upgrades, in order to keep abreast of research interests of applying researchers and their organizations
- Strategic partnership studies, e.g. through discovering and monitoring frequent (or otherwise prominent) funders of visitor scientists, as time slots on large-scale instruments can be considered grants-in-kind, hence recurring co-funding may indicate opportunities for permanent funders cooperation with a facility
- Research provenance chains that can include instruments where raw data was collected; this is important for research reproducibility and for informing potential research applicants about capabilities of particular instruments and facilities
- Giving proper credit to instrument scientists who may be less frequently mentioned nowadays as co-authors of peer-reviewed publications but deserve clear attribution of their work that contributes to quality research

In fact, there is no clear boundary between Open Science and impact studies traditionally supported by all sorts of research information management systems. Information services for Open Science can support impact studies, and potentially in novel ways, with better granularity and with community review that can raise the quality of impact studies and public trust in them. A few ongoing initiatives on the instruments metadata and attribution can support the Open Science cases and impact studies.

3   Ongoing Initiatives on the Instruments Attribution that Are Suitable for Large-Scale Instruments

3.1   Journal of Large-Scale Research Facilities (JLSRF)

Journal of Large-Scale Research Facilities (JLSRF) [4] is a peer-reviewed online Open Access journal with the editorial team from Jülich Research Centre [6]. The journal publishes articles that describe large-scale equipment intended for use by visitor scientists who are not affiliated with the institution operating the facility.

The articles are peer-reviewed by a reviewer board that is run by the journal; larger institutions that operate several facilities with multiple instruments are encouraged to set up their local reviewing body.

Articles can be attributed to the operating institution or the facility (corporate authors), yet people who compiled the article can be listed as contributors, which gives them a credit for their authoring of the instrument description. In any case, at least one human contact is provided for potential inquiries about the instrument.

An article published in JLSRF allows visitor scientists to cite large-scale instruments in their publications. Operators of large-scale facilities can refer to the respective article in JLSRF, too, e.g. on their websites or in their annual reports.

Every article is assigned with the DOI; an instrument upgrade description can be published as a new article with a new (modified) DOI.

Apart from the DOI, each article is supplied with Dublin Core metadata elements. These include citations (references) to papers and to other citable artefacts that may include other large-scale instruments, or previous versions of the same instrument, or a facility as a whole. This is an opportunity to give a rich information context to the facility instrument descriptions and include them, through citations, in a universal research discourse.

JLSRF is indexed by a few popular indexing platforms including OpenAire [8] and is recorded in Open Access monitoring databases such as SHERPA/RoMEO [9]. The articles metadata is harvestable via the widely known OIA-PMH interface.

Publishing articles about large-scale instruments in JLSRF can be the first reasonable step for facilities to develop best practices for clear instruments identification and for giving visitor scientists a handy mechanism for citing instruments.

3.2   RDA Persistent Identification of Instruments Working Group

The Research Data Alliance have recently endorsed a dedicated Working Group for Persistent Identification of Instruments [5]. The group collects case studies from various research disciplines, and aims to develop a common metadata model for instrument PID descriptions with the main purpose of using them by machine agents (software), compared to the case of JLSRF where instrument descriptions are mostly intended for human consumption.

Another difference from the JLSRF is scope: the use case of large-scale facility instruments has been supplied for the group consideration, but this RDA group is interested in all sorts of instruments, not necessarily large-scale instruments. As an example, a few use cases from geoscience and other disciplines are about the networks of sensors and other serial equipment. This makes the works of this RDA group, on one hand, universal, but on the other hand, the eventual metadata and associated information management practices may happen to be less suitable for a particular case of large-scale instruments. Another limitation is that this RDA group decided to focus on instruments for measurements (data collection) but some large-scale instruments, e.g. photon sources, can also be used for samples modification.

From facilities perspective, this RDA group works should be best viewed as a complementary effort to what the JLSRF have been successfully doing for years.

3.3 ORCID User Facilities and Publications Working Group

ORCID User Facilities and Publications Working Group [7] engages with information management specialists mostly from American large-scale research facilities and aims to promote ORCID persistent identifiers for facilities visitor scientists. The Group have developed a recommendation for facilities user offices to request ORCID IDs and personal ORCID API tokens from researchers who apply for facilities time, as well as to ask the researchers' consent for auto-populating their ORCID accounts with information about facilities time allocation. Once a time slot is allocated, the notice of it can be published by facility in the visitor scientist's ORCID's section devoted to grants or in other section devoted to resources that supported researcher.

There is no functionality within ORCID that allows linking particular papers in the ORCID Publications section with records in the Research Resources or Funding sections. It is the ORCID's view that a publication will get linked to a facility award as a grant-in-kind or to the facility instrument as a research-resource-in-kind when a researcher submits a manuscript for publication. It is the publisher's responsibility then to ask about research awards and resources that supported the paper in question.

Unless the link between a research paper and an instrument is requested by a publisher, it will be only possible to find out, using just an ORCID record, that a particular researcher used a certain facility instrument at a certain time. This will be enough for *some kinds* of pretty coarse impact studies and Open Science use cases but not for fine-grained assessment or for a sensible level of research reproducibility, so this approach that relies on publishers' best practices (that may be diverse across different publishers, too) has its natural limitations. Also facilities' reluctance, owing to privacy concerns and extra effort required, to request ORCID identifiers from visitor scientists and to auto-populate their ORCID records, can be an obstacle for the universal adoption of the ORCID-based mechanism of instruments attribution.

3.4   PANKOS Vocabulary

PANKOS vocabulary is an ontology of photon and neutron sources; it was one of the outcomes of PaNdata-ODI project (see under [10]). This kind of a semantic resource will be invaluable in fine-grained impact studies and for Open Science use cases.

The reason for this is that researchers can cite the entire facility in their papers, e.g. a synchrotron light source, or they can cite a particular instrument of it, or a particular experiment (investigation) that corresponds to a facility research award. There should be some means to make aggregations up to the instrument or to the facility level, in order to count all citations towards the impact of a particular instrument or a facility as a whole. More complex and more granular studies of a comparative nature can be considered, too, e.g. comparing impact of only the instruments that use the same or similar experimental technique across a few facilities.

Therefore, semantic links are required within vocabulary that allow to reason over the belonging of the instrument to a facility, as well as over the experimental technique used by the instrument. In PANKOS, this was achieved using Web Ontology Language (OWL) classes, which can be perceived as overcomplicated from modelling point of view and thus prevent the universal vocabulary adoption. The OWL modelling may also present an indirect obstacle for the vocabulary deployment in a variety of IT environments, as triple stores differ in flavours of OWL they can support.

The PANKOS can be a good starting point though for the design of a new universal vocabulary that will have enough expressivity to support the aforementioned modes of reasoning, but will not be overcomplicated or facility-specific. The vocabulary may include the notion of samples modification, not only of their characterization, which will make it applicable when a large-scale instrument is a part of a production line or is otherwise used for the alteration of exposed samples.

4   FREYA Project and Priorities for the Adoption of Large-Scale Instruments Metadata

FREYA project [11] aims to extend the infrastructure for persistent identifiers as an essential component of Open Science, in the EU and globally.

It is a view of FREYA that research communities should come up with their own use cases of using PID resolution services such as Crossref [12] or DataCite [13] for the promotion of research FAIR principles. In turn, research communities are expected to contribute their purpose-built research graphs, with all kinds of PIDs as nodes and with sensible relations between the nodes, into the interoperable federation of PID graphs and services built atop of them.

Communities that operate and use large-scale instruments may benefit from this FREYA vision and from services based on PID graphs. Metadata for large-scale facilities instruments will contribute to the graphs and can be adopted through the following routes that complement each other but will be best pursued in the following order:

- Textual descriptions and metadata in JLSRF, including DOIs suitable for citation of instruments in research papers and for their linking to other research artefacts

- Machine-interpretable metadata associated with instrument PIDs if/when the appropriate recommendation will be agreed by the RDA PIDINST WG
- Entries for the large-scale facilities instruments in a semantic vocabulary that allows modest machine reasoning, with the right balance between the vocabulary expressivity and simplicity
- The practice based on facility instruments registration in ORCID records can be further explored, but it involves a variety of stakeholders with different policies, which may hinder the universal adoption of ORCID recommendations

The semantic vocabulary can be a proper tool for eventually incorporating the other flavours of metadata for large-scale instruments. The vocabulary can include DOIs of the JLSRF articles and PIDs for the machine-actionable descriptions according to the RDA PIDINST WG recommendations. These PIDs can be related by a vocabulary entry with an indication of their respective purposes, and with a possibility to crosswalk between different PIDs for the same instrument.

Acknowledgements. This work is supported by funding from the Horizon 2020 FREYA project, Grant Agreement number 777523. The views expressed are the views of the author and not necessarily of the project or the funding agency.

References

1. European Open Science Cloud Declaration. https://ec.europa.eu/research/openscience/pdf/eosc_declaration.pdf. Accessed June 2018
2. Open Science Commons. https://documents.egi.eu/public/ShowDocument?docid=2410. Accessed June 2018
3. Mesot, J.: A need to rethink the business model of user labs? Neutron News **23**(4), 2–3 (2012)
4. Journal of large-scale research facilities (JLSRF). https://jlsrf.org/. Accessed June 2018
5. RDA Persistent Identification of Instruments Working Group. https://www.rd-alliance.org/groups/persistent-identification-instruments. Accessed June 2018
6. Forschungszentrum Jülich. http://www.fz-juelich.de/. Accessed June 2018
7. ORCID User Facilities and Publications Working Group. https://orcid.org/content/user-facilities-and-publications-working-group. Accessed June 2018
8. OpenAIRE initiative. https://www.openaire.eu/. Accessed June 2018
9. SHERPA/RoMEO. Publisher copyright policies & self-archiving information service. http://www.sherpa.ac.uk/romeo/. Accessed June 2018
10. PANdata: Photon and Neutron data infrastructure initiative. http://pan-data.eu/. Accessed June 2018
11. FREYA project. https://www.project-freya.eu/. Accessed June 2018
12. Crossref consortium. https://www.crossref.org/. Accessed June 2018
13. DataCite consortium. https://datacite.org/. Accessed June 2018
14. Wilkinson, M., et al.: The FAIR guiding principles for scientific data management and stewardship. Sci. Data **3**, 160018 (2016). https://doi.org/10.1038/sdata.2016.18

Agriculture, Food and Environment

Identification and Exchange of Regulated Information on Chemicals: From Metadata to Core Vocabulary

Alicja Agnieszka Dys[(✉)] [iD]

European Chemicals Agency, Helsinki, Finland
alicja.agnieszka.dys@gmail.com

Abstract. Regulatory bodies perform risk assessments of chemicals and produce regulatory outcomes: evaluations and decisions on chemicals and conditions of their use. Access to scientifically proven and already regulated information becomes crucial for their efficient work and consistent decisions. Exchanging and reusing information relies on common understanding of the main concepts. Here is the challenge: even if the regulations and industry standards provide definitions of chemical substance, the interpretation poses some issues. This paper introduces a concept of Regulated Substance and aims to highlight the complexity of implementing semantic interoperability on regulated information between different parties.

The regulatory activities of European Chemicals Agency (ECHA) overlap, follow or trigger activities performed by other authorities. Capabilities to exchange the information and having access to shared databases can increase regulatory benefits. The common initiative of European Commission, Publication Office, and EU agencies is looking into possibilities to exchange the information. One of the tools promoted by Publication Office – Core Vocabularies – is meant to facilitate interoperability between authorities. The initiative will build foundations for access to the public repositories of the regulated information and non-confidential scientific data for academia and researchers via Open Linked Data.

Keywords: Chemical substance · European Chemicals Agency (ECHA) · Regulated information · Semantic interoperability · Core vocabulary

1 Diversity in Chemical Substance Definitions

The information on substance identification is expressed by a number of descriptors – chemical identifiers. Although there are solid methods of determining chemical identity, the meaning of the specific set of descriptors differs depending on the context:

1. Legislations define handling substances for regulatory purposes in different ways (strict, inclusive, focused on hazardous properties, related to use, etc.)
2. Substance definitions in chemical databases vary in definition and scope

---

The above represents the opinion of the author and is not an official position of the European Chemicals Agency.

© Springer Nature Switzerland AG 2019
E. Garoufallou et al. (Eds.): MTSR 2018, CCIS 846, pp. 333–339, 2019.
https://doi.org/10.1007/978-3-030-14401-2_31

3. Chemical monitoring data by the means of analytical methods is focused on occurrence of chemicals and chemical mixtures
4. Location of the substance in supply chain determines its ontological and semantic fate

Agreeing on a consistent definition of chemical substance – a premise for enabling exchange of information – does not seem to be obvious. Referring to publicly available (not strictly academic) sources brings a few definitions of chemical substance [12]. The official IUPAC[1] definition of chemical substance is the following:

Definition 1: *Chemical substance is matter of constant composition best characterized by the entities (molecules, formula units, atoms) it is composed of. Physical properties such as density, refractive index, electric conductivity, melting point etc. characterize the chemical substance [1].*

A more generic character of the term 'chemical substance' is used by Chemical Abstracts Service (CAS), a division of the American Chemical Society - a source of chemical information for more than 130 million organic and inorganic substances:

Definition 2: *CAS Registry contains a wide variety of substances, including the world's largest collection of: Elements, Organic compounds, Inorganic compounds, Coordination compounds, Metals, Alloys, Minerals, Organometallics, Isotopes, Nuclear particles, Proteins and nucleic acids, Polymers, Nonstructurable materials (UVCBs) [2].*

The legal definitions are even broader, since they focus on substances or products that (potentially) enter the market. The regulatory programs under the remit of ECHA - REACH[2] (Article 3), CLP[3] (Article 2) and BPR[4] (Article 3 p. 2a) define a substance as:

Definition 3: *A chemical element and its compounds in the natural state or obtained by any manufacturing process, including any additive necessary to preserve its stability and any impurity deriving from the process used, but excluding any solvent which may be separated without affecting the stability of the substance or changing its composition [7].*

The definition goes beyond a pure chemical compound composed of a single molecule. The term covers both substances obtained by a manufacturing process and substances in their natural state, which can both include several components: main constituents that make up a significant part of that substance and are therefore used in substance naming and identification, impurities - unintentional constituents coming from the manufacturing process or from the starting material(s), additives - constituents which are intentionally added to stabilize the substance and only for this purpose. In case of the substances for which the number of constituents is high, the composition

---

[1] IUPAC International Union of Pure and Applied Chemistry.
[2] EC Regulation No. 1907/2006 on the Registration, Evaluation, Authorisation and Restriction of Chemicals.
[3] EC Regulation No. 1272/2008 on the Classification, Labelling and Packaging of substances and mixtures.
[4] EU Regulation No. 528/2012 concerning the making available on the market and use of biocidal products.

is to a significant extent unknown, or the variability of composition is large or unpredictable, a clear identification based on the chemical composition is not possible and these will need to be considered as a substances of Unknown or Variable composition, Complex reaction products or Biological materials (UVCB). Typically UVCBs should be identified by considering the origin material of the substance, the most relevant steps during the manufacturing process and, according to the specific case, other relevant parameters (in addition to what is known about their chemical composition).

Rotterdam Convention (PIC[5]) concerning the export and import of hazardous chemicals (Article 2a), also being implemented by ECHA, refers directly to the uses of substance and defines chemicals as follows:

Definition 4: *'Chemical' means a substance whether by itself or in a mixture or preparation and whether manufactured or obtained from nature, but does not include any living organism. It consists of the following categories: pesticide (including severely hazardous pesticide formulations) and industrial* [14].

As a comparison – a definition established in response to standardization needs in the regulatory program for medicinal products by European Medicinal Agency (EMA):

Definition 5: *Substance is any matter of defined composition that has discrete existence, whose origin may be biological, mineral or chemical. Chemical substance is type of substance that can be described as stoichiometric or non-stoichiometric single molecular entity and is not a protein or nucleic acid substance. (Health informatics - Identification of medicinal products - Data elements and structures for the unique identification and exchange of regulated information on substances* [8].

At this stage it can be already understood that establishing the sameness of a chemical substance based only on their chemical descriptors becomes impossible. Apart from the complexity of the structure (composition), there are other elements that are taken into consideration in building its identity (origin, manufacturing process, form or state). As it can be observed, the definition of a chemical substance varies depending on the overall purpose.

The legal acts mentioned before and the respective regulatory activities often focus on substance in the context of some product or use (and less on a theoretical molecule), whereas monitoring aims to capture occurrences of chemicals in different media, e.g. environment (air, soil, water) or human body. The issue of 'instantiation' of a chemical substance in the material world brings interesting aspects, since it is placed in different 'locations' [6]. Ontological status based on location can be described as:

chemical   substance → material → industrial   product → consumer   product → waste[6]

A change of location (lab, manufacture site, market, waste disposal) of chemical substance implies a change of the relevant relationships (contexts). Diversity of locations brings new contexts captured as 'metadata' and is enriched with regulatory aspects – a reason and purpose for which the substance is subject to regulation.

---

[5] Regulation (EU) 649/2012 concerning the export and import of hazardous chemicals.

[6] The symbol of 'arrow' implies a change of location and not a succession of events.

2 Existing Standards for Chemical Data Exchange

2.1 IUCLID and OECD Harmonized Templates

The OECD[7] Harmonized Templates (OHTs) are standard data formats used by governments and industry to exchange information on risk assessment of chemicals (studies determining chemicals' properties or their effects on human health and the environment) and for storing data on use and exposure [13]. OECD and the European Commission have agreed on a standard XML format for data storing and sharing. The International Uniform Chemical Information Database platform (IUCLID) implements the OHTs and the management of the IUCLID format is done by the European Chemicals Agency (ECHA) in collaboration with the OECD. ECHA's mandate originates from REACH Article 111: *'The Agency shall specify formats and make them available free of charge'.*

IUCLID is used in the implementation of various regulatory programs, facilitating the reuse and exchange of the data. IUCLID is also the main repository of scientific data in ECHA, covering the information about e.g.:

- Chemical substances managed by the company, namely their:
  - identity, composition, and supporting analytical data; reference information (chemical descriptors); classification and labelling in terms of hazard; physical/chemical properties, toxicological and eco-toxicological properties,
- Use of and exposure to chemical substances.

2.2 Use Descriptor System and Sector Use Maps

The information on the use of and exposure to chemicals is organized in six OECD Harmonized Templates, covering different locations of the chemical in supply chain: Manufacture; Formulating or re-packing; Uses at industrial sites; Widespread use by professional workers; Consumer uses; Service life. In order to improve communication about chemicals in supply chain and to promote safer use thereof, ECHA and several stakeholder organizations have developed a plan called Chemical Safety Report/Exposure Scenario Roadmap (CSR/ES Roadmap), for which several industry organizations and Member States have signed the commitment charter. Use maps are generated by downstream user sector organizations in a harmonized and structured way. The manufacturers and formulators benefit from getting standardized information on uses and conditions of use that help them to carry out the chemical safety assessments. The downstream users (distributors, resellers) receive realistic and useful exposure scenarios for communication generated by suppliers based on use maps. As a result, the information can be exchanged and shared in more efficient way. The following 'use map packages' have been developed under the CSR/ES Roadmap:

- Detergents and Maintenance Products, Cosmetics and personal care products,
- Fuels, Construction Chemicals, Plastics Converters,

---

[7] OECD - The Organisation for Economic Co-operation and Development.

- Crop Protection, Fertilizers,
- Solvents, Adhesives and Sealants, Imaging and printing products [5].

2.3   The European Product Categorization System (EuPCS)

The European Product Categorization System (EuPCS) is used to describe 'the intended use of a mixture' according to Article 45 and Annex VIII of the CLP Regulation, which states that a hazardous mixture must be assigned a single product category by the importer or downstream user. The EuPCS can also be used by Member State appointed bodies or poison centers to facilitate comparable reporting and monitoring of poisoning incidents at EU level.

The EuPCS covers the categories for mixtures that are within the scope of Article 45 of CLP – namely, mixtures classified as hazardous based on their health effects or physical properties. Other product categories, including 'Cosmetics, food and tobacco products', 'Medicinal products and medical devices' and 'Drugs of abuse', are out of scope and not included. The system is a five-level hierarchical tree containing approximately 250 product categories [4].

2.4   Classification and Communication of Hazard (GHS/CLP)

In the area of classification substances and mixtures as hazardous there is an internationally agreed-upon standard managed by the United Nations: The Globally Harmonized System of Classification and Labelling of Chemicals (GHS). The system divides hazards into types (physical, human health and environmental) and classifies them depending on its nature. Substances are assigned to the relevant hazard classes based on their intrinsic properties and their hazard classification is categorized according to the level of severity. The system has been implemented in European Union as the CLP Regulation and United States Occupational Safety and Health Administration standards. Within the ECHA regulatory remits, hazard classification and labelling standards, with the information structure and permissible values, are provided as IUCLID template. It enables receiving and exchanging the information about substance classified as hazardous in a standardized way.

2.5   ECHA Ontologies

Two projects, conducted by European Chemicals Agency (ECHA) in cooperation with the Organization for Economic Co-operation and Development (OECD) and other organizations, resulted in developing controlled vocabularies (ontologies) for several toxicological endpoints. The set of controlled vocabularies include definition of classes and hierarchical relationships, synonymous and homonymous, compilation of terms related to the endpoint, establishing of relationships, interactions and hierarchies between classes, object and numeric properties for each term and rules, where relevant. The objective was to improve the integration of experimental data from different sources and the following domains have been covered: Carcinogenicity, Repeated Dose Toxicity, Reproductive/Developmental Toxicity, Skin irritation/corrosion, Eye irritation/corrosion, Skin sensitization.

3   Use Case, Initiatives and Further Developments

Substances are at the core of ECHA's business, its strategic objectives, and regulatory activities. A concept of *Regulatory Substance* has been introduced to establish a repository of regulated substances and to implement substance-centric view across regulations, realized in ECHA Dissemination website as *Substance InfoCards* and *Brief Profiles* [3].

Definition 6: *Regulatory Substance is any material that is subject of one or more of the regulations under responsibility or within interest of ECHA. Substance can be of chemical or biological type. Regulatory Substances are individual or classified as group based on specific properties or structure and for regulatory purpose. An instance of Regulatory Substance is uniquely identified by Regulatory Master List Index (RML Index) and described by chemical descriptors: CAS number, EC number[8], IUPAC Name, other names, molecular formula, etc.*

The concept of Regulatory Substance is a potential 'common denominator' and enabler of interoperability between regulatory bodies, including ECHA's sister Agencies, European Commission and national authorities. The study performed by ECHA in 2017 in the context of *EU Chemicals Legislation Finder* has identified the main 55 EU legislations that deal with and relate to chemicals:

- 9 **chemical** legislations, 4 exposure to chemical agents and chemical safety,
- 13 **products** control legislations, e.g. cosmetics, toys
- 18 environmental-related legislation
  - waste (7), water (5), industrial emissions and accidents (3), air-related (3)
- 6 food **safety** and food contact material legislations, 5 health and **safety** at work

Out of the 55 legislations currently four are within ECHA's remit and the remaining ones are implemented by European Commission, EU agencies and national authorities. Dealing with the regulatory activities separately creates unnecessary burden for the regulatory bodies, therefore agencies have already established a practice of exchanging information. The issue propagates to other stakeholders (e.g. industry obliged to comply with legislation or consumers seeking safe product) and hampers access to information on a specific substance, especially when the chemical is used for various applications covered by different pieces of legislation.

The exchange of regulated information in their context and reuse of data is challenging and comes with many semantic interoperability questions implied by differences in legislations, the interpretation of administrative procedures, the absence of universal reference data, models, controlled vocabularies, etc. Semantic interoperability in the EU Member States is promoted by a dedicated program - *Interoperability Solutions for European Public Administrations* (ISA/ISA2) [9]. The program supports seeking agreement on fundamental ('core') concepts that can be represented as 'Core Vocabulary' using different formalisms (e.g. XML, RDF or JSON). During the discussions with European Commission and ECHA's sister-agencies (EFSA, EMA,

---

[8] Identifier assigned to substances for regulatory purposes by the European Commission.

ECDC[9]) it was discussed that a similar approach could be considered for exchanging the information about regulated chemical substances and products and facilitating access to information for interested parties. Agreement on common concepts will be the first step towards semantic interoperability.

References

1. McNaught, A.D., Wilkinson, A.: IUPAC. Compendium of Chemical Terminology. The 'Gold Book', 2nd ed. Blackwell Scientific Publications, Oxford (1997). https://goldbook.iupac.org/html/C/C01039.html. Accessed 15 June 2018
2. CAS (Chemical Abstract Service). http://www.cas.org/content/chemical-substances. Accessed 10 June 2018
3. ECHA Dissemination website. https://echa.europa.eu/information-on-chemicals. Accessed 10 June 2018
4. ECHA EuPCS (2018). https://poisoncentres.echa.europa.eu/eu-product-categorisation-system. Accessed 15 June 2018
5. ECHA Use Maps. https://echa.europa.eu/csr-es-roadmap/use-maps/concept. Accessed 15 June 2018
6. Ghibaudi, E., Cerruti, L.: Chemical substance, material, product, goods, waste: a changing ontology. Found. Chem. **19**(2), 97–123 (2017)
7. Guidance in a Nutshell for identification and naming of substances under REACH and CLP. ECHA, April 2017
8. Health informatics - Identification of medicinal products - Data elements and structures for the unique identification and exchange of regulated information on substances (ISO11238:2012)
9. Interoperability solutions for European public administrations (ISA), eGovernment Core Vocabularies (2012). https://joinup.ec.europa.eu/sites/default/files/document/2012-02/ISA_eGovernment-Core-Vocabularies_February2012.pdf. Accessed 10 May 2018
10. ISA Program, P.E.: ISA2 Handbook for using Core Vocabularies. Publications Office of the European Union, Luxemburg (2015)
11. IUCLID 6. https://iuclid6.echa.europa.eu/project-iuclid-6. Accessed 15 June 2018
12. Hastings, J., Adams, N., Ennis, M., Hull, D., Steinbeck, C.: Chemical ontologies: what are they, what are they for and what are the challenges. Cheminform. **3**(Suppl 1) (2011). https://www.ncbi.nlm.nih.gov/pmc/articles/PMC3083557/. Accessed 20 May 2018
13. OECD Harmonized Templates (2018). https://www.oecd.org/ehs/templates/. Accessed 01 June 2018
14. Rotterdam Convention on the Prior Informed Consent Procedure for Certain Hazardous Chemicals and Pesticides in International Trade (2015). https://eur-lex.europa.eu/legal-content/EN/ALL/?uri=CELEX:22003A0306(01). Accessed 15 June 2018

---

[9] EFSA - European Food Safety Agency; EMA - European Medicines Agency; ECDC - European Centre for Disease Prevention and Control.

Semantics for Data in Agriculture: A Community-Based Wish List

Caterina Caracciolo[1]([✉]), Sophie Aubin[2], Brandon Whitehead[3],
and Panagiotis Zervas[4]

[1] Food and Agriculture Organization of the United Nations, Rome, Italy
caterina.caracciolo@fao.org
[2] INRA, UAR 1266, DIST Délégation Information Scientifique et Technique,
Versailles, France
sophie.aubin@inra.fr
[3] CABI, Wallingford, UK
b.whitehead@cabi.org
[4] Agroknow, Athens, Greece
pzervas@agroknow.com

Abstract. The paper reports on activities carried within the Agrisemantics Working Group of the Research Data Alliance (RDA). The group investigated on what are the current problems research and practitioners experience in their work with semantic resources for agricultural data and elaborated the list of requirements that are the object of this paper. The main findings include the need to broaden the usability of tools so as to make them useful and available to the variety of profiles usually involved in working with semantics resources; the need to online platform to lift users from the burden of local installation; and the need for services that can be integrated in workflows. We further analyze requirements concerning the tools and services and provide details about the process followed to gather evidence from the community.

Keywords: Semantics · Agricultural data · Vocabularies · Ontologies

1 Introduction

Increasing attention is being devoted to the use of semantics to achieve data interoperability [1, 2]. However, challenges still remain in making the technology of broader use. The goal of the Agrisemantics Working Group (WG) within the Research Data Alliance (RDA) is to gather researchers and practitioners interested in the use of semantics in conjunction with agricultural data. In this paper we report on one activity of the group, aim at finding out what the main issues and bottlenecks the community experience when working with semantic resources, and what are the requirements to overcome them. "Semantic resources" in this context refers to "...structures of varying nature, complexity and formats used for the purpose of expressing the "meaning" of data" [3], be those textual or numeric. Controlled vocabularies, value lists, classification systems, glossaries, thesauri, and ontologies are all example of semantic structures. They may be expressed in a variety of formats, open or proprietary, machine-readable

© Springer Nature Switzerland AG 2019
E. Garoufallou et al. (Eds.): MTSR 2018, CCIS 846, pp. 340–345, 2019.
https://doi.org/10.1007/978-3-030-14401-2_32

or not. This broad definition then includes both the "vocabularies" as defined by W3C[1] (i.e., including metadata elements and value vocabularies, aka knowledge organization systems), and ontologies, be those lightweight or with richer descriptions and logical axioms.

Our first activity focused on delineating the applications of semantic resources in agriculture [3]. Now, we report on our second activity, aimed at surveying the real-life problems and bottlenecks that researchers and practitioners encounter when using semantic resources, together with their wishes and/or proposed solutions. We digested the input gathered from the community into requirements. The next step will be to distill our findings into a set of recommendations for e-infrastructures that aim at supporting researchers and practitioners in their work with agricultural data. We were particularly interested in identifying needs concerning: (a) access to useful semantic resources, (b) reusability of semantic resources either by human or machines, (c) tools and services to create, manage, improve, interlink, publish semantic resources, (d) use of semantic resources or services in applications and (e) standards and best practices to represent and exchange semantic resources.

2 Use Case Collection: Methodology and Results

Input was collected using a template, defined by the group chairs with feedback from the Agrisemantics WG members. Respondents were invited to answer 4 core questions (to describe the limitations or difficulties they face) and 4 additional questions concerning their role and the context of their work. All questions were open-ended, provided with some explanations expressed in the form of questions to guide respondents in articulating their answer.

As a result, we received 20 use cases. All use cases were summarized in a spreadsheet, then the requirements drawn from each use case were organized using an online mind map software. The graphical mind map was also used as a basis for discussion within the working group. The map together with all use cases are available from the RDA Agrisemantics Working Group web space[2]. The set of requirements resulting from this process were further discussed and finalized in the course of a workshop during the RDA P11 in Berlin (March 2018), with the participation of about 30 people. In the following, the requirements gathered are synthesized and presented.

We collected 20 use cases, from institutions based in 10 distinct countries from 4 continents (15 from Europe, 2 from North and 2 from South America, 1 from Asia), mostly from research organizations (15), 3 international organizations, 1 professional and 1 governmental organization.

From the use cases, it emerges that a number of different roles and backgrounds are involved in different tasks dealing with semantic resources, showing that the process of producing semantic resources is highly collaborative and requires various competencies. Also, virtually all tasks are mentioned in the use cases, from when semantic

---

[1] https://www.w3.org/standards/semanticweb/ontology.

[2] https://www.rd-alliance.org/deliverable-2-use-cases-and-requirements.

resources are first created to their retrieval and use in applications. The evidence we collected shows that there are as many toolkits as projects, covering all steps in the data life cycle and project workflow, from editing a semantic resource to its use in a given application. The great majority of use cases combine open source and ad-hoc tools, often developed in-house, while the commercial solutions adopted tend to be integrated platforms covering various phases of the semantic resources life cycle, for which no equivalent product is available for free and/or as open source. Almost half of the use cases mention of RDF technologies, in particular triple stores.

3 Requirements

The high level message collected is that semantic technologies/methodologies need to be made more accessible both in terms of skills and resources required for their development and use. In particular:

RQ1. Tools designed for use with semantic resources should also be accessible to non-ontologists. More specifically, more attention should be paid to graphical interfaces, terms used, support for validation, and for methodological support in each task.

RQ2. Online platforms are needed to lift the burden of local (or ad-hoc) installations and maintenance from users or individuals.

RQ3. Common tasks involving semantic resources (e.g. editing, format conversion, etc.) should be integrated, or integratable to form flexible and interoperable workflows, to minimize the breadth of skills required to work with semantic resources.

We further analyzed the last requirement above identifying four tasks: (1) Creation and maintenance (2) Mapping (3) Use in applications and (4) Discoverability and availability.

3.1 Creation and Maintenance

This phase includes all tasks involved in the creation and evolution of a semantic resource.

1. Editing tools should be designed having in mind that different users, and therefore competencies, are involved in various (sub)phases of the editing tasks. For example, it is important that domain experts are enabled to understand and provide feedback on the semantic resources implemented by the knowledge manager.
2. Tools used in different phases of the editing process should be integrated. Editing a semantic resource is often articulated in subtasks like eliciting and formalizing the knowledge, validating the resulting structure with domain experts, searching and reusing fragments from other resources or creating alignments with other sources. It should be possible to move from one activity to the other in an unfragmented way.
3. Tools should integrate methodologies for modeling, quality checking, and valida-tion. They may implement heuristics to warn risks and possibly suggest alternative modeling decisions or specific resources to reuse.

4. Online platform(s) should be available to those who cannot afford hosting and maintaining platform in-house. They are also important to enable collaborative work.

In the following, we provide specific requirements for each of the main task above. Then we discuss some issues related to availability and formats of semantic resources, as emerged from the use cases and the face-to-face discussion.

3.2 Mapping

This phase focuses on the alignment of semantic resources, consisting in the creation of mappings between them [4]. Here we refer to the mapping activity in general, independently of the type of mapping to establish, or of the reason for engaging in the task.

1. Tools should make available state-of-art algorithms for the automatic extraction of candidate mappings. Competitive algorithms too often remain as research products that require advanced computing skills to reuse in another context and, as such, are difficult to install and configure, have poor or no interface at all, and offer no support to users.
2. Tools should integrate methodologies and best practice to support users during the various steps involved in the process, including searching for existing mappings to reuse, supporting the actual mapping creation (in case of manual creation) or validating those automatically generated.
3. Promote a standard to represent mapping involving semantic resources in not or little machine-actionable formats, e.g., spreadsheets.
4. Promote a standard way to annotate spreadsheets with semantic resources, in particular column heading referring to common concepts of the domain.
5. Appropriate graphical interface should be available to allow users validate mappings independently from their skill level regarding semantics. This requirement is especially important considering the critical role that human validation plays in making mappings useful.

3.3 Use

Under this heading we group together tasks related to the actual use of semantic resources in applications. We discuss this group in isolation to emphasize the variety of factors essential to make semantic resources used and usable.

1. Services should be available that notify updates of a semantic resource to the application using it. This is to avoid that changes in a semantic resource are not reflected in the applications, causing delays in updates and possible breaks in the services provided by the application.
2. Appropriate interfaces, formats, training, and documentation should be made available to tool developers to encourage the introduction of semantics in end user applications. The use of semantic resources is too often perceived as something that requires very specialized knowledge, and a steep learning curve to achieve it.
3. "Low-level resources" should be created and made available by and to the community, and well maintained when already existing. Such "low-level" resources are of

fundamental importance in real-life applications as they represent the actual subjects of observation, measurement and research - e.g., crop varieties, livestock, pests.

4. Services and metrics to assess resources usage should be developed. Ways to quantify and evaluate their use could help maintainers prioritize their resources and effort, and funders get a grasp of the use of their funding.

3.4   Discoverability and Accessibility

This section focuses on all elements considered relevant to find and access semantic resources online. In this area, we support the recommendations made through the FAIR principles [5].

1. The use of global identifiers should be encouraged and supported. Global identifiers, e.g., URIs or DOIs, are the basis of accessibility over the web.
2. Automatic creation of metadata should be supported by tools to the greatest extent possible, leading to increased availability of metadata and better quality (e.g., up-to-date, rich or in consistent formats).
3. Datasets' metadata should always specify the semantic resources in them. Despite major metadata schemes, e.g., DCAT[3], do include properties for that purpose, these properties are often not supported by data and content management systems (i.e., services like CKAN[4], Dataverse[5], DataCite[6], and CrossRef[7]) or not enforced. This limits the possibilities of automatic search and integration of datasets.

3.5   Semantic Resources in Agriculture and Nutrition

While most of the input collected focused on tools and services, it also touched on the availability of semantic resources on specific topics. The main claims for such reference resources are: (1) to avoid duplicated efforts, and (2) to augment interoperability among datasets, information systems, and semantic resources themselves. Efforts should be made to:

1. Have machine-actionable reference lists of "entities" important to agriculture provided with global identifiers for use in applications, such as pests, diseases, livestock, agricultural activities (i.e., the "low-level resources" mentioned above).
2. Support the use of semantic resources in conjunction with quantitative data as the usefulness of many semantic resources developed to tag or index textual information data is limited when applied to numeric data qualified by measurements (e.g., different units, such as cubic tons or cubic meters, or different measuring methods, such as pH in water or in non-aqueous solutions).

---

[3] https://www.w3.org/TR/vocab-dcat/.

[4] https://ckan.org/.

[5] https://dataverse.org/.

[6] https://www.datacite.org/.

[7] https://www.crossref.org/.

4 Conclusions

Many of the requirements hint a need to publish existing semantic resources according to Semantic Web standards, to make them openly accessible, machine-readable, and exposed in triple stores with the twofold goal of increasing data interoperability and avoiding duplication. We appreciate that some initiatives are already being carried on in this sense (e.g. within GODAN and by individuals and organizations gathering around the RDA and GODAN communities) but, as also reported as a finding of our landscaping activity, this effort certainly needs to be further promoted.

We noticed that many of the requirements presented are not specific to agriculture. This matches our understanding of semantics as something general, cross-domain. Instead, what we found very domain specific is the community environment, characterized by the resources used, and the social side of the work, i.e. the terminology adopted, the type of training they have access to, and the expectations about interfaces and functionalities.

Considering that semantics is key to both efficient data discoverability and integrability to serve better research in agriculture, we call on the community of engineers and researchers who develop methods and tools to manipulate and use semantic resources to consider the requirements expressed in the use cases we collected and synthetized in this paper.

Acknowledgments. The work of Caterina Caracciolo contributing to this paper was supported by the Cross-Cutting project, funded by the Bill and Melinda Gates Foundation. The views expressed in this information product are those of the author and do not necessarily reflect the views or policy of FAO.

The work of Panagiotis Zervas presented in this paper has been partly supported by the AGINFRA PLUS Project that is funded by the European Commission's Horizon 2020 research and innovation program under grant agreement No 731001.

References

1. Haav, H., Kungas, P.: Semantic data interoperability: the key problem of big data. In: Big Data Computing. CRC Press (2014)
2. Villa, F., Balbi, S., Athanasiadis, I., Caracciolo, C.: Semantics for interoperability of distributed data and models: foundations for better-connected information. F1000Research **6** (2017). https://f1000research.com/articles/6-686/v1. Accessed 7 Feb 2019. (version 1; referees: 1 approved with reservations)
3. Aubin, S., Caracciolo, C., Zervas, P.: Landscaping the Use of Semantics to Enhance the Interoperability of Agricultural Data. Agrisemantics Working Group. https://www.rd-alliance. org/deliverable-1-landscaping. Accessed 22 Aug 2018
4. Shvaiko, P., Euzenat, J.: Ontology matching: state of the art and future challenges. IEEE Trans. Knowl. Data Eng. **25**, 1 (2013). https://doi.org/10.1109/TKDE.2011.253
5. Wilkinson, M.D., et al.: The FAIR guiding principles for scientific data management and stewardship. Sci. Data **3**(1), 160018 (2016). https://doi.org/10.1038/sdata.2016.18

Development of Methodologies
and Standardized Services for Supporting
Forest Economics

Thomas Katagis[1]($\boxtimes$), Nikolaos Grammalidis[2], Evangelos Maltezos[3],
Vasiliki Charalampopoulou[3], and Ioannis Z. Gitas[1]

[1] Laboratory of Forest Management and Remote Sensing,
AUTH, Thessaloniki, Greece
thkatag@for.auth.gr
[2] Information Technologies Institute, CERTH, Thessaloniki, Greece
[3] Geosystems Hellas S.A., Athens, Greece

Abstract. In the Mediterranean region, many types of forests are non-productive or degraded, although they could substantially contribute to growth of local economies. In Greece, 30% of the total area is covered by forests, however their contribution to the GDP is almost non-existent. An example is the chestnut production in Thessaly region of Greece, and especially in Mouzaki municipality, which is almost abandoned due to insufficient agricultural policies concerning establishment of alternative crops, and consequently leads to loss of potential income for the rural economy. The ARTEMIS project, funded by the Greek Secretariat for Research and Technology, aims at delivering an innovative information platform providing systematically high quality Earth Observation based products and services for monitoring forest health and supporting eventually the growth of forestry related economy and market. The architecture of the proposed platform will incorporate new OGC/ISO technologies, while the applicability of existing metadata standards for management of geospatial datasets will be evaluated. A pilot implementation of the developed system will be conducted in a selected area in Thessaly region of Greece.

Keywords: Forest economics · Forest monitoring · Earth Observation ·
Forestry metadata

1 Introduction

Forests provide a wide range of products and ecosystem services, including wood supply, food security, raw materials, energy resources, biodiversity conservation. In addition, forests provide a multitude of environmental, social and cultural benefits related to climate regulation, human health, recreation, fresh water supply, to name just a few. At the same time, forests provide substantial economic benefits at local to national level through wood and non-wood related industries and investments in the forest sector [1]. More specifically, economic benefits are usually measured in monetary terms and may include: income from employment in the sector; the value of the production of goods and services from forests; and the contribution of the sector to the

© Springer Nature Switzerland AG 2019
E. Garoufallou et al. (Eds.): MTSR 2018, CCIS 846, pp. 346–351, 2019.
https://doi.org/10.1007/978-3-030-14401-2_33

national economy, energy supplies and international trade. The economic viability or sustainability of the sector can be assessed by measures such as the profitability of forest enterprises or the level of investment. Currently, the EU strategy aims to place forests and the forest sector at the heart of the path towards a green economy and to value the benefits that forests can sustainably deliver, while ensuring their protection.

In the Mediterranean region, many types of forests are non-productive or degraded, although they could substantially contribute to local economies, at least [2]. For example, in Greece, 30% of the total area is covered by forests but their contribution to the GDP is almost non-existent. An example is the chestnut production in Thessaly, Greece, and especially at the forests of Mouzaki municipality, which is almost abandoned due to insufficient agricultural policies concerning establishment of alternative crops and the lack of support policies for enhancing rural economies, thus forcing younger populations to move to urban areas.

A sustainable forest management that would also foster commercial exploitation of forest resources and market development of non-wood products should take into account the following: (a) selection of crops, (b) compliance with rules and protocols; and (c) adaptation and modification of cultivation practices using new monitoring technologies, such as remote sensing, near-real-time satellite meteorology combined with rural data and ICT/computer vision technologies.

The ARTEMIS project, funded by the Greek Secretariat for Research and Technology, aims at delivering an innovative information platform providing systematically high quality products and services for assessing forest condition and threats, both abiotic and biotic. The proposed services and products will be potentially useful for exploitation of raw materials, for creation of product certifications and for supporting market development of non-wood goods thus increasing employment and healthy economic growth. This monitoring system will be capable of processing multi-scale forest related geospatial and in-situ datasets and will be initially implemented for chestnut or similar cultivations. Based on the data requirements of ARTEMIS, we are going to evaluate the applicability of existing metadata standards in our application in order to select/define an appropriate forest information metadata standard, while the ISO 19115 will be used for describing geospatial metadata.

2 Proposed Approach

The proposed methodological approach of ARTEMIS is displayed in Fig. 1. The envisaged output is the creation of a reliable forest health monitoring platform based on the seamless integration of Earth Observation data and products as well as data stemming from a multi-sensor system designed to assess the status and changes of indicators of forests health condition. Modern state of the art remote sensing technologies will provide the means for wide coverage measurement of forest health with reasonable accuracy.

The satellite data to be used will be provided from modern satellite receivers (spectral, hyperspectral and SAR) [3, 4]. Particular emphasis will be given to satellite data and products provided from the European Union's Earth Observation Copernicus Program[1]. Satellite data from the Sentinel missions and other contributing satellites offer high temporal and spatial resolution and facilitate systematic vegetation monitoring.

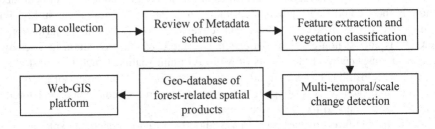

Fig. 1. Proposed methodology for forest monitoring

The main methodological steps related to data processing and algorithm development can be summarized as follows:

- Collection and pre-processing of satellite images and vector datasets from multiple sources (aerial, terrestrial field measurements, existing spatial databases). Radar (SAR) and optical and images from Sentinel-1&2 missions respectively and contributing satellites will be employed.
- Development of advanced semi-automated techniques for classification and mapping of vegetation types and species. Such techniques will be based on advanced deep learning techniques (e.g. Convolutional Neural Networks, CNNs), dual tree complex wavelet transform [5], and texture and dynamic feature analysis [6, 7].
- Appropriate combinations of SAR polarities (Sentinel-1 VV, VH and VH/VV) will be selected to identify different land uses and distinguish between different types of vegetation or crops.
- Specific vegetation indices will be selected, which are related both to plant physiology characteristics, and structural variations of forests. Indicators based on visible and infrared wavelengths such as the broadband NDVI, SR and EVI, and narrowband indices using reflectance at specific wavelengths (e.g. TCARI and MCARI1 indices) will be investigated.
- Synthesis of indicators to create multi-temporal forest condition/health maps.
- Development of a time series analysis algorithm, based on vegetation indices, for accurate spatio-temporal monitoring of vegetation changes. Forest areas and cultivations will be monitored by combining multi-modal satellite imagery and their derivatives (vegetation and health indicators). The aim is to identify and discriminate areas of gradual (plant disease, water stress) or abrupt (logging, fires) change.

The final step is to design and develop the architecture of the WEBGIS platform that will incorporate the following features: (a) Free access to the products by the users

---

[1] http://copernicus.eu/main/sentinels.

by implementing new OGC/ISO technologies for the dissemination and processing of data through services (WMS, WFS, WCS, WPS), (b) Development of an online platform for data processing folders and databases in near real time; (c) Development of specific software that will test, homogenize and merge the measurements that will result from field campaigns. For faster processing operations, it will be possible to automatically create pyramids and thumbnails when listing new data and convert their metadata according to ISO 19115, the industry standard for geospatial metadata. The display and navigation will be in two (2D) or three (3D) dimensions for improved visualization of the forests. The developed algorithms and chains will be imported to the system and will be executed as a Web Processing Service (WPS). Finally, the user or stakeholder will be able to create a database search form via SQL queries and visualize the results on the map, as well as to generate reports through an Incident Reporting module.

The proposed approach will be evaluated within a pilot setup of the system for selected forests in Mouzaki municipality, in the Thessaly region, Greece during a 14 month period. During this period, the services will be implemented and evaluated extensively in selected forest areas with chestnut trees. Producers will be trained to use the new service and become familiar with the modern geospatial technologies.

3 Forestry Metadata Formats

Metadata is data about other data [8] and have a vital role for digital information management as they facilitate search, allowing users to identify important information and resources. For the specific fields of agriculture and forestry, a recent overview of the standards of metadata areas is provided in the work by Santos and Riyuiti [9]. Specifically, a number of standards (Dublin Core, Darwin Core, AgMES, AGRIS, Agrovoc, AgroXML, agXML) are reviewed and their scope of use and characteristics are described and their quality is assessed. A metadata schema for forestry related information resources based on the Dublin Core Metadata (DCMI) was developed by NEFIS project [10]. This model is then extended in Tilsner [11], where a metadata model for the European Forest Information and Communication Platform (EFICP) is presented, in order to support online access and exchange of forestry specific statistical data. Beyond Europe, other initiatives include the Canadian National Forest Information System and the GeoGratis portal [12]. The latter infrastructures focus on interoperability between geospatial data sources and provide web services to geospatial information, based on the Open Geospatial Consortium (OGC) Standards.

Based on the data requirements of ARTEMIS, we are going to evaluate the applicability of these standards and related geospatial formats (e.g. shapefile, Geotiff, geodatabase, .xls, xml, etc.) in our application in order to define an appropriate forest information metadata standard. Commercial and open-source metadata software tools, designed for data integration in database systems, will be additionally evaluated. In order to ensure compatibility with the requirements of INSPIRE[2] directive on geo-referenced

---

[2] http://inspire.ec.europa.eu/documents/Metadata/MD_IR_and_ISO_20131029.pdf.

data, it is strongly recommended to apply the rules laid down in ISO 19115 for creating a metadata profile. A good example of an INSPIRE-based profile for geographic metadata that can be employed, is the European Environment Agency (EEA) Metadata Profile[3], which has been developed to meet the needs and demands for interoperability of metadata. Due to ARTEMIS requirements, two basic categories of metadata are foreseen:

- *Metadata related to the final geospatial products and corresponding services.* These products will contain detailed information on forest condition, vegetation species, temporal changes, etc., as described previously. ARTEMIS will perform an extensive review on established schemes as implemented by international agencies. For example, the EUNIS habitat classification will be reviewed, which is the classification standard for the INSPIRE Directive. EUNIS is a comprehensive pan-European system that facilitates harmonized description and collection of habitat data across Europe. The pan-European components of the Copernicus Land Monitoring Service will be also considered. These include the CORINE Land Cover classification scheme, as well as the High Resolution (HR) Layers. Specific attention will be given to the Forest HR Layer.
- *Metadata related to Earth Observation (EO) and remote sensing data.* A common metadata framework will be defined to support metadata from all ARTEMIS input data sources, and especially the remote sensing ones, based on recent geospatial metadata standards, such as the ISO 19115. Given the abundance of EO imagery mainly due to free data access policies for Landsat and Copernicus missions, the thorough study and mapping of metadata can greatly benefit research and operational applications. Existing comprehensive guides, such as the NASA ESDIS Unified Metadata Model (UMM), and software libraries, e.g. the HDF-EOS5 Data Model[4], are extensively utilized for management of EO metadata information. The continuous and seamless data flow within the ARTEMIS platform will require a specific adaptation of these standards.

4   Conclusions

A new approach for forest monitoring is presented aiming at preserving the quality, health and sustainable development of economic forests and particularly chestnut forests. The forest health platform outputs are expected to provide timely and updated information on forest condition, which will be considered a valuable supplement to standard forest management plans and reporting at regional level. Furthermore, the proposed monitoring system will promote health status reporting at broad scales, beyond local needs, enhancing cooperation among various agencies. Through the incorporation of widely accepted metadata standards and formats, the establishment of

---

[3] https://taskman.eionet.europa.eu/projects/public-docs/wiki/Cataloguemetadata_guidelines.

[4] https://cdn.earthdata.nasa.gov/conduit/upload/4880/ESDS-RFC-008-v1.1.pdf

links and potential collaborations with current platforms, such as the ESA driven Forestry Thematic Exploitation Platform (Forestry TEP) and forest information agencies (European Forest Institute, EFI) will be promoted.

Acknowledgements. This work was prepared in the framework of the ARTEMIS project, which is co-financed by the European Union and Greek national funds through the Operational Program Competitiveness, Entrepreneurship and Innovation, under the call RESEARCH – CREATE – INNOVATE (project code: T1EDK-01577).

References

1. Joint Research Centre Homepage. http://forest.jrc.ec.europa.eu/activities/forest-ecosystem-services/. Accessed 09 June 2018
2. Allard, G., et al.: State of Mediterranean Forests 2013 (2013)
3. Addabbo, P., Focareta, M., Marcuccio, S., Votto, C., Ullo, S.L.: Contribution of sentinel-2 data for applications in vegetation monitoring. ACTA IMEKO **5**, 44 (2016)
4. Dostálová, A., Hollaus, M., Milenković, M., Wagner, W.: Forest area derivation from sentinel-1 data. ISPRS Ann. Photogram. Remote Sens. Spat. Inf. Sci. **III-7**, 227–233 (2016)
5. Kingsbury, N.: A dual-tree complex wavelet transform with improved orthogonality and symmetry properties. In: Proceedings of 2000 International Conference on Image Processing 2000, vol. 2. IEEE (2000)
6. Dimitropoulos, K., Barmpoutis, P., Kitsikidis, A., Grammalidis, N.: Classification of multidimensional time-evolving data using histograms of Grassmannian points. IEEE Trans. Circ. Syst. Video Technol. **28**(4), 892–905 (2016)
7. Dimitropoulos, K., Barmpoutis, P., Kitsikidis, A., Grammalidis, N.: Extracting dynamics from multi-dimensional time-evolving data using a bag of higher-order linear dynamical systems. In: International Conference on Computer Vision Theory and Applications (VISAPP 2016), Rome, Italy, February 2016
8. Weibel, S.: Metadata: the foundations of resource description. D-Lib Magazine. http://www.dlib.org/dlib/July95/07weibel.html. Accessed 09 June 2018
9. Santos, C., Riyuiti, A.: An overview of the use of metadata in agriculture. IEEE Lat. Am. Trans. **10**, 1265–1267 (2012)
10. Schuck, A., Green, T., Requardt, A., Richards, T.: A metadata schema for forest information resources. The FBMIS Group **1**, 11–21 (2006)
11. Tilsner, D., et al.: Metadata model for the European forest information and communication platform. Int. J. Spat. Data Infrastruct. Res. **2**, 112–131 (2008)
12. Goodenough, D.G., et al.: Grid-enabled OGC environment for EO data and services in support of Canada's forest applications. In: 2007 IEEE International Geoscience and Remote Sensing Symposium, pp. 4773–4776. IEEE (2007)

Open Repositories, Research Information Systems and Data Infrastructures

Open Citation Content Data

Mikhail Kogalovsky[3] , Thomas Krichel[1], Victor Lyapunov[1],
Oxana Medvedeva[1], Sergey Parinov[1,2(✉)] , and Varvara Sergeeva[1]

[1] Russian Presidential Academy of National Economy and Public
Administration (RANEPA), Moscow, Russia
`sparinov@gmail.com`
[2] Central Economics and Mathematics Institute of RAS (CEMI RAS),
Moscow, Russia
[3] Market Economy Institute of RAS (MEI RAS), Moscow, Russia

Abstract. There are several projects in the research community to make the citation data extracted from research papers more re-usable. This paper presents results from the CyrCitEc project to create a publicly available source of open citation content data extracted from PDF papers available at a research information system. To reach this aim the project team has created four outputs: (1) an open source software to parse papers' metadata and full text PDFs; (2) an open service to process papers' PDFs to extract citation data; (3) a dataset of citation data, including citation contexts (currently mostly for papers in Cyrillic); and (4) a visualization tool that provides users insight into the citation data extraction process and gives some control over the citation data parsing quality.

Keywords: Open data · Citation content · CyrCitEc · RePEc · Socionet

1 Introduction

Currently there is a clear trend in the research community to make the citation data extracted from research papers more re-usable. One example is the OpenCitations project. Its main aim is "the creation and current expansion of the Open Citations Corpus (OCC), an open repository of scholarly citation data made available under a Creative Commons public domain dedication, which provides in RDF accurate citation information (bibliographic references) harvested from the scholarly literature" (http://opencitations.net/). As of June 1, 2018 this project provides references from 302,758 citing bibliographic resources. It contains information about 12,830,347 citation links to 6,549,665 cited resources.

The primary focus of the OpenCitation project is the references from research papers. Another part of the citation data that also available in research papers is the citation content or context.

In recent years, methods for analyzing the content of citations have been actively developed. Some studies (Ding et al. 2014) present a concept of the content-based citation analysis (CCA), which addresses a citation's value. It became a common view that "the text of citation context is used to characterize publications for various applications, such as publication summarization, survey article generation and

E. Garoufallou et al. (Eds.): MTSR 2018, CCIS 846, pp. 355–364, 2019.
https://doi.org/10.1007/978-3-030-14401-2_34

information retrieval" (He and Chen 2017). Other authors wrote: "the extraction of citation contexts is a preliminary step to any statistical, distributional, syntactic or semantic analysis" (Bertin and Atanassova 2018). Also "to capture document usage, we observe that the context in which one document cites another tends to reflect how a document is used, namely, within a document, people tend to cite other documents for very precise reasons" (Berger et al. 2017).

One of few already existing sources of open citation content data is the In-text Reference Corpus (InTeReC) available at https://zenodo.org/record/1203737. Currently the InTeReC dataset provides 314023 sentences containing in-text references (also called as the in-text citations) together with other useful data. The sentences are extracted from 90,071 research articles published by PLOS up to September 2013 (Bertin and Atanassova 2018).

A full text of each sentence in InTeReC (Bertin and Atanassova 2018) is supplemented by:

- a journal title;
- DOI of the article from which the sentence was extracted;
- size of the article, as number of sentences, and a position of the sentence in the article, as number of sentences from the beginning of the article;
- size of the section, as number of sentences, and a position of the sentence in the section, as number of sentences from the beginning of the section;
- section type (introduction, method, results, etc.);
- a list of verb phrases that occur in the sentence.

Our project CyrCitEc[1] provides a new source of open citation content data. The project is funded by the Russian Presidential Academy of National Economy and Public Administration (RANEPA, http://www.ranepa.ru/eng/). The first result of this project was presented in (Barrueco et al. 2017).

The project has two main aims: (1) to create the CyrCitEc system - a public service for processing available research papers full text (particularly, in PDF and with a focus on Social Sciences), in order to build and regularly update an open dataset of citation relationships and citations content; (2) to use the citation content data for developing methods of qualitative citation analysis, which can be used for improving of current practice of a research performance assessment.

The project builds a pilot version of open scholarly infrastructure (Bilder et al. 2015) based on the following pillars:

1. Open distributed architecture. The project provides a concept, open source software[2] and an initial core infrastructure for interoperable systems, which are processing citation relationships and its content from research papers' full text.
2. Two initial nodes of this core infrastructure, presented by interacting CitEc (http://citec.repec.org/) and CyrCitEc systems. Currently these nodes are exchanging by citations data. The nodes have a specialization on processing papers in specific

---

[1] https://github.com/citeccyr/CyrCitEc_method.

[2] https://github.com/citeccyr.

languages: Romano-Germanic languages by CitEc and Russian by CyrCitEc. Other nodes, e.g. specialized on processing citation data in languages, like Chinese, Japanese, Arabic, etc., could be added by the same way. There is also an intention to integrate data about references into the OpenCitations Corpus (http://opencitations.net/).

3. Transparency. It allows publishers, authors and readers of papers to see how the citation data of their papers are extracted by the system and to trace why some papers' references/in-text citations are not processed or not counted.
4. Better representation and usability of citation data by its deeper integration with research information system tools and services.
5. Enrichment facilities. The system provides tools for authors of papers to enter additional data to correct errors of processing citations found in their papers and to enrich their citation relationships, e.g. by qualitative characteristics of their motivation for citing papers of other authors, etc.
6. Public control. Readers of papers can see how authors used enrichment facilities to increase their number of citations. Thus, they will be able to react to authors misbehaviour.

CyrCitEc takes papers' metadata from the Socionet (https://socionet.ru/), which also includes a full set of metadata from RePEc (http://repec.org).

Comparing with InTeReC, the CyrCitEc system has following main differences:

(a)   an openness for adding new papers for processing by the system. The papers just have to be added to a Socionet or into RePEc;
(b)   the system works as a part of an infrastructure, i.e. in everyday mode it automatically processes all new available papers and updates citation content data;
(c)   the input papers are in PDF (InTeReC works with papers in XML).

Unlike of InTeReC authors using the term "in-text reference", we in CyrCitEc use the term "in-text citation". It is defined as: "the in-text citations of publications are the citations referred to this publication in the full text of other publications cited this publication. The text around the in-text citation is the citation context text" (He and Chen 2017).

The second section of the paper presents the open citation content data provided by the CyrCitEc project for public re-use.

In the third section, we describe a visualization tool of the citation content data which creates a transparence on how the citation data is produced step by step. It also allows some public control over results of citation data parsing.

The last section briefly discusses possible further development of this project.

2   Open Citation Content Data from the CyrCitEc Project

In the beginning of June 2018, CyrCitEc processed 220 collections of papers with 100,553 publications in total (see Table 1 for more statistics). The biggest part of this set are 157 Russian academic journals covering different academic disciplines and provided by the NEICON consortium. There are also research papers series in Russian and English languages provided by Russian Universities (RANEPA, Higher Scholl of Economics, etc.) and by research organizations of Russian Academy of Sciences.

An approach used by CyrCitEc for the citation content data parsing was presented in (Parinov 2017).

All extracted by CyrCitEc project citation data and processing log files are publicly available at http://cirtec.ranepa.ru/data/. This storage is organized as nested folders with names based on Socionet IDs of processed papers. A processed paper's folder contains: (a) JSON version of PDF papers (the file 0.pdf-stream.json), which was used for parsing citation data; (b) file "summary.xml" with the parsed citation data; and (c) reports about errors in processing the paper and parsing citation data (files with extensions ".err" and ".log").

A single in-text citation includes following data:

(1) a text string of how this in-text citation is occurred in a paper content, e.g. a number or an author name in square or round brackets (the tag <Exact> in the example below);
(2) a link to a reference, mentioned in this in-text citation (the tag <Reference> below);
(3) text coordinates of the in-text citation, i.e. a serial number of the first and the last in-text citation symbols counting from the begging of the paper's content (tags <Start> and <End>);
(4) citation contexts located at the left and at the right according the in-text citation; it includes at least 200 symbols expanded for taking a whole sentence (tags <Prefix> and <Suffix>).

An example of parsed data for one in-text citation:

```
<intextref>
  <Prefix>… countries and Soviet republics</Prefix>
  <Suffix>; Gokhberg, Kuznetsova, 2011]. …</Suffix>
  <Start>8757</Start>
  <End>8781</End>
  <Exact>[Gokhberg et al., 2009</Exact>
  <Reference>20</Reference>
</intextref>
```

Source: https://goo.gl/vfNRgJ

The in-text citation from the example above has a link with a reference having the number 20 in the paper. CyrCitEc parsed for this reference following data:

```
<reference num="20" start="54464" end="54654"
  author="Gokhberg Kuznetsova …" title="Towards …"
  year="2009"
  handle="repec:oup:scippl:v:36:y:2009:i:2:p:121-126">
<from_pdf>Gokhberg L., Kuznetsova T., Zaichenko
  S. (2009) Towards a New Role of Universities in Russia:
  Prospects and Limitations. Science and Public Policy,
  vol. 36, no 2, pp. 121-126.</from_pdf>
</reference>
```

Source: https://goo.gl/vfNRgJ

XML data of the example above includes following subtags and attributes:

(a) subtag `<from_pdf>` - extracted raw data of a reference (some publishers provide reference data within the papers' metadata, see the subtags `<from_metadata>` in the example at https://goo.gl/tKRZF1);

(b) attribute num - a serial number of the reference in the paper's list of references;

(c) attributes `start` and end - text coordinates of the reference, which are numbers of the first and the last symbols of the reference counted from the beginning of the initial PDF document's text;

(d) attribute url - contains a proper URL, if there is one in data of the tag `<from_pdf>`;

(e) attributes `author`, `title` and year are extracted from the raw reference data in the tag `<from_pdf>` and used for different purposes, e.g. for searching the in-text citations at Socionet for linking the reference with metadata of the same paper (creating a citation relationship for this reference), etc.;

(f) attribute handle - contains ID of the paper at Socionet, if the linking procedure for this reference was successful.

These data about in-text citations and references are supplemented by the ID of paper's metadata (see `<source handle=` in the example below) and by the URL of the source full text PDF of the paper (see `<futli url=` below). Having the paper's metadata ID and using Socionet API one can take all available information about this paper, including its title, abstract, authors, etc.

```
<source handle="repec:hig:fsight:v:11:y:2017:i:4:…">
<futli url="https://foresight-journal.hse.ru/data/…">
```

Source: https://goo.gl/vfNRgJ

Comparing with InTeReC, the CyrCitEc data have following main differences:

1. the citation content is organized as two text strings: at the right and at the left side according the in-text citation location; and it can provides several sentences instead of one sentence in InTeReC;

2. a broader set of attributes for citation content, like reference data linked with in-text citation, etc.
3. in-text citation's coordinates as number of symbols (InTeReC counts sentences);
4. current version of CyrCitEc citation data has no associations with the type of paper's sections that exists in InTeReC.

Citation data generated by CyrCitEc system provides more opportunities for a citation content analysis (Parinov 2017) and allow different types of visualization of this data, one of which is presented below.

3 Visualization Tool for the Open Citation Content Data

To make the open citation content data more usable, the project team created a visualization tool. The tool presents daily updated aggregated statistics about parsing results for each collection of papers. The tool is publicly available at http://cirtec.ranepa.ru/stats.html.

series	[1] records	[2] with futli	[3] with WARCs	[4] with PDF WARCs	[5] with JSON
RePEc:bkr:wpaper	26	26	21	17	17
RePEc:cas:wpaper	26	26	20		
RePEc:cfr:cefirw	228	228	170	164	160
RePEc:eer:wpalle	240	240	194		
RePEc:eus:ce3swp	26	26	23	23	23
RePEc:eus:wpaper	53	53	42	42	40
RePEc:gai:gbchap	37	37	37	36	36

Fig. 1. Visualization tool's main page, a fragment (source: http://cirtec.ranepa.ru/stats.html)

The main page of the visualization tool (see a fragment at Fig. 1) provides a general overview of processed data by collections of papers (collections in rows). For each collection it presents three groups of statistics: (a) numbers of papers processed on different stages of the CyrCitEc utilization (columns [1]–[5], visible at Fig. 1); (b) numbers of papers' JSON versions which contain (or not) some citation data (columns [6]–[9], presented in Table 1); (c) numbers of found (or not) different types of citation data (columns [a]–[e], presented in Table 1).

Table 1 gives additional information about the main page content (on 2018.06.01): (1) in the "Tag of column" and "Legend to column" there are short names and descriptions of data presented in columns of the visualization tool' main page; (2) in the "Totals" - aggregate statistics about different aspects of processing of research papers from all collections; (3) in the "Collection" - statistics for all papers of a sample collection (citation data used in the previous section belong to a paper from this collection).

Table 1. Visualization tool's main page content, a fragment (on 01.06.2018)

Tag to column	Legend to column	Totals	Collection
Series	List of processed collections of papers	220	RePEc:hig:fsight
[1]	Metadata records available	100553	262
[2]	Records with links to paper's full text	91929	262
[3]	Records at Web ARChive (WARC)	86882	216
[4]	PDF files in Web ARChive	67048	213
[5]	PDF files converted to JSON	66802	207
[6]	JSON files with found reference sections	49129	95
[7]	JSON with in-text citations	45580	94
[8]	JSON files with citation relationships	18977	75
[9]	JSON files with non-mentioned references	18617	92
[a]	Total references	865042	3455
[b]	Total citation contexts	735709	4041
[c]	Total mentioned references	806680	2700
[d]	Total citation relationships	47052	597
[e]	Total non-mentioned references	129333	755

The legends for the main page columns [1]–[5], listed in Table 1, explain functions of the CyrCitEc utilization stages. The first two stages are: taking all available papers' metadata from Socionet and specify which of them have a link to a paper's full text. At the stage "[3] records at Web ARChive" the system uploads available papers' full texts into a web archive based on the WARC archive format[3]. The next stage "[4] PDF files in Web ARChive" selects only PDF from all available papers' full text formats. The stage "[5] PDF files converted to JSON" determines which PDFs have a text layer and are not corrupted. After conversion only these files have a proper JSON format and can be processed further for the citation data parsing.

Data in cells with tags [6]–[9] show following amounts of:

- papers with recognized list of references (49,129 of 66,802 are available for analysis);
- papers with recognized in-text citations (45,580 of 49,129 papers have recognized in-text citations);
- papers with references which we linked with metadata of the same papers available at Socionet (18,977 of 49,129 papers have at least one citation relationship);
- papers with non-mentioned references (18,617 of 49,129 papers have non-mentioned references).

Data in cells with tags [a]–[e] contain total numbers of following types of extracted citation data:

- references ([a]);
- citation contexts, which include at least one in-text reference ([b]);

---

[3] https://en.wikipedia.org/wiki/Web_ARChive.

- references for which there are at least one in-text reference ([c]);
- references linked with metadata of the same paper ([d]); and
- references without mentions in text ([e]).

The column "series" (left at Fig. 1) contains ID of collections, which currently have being processed by CyrCitEc. If some ID in the column has no link, it means that in this collection there are no papers with recognized list of references. In such cases the system cannot produce the citation statistics for this collection. If the link exists, it opens a page with a list of citation data by the collection's papers. Table 2 shows an example of statistics for a single paper in the list. A paper for this example is the same which citation data is used in the previous section.

Table 2. Aggregate citation statistics for a single paper (on 01.06.2018)

Paper handle	RePEc:hig:fsight:v:11:y:2017:i:4:p:84-95
[a] references	40
[b] reference contexts	45
[c] contexts by reference	34
[d] linked references	7
[e] references without contexts	6

For each paper, presented by its ID (see the "paper handle" in Table 1), the system provides following data:

- number of recognized references with a link to a list of them;
- number of recognized citation contexts, which should include mentions of one or more references;
- number of references mentioned in a paper;
- number of references with available metadata of the same papers;
- number of non-mentioned references in a paper.

All values on this page have links to further details. E.g. a link from paper's ID opens paper's metadata page at Socionet. Links from numbers at this page open list of appropriate entities, like recognized references, extracted citation contexts, etc.

Figure 2 presents a fragment of a list of non-mentioned references of a paper. Each non-mentioned reference in the list have a hyperlink called "check this in PDF content". This link opens the paper's PDF where the non-mentioned reference is highlighted as an annotation. One can check is the reference really not mentioned and if it is a technical error he/she can report about this to initiate improvements of citation data parsing software.

The 6 references without contexts in paper RePEc:hig:fsight:v:11:y:2017:i:4:p:84-95

17

Gertner J. (2012) The Idea Factory: Bell Labs and the Great Age of American Innovation, New York: Penguin Group.
(check this in PDF content)

24

Kuzyk M., Grebenyuk A., Kakaeva E., Manchenko E., Dovgiy V., pp. 84–95
(check this in PDF content)

26

Fig. 2. A fragment of non-mentioned references list

Columns [1]–[5] of the main page (see Fig. 1) also provides links to papers missed at different stages of the CyrCitEc processing. Table 3 shows an example of how numbers of papers are changed step by step of their processing by the system.

Table 3. Numbers of processed papers for a collection (on 01.06.2018)

Series	[1]	[2]	[3]	[4]	[5]
RePEc:hig:fsight	262	262	216	213	207

The same numbers in columns [1] and [2] means that all available papers metadata have links to papers' full text. A number in the column [3] is less than the number in [2] since for 42 papers the system cannot download them for parsing citation data. The column [4] has number in 3 papers less than in [3] what means that these 3 papers are not PDF. A difference between numbers in the column [5] and [4] means that 6 papers cannot be converted to JSON format for further processing, since, e.g. the papers have no text layer or corrupted.

For all cases when there are differences between numbers in neighbor columns the system provides links to pages with list of missed papers. Using this feature one can see which papers were out of processing by CyrCitEc and figure out why.

4   Conclusion

The CyrCitEc project provides for public re-use four main outputs: (1) the open source software to parse and manage citation data; (2) the open service to process paper's PDFs to extract citation data; (3) the dataset of citation data, including citation contexts; and (4) the visualization tool to provide for users a transparence on how extraction of citation data works and a public control over results of parsing citation data. These outputs working together create a new type of openness for the citation content data. Based on such openness and transparence the research community can have the citation data with better quality. It also opens opportunities to improve scholarly citation practice and to develop scholarly communications.

Comparing with other open citation services, the CyrCitEc system currently provides more data for the citation content analysis and gives the research community better transparency for public control over the citation data/indicators correctness and quality.

References

Barrueco, J.M., Krichel, T., Parinov, S., Lyapunov, V., Medvedeva, O., Sergeeva, V.: Towards open data for the citation content analysis. arXiv preprint arXiv:1710.00302 (2017)

Berger, M., McDonough, K., Seversky, L.M.: cite2vec: citation-driven document exploration via word embeddings. IEEE Trans. Vis. Comput. Graph. **23**(1), 691–700 (2017)

Bertin, M., Atanassova, I.: InTeReC: in-text reference corpus for applying natural language processing to bibliometrics. In: Proceedings of the Seventh Workshop on Bibliometric-Enhanced Information Retrieval (BIR), Grenoble, France, pp. 54–62. CEURWS.org (2018)

Bilder, G., Lin, J., Neylon, C.: Principles for open scholarly infrastructures. In: Blog "Science in the Open" (2015)

Ding, Y., Zhang, G., Chambers, T., Song, M., Wang, X., Zhai, C.: Content-based citation analysis: the next generation of citation analysis. J. Assoc. Inf. Sci. Technol. **65**(9), 1820–1833 (2014)

He, J., Chen, C.: Understanding the changing roles of scientific publications via citation embeddings. arXiv preprint arXiv:1711.05822 (2017)

Parinov, S.: Semantic attributes for citation relationships: creation and visualization. In: Garoufallou, E., Virkus, S., Siatri, R., Koutsomiha, D. (eds.) MTSR 2017. CCIS, vol. 755, pp. 286–299. Springer, Cham (2017). https://doi.org/10.1007/978-3-319-70863-8_28

The Case for Ontologies in Expressing Decisions in Decentralized Energy Systems

Elena García-Barriocanal, Miguel-Ángel Sicilia[✉],
and Salvador Sánchez-Alonso

Computer Science Department, University of Alcalá,
Polytechnic Building. Ctra. Barcelona km. 33.6,
28871 Alcalá de Henares, Madrid, Spain
{elena.garciab,msicilia,salvador.sanchez}@uah.es

Abstract. Advanced in technologies for the decentralization of applications have enabled micro-grid energy systems that do not rely on central control and optimization but are controlled by their owners. This may eventually enable consumers or intermediaries to specify concrete and diverse conditions on the supply that not only concern throughput, price and stability but also elements as provenance (e.g. that energy is produced from renewable sources) or locality among others. Blockchain technologies have emerged as a possible solution for the integration of the stream of events generated by smart meters and networks, providing tamper-proof ledgers for offerings, transactions and traces. However, that requires languages for expressing conditions that might become complex and have to be executed locally. In this paper, we review the state of decentralization in micro-grids and its requirements, and discuss the role of ontologies as support for expressing constraints in those networks.

Keywords: Microgrids · Transactive energy · Blockchain ·
Decentralization · Ontologies

1 Introduction

Dozens of energy blockchain startups have emerged in the last years, and large energy companies also have a stake in this new technology. Some of these startups as Grid+[1] are looking to implement blockchain technology into wholesale electricity distribution, i.e. on connecting end-users with the grid, allowing them to trade and buy energy directly from the grid rather than from retailers. However, a majority of blockchain energy projects focus on building peer-to-peer (P2P) grid networks, in which entities – often called *Distributed Energy Resources* (DER) – (as, for example, photovoltaic systems) trade and buy excess energy between one another, without a central or wholesale entity. An example is Power Ledger[2], which is currently deploying pilots at several countries, and

---

[1] https://gridplus.io.
[2] https://powerledger.io/.

© Springer Nature Switzerland AG 2019
E. Garoufallou et al. (Eds.): MTSR 2018, CCIS 846, pp. 365–376, 2019.
https://doi.org/10.1007/978-3-030-14401-2_35

others are expected to emerge in the near future, as regulations progressively enable transactive energy use cases [2].

Distributed ledger technologies have been considered a key enabler of such energy decentralized systems, so that transactions are traceable, transparent and tamper-proof even in the case of a trustless environment. Blockchain technologies offer a reliable, relatively low-cost way for financial or operational transactions to be recorded and validated across a network with no central point of authority, and may enable easier switch of provider among other envisioned applications [5]. Other distributed ledger technologies as *tangles* [20] may also be applicable to energy micro-grids, but they are still in a process of inception, so that we leave their study to future work.

Some proof of concept applications [14] and limited case studies [16] of those technologies have recently been reported. This allows for the study of the data models and required supported semantics for those transactions to support the requirements of interchange that are specific to the context of emerging microgrids. Blockchain technologies have also applications in oil&gas distribution and also as mere registries of transactions on current centralized grids, but we focus here on decentralized systems, while the models discussed may have an application in other contexts also.

Adopting a P2P approach entails that production and consumption may be directly controlled by users or intermediaries to some extent, which poses new challenges to the expression of preferences of autonomous systems taking independent decisions. This in turn requires expressing those conditions on shared conceptualizations and data models. Ontologies have yet been proposed to model the business networks that operate over blockchains. For example in [22], the *Blockchain Business Network Ontology* (BBO) is proposed, that covers a model of networks, participants and communications. However, these models are generic and do not provide means to model complex conditions on the transactions that are essential for the use case of decentralized energy systems. Further, the nature of energy production requires taking decisions over streams of data, which constrains the way in which local decisions are to be taken that need to be accounted for. In the modeling of blockchain based transactions, several works [9,15] have reused and applied the *Resource-Event-Agent* (REA) ontology, originally proposed and later revised by McCarthy [11] as a generalized accounting model. REA-based ontologies provide a point of departure for that modeling, but its suitability for decentralized energy systems needs further inquiry.

In this paper, we report ongoing work in modeling the conditions and requirements of parties involved in decentralized energy systems. We depart from previous work on models for economic transactions and discuss how these can be aligned with ontologies specific to energy systems, and with the emerging use cases of decentralized energy systems, and discuss a high-level model for local decisions of agents in that context. The focus is on delineating the main components of a solution and the role of ontologies and decision steps, rather than on implementation details, so that the discussion is kept at a high level and pseudocode is used for illustration.

The rest of this paper is structured as follows. Section 2 briefly reviews the state of decentralized energy networks and ontologies in the energy domain. Then, in Sect. 3 the requirements for a model specific to decentralized energy systems are discussed. Section 4 presents the model based on examples. Finally, conclusions and outlook are provided in Sect. 5.

2 Background

2.1 Decentralized Energy Networks

The Brooklyn microgrid [16] is a pioneering case study of a blockchain-based microgrid energy market without the need for central intermediaries. The main arguments for using a blockchain in a decentralized energy trading system are those related to security. Pop et al. [18] describe the use of Ethereum for the registration of the production and consumption in a microgrid and also covering restrictions and rules, using existing datasets for testing purposes. Aitzhan and Svetinović [3] reported a proof-of-concept for a decentralized energy microgrid using blockchain technology, multi-signatures, and anonymous encrypted messaging streams, enabling peers to anonymously negotiate energy prices and securely perform trading transactions. In [17] blockchain-supported smart contracts are also used for coordination control, thus contributing to optimization under constraints in a microgrid.

All the above mentioned examples are cases and prototypes demonstrating the potential of the technologies for particular cases. A common theme across them is the registration of facts about production and consumption, along with that of rules and requirements. For these solutions to eventually become interoperable, a shared model is needed, encompassing the specifics of microgrids as the main use case. In microgrids, where end users gather, the criteria for trading or exchange is not limited to prices or technical parameters as flexibility, but it may encompass additional concerns as for example, the kind of generation device. Imbault et al. [14] describe a proof of concept for a blockchain-based support of proof that electricity has been generated from a renewable energy source (*eco-certificates*); such certificates are an example of a possible condition that could appear in the preferences of energy consumers.

2.2 Ontologies and Models for the Energy Domain

There are a limited number of models for energy generation aimed at interoperability reported in the literature. Sikorski et al. [23] describe an ontology for capturing blockchain data in the context of an electricity market, but it does not relate to the energy domain, but to the internal entities in the blockchain. The Electricity Market Ontology (ELMO) [4] is an early attempt to model a shared understanding of concepts and procedures regarding the operation of the electricity market, initially devised for the Greek market, but reusable to other jurisdictions. Grassi et al. [13] describes an ontology structured around five models: device, energy, context, user and service.

Some multi-agent research encompasses also models for energy production [6,12] including physical as well as operational management concepts as needed for distributed agent communication.

All the previous research mentioned has not considered the new context of distributed ledger based support for decision, but it is useful as a basis for describing the main elements included in such decision making processes.

3   Requirements

The working of a microgrid and of decentralized energy networks is made up of a number of differentiated concerns that need to be addressed separately. From the analysis of existing models and the needs of decentralization, these include at least the following:

- Resources, i.e. the properties and configuration of units, be them individual, aggregated or even virtual. Each of them are capable of consuming and producing, and have some attributes that describe them and should be made visible to consumers, as they could be considered in decision making.
- Market, i.e. the expression of requirements and transactions that ends up in the dynamics of pricing, and overall network properties including congestion or under-utilization.
- Service. The actual service and how it is traced by the system. This can be hypothesized to come from energy prosumption information collected from smart metering devices.
- Context. This comprises external data that may affect the decisions of individual users or DERs based on external data. This opens the system to external conditions, e.g. weather forecasts that may affect future prices.

It is important to understand that in current accounts of energy demand, energy provenance is important. Even though the actual provision can be considered fungible, consumers may impose rules on the kind of resources used for generation, typically this concerns the use of renewable sources as an ethical concern. In consequence, the conditions on energy provision are at the granularity of individuals, be them consumers or prosumers. Further, there is an interaction of proposals and incentives that are exchanged in the network to shift future consumption profiles.

Some of the existing proposals for decentralized energy as *Overgrid* [7] propose an automatic control distributed demand response implemented over P2P. Other proposals as [18] give a degree of control to DER but still there is a global optimization scheme based on a set of linear equations. We consider here **autonomy** as the first design commitment, so that DERs and users are capable of expressing their own conditions over production and consumption and network-wide concerns. The second design principle is that of **flexibility** so that those conditions can be changed at any time, and the language for expressing them could incorporate any contextual information and also evolve over time. These principles call for rich languages for expressing those conditions along with interoperable descriptions.

4 Proposed Model

4.1 Base Model

Here we depart from the work of Laurier et al. [15] on the unified REA-ontology called REA^2 that formalises both the dependent and independent dimensions of collaborating business entities in one view. Table 1 summarizes the main mappings of terms in existing ontologies ELMO [4] and Energy Ontology (EO) [13], that are relevant in energy grids, to REA^2 terms.

Table 1. Main elements for energy grids and their mapping to REA^2

REA^2 element	Description	Examples
EconomicAgent, TradingPartner	Entities participating as prosumers (DERs), Distributed System Operators (DSO) or users	elmo:Participant, eo:PowerProducer, eo:PowerConsumer
Contract	Enforceable agreement among partners	elmo:Right/Obligation
Commitment	Set of conditions to be met in a contract, or expression of needs	elmo:Right/Obligation
EconomicResource	Anything of value	-

We have not found in existing energy-related ontologies reference to the modeling of economic resources in an explicit, differentiated way. However, it is important to clearly differentiate between energy resources as assets and as economic resources. Particularly in our context of decentralization, the modeling of tokens is important to allow for mechanism design [21], i.e. the mechanisms devised by token issuers in an attempt to produce some form o desired emergent behaviour. For example, *Power Ledger* uses a combination of a token called *Sparkz* in which the actual energy transactions are settled with a token *POWR* that serves as a "smart bond" in a second level. In any case, a concept of Token is in this context similar to conventional fiat-money based prices, but it may have additional implications in the decision process. For example, some tokens may be driven by smart contracts that produce externalities to the network of token-holders or even to third parties (e.g. donations enforced by the contract). This may in some cases be subject to consumer preferences beyond the interchange rates of the token.

It should be noted that the actual system is decentralized, individual DER receive offerings to change their consumption or production profile, which eventually become contracts, that will later be subject to scrutiny as the actual service, due to different conditions, may be below the promised. In consequence, matching conditions is done in two stages:

- Pre-service stage, i.e. when dealing with offerings and contracts.
- Post-service stage, checking what actually occurred as recorded in transactions in the ledger.

It is also important to understand that contracts in the system may be violated, as also occurs with regular contracts, usually for non predictable reasons as external conditions or congestion. These may be subject to penalties or liabilities specified in the contracts themselves, and these consequences can be enforced by the blockchain, based on post-service transaction inspection.

It should be noted that all offerings and transactions are actually timed, as they are for a specific period of time, typically an offering will be for a given time span. We do not deal here with the problems associated to determining shared time in a distributed system, but it should be addressed at the implementation stage. In any case, the model can be conceptualized as a stream of `Offer` instances that the autonomous component (agent) matches against a set of preferences, determining the observable behaviour of the agent. Figure 1 shows a summary of the three main actor roles (producers and operators, external sources of information and the agents acting on behalf of consumers) and the main data streams that interact with the distributed ledger. Producers provide a stream of time-bounded offerings for which REA concepts can be used as a model, combined with descriptions of the producers and its characteristics using energy-market specific ontologies. Other external sources are also pushing a stream of data that is relevant to decision making using some oracle mechanism (discussed later). These may use any kind of ontologies, e.g. those describing environmental conditions. Finally, consumer agents take the all the previously mentioned information and decide on the offerings. This eventually results in REA contracts (not to be confused with "smart contracts", a blockchain-specific term) to be recorded on the ledger.

Note that the registry of transaction would still be subject to post-service inspection, on the basis of the actual service provided, but this is not dealt with here.

The setting describes extends current proposed pilots, e.g. in [16] there is a market mechanism with offers for sell and buy in time slots, a double auction mechanism and some "payment rules". Here we add the possibility of a complex,

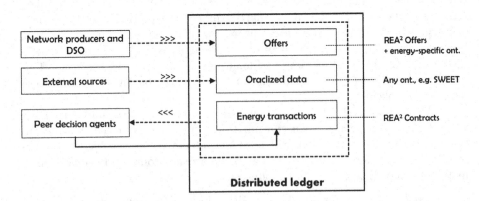

Fig. 1. Main actors, role of the distributed ledger and use of ontologies

automated decision model beyond prices that controls the generation of buy bids (it may also be applied to sell bids but we do not consider it here). It should be noted that optimization as proposed in [17] should be reconsidered in this context, as the constraints of consumer agents are arbitrary and may not be aligned among them, as the main design principle is autonomy.

4.2   Conditions over Transactions

In a decentralized system, entities may offer others some opportunities to buy consumption (including barter or using tokens, but we do not deal with those specificities here). This requires the introduction of an `Offer` concept, which in REA may be compared to the concept of the same name or that of *Quote* that bear the same structure as contracts that have not been accepted by all parties in a contract.

In our case, the parties specify the requirements of acceptable offers as part of the description of the entity that we will call here `DER`. Then, when an offering is evaluated, there is a need to check if the clauses of the offer, which are similar to commitments, comply with those associated to the DER *at current time*. The following example expressed in a SWRL-like syntax[3] contains the preferences as a custom built-in `complies-req`.

```
Offer(?o), DER(?der), producer(?o, ?der),
ext:complies-req(?o, ?der) -> AcceptableOffer(?o)
```

It should be noted that such rules act as filters on the stream of offerings, and they may include elements of a various kind, including locality, external conditions or even some form of recording of the past. The following pseudocode for `complies-req` includes the main kinds of conditions:

- Source of energy, expressed as type of producer or having some certificate of provenance.
- External conditions as weather forecasts.
- Conditions on the producer itself, as the proximity of the producer,
- Past history of the producer, e.g. reliability based on past service failure events.

The categories of conditions may also include those expressed on the overall characteristics or profile of the network as a whole (e.g. load or congestion), especially if decisions are made by a Distribution System Operator (DSO) or intermediary on behalf of users.

It should be noted that there can be different sets of conditions that consider acceptable an offering, so that `complies-req` is actually checking $C_1 \vee C_2, \ldots \vee C_n$ where each C_i is a conjunction of clauses as the following one.

---

[3] We use here similar syntax, but not strictly SWRL conformant rules. They are intended as production rules pseudocode and not as direct axioms on OWL ontologies.

```
?der owl:type (FVProducer or hasCertificate.GreenCert)
?weather-cond[?o.start, ?o.end] not Stormy
?der.locality in ?user.region
service_failures(?der, ?now, ?now - timedelta("3m") < 10
```

The requirements associated to the DER may be simple or complex, and eventually require the use of additional ontologies. This is the key problem of interoperability that may be mitigated by reusing ontologies, e.g. in the previous pseudocode by referring to Metereological phenomena concepts in the *Semantic Web for Earth and Environment Technology Ontology* (SWEET) [19]. By default, if the requirements on the DER include elements not present in the offering, the offer is not accepted, assuming that not knowing is failure. As the offers are a stream, they need to be windowed in some form, so that decisions on best offers are made at configurable points. The following would be an example decision criteria for a set of acceptable offerings for a given window using pseudocode that expresses a local optimization problem.

```
minimize:
    sum(o.price in AcceptableOfferings)
      + sum(o.cfp in AcceptableOfferings)
subject_to:
    (time_span(o in AcceptableOfferings)) covers time_span(window)
    (power(o in AcceptableOfferings)) >= power_req(window)
```

The idea is that of using optimization solvers over the filtered stream of acceptable offers, subject to covering demand on the period. In the previous example, cfp stands for some metric of carbon footprint associated to the offering, provided that under some set of conditions C_k (similar to the one described above) the user may consider acceptable non-renewable sources. Unit ontologies [24] could be used to express quantities and measures. Of course this is just an illustrative example. It should be noted that the filtering as a pre-processing step may eventually make the decision problem fail, and then the market competition for production bids may also require recomputing the requested profile. For these cases, there may be defaults or failback mechanisms, and it also imposes an important requirement on performance, that might limit the expressivity of the language expressing the preferences.

Once the requested profile of an agent succeeds, it produces the corresponding blockchain transactions that become the Contracts to be served by producers. At post-service, the transactions actually recorded in the blockchain can be inspected for compliance with the original contracts. The following SWRL-like fragment shows the matching and represents the compliance check of each commitment using a noncompliant-effect custom built-in:

```
IncrementEvent(?ie), DecrementEvent(?de), duality(?ie, ?de),
Contract(?c), Commitment(?cm), clause(?c, ?cm), fulfillment(?cm, ?ie),
ext:noncompliant-effect(?cm ?ie, ?de)  -> violated(?c, ?cm)
```

That represents a template for checking violations provided that actual service is recorded automatically in the blockchain (e.g. via IoT communication with smart meters). Finally, violated commitments would be processed to apply the penalties or corrective actions, as specified in the commitments. Commitments by default include the profile of the offerings accepted, but this can be verified thanks to the immutability of data in the blockchain.

4.3   Mapping to Existing Blockchains

The model presented so far is independent of the technical implementation details of distributed ledgers. These concrete technology pieces provide the support for immutable and permanent storage of transactions, i.e. the full history of `EconomicEvents` with all their context associated. However, there are parts of that history that are explicitly stored while others are implicit. For example, a `Contract` will be (at least to some extent) realized in smart contract code and independent of any concrete party, which is of a different nature than the actual transactions based on that contract.

This is related to the different ontology layers described by de Kruijff and Weigand [9] as *datalogical, infological* and *essential.* The latter is actually a small subset of the REA ontology, and the *infological* layer contains only a few high level terms as transaction, ledgers or accounts that could be represented using REA elements also. The *datalogical* layer deals with modeling the details of the implementation: nodes, blocks, miners, wallets, IoT devices [8] etc. and it is of little interest here, as its use cases are far from our present concerns. However, the deployment of a model like the one sketched in this paper on a concrete blockchain would not require such a implementation ontology, but rather a mechanism to use ontologies as a supplement to the functioning of the blockchain. An example of such idea can be found in [10].

The two major implications for current blockchain technologies for such a model are (i) programming model and (ii) the limitations inherent to isolation of smart contracts. The programming model for the time-based decisions sketched requires streaming or reactive approaches, in which clients can take a stream of validated offerings with related information and make decisions. This requires low transaction fees and high throughput that cannot be achieve in some of the current public networks as Ethereum[4]. An example of a new development implementing dataflow in smart contracts is Ziliqa[5] and energy-specific blockchains are also proposed, notably the one of the Energy Web Foundation[6]. However, the approach to conditions and optimization as described do not necessarily fit the constrained languages of such blockchains, so further research on that area is required concerning rule-based and constraint optimization computations.

Regarding the problems of isolation of smart contracts (which in principle restrict the use of data external to the blockchain), the standard solution to

---

[4] At the time of this writing, however, Ethereum is experimenting changes to solve those problems.

[5] https://zilliqa.com.

[6] https://energyweb.org/.

date is using *oracles*, with the limitations that they may introduce single points of failure. Some proposals for decentralized oracles (as Astraea [1]) are possibly providing solutions to such problems in the near future.

5   Conclusions and Outlook

The adoption of power generation systems that are able to produce from renewable sources and share it or use the excess capacity has opened new possibilities for decentralized energy systems. Distributed ledger technologies as blockchains are key enablers for these new approaches to decentralization.

If maximum autonomy and flexibility to participants is sought as a design criteria, the behaviour of the micro grid cannot be represented by a fixed set of equations or rules or a distributed algorithm, even in P2P settings. Instead, a model is required that accounts for all aspects of the provision, including resources, market, service and context and that is distributed across decision-capable agents.

Several ontologies specific to the energy domain have been proposed to date, some of them with a considerable level of detail in representing equipment and devices. However, they do not provide a sound model for the economic events underlying the supply-demand models required. Further, there is a need to account for elements that are specific of highly decentralized micro-grids in which participants have a large degree of autonomy. For the former, we have proposed the use of the REA^2 ontology that accounts both for party-specific and independent views of the transactions. For the latter, the use of ontologies (combined with rules or other procedural computation mechanisms as optimizers) allow for declarative specifications that can be matched in a distributed way. These when combined with blockchains and smart contracts for the automation of the commitments provide the required flexibility in expressing needs and constraints of any kind.

Future work should advance in the complete specification of the different elements of the model, and its associated mechanisms for distributed operation. In the implementation side, work is needed on the suitability of current distributed ledger technologies to fit the requirements posed by the model of operation presented here.

References

1. Adler, J., Berryhill, R., Veneris, A., Poulos, Z., Veira, N., Kastania, A.: Astraea: A Decentralized Blockchain Oracle. arXiv preprint arXiv:1808.00528 (2018)
2. Aguero, J.R., Khodaei, A.: Grid modernization, DER integration & utility business models-trends & challenges. IEEE Power Energy Mag. **16**(2), 112–121 (2018)
3. Aitzhan, N.Z., Svetinovic, D.: Security and privacy in decentralized energy trading through multi-signatures, blockchain and anonymous messaging streams. IEEE Trans. Dependable Secure Comput. **15**(5), 840–852 (2016)

4. Alexopoulos, P., Kafentzis, K., Zoumas, C.: ELMO: an interoperability ontology for the electricity market. In: Proceedings of the International Conference on e-Business, pp. 15–20 (2009)
5. Basden, J., Cottrell, M.: How utilities are using blockchain to modernize the grid. Harvard Business Review (2017)
6. Chappin, E.J., Dijkema, G.P., van Dam, K.H., Lukszo, Z.: Modeling strategic and operational decision-making-an agent-based model of electricity producers. In: Proceedings of the 21st Annual European Simulation and Modelling Conference (ESM2007), St. Julian's, Malta, pp. 22–24 (2007)
7. Croce, D., Giuliano, F., Tinnirello, I., Galatioto, A., Bonomolo, M., Beccali, M., Zizzo, G.: Overgrid: a fully distributed demand response architecture based on overlay networks. IEEE Trans. Autom. Sci. Eng. 14(2), 471–481 (2017)
8. D'Elia, A., Viola, F., Roffia, L., Azzoni, P., Cinotti, T.S.: Enabling interoperability in the internet of things: a OSGi semantic information broker implementation. Int. J. Semant. Web Inf. Syst. (IJSWIS) 13(1), 147–167 (2017)
9. de Kruijff, J., Weigand, H.: Understanding the blockchain using enterprise ontology. In: Dubois, E., Pohl, K. (eds.) CAiSE 2017. LNCS, vol. 10253, pp. 29–43. Springer, Cham (2017). https://doi.org/10.1007/978-3-319-59536-8_3
10. García-Barriocanal, E., Sánchez-Alonso, S., Sicilia, M.-A.: Deploying metadata on blockchain technologies. In: Garoufallou, E., Virkus, S., Siatri, R., Koutsomiha, D. (eds.) MTSR 2017. CCIS, vol. 755, pp. 38–49. Springer, Cham (2017). https://doi.org/10.1007/978-3-319-70863-8_4
11. Geerts, G.L., McCarthy, W.E.: An ontological analysis of the economic primitives of the extended-REA enterprise information architecture. Int. J. Account. Inf. Syst. 3(1), 1–16 (2002)
12. Gnansounou, E., Pierre, S., Quintero, A., Dong, J., Lahlou, A.: A multi-agent approach for planning activities in decentralized electricity markets. Knowl.-Based Syst. 20(4), 406–418 (2007)
13. Grassi, M., Nucci, M., Piazza, F.: Towards an ontology framework for intelligent smart home management and energy saving. In: Proceedings of the IEEE International Symposium on Industrial Electronics (ISIE), pp. 1753–1758. IEEE (2011)
14. Imbault, F., Swiatek, M., De Beaufort, R., Plana, R.: The green blockchain: managing decentralized energy production and consumption. In: Proceedings of the 2017 IEEE International Conference on Environment and Electrical Engineering and IEEE Industrial and Commercial Power Systems Europe (EEEIC/ICPS Europe), pp. 1–5 (2017)
15. Laurier, W., Kiehn, J., Polovina, S.: REA 2: a unified formalisation of the resource-event-agent ontology. Appl. Ontol. 13, 1–24 (2018)
16. Mengelkamp, E., Gärttner, J., Rock, K., Kessler, S., Orsini, L., Weinhardt, C.: Designing microgrid energy markets: a case study: the Brooklyn Microgrid. Appl. Energy 210, 870–880 (2018)
17. Münsing, E., Mather, J., Moura, S.: Blockchains for decentralized optimization of energy resources in microgrid networks. In: Proceedings of the 2017 IEEE Conference on Control Technology and Applications (CCTA), pp. 2164–2171. IEEE (2017)
18. Pop, C., Cioara, T., Antal, M., Anghel, I., Salomie, I., Bertoncini, M.: Blockchain based decentralized management of demand response programs in smart energy grids. Sensors 18(1), 162 (2018)
19. Raskin, R.G., Pan, M.J.: Knowledge representation in the semantic web for Earth and environmental terminology (SWEET). Comput. Geosci. 31(9), 1119–1125 (2005)

20. Red, V.A.: Practical comparison of distributed ledger technologies for IoT. In: Proceedings of the SPIE Defense + Security Conference, vol. 10206, p. 102060G (2017). https://doi.org/10.1117/12.2262793
21. Samadi, P., Mohsenian-Rad, H., Schober, R., Wong, V.W.: Advanced demand side management for the future smart grid using mechanism design. IEEE Trans. Smart Grid 3(3), 1170–1180 (2012)
22. Seebacher, S., Maleshkova, M.: A model-driven approach for the description of blockchain business networks. In: Proceedings of the 51st Hawaii International Conference on System Sciences, pp. 3487–3496 (2018)
23. Sikorski, J.J., Haughton, J., Kraft, M.: Blockchain technology in the chemical industry: machine-to-machine electricity market. Appl. Energy 195, 234–246 (2017)
24. Zhang, X., Li, K., Zhao, C., Pan, D.: A survey on units ontologies: architecture, comparison and reuse. Program 51(2), 193–213 (2017)

Author Index

Printed in the United States
By Bookmasters